THE ART OF CLASSIC SCI-FI MOVIES

FRONT COVER: Detail from *Forbidden Planet* (1956) US poster.

BACK COVER (LEFT TO RIGHT): *Alraune* (1918) German poster. *The War of the Worlds* (1953) US poster. *The Green Slime* (1968) Italian poster. Art by G.D. Stefano.

PAGE 1: Detail from *Alraune* (1918) German poster. Art by C. Eisen.

PAGE 2: Detail from *The X from Outer Space* (1967) Italian poster.

PAGE 3: *The War of the Worlds* (1953) Spanish promotional herald/handbill.

PAGE 4: Detail from *The Brain* (1962) Spanish poster.

PAGE 5: Detail from *Super Giant* (1957) 1961 Italian poster. Art by Arnaldo De Amicis.

www.elephantbookcompany.com

Published in 2023 by Applause Theatre & Cinema Books
An Imprint of Rowman & Littlefield Publishing Group, Inc

Trade Book Division Editorial Offices:
64 South Main Street, Essex, Connecticut 06426

Elephant Book Company Editorial director: Will Steeds
Book design: Martin Stiff at Amazing 15. www.amazing15.com

Printed in China

Library of Congress Cataloging-in-Publication Data is available upon request.

ISBN 9781493071036

www.applausebooks.com

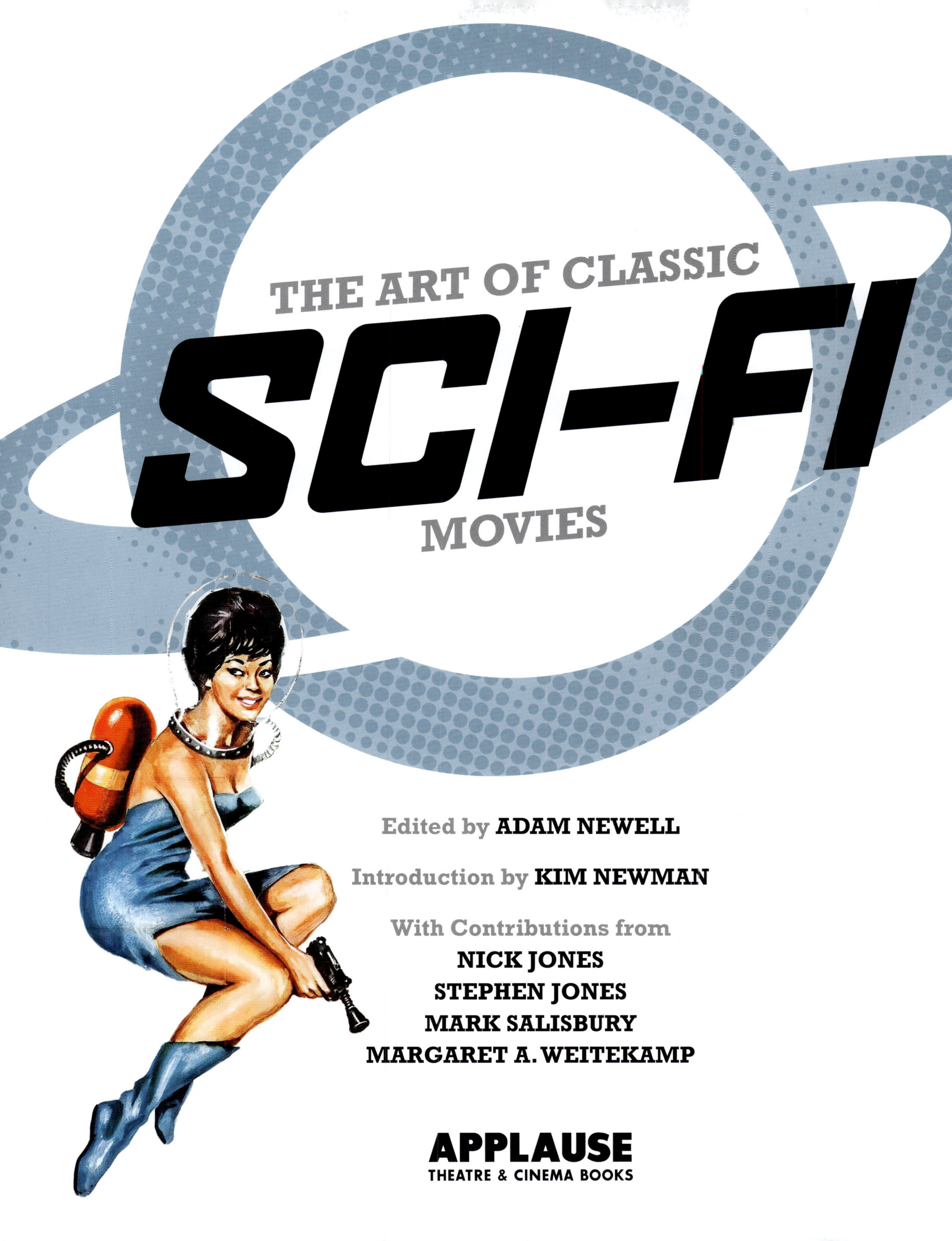

THE ART OF CLASSIC SCI-FI MOVIES

Edited by **ADAM NEWELL**

Introduction by **KIM NEWMAN**

With Contributions from
NICK JONES
STEPHEN JONES
MARK SALISBURY
MARGARET A. WEITEKAMP

APPLAUSE
THEATRE & CINEMA BOOKS

CONTENTS

THE 1960s..................... 198

THE 1970s..................... 274

INTRODUCTION

SF: THE CLASSIC ERA
By Kim Newman

Science fiction existed before cinema, but only just . . . Antecedents of SF can be found as far back as Lucian of Samosata's *A True Story*—a second century work which features the first fictional trip to the moon and encounters with alien life-forms . . . though, crucially, Lucian was making fun of the already well-established tradition of the far-fetched traveler's tale. Among the most famous works of proto-science fiction are Thomas More's *Utopia* (1516), Cyrano de Bergerac's *The Other World: Comical History of the States and Empires of the Moon* (1657), Jonathan Swift's *Gulliver's Travels* (1726) and Mary Shelley's *Frankenstein, or: The Modern Prometheus* (1818).

PREVIOUS SPREAD: Detail from a US one-sheet for *The War of the Worlds* (1953). See also page 15.

ABOVE: Giant spiders on the Moon! An illustration by Scottish artist William Strang from an 1894 edition of Lucian's second-century work, *A True Story*.

OPPOSITE: English artist Warwick Goble was the first to visualize Wells's Martian tripods. His illustrations appeared with the first publication of *The War of the Worlds*, when it was serialized in *Pearson's Magazine* in 1897.

Science fiction couldn't really take off as a form until the ascent of the scientific method, so it really emerged in the nineteenth century in parallel with unprecedented technological advances. Authors like E.T.A. Hoffman and Edgar Allan Poe proposed fanciful (often macabre) uses for mesmerism, galvanism, ventriloquism, Darwinism, automata, and the like. Others imagined a future world devastated by plague or war, or transformed into a paradise by some political or philosophical movement.

Jules Verne began his series of imaginary voyages with the 1851 short story "A Drama in the Air" (subtitled "A Voyage in a Balloon")—combining then high-tech means of aviation with the very sexy nineteenth century science of geography—and soon expanded the envelope by speculating about travel to underground lost worlds in *Journey to the Centre of the Earth* (1864), into space in *From the Earth to the Moon* (1865) and under the ocean by submarine in *20,000 Leagues Under the Sea* (1869–70). Verne was a hard science man and insisted his imagined technologies were plausible—just as he gave a realistic, copiable timetable for the trip taken in *Around the World in 80 Days* (1872). His rival and successor H.G. Wells was less timid. Verne sent his explorers into lunar orbit with dynamite and a big gun (which, while seemingly plausible, wouldn't actually work) while Wells's

TOP: Russian poster for *Cosmic Voyage* (1936). This Soviet silent film was one of the first to attempt to depict "realistic" spaceflight.

ABOVE: The cover of the US "herald" leaflet for *Metropolis* (1927) featured, as did much of the film's promotional material, star Brigitte Helm in her guise as Rotwang's robot.

OPPOSITE: A looming Raymond Massey in this UK poster promoting the first run of *Things to Come*. H.G. Wells helped to adapt his own 1933 "future history" novel for the big-budget production, which premiered at London's Leicester Square Theatre on 23 February 1936.

The First Men in the Moon (1901) use a diving bell covered in antigravity paint (which doesn't actually exist, so its efficacy can't be disproven).

More than any other writer, the restless, lively Wells was responsible for invigorating what was then called scientific romance and turning it into science fiction. In a short decade, he dashed off a series of major works—*The Time Machine* (1895), *The Island of Doctor Moreau* (1896), *The Invisible Man* (1897), *The War of the Worlds* (1897), and a raft of short stories built around startling concepts like super-speed, attacks by sea-creatures or insects, and man-eating plants. While Wells was turning out his great SF novels, the cinema was being born—developed out of flipper books, magic lantern shows, the zoetrope, praxinoscope, and other primitive gadgets into the moving pictures exhibited by the Lumière Brothers. Wells even partnered with British film pioneer Robert W. Paul to patent what sounds like a theme park ride—patrons would sit on a replica of the Time Machine and film would be projected on all the walls of a room to provide the experience of rushing through centuries to the past or future.

The Wells–Paul project was never realized, but the pioneer Georges Méliès took on the job of bringing the visions of Verne and Wells to the screen, incidentally developing the art of movie special effects. Méliès's *A Trip to the Moon* (1902) scrambles elements of the lunar voyages of the two authors—Verne's space-gun, which is fired off by chorus girls from the Folies Bergère, and Wells's capering insectile Selenites, who explode in puffs of smoke when struck with an umbrella. Between *A Trip to the Moon* and *Star Wars* (1977), the story of science fiction in multiple media—novels, magazines, illustration, comic strips, comic books, propaganda, satire, radio, television, advertising—is complicated and exciting, and continually fuels the development of SF cinema.

Among film genres, science fiction is the widest ranging and hardest to pin down. All Westerns, swashbucklers, rom-coms, horror films, and detective stories have elements in common with all other entries in those genres that can be ticked off and categorized. Science fiction can feature anywhere, as witness: *The Phantom Empire* (1935), a science fiction Western; *Flash Gordon* (1936), a science fiction swashbuckler; *The Perfect Woman* (1949), a science fiction rom-com; *The Thing from Another World* (1951), a science fiction horror film; and *The Magnetic Monster* (1953), a science fiction detective story. Indeed, amid so many genre hybrids it's hard to find a film that's *just* science fiction—save for Fritz Lang's *Metropolis* (1927) and the multi-authored *Things to Come* (1936). These are futurist visions dotted with technological prophecies and tell stories torn between the rival strains of dystopia (the future will be horrible) and utopia (the future will be wonderful). Wells pooh-poohed *Metropolis* as "quite the silliest film," discerning in its magnificence traces of his own early works, but his own 'answer' in *Things to Come* is as often clunky or ridiculous as it is awe-inspiring. Both pictures, like *Blade Runner* (1982), required massive innovations in effects technology, were hugely expensive commercial disappointments, exist in multiple confusing versions, proved hugely influential on other films, provided images and ideas that would be referenced for decades to come, and have recently been restored to something approaching their full glory.

There were other, comparable big-budget SF efforts before World War II: Lang's *Woman in the Moon* (1929), the satirical Hollywood musical *Just Imagine* (1930),

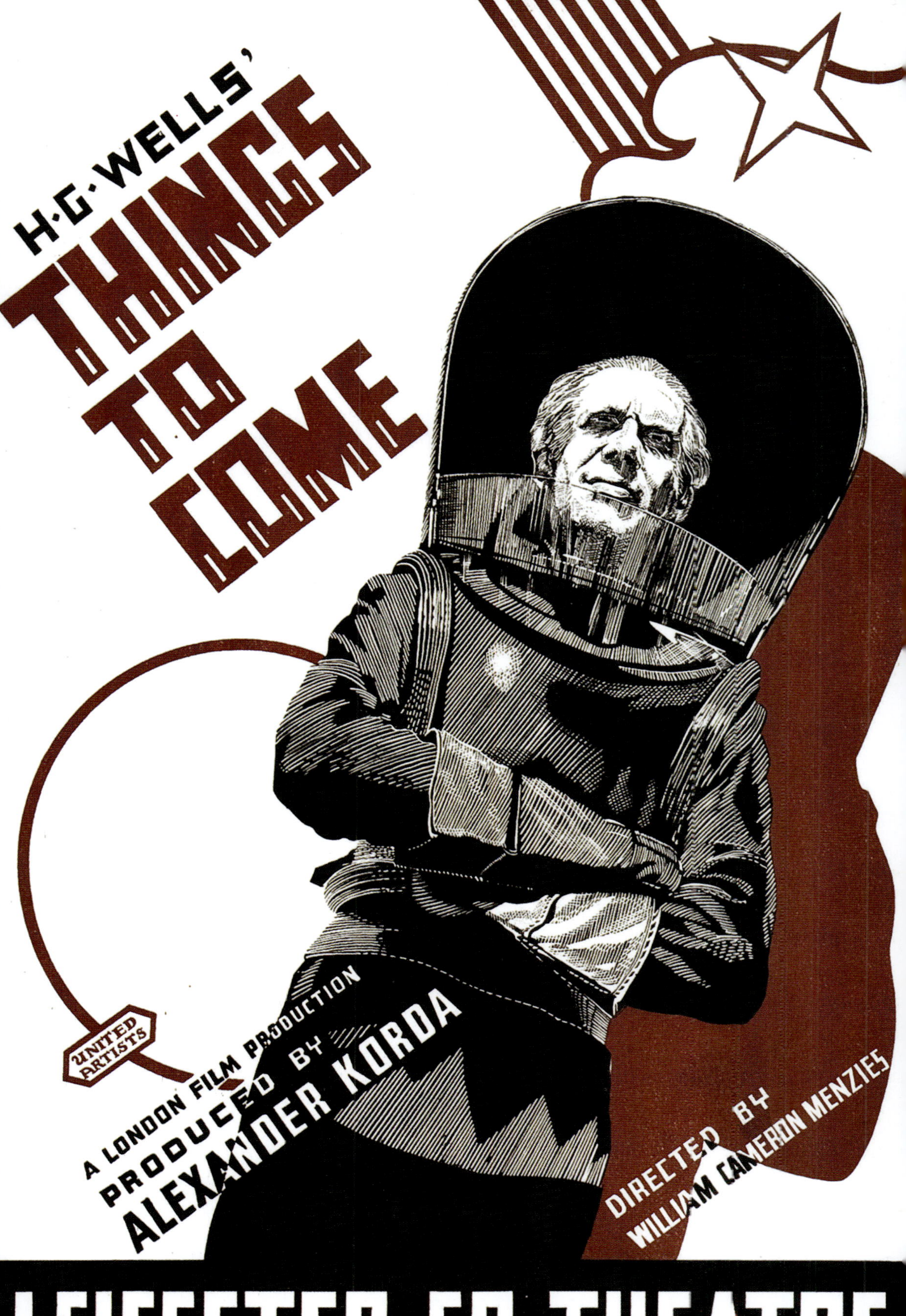
H·G·WELLS'
THINGS TO COME
UNITED ARTISTS
A LONDON FILM PRODUCTION
PRODUCED BY
ALEXANDER KORDA
DIRECTED BY
WILLIAM CAMERON MENZIES
LEICESTER · SQ · THEATRE
Props: LEICESTER SQUARE ESTATES LTD.
Managing Director: JACK BUCHANAN.
General Manager: Alexander Stevenson.

ABOVE LEFT: US lobby card for the penultimate chapter of the 13-part serial *Flash Gordon* (1936), based on Alex Raymond's newspaper comic strip.

ABOVE RIGHT: US insert poster for *Rocket Ship*, a condensed, 72-minute feature film version of the 1936 *Flash Gordon* serial, released in 1949. In the early 1970s, young filmmaker George Lucas wanted to make a new Flash Gordon movie; when he couldn't get the rights, he wrote his own SF saga instead…

OPPOSITE: It took until 1953 for H.G. Wells's *The War of the Worlds* to be adapted for film. Paramount's big-budget, modern-day take replaced the Martians' tricky-to-create tripods with legless hovering ships, as depicted on this bold, silk screen style US one-sheet.

and the Soviet spaceship saga *Cosmic Voyage* (1936). But the dominant mode of film science fiction was set by James Whale's *Frankenstein* (1931) and *The Invisible Man* (1933), adaptations of key SF novels made in the style of Universal Studios' recent horror hit *Dracula* (1931). Mad science and monsters were the order of the day, and other studios chipped in with Dr Moreau and Dr Jekyll. Many an electric arc crackled, retort bubbled, pile of slime shifted into life and rampage ensued. These were the Awful Warning films, keyed to a generation that had soured on science during a war of mechanized death on a huge scale, or worried about being put permanently out of work by robots or automation. The only forward-looking, gee-isn't-science-great movies were coming from dictator nations like Germany or the USSR—while American space-faring science fiction virtually ignored the thriving pulp magazines in favor of comic strips that could be turned into serials. Flash Gordon and Buck Rogers fought Ming of Mongo and Killer Kane, who were respectively an outer space despot in the Hitler-Stalin mode and a super-racketeer of the far future.

After World War II, the exciting, terrifying prospect of the unleashed atom became all-pervasive culturally . . . with pessimists conceiving of the devastation of civilization in worldwide atomic warfare and optimists thrilled by the possibility of atom-powered fridges and washing machines. A few techies even got excited about computing machines, which began to feature in more and more SF yarns. Before 1950, science fiction tended to be dismissed by grown-ups as "Buck Rogers stuff." Hollywood relegated to Saturday morning cheapies the sorts of

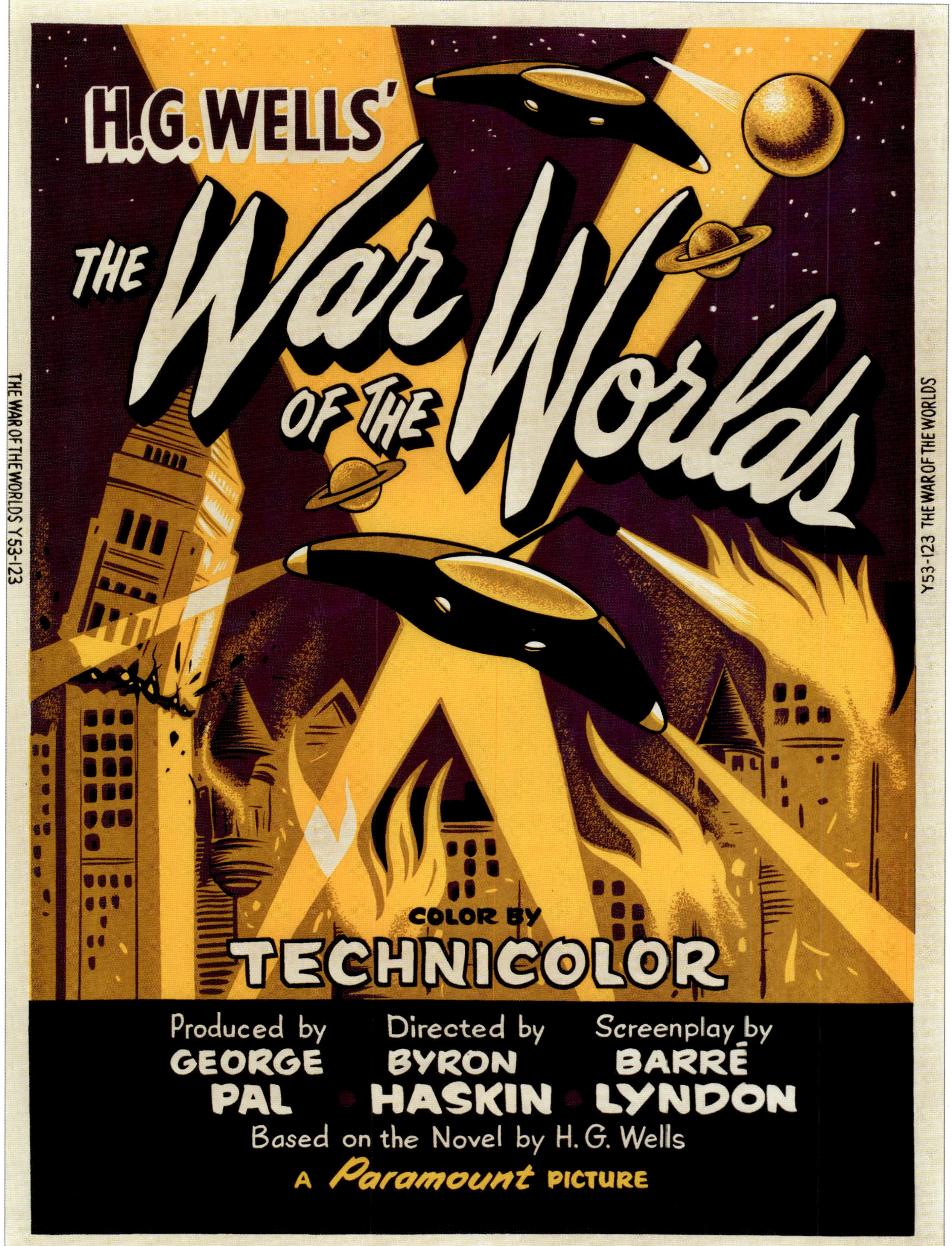
H.G. WELLS'
THE War OF THE Worlds
COLOR BY
TECHNICOLOR
Produced by
GEORGE
PAL
Directed by
BYRON
HASKIN
Screenplay by
BARRÉ
LYNDON
Based on the Novel by H. G. Wells
A Paramount PICTURE
THE WAR OF THE WORLDS Y53-123
Y53-123 THE WAR OF THE WORLDS

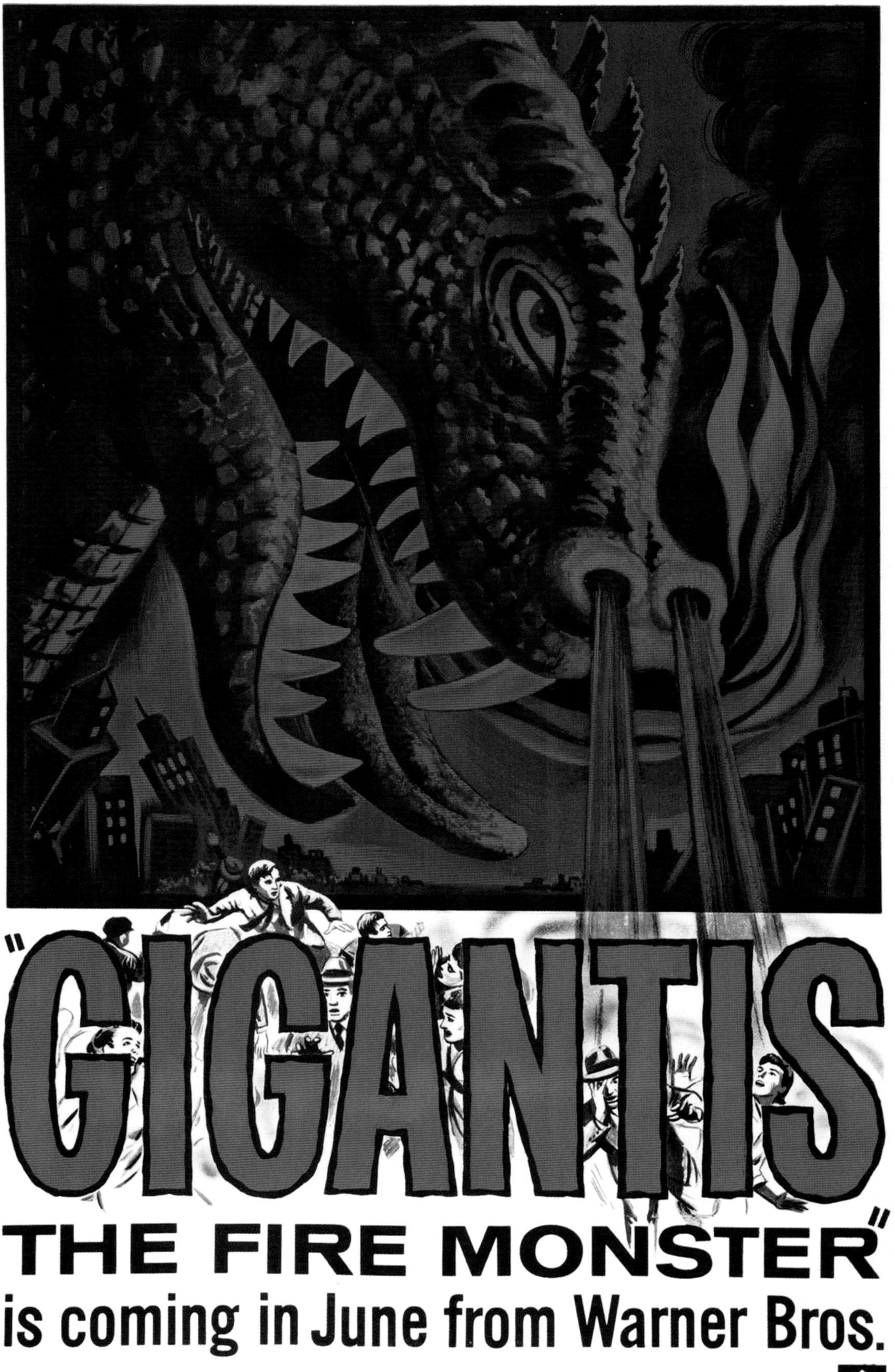

"GIGANTIS
THE FIRE MONSTER"
is coming in June from Warner Bros.

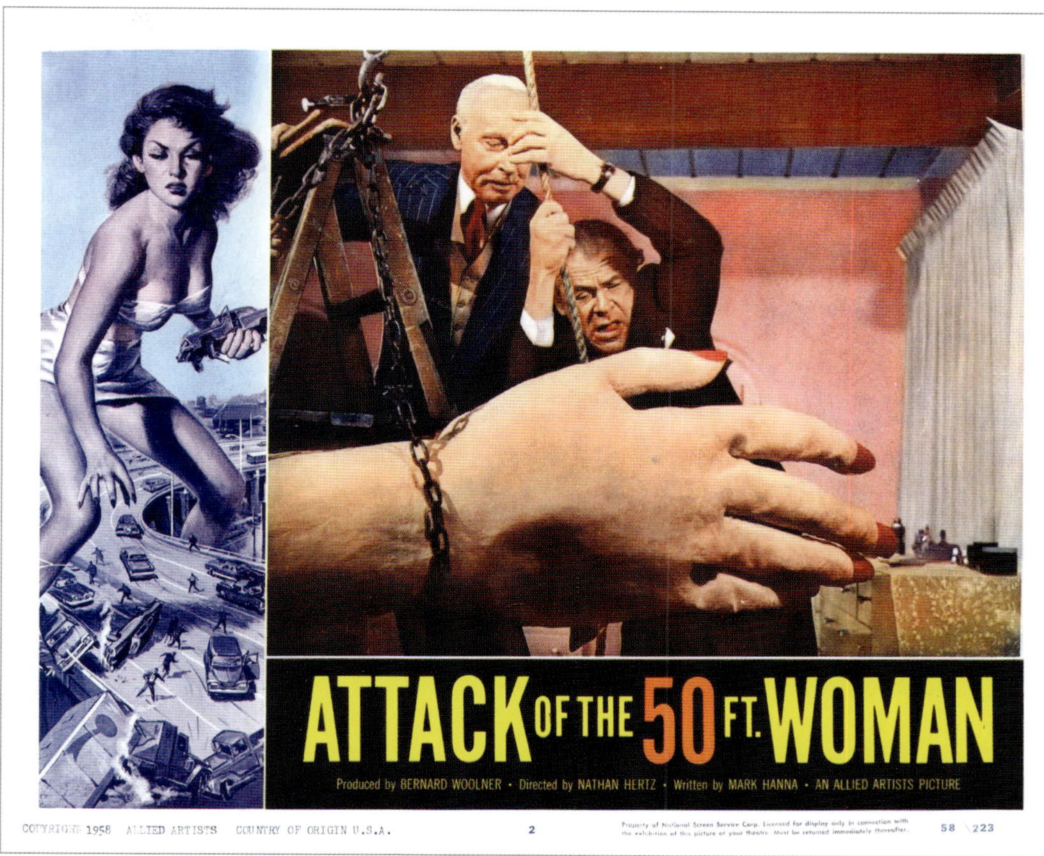

subjects (space opera, superheroes) who would after 1977 come to dominate the big budget production schedules of major studios and the box office charts. In the 1950s, things almost changed—Howard Hawks made *The Thing from Another World*, Fox featured an alien and a killer robot in a thoughtful fable *The Day the Earth Stood Still* (1951), Paramount had George Pal produce *The War of the Worlds* (1953), MGM backed the adult space opera *Forbidden Planet* (1956), Warner Bros. unleashed giant atomic ants in *Them!* (1954), and Universal added the Gill Man, the Mole People, and the Shrinking Man to their monster roster. Japan and the UK got in on the act with the Godzilla and Quatermass movies, which were—at least initially—much more sophisticated than the run of creature-on-the-loose quickies. Perhaps it was the shadow of the mushroom cloud, but suddenly SF didn't seem to be silly any more.

Of course, silliness came along quickly—often in splendid, subversive, startling forms. Going from the relative sobriety of *The Incredible Shrinking Man* (1957) to the demented glee of *Attack of the 50 Foot Woman* (1958) in only a year is remarkable, and there's a shift in aesthetics from the careful, impressive, meticulous effects work of Jack Arnold's film to the rough-and-ready, doesn't-quite-match-the-poster feel of the cash-in . . . but both movies attain pop culture immortality. The SF films of the first half of the '50s were aimed at adults but tended to connect with kids who cherished the robots, scary aliens, flying saucers, and ray guns (all elements carried over from Flash and Buck). Their successors in the next phase were aimed at teenagers in drive-ins, and reduced the messages to flip, sometimes cynical throwaways while turning up the rock 'n' roll and bringing on the bug-eyed monsters. Roger Corman was the biggest talent in this arena, making films

OPPOSITE: Striking US advance (or "teaser") one-sheet for *Gigantis The Fire Monster* (1959). The film was in fact a heavily re-edited, re-dubbed version of Toho's first Godzilla sequel, *Godzilla Raids Again* (1956). The origins of the main US movie poster format, the 27-by-41-inch one-sheet, date back to 1909, when Edison's General Film Company standardized promotional material supplied to movie theaters, where frames of that size had been installed.

ABOVE: This US lobby card for *Attack of the 50 Foot Woman* (1958) betrays the fact that the film's SFX budget was not up to matching on screen the sheer brilliance of Reynold Brown's one-sheet poster art, used on the left of the card.

TOP: A day-glo US one-sheet for *Barbarella* (1968) featuring Jane Fonda doing her thing.

ABOVE: US half-sheet for *Conquest of the Planet of the Apes* (1972). The fourth entry in the franchise told of an ape rebellion in the far-off year 1991.

OPPOSITE: British artist Philip Castle's airbrushed art, and lettering design, were used around the world on the posters for Kubrick's *A Clockwork Orange* (1971), including this commercially available "personality poster." "Stanley wanted the bowler hat just right... they sent me the hat to get it right," Castle remembered.

as bizarre and somehow perfect as *It Conquered the World* (1956), *Not of This Earth* (1957), and *Attack of the Crab Monsters* (1957), with weird-looking creatures whipped up on a low budget and a general buzz of ideas. Edward D. Wood didn't make the poorest films in the field, though the fascinating inadequacies of *Plan 9 From Outer Space* (1958) are remembered more fondly than the mere competence of, say, *Riders to the Stars* (1954).

Somber, sober, doom-laden SF continued to be an occasional crossover genre, whether in the allegorical form of Don Siegel's *Invasion of the Body Snatchers* (1956) or the nuclear war sermon of Stanley Kramer's *On the Beach* (1959). Films added color, 3D, widescreen and stereophonic sound to compete with television—where SF already had a new dawn with kids' stuff like *Captain Video*, and more serious efforts like *Science Fiction Theater*. 1950s-style cheapo monster-on-the-loose science fiction kept being made—indeed, thanks to the SyFy Channel, it's still being made—even as more money was expended on effects R&D in parallel with the suddenly-booming, post-*Sputnik* space race, which encouraged filmmakers to look to the moon and beyond as achievable destinations. In the 1960s, SF seeped into the James Bond superspy movies in the form of gadgets and missiles and eventually the space piracy of *You Only Live Twice* (1967). And Stanley Kubrick, an American filmmaker resident in the UK, made three masterpieces in a row in different SF subgenres . . . the edge-of-doom nightmare comedy *Dr Strangelove, or: How I Learned to Stop Worrying and Love the Bomb* (1964), the epic space opera *2001: A Space Odyssey* (1968), and the scurrilous dystopian satire *A Clockwork Orange* (1971).

Kubrick's vision was dominant in filmed SF for a decade, before George Lucas, Steven Spielberg, Ridley Scott, and James Cameron (all, in one way or another, influenced by Kubrick) took things in other directions—but he was not the whole show. Television got in on the act by creating lasting, ever-mutating franchises in *Doctor Who* (1963–) and *Star Trek* (1966–), which opened up universes (and, eventually, multiverses). The colorful, explosive 1960s rebooted *Flash Gordon* in sexier, satirical form in *Planet of the Apes* (1968) and *Barbarella* (1968). Then the dour, paranoid 1970s let loose Michael Crichton's odd mix of technophilia and technoparanoia in *The Andromeda Strain* (1971) and *Westworld* (1973). Russia, Japan, Great Britain, and other countries had their own distinctive take on SF, and turned out films as revealing of national concerns as anything coming out of Hollywood.

All the while, magazine SF kept being published and many name authors—Arthur C. Clarke, Robert Heinlein, Ray Bradbury, John Wyndham, Philip K. Dick, Michael Moorcock, J.G. Ballard, Harlan Ellison—were tapped in various ways by the movies. The modern Marvel Universe began when the Fantastic Four were exposed to cosmic rays on a manned space flight, just like the astronaut in *The Quatermass Xperiment* (1955)—as filmed SF fed into comics, spurring yet another mushroom growth of ideas, characters, and plots that would last for decades. Many of the films, characters, writers, and concepts covered in this general introduction remain active franchises in the 2020s—the decade when *Soylent Green* (1973) and *A Boy and His Dog* (1975) suggested humanity would revert to cannibalism.

It's been a trip since *A Trip to the Moon* . . .

. . . and we're still rushing ahead into the future.

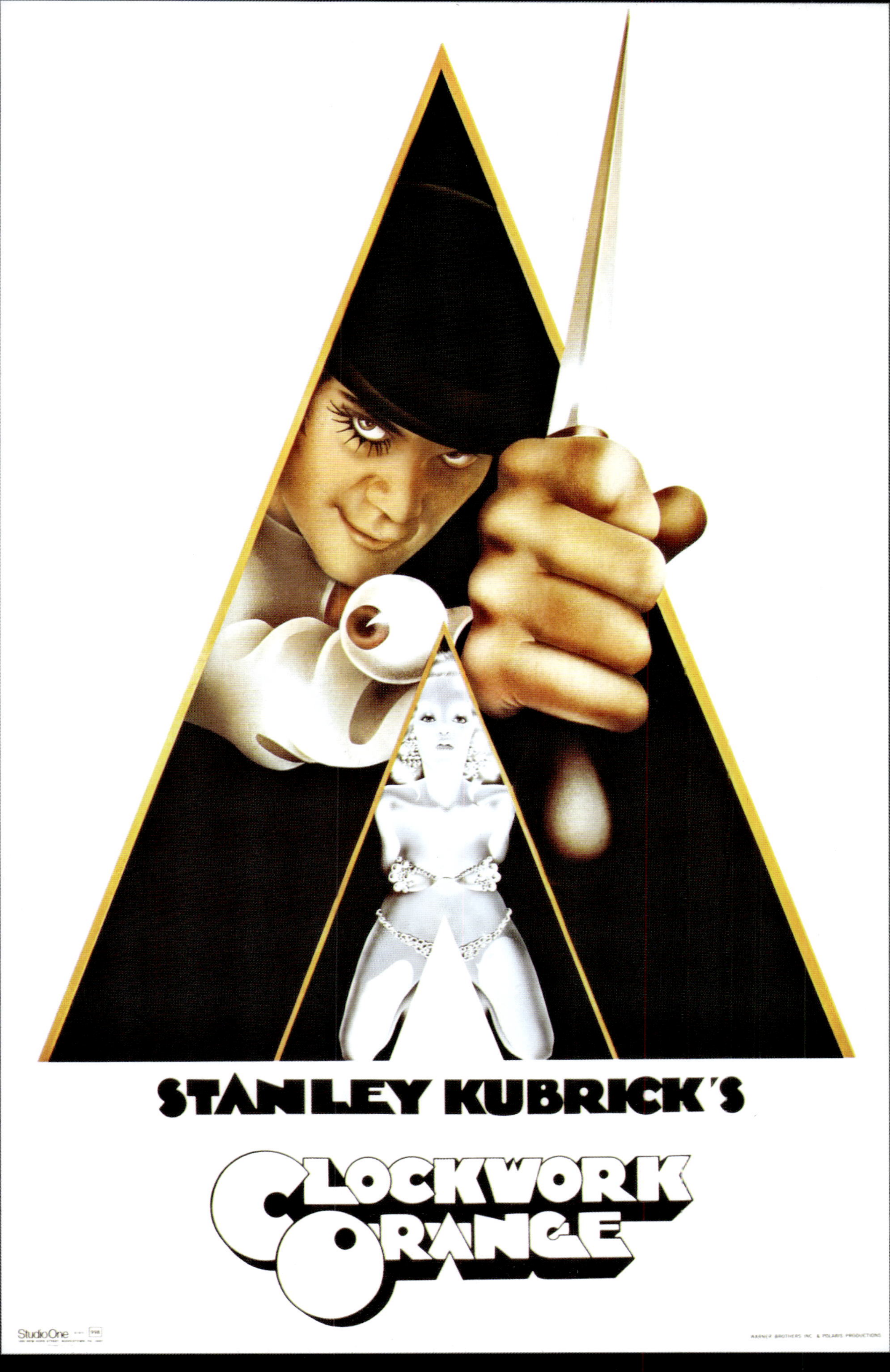
STANLEY KUBRICK'S
CLOCKWORK ORANGE
Studio One

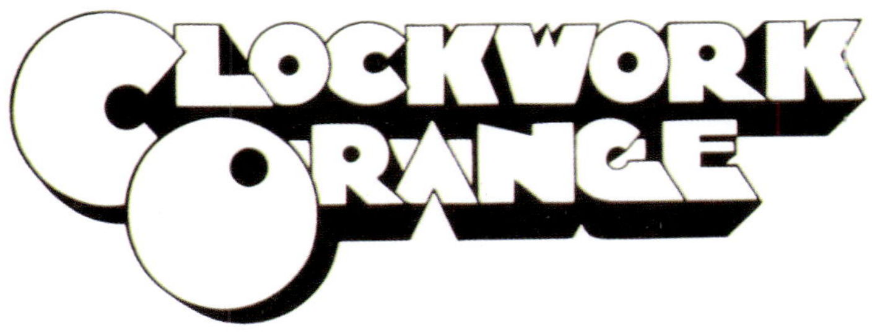

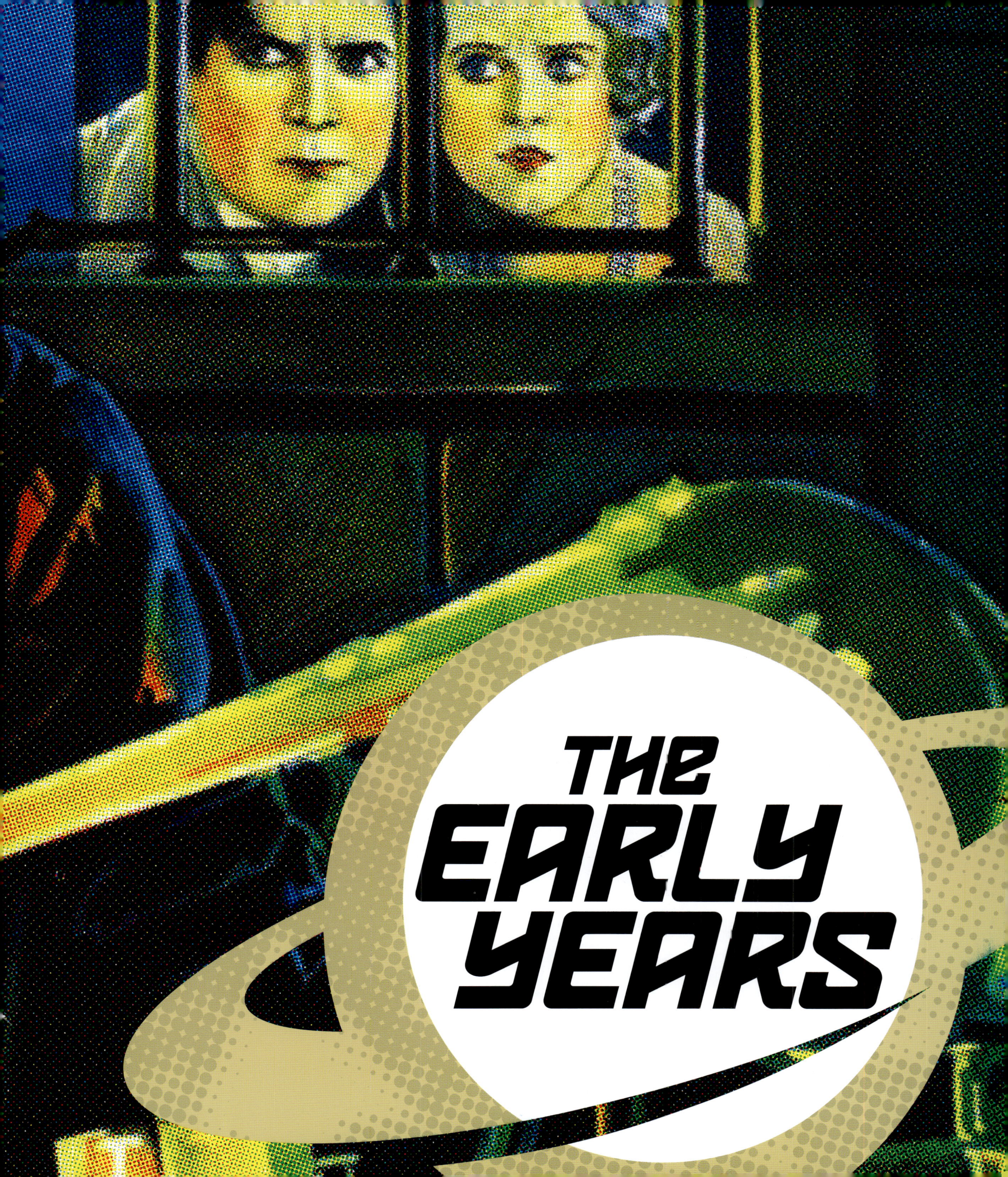
THE
EARLY
YEARS

Stephen Jones on *The Invisible Ray* and *The Phantom Creeps*

Unlike Europe—where what was then called "scientifiction" (a term coined by Hugo Gernsback, founder of *Amazing Stories* magazine) had been around since the silent days—Hollywood was slow to embrace the genre in motion pictures. In an odd way, with notable exceptions such as the 1930 futuristic musical *Just Imagine*, early American science fiction films were more likely to be disguised as horror movies, with the scientific elements subsumed within a distinctly gothic atmosphere.

PREVIOUS SPREAD: Detail from the US one-sheet for the mad scientist drama *Drums of Jeopardy* (1931).

BELOW: A suggestion for a costumed publicity stunt from a pressbook for *The Invisible Ray* (1936).

OPPOSITE: The film's stunning stone litho French poster.

The sleek robots and spaceships of *Metropolis* (1927) and *Woman in the Moon* (1929) became the ever-bubbling beakers of *Doctor X* (1932) or the fog-shrouded English village of *The Invisible Man* (1933) in the hands of Hollywood filmmakers.

Whereas countries like Germany, France, and Britain looked to the future and the stars with productions like *F.P.1 Doesn't Answer* (1932), *The Tunnel* (1935), and *Things to Come* (1936), the big American studios—mostly all run by European émigrés such as Universal Pictures' "Uncle" Carl Laemmle—turned to the past and their own heritage to imbue their fantasies with a Mittel-European charm.

One notable example of this trend was Universal's *The Invisible Ray* (1936), which can arguably be called America's first serious science fiction movie, despite the studio's attempts to sell it as something completely different.

Originally announced as *The Death Ray* and touted on the advertising as ". . . delving into new, strange fields of mystery!" (about as close as Universal could come to calling it "science fiction"), the studio co-starred its top terror team of Boris Karloff (top-billed by just his surname as "The Luminous Man") and Bela Lugosi for the third time as screen rivals.

However, despite its scientific premise and a plot that resembled H.P. Lovecraft's 1927 story "The Colour Out of Space," the studio still insisted on dressing it up in the old-world trappings that audiences had come to expect from its horror output. Makeup man Jack P. Pierce decked Karloff out in a curly black wig and moustache for his role as schizophrenic scientist Dr. Janos

Universal Film S.A. présente:
BORIS
KARLOFF
ET
BELA LUGOSI
DANS
LE RAYON INVISIBLE
(THE INVISIBLE RAY)
AVEC
FRANCES DRAKE
ET FRANK LAWTON
UNIVERSAL
Mise en scène de Lambert HILLYER
IMP. de la CINÉMATOGRAPHIE FRANÇAISE 29. R. Marsoulan . PARIS
Dépôt légal N° 268 _ 1

TOP: *The Phantom Creeps* (1939) featured as an 8-page photo strip adaptation in the sixth and final issue of All-American Publications' *Movie Comics*.

ABOVE: The US one-sheet poster, like most of the promotional material for *The Phantom Creeps*, featured Dr. Zorka's robot as prominently as star Bela Lugosi.

Rukh, who from his Carpathian observatory has discovered through his super-scientific telescope that eons ago a gigantic meteorite landed in Africa containing an unknown element which he calls "Radium X." With the help of Dr. Felix Benet (Lugosi, in one of the most controlled performances of his career) and Sir Francis Stevens (Walter Kingsford), he mounts an expedition into the jungle to find the impact site.

Unfortunately, after setting out from camp alone, Rukh becomes contaminated by the radioactive element and his touch proves instantaneously fatal (as represented by John P. Fulton's glow-in-the-dark photographic effect). Dr. Benet creates a temporary antidote, but when he later tries to pass off the curative effects of Radium X to the scientific community of Paris as his own discovery, an ever-more unhinged and embittered Rukh decides to get his revenge on the members of the expedition, killing Stevens and his wife, along with Dr. Benet in a memorable confrontation between the two great horror stars.

After Rukh almost murders his wife (Frances Drake, who replaced the originally announced Gloria Stuart) and her new husband (Frank Lawton), his mother (Violet Kemble Cooper) destroys the antidote serum and the remorseful scientist promptly bursts into flame, consumed by the alien poison flowing through his body.

Original director Stuart Walker (*WereWolf of London*) was dissatisfied with John Colton's screenplay and asked for a three-day delay before shooting started. Universal turned down his request and replaced him with Western journeyman director Lambert Hillyer (who, despite going $68,000 over the designated $166,875 budget and a reported 25 days over schedule, was rewarded that same year with *Dracula's Daughter*).

Despite being marketed and reviewed as a horror film, *The Invisible Ray* was a box office success and introduced many concepts that would later become staples of science fiction movies for years to come.

The one area of cinema where science fiction *did* flourish during the 1930s was in the serials. Perhaps because they were considered juvenile fare, such multi-chapter plays as *Undersea Kingdom* (1936), *Flash Gordon* (1936), *Flash Gordon's Trip to Mars* (1938), and *Buck Rogers* (1939) were often derived from comic strips, and contained all the robots, rocket ships, and ray-guns that were missing from the mainstream movies of this period.

Whereas Boris Karloff (mostly) chose his projects with care, the same could not be said about Bela Lugosi, who seemed to take anything that was offered strictly for the money. A good example of this is *The Phantom Creeps*, a 12–chapter serial released by Universal in January 1939. The last of five serials Lugosi made during the 1930s, the actor—in a performance light-years removed from his nuanced appearance in *The Invisible Ray* just three years earlier—starred as Dr. Alex Zorka, a crazed scientist who uses his eight-foot humanoid robot (one of the most memorable screen creations of the decade, played by stuntman Edwin "Bud" Wolfe), "devisualizer" belt, mechanical spiders, and suspended animation formula derived from a meteorite fragment to attempt world domination from his subterranean laboratory.

Co-directors Ford Beebe and Saul A. Goodkind kept the action moving swiftly along in cliffhanger episodes with titles such as "The Menacing Power," "Death

Stalks the Highways," "Invisible Terror," "The Iron Monster," and "Phantom Footprints," while stock footage from various Universal productions—including a clip from *The Invisible Ray* in which Karloff "doubles" for Lugosi—helped alleviate the budgetary restraints.

Unfortunately, the money didn't stretch to the invisibility effects of Zorka's devisualizer belt which, instead of utilizing John P. Fulton's superior optical effects from the studio's Invisible Man films, opted for a moving smudge on the film.

It would be just over another decade before George Pal's production of *Destination Moon* (1950) would truly usher in the atomic age of filmmaking, but it would be such nascent genre titles as *The Invisible Ray* and *The Phantom Creeps* that started to form the basis of the Hollywood science fiction boom which was to come . . .

ABOVE: Title lobby card. Other lobbies were produced for each of the 12 "spine-shivering" chapters. This title card incorporated comic strip-style illustrations among the photos.

A TRIP TO THE MOON

When Georges Méliès (1861–1938) cashed out of his family's luxury shoe business to buy Robert-Houdin's theater of magic in Paris, his aim was to become a stage illusionist; after an 1895 meeting with the Lumière brothers, he introduced short films into his act, and became the father of movie special effects as well. Though *A Trip to the Moon* (*Le Voyage dans la Lune*, 1902) is considered to be the first science fiction film, Méliès's earlier short *The Astronomer's Dream* (*La Lune à un mètre*, 1898) had explored similar imagery, and even inspired an attraction at the 1900 Paris Exposition (poster above). *A Trip to the Moon* had a variety of sources, including Jules Verne's novels *From the Earth to the Moon* (1865) and *Around the Moon* (1870), featuring a projectile spaceship (illustrations left), and Jacques Offenbach's operatic parody of Verne's work (poster far left). H.G. Wells's book *First Men in the Moon* (1901) was also in the mix, but the resulting film was very much Méliès's, from pre-production art to final frame. He even sketched out a potential poster design (opposite bottom left).

In later life, Méliès considered the film "not one of my best, but people are still talking about it thirty years later! It left an indelible trace because it was the first of its kind. In short it is considered my masterpiece—and I can only bow and agree."

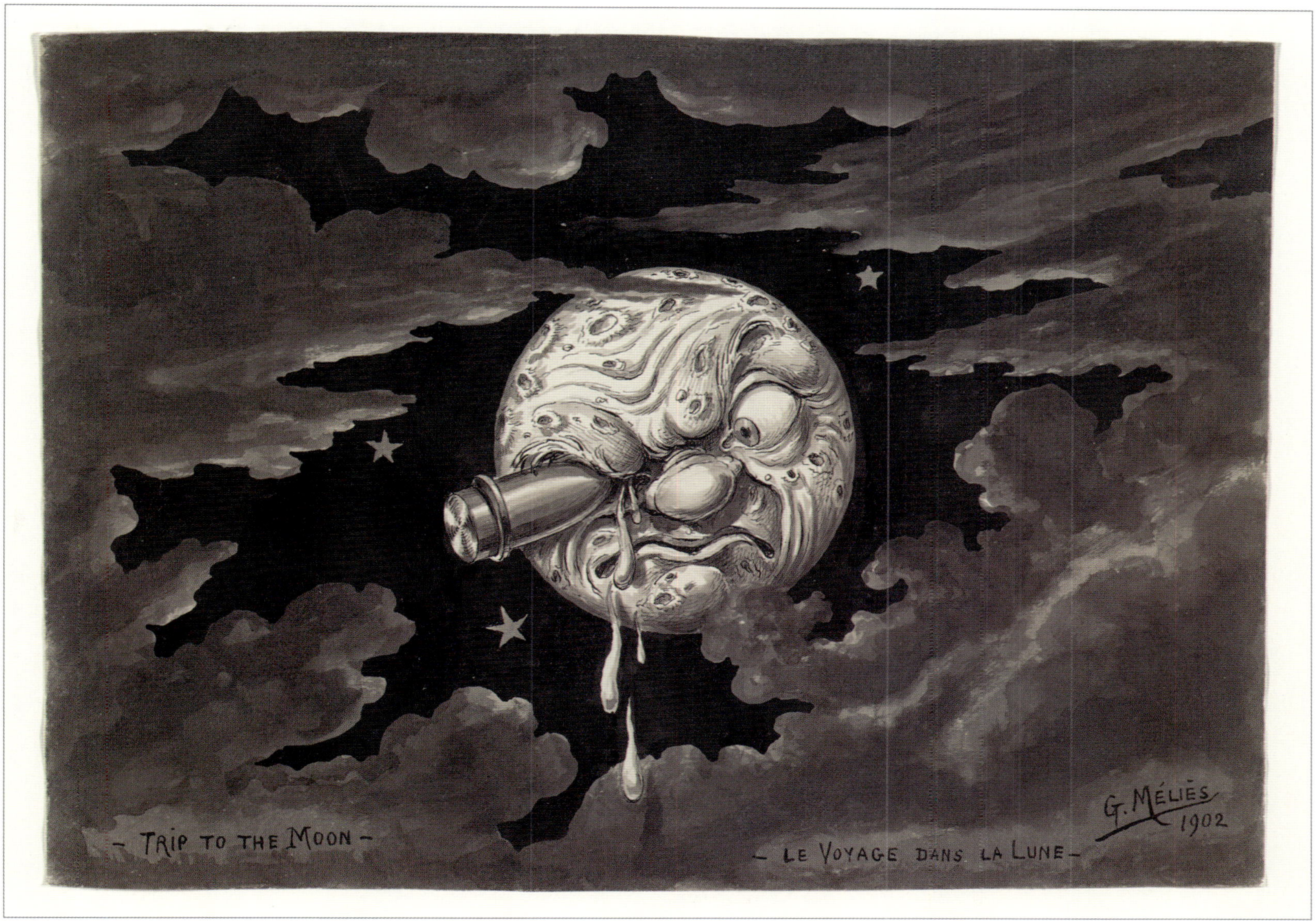

- TRIP TO THE MOON -
- LE VOYAGE DANS LA LUNE -
G. MÉLIÈS 1902

EARLY SILENTS

Just as bestselling books are signed up for movie adaptations today, early silent filmmakers were on the lookout for other Jules Verne-style authors to inspire them. Fellow Frenchman Albert Robida was, usefully, an illustrator as well as a novelist, and his 1879 novel (illustration top left) became the Italian epic *The Extraordinary Adventures of Saturnino Farandola* (*Le avventure straordinarissime di Saturnino Farandola*, 1913). No poster survives, but as the film frames show, the eponymous hero went under the water, and into the air, fighting an armored balloon battle against Verne's globetrotting hero, Phileas Fogg.

Other early SF outings include more intrepid explorers, this time with a flying machine, in Georges Méliès's *The Conquest of the Pole* (*À la conquête du pole*, 1912), Charles Ogle as the Monster and Alan Holubar as Captain Nemo in the first adaptations of Mary Shelley's *Frankenstein* (1910) and Verne's *20,000 Leagues Under the Sea* (1916), and John Gottowt as a visiting alien in the German production *Algol* (1920). The Danish film *Himmelskibet* (1918), arguably the first cinematic space opera, was released in the US as *A Trip to Mars*, with advertising trumpeting the "more than $100,000 of mechanical devices" on screen. The Soviet film *Aelita* (1924) featured a romance with the Queen of Mars (as seen on the domestic poster, opposite bottom), albeit only in the mind of the daydreaming protagonist.

HIMMELSKIBET
FILMSKUESPIL AF SOPHUS MICHAËLIS OG OLE OLSEN
ISCENESAT AF HOLGER-MADSEN. OPTAGET AF NORDISK FILMS Co
I HOVEDROLLERNE:
GUNNAR TOLNÆS • LILLY JACOBSSON

"A TRIP TO MARS"
"A Revelation!"
Truly, a Remarkable
Novelty Feature
with
An All Star Cast
5,000 Actors,
50 Gorgeous Settings,
$100,000 Worth of
Mechanical Devices
You Can Now Make Reservations
for Territorial Rights
TOWER FILM CORP.
71 West 23rd St. New York City

КИНО-
УНИОН
ТЕАТР
Большая Проломная улица, дом № 42-8, телефон № 6-21.
АЭЛИТА
14 15 16 17
ОКТЯБРЯ
14 15 16 17
ОКТЯБРЯ
Производство
Межрабпом-Русь
Москва.
Постановка
Режиссера
Я.А Протазанова

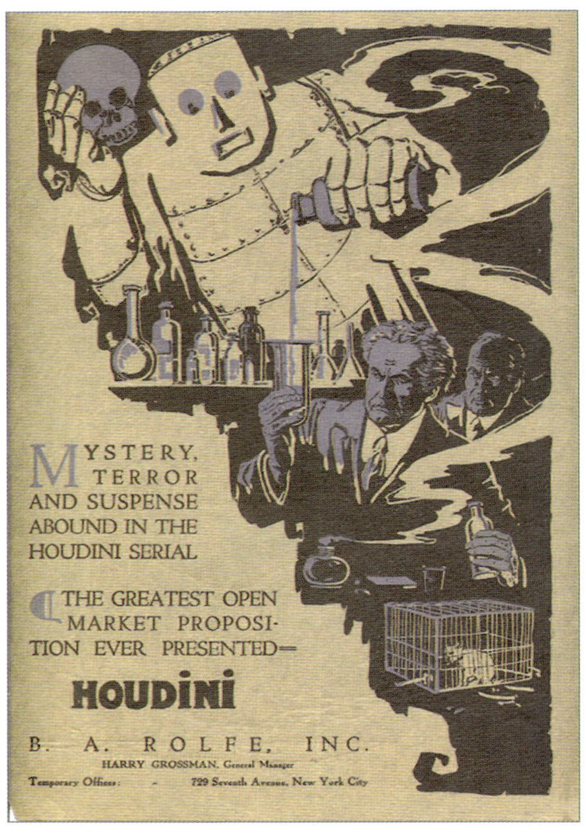
MYSTERY, TERROR AND SUSPENSE ABOUND IN THE HOUDINI SERIAL
THE GREATEST OPEN MARKET PROPOSITION EVER PRESENTED—
HOUDINI
B. A. ROLFE, INC.
HARRY GROSSMAN, General Manager
Temporary Offices: - 729 Seventh Avenue, New York City

You Cannot Keep Him Out of Your Theatre—
Houdini
ROLFE PRODUCTIONS, Inc.
HARRY GROSSMAN, Genl. Mngr.
Temporary Office:
729 Seventh Ave., New York

8e EPISODE UN PLAN DIABOLIQUE
HOUDINI
le Maître du Mystère
GRAND ROMAN CINEMA
ADAPTÉ PAR
EDITÉ PAR
PATHÉ
PUBLIÉ DANS
L'ORDRE PUBLIC

HOUDINI
LE MAÎTRE DU MYSTÈRE
GRAND ROMAN CINÉMA
Adapté par
Mr J. PETITHUGUENIN
ÉDITÉ PAR
PATHÉ
PUBLIÉ DANS
L'ORDRE PUBLIC
FIRST NATIONAL EXHIB CIRCUIT

B·A·ROLFE PRESENTS
HOUDINI
IN
The MASTER MYSTERY
BY ARTHUR B. REEVE AND CHARLES A. LOGUE
DIRECTED BY BURTON KING
EPISODE TEN
B.A. ROLFE PRODUCTIONS
OCTAGON FILMS, INC.

HOUDINI'S AUTOMATON

In 1918, the Hungarian-born escapologist Harry Houdini was up there with Charlie Chaplin as one of the most famous people in America, if not the world. He'd featured in many newsreel shorts, but his first proper acting role came that year in *The Master Mystery*, a 15-part serial advertised to movie theater owners as "The greatest open market proposition ever presented."

Houdini played an agent of the Department of Justice, foiling the dastardly shenanigans of a team of patent thieves. The somewhat random plot was all just an excuse to set up what the audience was there for: a series of daring escapes for our hero, from shackles, a straitjacket, handcuffs, an electric chair, a vat of acid… though disappointingly he did not actually hang from a cliff at any point.

Harry didn't have much range as an actor, and his stonier-than-Buster-Keaton expression is faithfully reproduced on the posters, which stress the Houdini name, but also all include the serial's other big visual draw: Q the Automaton, which was the first humanoid robot to appear on film. Even if Q eventually turned out to be a human baddie in a powered exoskeleton suit (still a first!), it was a significant SF milestone, predating *Metropolis* by almost a decade, and even the coining of the word "robot" by Czech artist Josef Čapek in 1920. Floyd Buckley, the actor in the suit, had an even bigger footnote in history to boast of: he was the voice of Popeye on radio in the '30s. Houdini made a few more films, though gave up on the movie business in 1923, canny showman that he was, because "the profits are too meager."

METROPOLIS

Fritz Lang's futuristic man-versus-technology epic *Metropolis* (1927) enjoys a towering reputation today, even if it was dismissed at the time as "quite the silliest film" by H.G. Wells. Marketed with various images around the world (see the key on p312 for details), the German three-sheet (opposite left), with art by Heinz Schulz-Neudamm, is the most famous: it became the most valuable single movie poster of all time when one of the four known remaining copies sold for $690,000 in 2005, reportedly to Leonardo DiCaprio.

Though many viewers would disagree, Lang himself was dubious about the worth of his film in later years, telling an interviewer for *Sight & Sound* magazine in 1967, "All right, so man has to live with the machine. Is that a message today? He still has to live with himself first."

METROPOLIS
MANUSKRIPT: THEA VON HARBOU
MUSIK: GOTTFRIED HUPPERTZ
EIN FILM VON FRITZ LANG
IN DEN HAUPTROLLEN:
BRIGITTE HELM · GUSTAV FRÖHLICH,
ALFRED ABEL, RUDOLF KLEIN-ROGGE, THEODOR LOOS, FRITZ RASP, HEINRICH GEORGE
AN DER KAMERA: KARL FREUND, GÜNTHER RITTAU
UFA
UFA FILM IM VERLEIH DER PARUFAMET

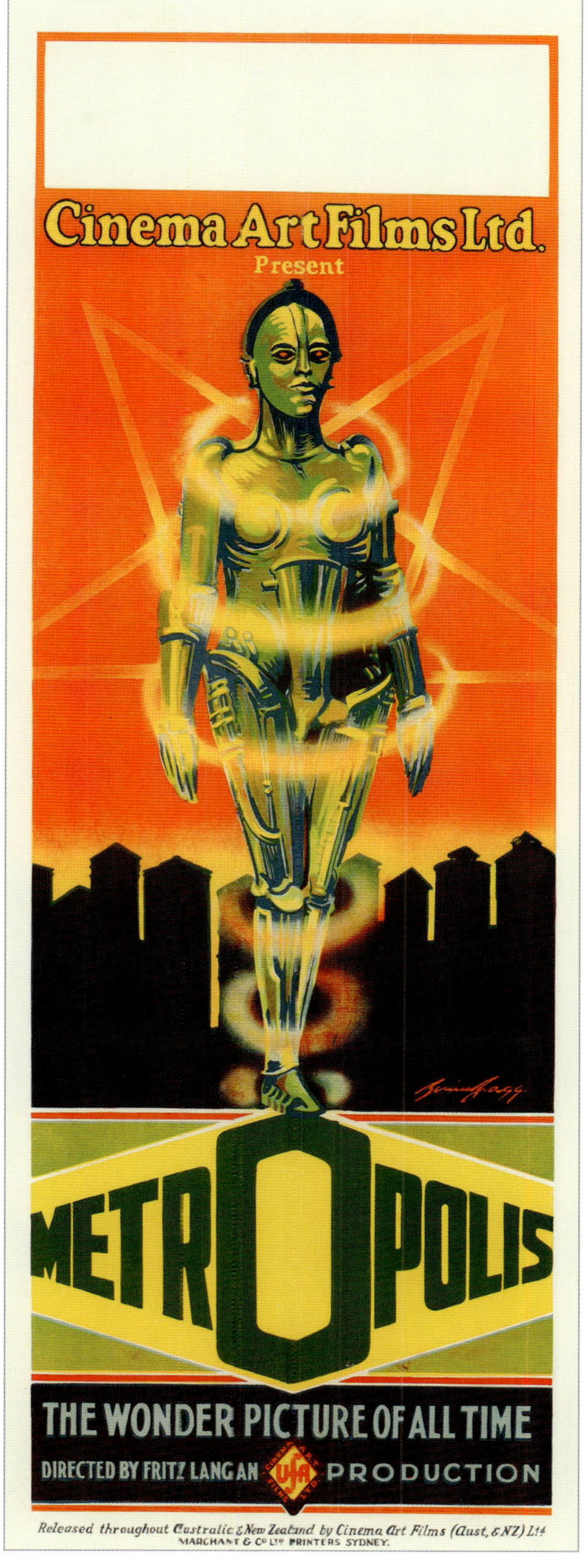
Cinema Art Films Ltd.
Present
METROPOLIS
THE WONDER PICTURE OF ALL TIME
DIRECTED BY FRITZ LANG AN UFA PRODUCTION
Released throughout Australia & New Zealand by Cinema Art Films (Aust. & NZ) Ltd.
MARCHANT & Co Ltd PRINTERS SYDNEY.

L'ALLIANCE CINÉMATOGRAPHIQUE EUROPÉENNE
PRÉSENTE UNE PRODUCTION UFA
RÉALISÉ PAR
FRITZ LANG
D'APRÈS LE SCÉNARIO DE
THEA von HARBOU:
Boris Bilinsky
METROPOLIS.

ASLUND
METROPOLIS
DEN STORA FILMEN OM FRAMTIDENS JÄTTESTAD
MED DEN NYA UNGA UFA-STJÄRNAN
BRIGITTE HELM
SAMT GUSTAV FRÖLICH OCH ALFRED ABEL
ENSAMRÄTT: A.B. UFAFILM-STOCKHOLM

Paramount Pictures
METROPOLIS
DIRECTED BY FRITZ LANG
ADAPTED BY CHANNING POLLOCK
AN UFA PRODUCTION
a Paramount Picture

METROPOLIS
Directed by FRITZ LANG
Paramount Pictures

ALLT för ALLA
Nr 8
10 öre
Veckans prisfråga:
Hur många "kusar" bakas på krono-
bageriet i Stockholm fred. 23 mars i år.

Thea von Harbou
METROPOLIS
ROMAN

METROPOLIS
WARDOUR
AUBREY HAMMOND
by Thea von Harbou
«the book sensation of Europe»

METROPOLIS
GRAUL
30 Pfg
UFA MAGAZIN
Sondernummer

EJT.

WILLY FRITSCH

GERDA MAURUS

EN FRITZ LANG FILM

J. OLSÉNS LITOGR. ANST. STHLM

WOMAN IN THE MOON

Like *Metropolis*, *Woman in the Moon* (*Frau im Mond*, 1929) was shot by Fritz Lang in Germany, and was based on a story by his wife, Thea Von Harbou (they later divorced when she joined the Nazi party). The plot has not held up well—a love triangle during a trip to the moon, which has a breathable atmosphere, to find gold—but it's the rocket science that's remarkable, presenting concepts that would become the norm to a mass audience for the first time, including a multi-stage rocket (star of all the posters and marketing), and a countdown to launch from ten.

"The scientific world is becoming rocket-conscious," announced *Popular Mechanics* in its March 1930 cover story on the film. "Perhaps it is an exaggeration to talk of reaching the moon," the US magazine cautioned, but the movie's technical advisor, rocketry pioneer Hermann Oberth, was reported to believe that soon "rockets may be speeding across the Atlantic bearing mail. Within four years, there may be passenger rockets."

BRIGITTE HELM

Though her debut as Maria (and her robot double) in *Metropolis* remains her best-remembered role, German actress Brigitte Helm (1906–96) went on to make over 30 movies. Several returned her to the SF genre: she played the Queen of Atlantis in the lost world melodrama *L'Atlantide* (1932), the love interest in the special-effects-laden alchemy tale *Gold* (1934), and starred in both silent and sound productions of Hanns Heinz Ewers oft-filmed novel *Alraune* as the amoral, promiscuous fruit of a scientist's genetic experiments—a "vamp" rather than the literal vampire Eric Rohman's Swedish poster for the 1928 silent version suggests (opposite). Rohman (1891–1949) painted over 7,000 posters, often for his brother, who managed a chain of movie theaters. He had a simple style that nevertheless got to the heart of the story, and worked incredibly quickly, admitting "I can watch the film at 10am and deliver the poster at 3pm."

VAMPYREN
EN MODERN SAGA OM ETT HEMLIGHETSFULLT KVINNLIGT NATURVÄSEN
EFTER HANNS HEINZ EWERS' ROMAN "ALRAUNE".
BRIGITTE HELM · IVAN PETROWITJ
PAUL WEGENER
ROHMAN
REGI: HENRIK GALEEN. OFFICIN: AMA FILM, BERLIN.
ENSAMRÄTT: A-B. CONTINENTALFILM, STOCKHOLM.

What's the World Coming to in 1940?

How will we live, love and settle world affairs when television will take the place of newspapers and telephones—When airplanes, dirigibles and helicopters will take off from roofs—When women will wear trousers—And there can be no War?

Thrilling – Spectacular
Imaginative – Romantic

HIGH TREASON

In the wake of *Metropolis*, the UK production *High Treason* (1929) presented another story of conflict and romance in an art-deco future. The film's publicity pressbook stressed the innovations on display: "Television in everyday use, news simultaneously broadcast in sound and picture, the Channel Tunnel in operation, the nightclub of the future with its mechanical instruments for jazz music and lady fencers as cabaret turns; fashions of 1940, with plus fours for the women and soft silk shirts and knee breeches for the men; in short, an age of scientific marvels and sartorial surprises." Alas, *The New York Times* dismissed the film as "a farrago of nonsense" and it flopped horribly.

Tiffany presents
HIGH TREASON
with
JAMESON THOMAS
BENITA HUME
HUMBERSTON WRIGHT
A GAUMONT - TIFFANY
ALL DIALOGUE
PRODUCTION

JUST IMAGINE

Now largely forgotten, *Just Imagine* (1930) was in many ways America's answer to *Metropolis*. Hollywood being Hollywood, this big-budget vision of a future society was a comedy musical, with a trip to Mars—complete with performing orangutans—thrown in. It's worth remembering though for its art direction, which gained the first ever Oscar nomination for an SF film. The production design has a considerable legacy. Footage of the huge cityscape model (below) was recycled in both *Flash Gordon* (1936) and *Buck Rogers* (1939). The whizz-bang electrical lab machinery created by Kenneth Strickfaden for the scene in which a man from 1930 is revived in 1980 was reused to classic effect in *Frankenstein* (1931). A notable failure at the box office, *Just Imagine* was the last "straight" SF movie from a major US studio until the 1950s.

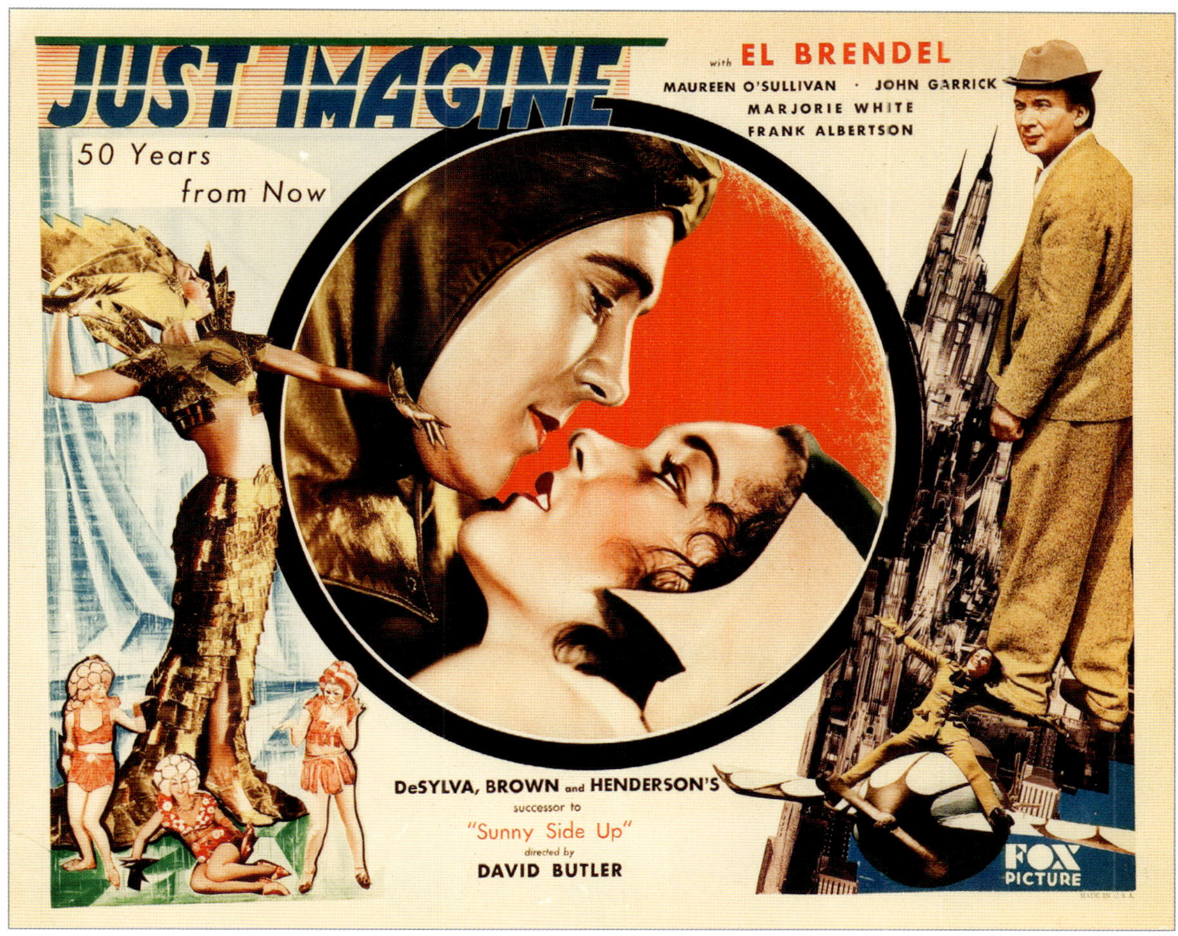
JUST IMAGINE
50 Years
from Now
with EL BRENDEL
MAUREEN O'SULLIVAN · JOHN GARRICK
MARJORIE WHITE
FRANK ALBERTSON
DeSYLVA, BROWN and HENDERSON'S
successor to
"Sunny Side Up"
directed by
DAVID BUTLER
FOX PICTURE

JUST IMAGINE
DeSYLVA, BROWN and HENDERSON'S
Fox Movietone successor to "Sunny Side Up"
with
EL BRENDEL
MAUREEN O'SULLIVAN · JOHN GARRICK
MARJORIE WHITE
FRANK ALBERTSON
Story, dialog and songs by
DeSYLVA, BROWN and HENDERSON
Dances staged by SEYMOUR FELIX
Directed by
DAVID BUTLER
FOX PICTURE

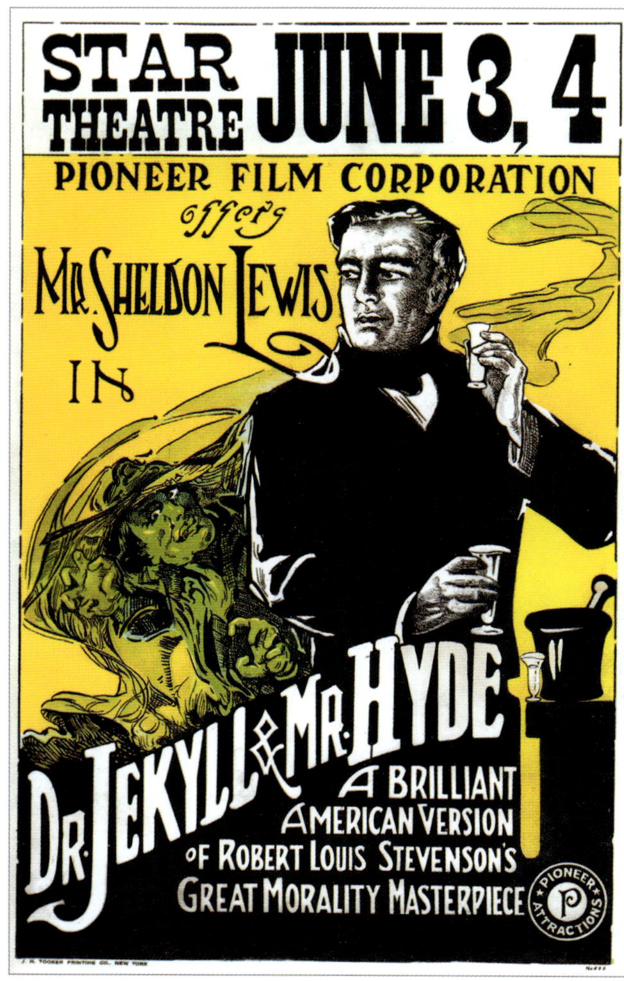

MAD SCIENTISTS

Considering its status as the first "modern" SF novel, it's no surprise that *Frankenstein* (1818) has proved to be an enduring influence on the genre in film, both in terms of actual adaptations, and the countless other mad scientists and crazed doctors who have followed in the footsteps of Mary Shelley's original. As early as 1916, the 16-part serial *The Crimson Stain* was being billed as "the story of a modern Frankenstein," though it's more of a Jekyll-and-Hyde tale of a scientist with a formula that turns him into a criminal alter ego. (Robert Louis Stevenson's 1886 novella has of course been directly adapted many times: 1920 and 1931 versions starred "Mr. Sheldon Lewis" and Fredric March respectively.) Though the doctor himself was played by Colin Clive, it was Boris Karloff as his Monster who became synonymous with the name in *Frankenstein* (1931), a smash hit which launched the Universal franchise that continued in 1935 with *Bride of Frankenstein*. The page from the latter's pressbook (overleaf), supplied to theater owners as a "catalog" of available posters and promotional material, gives a tantalizing glimpse of some poster designs where no remaining copies are known to exist.

Other early examples of the mad scientist trope featured in this selection include Warner Oland as Dr. Boris Karlov (no relation) in *The Drums of Jeopardy* (1931), Charles Laughton as Dr. Moreau in *Island of Lost Souls* (1932), Lionel Atwill as the sinister *Doctor X* (1932), and Bill Woods in the delirious schlockfest *Maniac* (1934), judged by critic Danny Peary, who has put in the hours when it comes to this sort of thing, as the very worst film ever made.

TIFFANY
presents
"The DRUMS of
JEOPARDY"
with
WARNER OLAND
JUNE COLLYER · LLOYD HUGHES
HALE HAMILTON · WALLACE MAC DONALD · GEORGE FAWCETT
STORY BY
HAROLD MAC GRATH
AND ALL-
STAR CAST
DIRECTED BY
GEORGE B. SEITZ
Recorded by RCA PHOTOPHONE

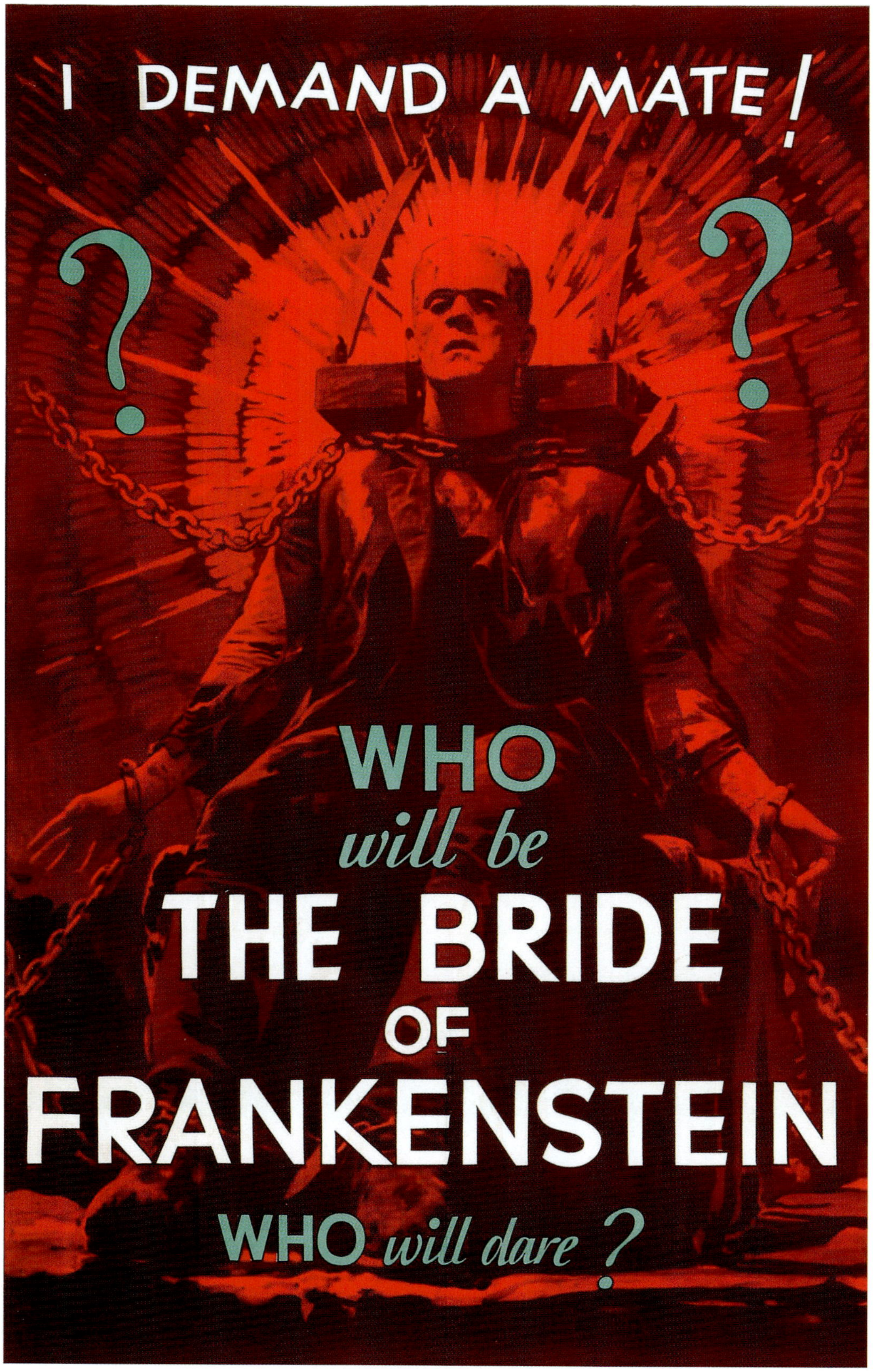

I DEMAND A MATE!
? ?
WHO
will be
THE BRIDE
OF
FRANKENSTEIN
WHO will dare ?

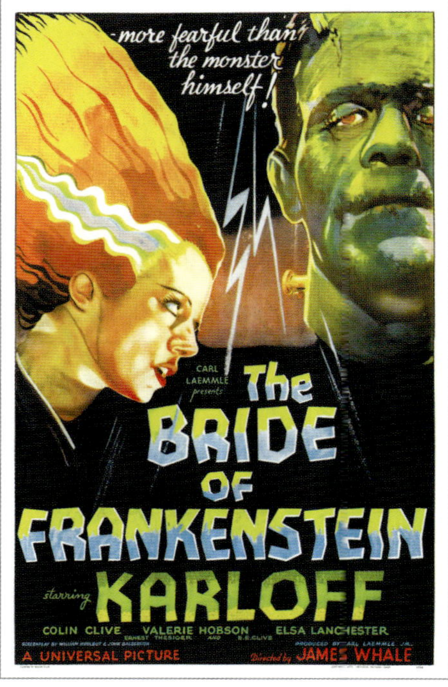
more fearful than the monster himself!
CARL LAEMMLE presents
The BRIDE OF FRANKENSTEIN
starring KARLOFF
COLIN CLIVE VALERIE HOBSON ELSA LANCHESTER
A UNIVERSAL PICTURE
Directed by JAMES WHALE

ROAD SHOW POSTERS
THE MONSTER DEMANDS A MATE!
KARLOFF
BRIDE OF FRANKENSTEIN.
JAMES WHALE
BRIDE of FRANKENSTEIN
KARLOFF
JAMES WHALE
NOTE: SEE OTHER STYLE POSTERS ON INSIDE PAGES!
I DEMAND A MATE!
WHO will be THE BRIDE OF FRANKENSTEIN
See other style posters on inside pages

REGI: ROUBEN MAMOULIAN
DR. JEKYLL och
MR. HYDE
BERÄTTELSE FÖR FILMEN EFTER EN ROMAN AV ROBERT LOUIS STEVENSON.
FREDRIC MARCH
MIRIAM HOPKINS ROSE HOBART
EN FILM FRÅN PARAMOUNT

Out-Thrills Them All!
"DOCTOR X"
LIONEL ATWILL
FAY WRAY LEE TRACY
DIRECTED BY MICHAEL CURTIZ

H.G. WELLS' "ISLAND of LOST SOULS"
with
CHARLES LAUGHTON
BELA LUGOSI
RICHARD ARLEN
LEILA HYAMS
and
The PANTHER WOMAN
a Paramount Picture

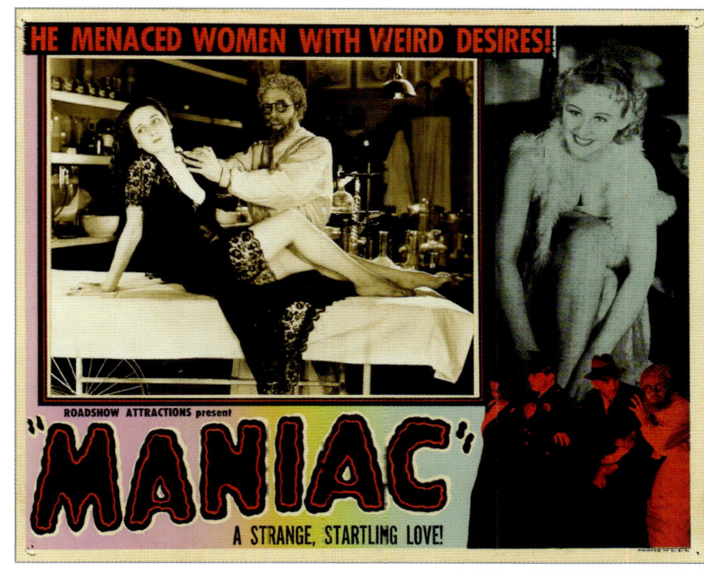
HE MENACED WOMEN WITH WEIRD DESIRES!
ROADSHOW ATTRACTIONS present
"MANIAC"
A STRANGE, STARTLING LOVE!

LOST WORLDS

"See Gigantic Prehistoric Monsters Battle Modern Lovers" puffed promotional material for *The Lost World* (1925), an early example of an SF subgenre that is still going strong: the same tagline applies equally well to *Jurassic World Dominion* (2022). Willis O'Brien's groundbreaking stop-motion creature effects in the short film *The Ghost of Slumber Mountain* (1918) were just a dry run for his work in the 1925 adaptation of Arthur Conan Doyle's already classic 1912 novel *The Lost World.* The film climaxed with a brontosaurus running amok in modern day London, though the poster—accuracy be damned!—substituted a more ferocious looking T. Rex.

Actor Lionel Barrymore shared the posters for the Jules Verne adaptation *The Mysterious Island* (1929) with a giant octopus (overleaf), but there was no question as to the main focus of the promotional art for O'Brien's effects masterpiece, *King Kong* (1933). The human cast got a bit more of a look-in on the posters for the quickie sequel *The Son of Kong*, released the same year. Scriptwriter Ruth Rose knew that the tight schedule and budget meant she couldn't compete with the first film. The result was a slightly goofy 69 minutes, but as Rose admitted, her motto was, "If you can't make it bigger, make it funnier."

First National Pictures Inc. presents
The Lost World
Sir Arthur Conan Doyle's
stupendous story
By arrangement with
Watterson R. Rothacker
Research and technical director
Willis H. O'Brien
With
Bessie Love
Lewis Stone
Wallace Beery
Lloyd Hughes
FIRST NATIONAL PICTURES
A First National Picture
Printed in U.S.A.

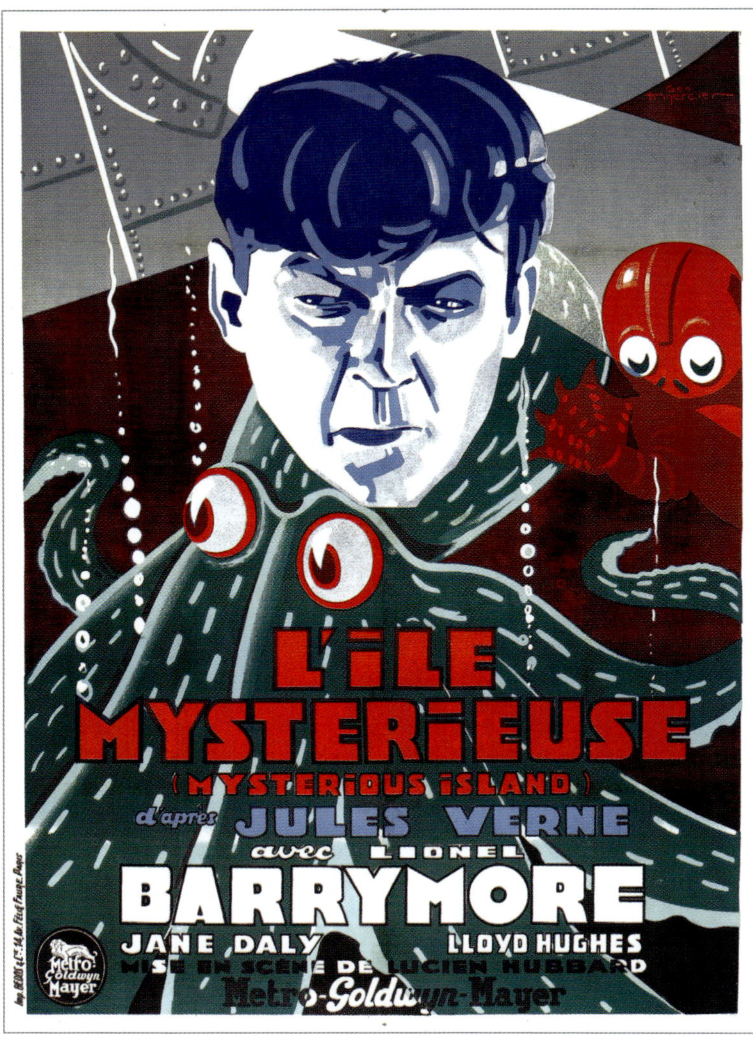
L'ILE
MYSTERIEUSE
(MYSTERIOUS ISLAND)
d'après JULES VERNE
avec LIONEL
BARRYMORE
JANE DALY
LLOYD HUGHES
MISE EN SCÈNE DE LUCIEN HUBBARD
Metro-Goldwyn-Mayer

DEN
HEMLIGHETS-
FULLA ÖN
(MYSTERIOUS ISLAND)
EFTER JULES VERNES ROMAN
LIONEL
BARRYMORE
LLOYD
HUGHES
Metro-Goldwyn-Mayer
ENSAMRÄTT: FILM-A.-B. LE MAT-METRO-GOLDWYN, STOCKHOLM

The mysterious Island
LIONEL BARRYMORE
LLOYD HUGHES
and JANE DALY
From the book by Jules Verne
Screen play by Lucien Hubbard
Directed by Lucien Hubbard...
PHOTOGRAPHED BY TECHNICOLOR PROCESS
A Metro Goldwyn Mayer PICTURE

The MYSTERIOUS Island
LIONEL
BARRYMORE
LLOYD
HUGHES
A Metro-Goldwyn-Mayer PICTURE
PHOTOGRAPHED BY TECHNICOLOR PROCESS

C.Finel 33
ATELIER G.P.HESS
RKO Radio Pictures
avec
FAY WRAY
ROBERT ARMSTRONG & BRUCE CABOT
Une Production de COOPER et SCHOEDSACK
D'APRÈS UN SCÉNARIO DE EDGAR WALLACE ET MERIAN C. COOPER
KING KONG
DIALOGUE FRANCAIS de PAUL BRACH
Distribué par la COMPAGNIE UNIVERSELLE CINÉMATOGRAPHIQUE, 40, r. Vignon, PARIS (9)
Imp. des PRESSES UNIVERSITAIRES DE FRANCE 49, Boulᵈ Sᵗ Michel, PARIS

KING KONG
FAY WRAY
ROB'T ARMSTRONG
BRUCE CABOT
A PERSONALLY DIRECTED
MERIAN C. COOPER
ERNEST B. SCHOEDSACK
PRODUCTION

CRESCENT THEATRE PONTIAC
SATURDAY
MAR. 17
NEW THRILLS!
NEW ADVENTURE!
NEW ROMANCE!
SON OF KONG
ROBERT ARMSTRONG · HELEN MACK
FRANK REICHER · JOHN MARSTON
VICTOR WONG · LEE KOHLMAR · ED. BRADY
DIRECTED BY ERNEST B. SCHOEDSACK
MERIAN C. COOPER, Executive Producer
©2004 HeritageComics.com

You'll Never Forget the Twelve Foot Prehistoric Ape with the Human Heart!
SON OF KONG
SEE THEM ALL!...
THE CANNIBALS!
THE SEA SERPENT!
PREHISTORIC BEASTS!
THE EARTHQUAKE!
These were the perils she faced with the man she loved on the Isle of Kong!
Man the sails! Take this cruise of bold adventure to the strange and dangerous land where mighty monsters of the infant world guard the fabled wealth of ages past!
With
ROBERT ARMSTRONG
HELEN MACK
FRANK REICHER
JOHN MARSTON
VICTOR WONG
LEE KOHLMAR
ED BRADY
Directed by
ERNEST B. SCHOEDSACK
RKO Radio

CONSTRUCTING THE FUTURE

A floating airport in the Atlantic was the focus of the German drama *F.P.1* (1932), an early talkie also shot in French and English versions to maximize international box office (hence the text-free poster, far right, produced for foreign distribution). It was based on a novel by Curt Siodmak (1902–2000), who after leaving his native Germany co-wrote the script for another film about a futuristic construction project. "I went to England and was making good money writing for British International and Gaumont-British," Siodmak remembered. "I received £200 for the screenplay of *Transatlantic Tunnel*, in 1935. It was the first British film that used American actors." The posters highlight GB's "Eight star special" of largely imported Hollywood talent. Siodmak ended up in Tinseltown himself, becoming best known for writing *The Wolf Man* (1941), but remained rueful about his place in the hierarchy: "Irving Thalberg once said: 'The most important man in the motion picture business is the writer. Don't ever give him any power!' I haven't met a writer yet who owns a yacht like producers or directors. But don't let them kid you. Where would they be without writers?"

GB's Eight Star Special
Richard DIX
Leslie BANKS
TRANSATLANTIC TUNNEL
NEW YORK to LONDON
Madge EVANS
Helen VINSON
C. Aubrey SMITH
Basil SYDNEY
Special portrayals by Mr. George Arliss and Mr. Walter Huston
A GB PRODUCTION
DIRECTED BY
MAURICE ELVEY
LITHO IN U.S.A.
THIS POSTER IS THE PROPERTY OF THE TWENTIETH CENTURY-FOX FILM CORP. IT IS LEASED – NOT SOLD
COPYRIGHT by TWENTIETH CENTURY-FOX FILM CORP. MCMXXXV
TOOKER-MOORE LITHOGRAPH CO., Inc. N.Y.

THINGS TO COME

"A film for the making of which every resource and discovery of modern film technique has been employed" announced a press ad for *Things to Come* (1936), and it wasn't an empty boast. The big-budget British production, based on a treatment by H.G. Wells, told an epic story of mankind from 1940 to 2036, though the original release posters tended to concentrate on the eye candy of the final, twenty-first century sequence. They are also a rare example of the writer getting top billing, though it didn't last: posters for an Italian re-release in the 1950s (p56 top) neglected to mention Wells, as did a Mexican lobby card (p56 bottom right), which used twentieth century imagery, and noted that the English title was "Come to Things." Whatever it's called, the film remains a triumph of production design. As Sir Christopher Frayling wrote in his monograph on the movie, "*Things to Come* is to modernism as *Blade Runner* is to post-modernism."

H.G. WELLS'
"THINGS TO COME"
An
ALEXANDER KORDA
PRODUCTION
WITH RAYMOND MASSEY · RALPH RICHARDSON · SIR CEDRIC HARDWICKE · PEARL ARGYLE
MARGARETTA SCOTT
and a cast of 20.000
Directed by WILLIAM CAMERON MENZIES
A LONDON FILM Released thru UNITED ARTISTS

MINERVA FILM
RAYMOND MASSEY MARGARETTA SCOTT
RALPH RICHARDSON CEDRIC HARDWICKE
JOHN CLEMENTS
NEL 2000 GUERRA O PACE?
(VITA FUTURA)
Regia di
WILLIAM CAMERON MENZIES

Raymond MASSEY Margaretta SCOTT
Ralph RICHARDSON Cedric HARDWICKE
John CLEMENTS
MINERVA FILM
NEL 2000 GUERRA O PACE?
(VITA FUTURA)
Regia di
WILLIAM CAMERON MENZIES

PRODUCCION:
ALEXANDER KORDA
H.G. WELLS
LA VIDA FUTURA
RAYMOND MASSEY · PEARL ARGILE
RALPH RICHARDSON

H.G.WELLS'
Things to come
A LONDON FILM PRODUCTION
DIRECTED BY WILLIAM CAMERON MENZIES
PRODUCED BY ALEXANDER KORDA.
DISTRIBUTED BY

TERROR, MUERTE, DESTRUCCION DEL MUNDO... POR BOMBAS ATOMICAS Y COHETES TELE-DIRIGIDOS..!
EL MUNDO EN GUERRA
(COME TO THINGS)
RAYMOND MASSEY
MARGARETA SCOTT
LA CIVILIZACION RESURGIRA EN UN MUNDO NUEVO, DE HOMBRES... O DE BESTIAS?
DIALOGADA EN INGLES CON TITULOS EN ESPAÑOL!
OPERADORA DE PELICULAS, S. A. de C. V.
Acapulco 38
Tels. 14-46-42 y 14-46-48
Mexico 7, D.

H.G. WELLS
LONDON FILM
tider skola komma...
PROD: ALEXANDER KORDA
SVENSK DIALOG
UNITED ARTISTS
MED RAYMOND MASSEY SIR CEDRIC HARDWICKE
MARGARETTA SCOTT RALF RICHARDSON
REGI: WILLIAM CAMERON MENZIES
ENSAMRÄTT: UNITED ARTISTS AKTIEBOLAG, STOCKHOLM.

FLASH GORDON

When he was offered the role that would define his career, Larry "Buster" Crabbe wasn't convinced: "I honestly thought *Flash Gordon* was too far-out, and that it would flop at the box office. God knows I'd been in enough turkeys; I didn't need another one." The first serial in 1936 was far from a turkey, leading to *Flash Gordon's Trip to Mars* (1938), which was opportunistically re-released in a feature film edit as *Mars Attacks the World* just a week after Orson Welles's infamous *War of the Worlds* radio broadcast. *Flash Gordon Conquers the Universe* (1940) lowered the budget by recycling footage, as Crabbe recalled: "Universal had a library full of old clips: Flash running from here to there, Ming going from one palace to another, exterior shots of flying rocket ships and milling crowds. It saved a lot of production time, but I thought it was a poor product." The posters had a similarly rushed, cut-and-paste look.

AN EYE FOR AN EYE
FINAL CHAPTER
OF THE NEW UNIVERSAL PICTURE
FLASH GORDON'S TRIP TO MARS
WITH LARRY "Buster" CRABBE as "FLASH GORDON"
JEAN ROGERS . . . . . as "Dale Arden"
CHARLES MIDDLETON . as "Emperor Ming"
FRANK SHANNON . . . . as "Dr. Zarkov"
BEATRICE ROBERTS . . . as "Queen Azura"
RICHARD ALEXANDER . . as "Prince Barin"
MONTAGUE SHAW . . . . as "Clay King"
DIRECTED BY FORD BEEBE AND ROBERT HILL
OWNED AND COPYRIGHTED BY KING FEATURES INC. JANUARY 7, 1934
ORIGINAL STORY AND SCREEN PLAY BY WYNDHAM GITTENS · NORMAN S. HALL · RAY TRAMPE · HERBERT DALMAS
from ALEX RAYMOND'S astonishing Newspaper Strip

YOUR FAVORITE NEWSPAPER ADVENTURE HERO ON THE SCREEN AGAIN!
The New UNIVERSAL presents
"FLASH GORDON'S TRIP TO MARS"
WITH
LARRY "Buster" CRABBE
AS "FLASH GORDON"
JEAN ROGERS AS "DALE ARDEN"
CHAS. MIDDLETON AS "EMPEROR MING"
FRANK SHANNON AS "DR. ZARKOV"
BEATRICE ROBERTS AS "QUEEN AZURA"
RICHARD ALEXANDER AS "PRINCE BARIN"
MONTAGUE SHAW AS "CLAY KING"
FROM ALEX RAYMOND'S ASTONISHING NEWSPAPER STRIP
DIRECTED BY FORD BEEBE AND ROBERT HILL
15 STARTLING CHAPTERS OF FURTHER ADVENTURES ON A NEW PLANET!

MARS ATTACKS THE WORLD
WITH
LARRY BUSTER CRABBE
JEAN ROGERS · CHARLES MIDDLETON
FRANK SHANNON · BEATRICE ROBERTS
A FILMCRAFT PICTURE

UNIVERSAL INTERNATIONAL presenta
UN VIAJE A MARTE
(FLASH GORDON TRIP TO MARS)
Larry "Buster" GRABBE
Jean ROGERS
CHARLES MIDDLETON · BEATRICE ROBERTS
15 EXTRAORDINARIOS EPISODIOS!
ES UNA PELICULA UNIVERSAL INTERNATIONAL
DIST. POR EAGLE LION DE MEXICO, S.A. · PASEO DE LA REFORMA 153

FLASH Gordon
INTERPRETADO POR
LARRY BUSTER CRABBE
En
PANTALLA PANORAMICA
MONSTRUOS DE LA ERA ATOMICA!
ELLOS CONQUISTAN MUNDOS Y DESTRUYEN PLANETAS CON SU PODER ATOMICO!
UN VIAJE a MARTE
Con
JEAN ROGERS
CHARLES MIDDLETON
FRANK SHANNON
BEATRICE ROBERTS
DISTRIBUIDA POR DIST. CONTINENTAL FILMS, S. A. MONTERREY 101 Desp. 209 y 210 MEXICO 7, D. F.

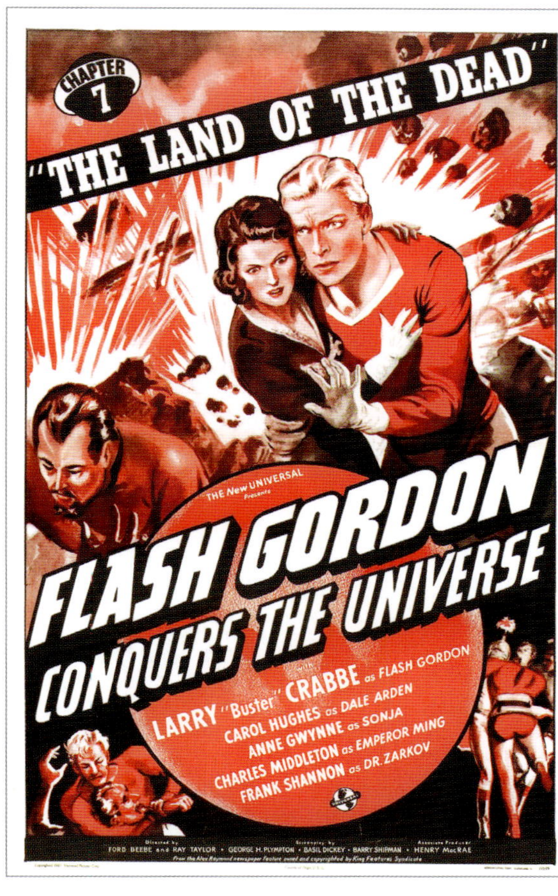

CHAPTER 7
"THE LAND OF THE DEAD"
THE New UNIVERSAL presents
FLASH GORDON
CONQUERS THE UNIVERSE
LARRY "Buster" CRABBE as FLASH GORDON
CAROL HUGHES as DALE ARDEN
ANNE GWYNNE as SONJA
CHARLES MIDDLETON as EMPEROR MING
FRANK SHANNON as DR. ZARKOV
Directed by FORD BEEBE and RAY TAYLOR • Screenplay by GEORGE H. PLYMPTON • BASIL DICKEY • BARRY SHIPMAN • Associate Producer HENRY MacRAE
From the Alex Raymond newspaper feature owned and copyrighted by King Features Syndicate

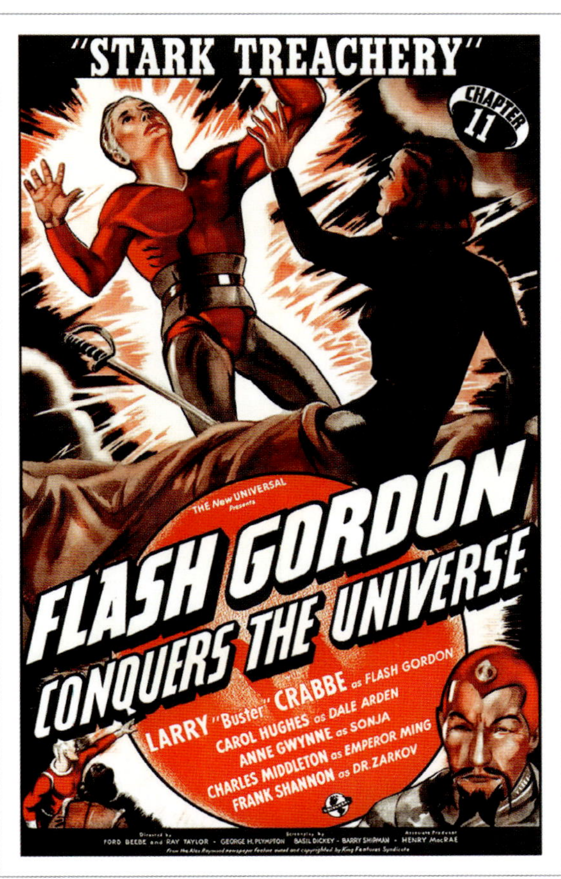

"STARK TREACHERY"
CHAPTER 11
THE New UNIVERSAL presents
FLASH GORDON
CONQUERS THE UNIVERSE
LARRY "Buster" CRABBE as FLASH GORDON
CAROL HUGHES as DALE ARDEN
ANNE GWYNNE as SONJA
CHARLES MIDDLETON as EMPEROR MING
FRANK SHANNON as DR. ZARKOV
Directed by FORD BEEBE and RAY TAYLOR • Screenplay by GEORGE H. PLYMPTON • BASIL DICKEY • BARRY SHIPMAN • Associate Producer HENRY MacRAE
From the Alex Raymond newspaper feature owned and copyrighted by King Features Syndicate

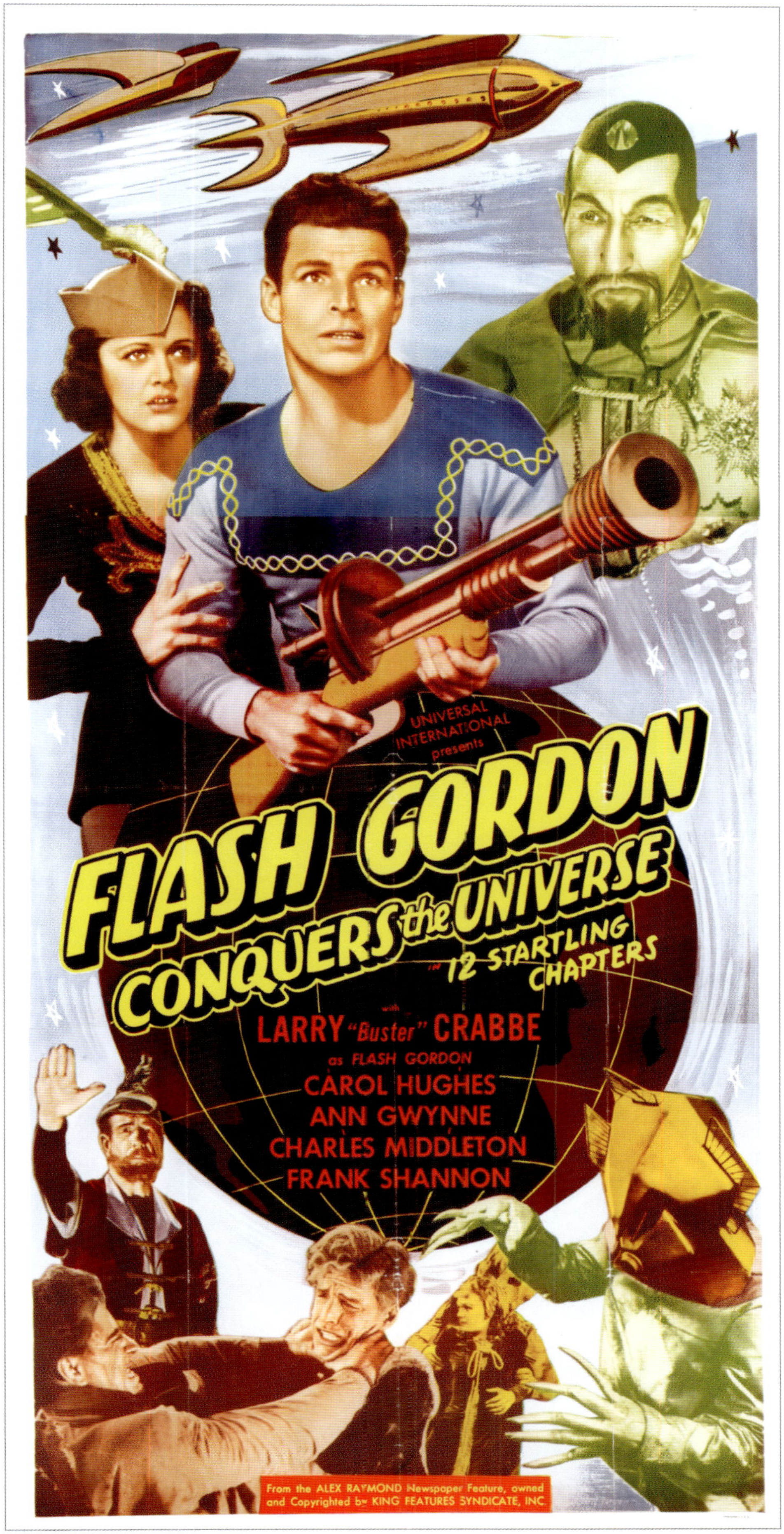
UNIVERSAL INTERNATIONAL presents
FLASH GORDON
CONQUERS the UNIVERSE
in 12 STARTLING CHAPTERS
with
LARRY "Buster" CRABBE
as FLASH GORDON
CAROL HUGHES
ANN GWYNNE
CHARLES MIDDLETON
FRANK SHANNON
From the ALEX RAYMOND Newspaper Feature, owned and Copyrighted by KING FEATURES SYNDICATE, INC.

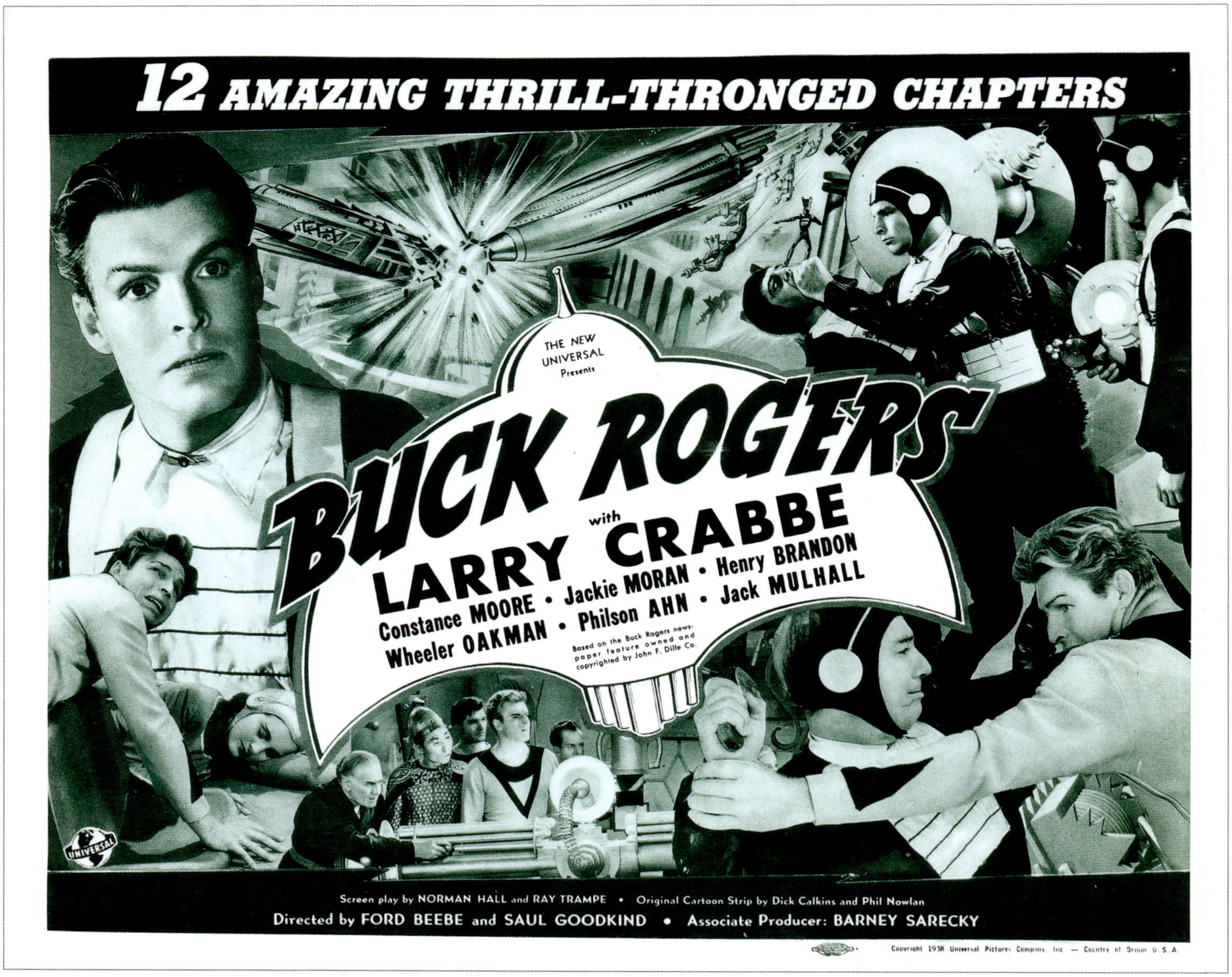
12 AMAZING THRILL-THRONGED CHAPTERS
THE NEW UNIVERSAL Presents
BUCK ROGERS
with
LARRY CRABBE
Constance MOORE • Jackie MORAN • Henry BRANDON
Wheeler OAKMAN • Philson AHN • Jack MULHALL
Based on the Buck Rogers newspaper feature owned and copyrighted by John F. Dille Co.
UNIVERSAL
Screen play by NORMAN HALL and RAY TRAMPE • Original Cartoon Strip by Dick Calkins and Phil Nowlan
Directed by FORD BEEBE and SAUL GOODKIND • Associate Producer: BARNEY SARECKY
Copyright 1938 Universal Pictures Company, Inc. — Country of Origin U.S.A.

"THE UNKNOWN COMMAND"
Chapter 6
THE NEW UNIVERSAL Presents
BUCK ROGERS
with
LARRY CRABBE
Constance MOORE • Jackie MORAN • Henry BRANDON
Wheeler OAKMAN • Philson AHN • Jack MULHALL
Directed by FORD BEEBE and SAUL GOODKIND • Associate Producer: BARNEY SARECKY

THE NEW UNIVERSAL Presents
BUCK ROGERS
with
LARRY CRABBE
Constance MOORE • Jackie MORAN • Henry BRANDON
Wheeler OAKMAN • Philson AHN • Jack MULHALL
12 AMAZING THRILL-THRONGED CHAPTERS

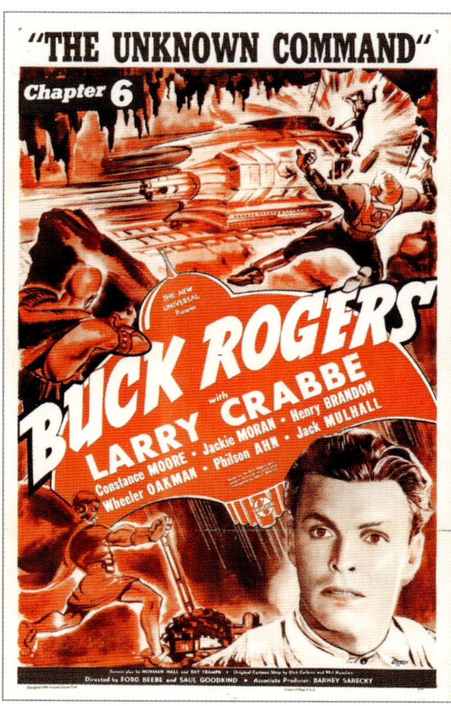

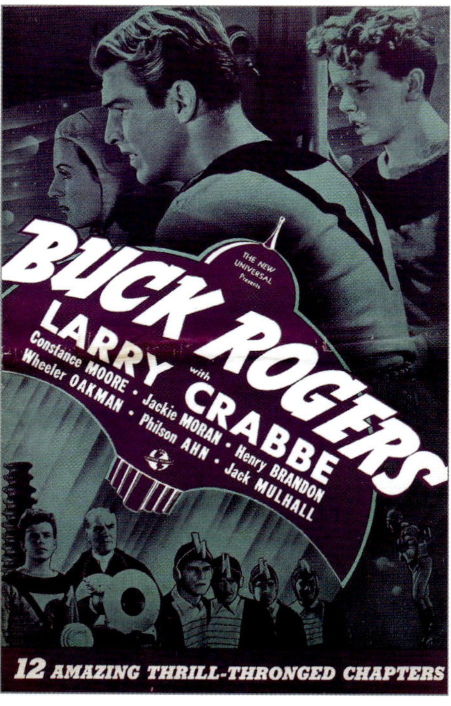

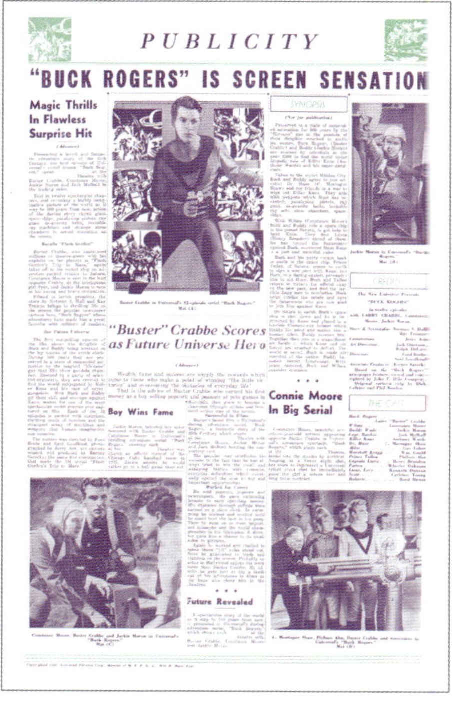

PUBLICITY
"BUCK ROGERS" IS SCREEN SENSATION
Magic Thrills In Flawless Surprise Hit
"Buster" Crabbe Scores as Future Universe Hero
Boy Wins Fame
Connie Moore In Big Serial
Future Revealed

SHOWMANSHIP

WORK WITH PAPER TO BOOST BOTH PICTURE AND DAILY STRIP

Buck Rogers, sensational new chapter play, has been made from the internationally famous cartoon created by John F. Dille and drawn by Lieutenant Dick Calkins from story by Phil Nowlan. Appears in over 100 newspapers whose combined circulations run well into the millions. Newspapers carrying the strip and the full colored Sunday page provide ready-made tie-ups with unlimited possibilities for extra publicity and exploitation to help your campaign. Work out a mutually advantageous arrangement with the local newspaper carrying the cartoon, whereby you will plug the newspaper strip and the newspaper will plug the motion picture.

Offer Your Full Co-operation

The editor should be glad to cooperate if you run a slide or trailer on your screen drawing attention to the newspaper feature. Make up a board for your lobby, as indicated in the sketch, featuring the Sunday colored page carrying the paper's masthead. For an advance stunt get a quantity of newspaper pages featuring the Buck Rogers cartoon and give them away in your theatre. Imprint this line on page: FOR THE FIRST TIME, YOUR FAVORITE NEWSPAPER HERO, COMES TO VIVID, STARTLING LIFE ON THE SCREEN! SEE HIM AT THE RIVOLI THEATRE EVERY SATURDAY! FOLLOW HIS AMAZING ADVENTURES IN THE BLANK CITY NEWS EVERY DAY! As a good will gesture and for extra publicity arrange a matinee for the paper's newsboys.

In return for your promotional efforts in behalf of the paper, the editor should give considerable assistance to publicizing the picture. Get him to use a tie-up line calling attention to Buck Rogers amazing screen adventures, on the page featuring the Buck Rogers cartoon. Place banners on the paper's delivery trucks, use the herald as an insert for the newspaper, make up special cards to place on the newsstands, and get the paper to run an ad featuring their newspaper cartoon and calling attention to the motion picture.

Following is a partial list of newspapers carrying the Buck Rogers cartoon.

(Sketch suggests display board tying-in paper feature with film.)

A Partial List of Newspapers

"Planet" Shadow Box

Built to represent the sky, with stars, planets and rocket ships in motion, this shadow box can be constructed by the house artist at little expense. Planets can be ordinary rubber balls of different sizes, painted a silver color. Around middle of ball place a flat cardboard halo as indicated. Hang from top of box by invisible wire or thread. Also suspend poster cut-out rocket ships, or the regular Buck Rogers space ships carried by toy stores. Back wall is endless piece of muslin or canvas, painted blue to represent sky. To secure effect of motion for rocket ships and planets, mount cloth sky on rollers placed at each side of box, with an endless belt attached to bottom of rollers and hooked up to a slow geared motor to keep sky moving in opposite direction from which rocket ships are heading. Sky background in motion will give effect of ships and planets rushing through space. Cut out stars and planets in cloth sky and cover with silver transparencies. Place flasher light behind to make stars appear stationary. Illuminate interior of box with concealed blue light.

THRILL LINES

See! Blazing rocket ships plunge through space!
Humans travel by radio!
The astounding atom chamber!
Amnesia Helmets!
Giant death ray machines!
Disintegrating guns!
Strange Tele-eyes!
Men turned into human Robots!
War between the planets!
Mountains crumble into dust!
The Paralyzing Machine!
The Hidden City!
Invisible Ray Guns!
Life on the Planet Saturn!
Space ships explode!
Mysterious effect of Nirvano Gas!
Degravity Belts!
Disintegrating Chambers!
Battles in the stratosphere!
Frightful wars of the future!
The animal like Zugg men!
The bombing of Saturn!
Earth men annihilate strange world bandits!
Amazing creatures on strange planets!
Cities that stagger the imagination!
Buck Rogers heroic battles to save the Earth *See!*

WHAT HAPPENS NEXT?

Plant contest with newspaper offering guest tickets for best letters explaining how the predicament with which each chapter closes, is cleared up. Prizes go to letters that come closest to actual action in film.

Bring Out the Local Buck Rogers

Plant a contest with the newspaper to find the local athlete who most closely resembles and measures up to the physical specifications of Larry "Buster" Crabbe, star of "Buck Rogers." Have contestants send their photos and measurements to the newspaper, which should publish them along with the photo and measurements of the star. Paper can provide a voting coupon for readers to use in selecting a winner.

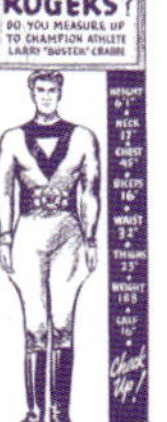

Promote merchandise from local merchants for prizes for winning entry. Make a display of the prizes in your lobby giving each contributing merchant a credit card. Start the stunt well in advance of the showing of the film and present the winner from your stage on opening night. Introduce winner at all local affairs such as, sporting events, dances, etc.

Sketch indicates illustration for newspaper announcement or a lobby display. Specifications on board are Larry Crabbe's measurements.

DISPLAY LINES

For the first time . . . your favorite newspaper hero comes to vivid . . . startling . . . life on the screen!

Unforgettable sights and adventures! See Buck Rogers wield mechanical marvels . . . mighty inventions of this world . . . against weird, destructive forces of menacing super-planets!

See the terrific battle of strange worlds! Zoom from planet to planet in space ships! Follow the amazing adventures of Buck and his buddies in the astounding 25th century!

Buck Rogers battles the universe . . . to save the Earth! Crashing into strange worlds! . . . blasting terrific obstacles! . . . fighting fantastic foes!

Astounding battles with amazing creatures on strange planets! Your newspaper friends . . . Buck Rogers, Wilma, Buddy, Dr. Huer . . . now electrify the screen!

Buck Rogers saves the Earth from annihilation! . . . in the most incredible . . . thrilling . . . adventure story ever packed into 12 chapters of enthralling entertainment!

A new chapter play of the 25th century to thrill and amaze you! Strange world adventures! Amazing escapades! Don't miss a single chapter!

The world of the future! The most amazing spectacle ever caught by cameras!

Sell Chapter Titles

Each chapter title can be effectively sold, week after week, with the chapter board illustrated in the sketch. Mount action stills from current chapter on the board each week. Have house artist paint and flitter planets and stars. Use poster cut-out heads as indicated. The 12 chapter titles in sequence are: "Tomorrow's World," "Tragedy of Saturn," "The Enemy's Stronghold," "The Sky Patrol," "The Phantom Plane," "The Unknown Command," "Primitive Urge," "Revolt of the Zuggs," "Bodies Without Minds," "Broken Barriers," "A Prince in Bondage," and "War of the Planets."

25th Century "Radio" To Make Lobby "Broadcasts"

Have a local radio man rig up a set as indicated in the illustration. It does not have to be a real one but should give impression of reality. Give it streamlined futuristic design. Hook up a microphone and loud speaker set so that some one inside theatre can broadcast through it. Dress a man in Buck Rogers costume as shown and station him at set. Use copy and layout indicated. Following message is suggested for broadcasting through loud speaker:

"Buck Rogers calling Dr. Huer! Buck Rogers calling Dr. Huer! Prepare all on earth for an attack by Killer Kane and his warriors from Saturn! Organize all Earth fighting men! . . . paralyzer guns! . . . space ships! . . . disintegrator guns! Hurry! Hurry! Buddy, Wilma and myself will join Earth forces immediately! This is Buck Rogers calling from "Saturn."

Contact the P.T.A.'s

Local Parent-Teacher Associations can prove of great value in helping you sell Buck Rogers. Always ready to promote a good cause, they should go for the scientific background of the film and the clean, stirring adventures of famed athlete Larry Crabbe. If possible, give them a special screening of the first chapter. Get them to indorse Buck Rogers. Quote their indorsement in your ads and in your lobby. Have them talk about the film at home and in class. Arousing their interest will provide an effective means of reaching the youngsters.

"TELE" STILL DISPLAY

The WORLD of the FUTURE!
BUCK ROGERS with LARRY CRABBE

Behind circular panel place a cardboard disc on which you have mounted several production stills. Arrange this disc so that it turns on a motor or can be turned by hand, in order that various stills will appear in glass covered opening.

Telescope Stunt

Promote telescope from optical store and set it up outside theatre. Have man dressed as Buck Rogers to guard it. Use this copy:

You can see the planets through this telescope . . . but to see the fantastic life on these strange worlds don't miss the thrilling film, Buck Rogers, now playing, Rivoli Theatre!

"ROBOT" BALLY

Strange world adventures of "Buck Rogers" can be effectively sold with street ballyhoo indicated in the sketch, suggested by outfit worn by Robot men in film. A local costumer can supply the black shirt, black riding breeches and black boots. Helmet can either be fashioned by a tinsmith or else made by your house artist of cardboard painted silver, or covered with tinfoil. For weapon, obtain a Buck Rogers Disintegrator from a toy shop.

Newspaper Art Contest

Following newspaper story describes an advance contest that should appeal to the local editor.

PRIZES FOR BEST ART SHOWING BLANK CITY OF THE 25th CENTURY

What will Blanktown look like in the 25th century? Will it be a city of chromium and steel designed in fantastic shape? Will it be built in levels, have airplane landing fields on top of buildings? Will our old, familiar landmarks be gone, replaced by streamlined construction for the Blanktown resident of the future?

Inspired by the amazing chapter play, Buck Rogers, depicting strange worlds and fantastic adventures of the 25th century, the Daily News is offering guest tickets to see this unusual film, for the 25 best pen and ink drawings of your conception of Blanktown as you think it will look in the 25th century. Drawings must be submitted not later than Friday. Send them to the Buck Rogers Editor, care of this paper.

"Space-Ship" Bally

Have house artist follow design indicated in sketch for a trick body to place over chassis of small automobile. Paint in brilliant reds, greens and yellows. Dress driver in helmet and goggles. Use copy shown.

MODEL SPACE-SHIP CONTEST

Streamlined, unusual appearing space ships of the future used by Buck Rogers, suggest a model space-ship building contest which should net some extra advance publicity for the film. Tie-up with newspaper for stories on the contest, publication of stills showing ships used in film, and pictures of the work contributed by contestants. Get cooperation of Boy Scout headquarters, schools, toy shops and people interested in model building.

Promote prizes from local sporting goods shops, stores selling Buck Rogers toys, and also offer a pair of guest tickets to see chapter one to all entrants. Hold model exhibit in lobby and in store windows. Get newspaper aviation editor, car, plane or industrial designer, and theatre manager to act as judges.

A Local Buck Rogers Club Holds Interest!

ORGANIZE EARLY WITH NEWSPAPER BACKING

Great popularity of Buck Rogers cartoon should pave way for a Buck Rogers Strange World Adventures Club, excellent medium to maintain youngster interest for the 12 chapters and to build good will. Get newspaper running cartoon to cooperate with announcement stories, notices of meetings, club news. Call your organization meeting well in advance of the showing of the film to pep up the youngsters on the idea.

Stage A Big Parade

On opening day of first chapter have club members parade to theatre. Get them to dress in Buck Rogers costumes. Give prizes to youngsters wearing most novel and original 25th century costumes. Get Boy Scout cooperation and have a scout or other boys' band lead the parade. Award Buck Rogers novelties to members with best attendance records at chapter showings. Give each youngster joining, one of the club membership cards illustrated.

Membership Card

A mat is available at your Universal Branch. Ask for Exploitation Service Mat. No. BR-2.

Club Buttons

Printed in two bright colors on heavy celluloid, in diameter. … PHILADELPHIA BADGE CO., 942 MARKET STREET, PHILADELPHIA, PA.

10¢
SPACE • JUNGLE • WESTERN
BUSTER CRABBE
THE AMAZING ADVENTURES OF
BUSTER CRABBE
FEB.
NO. 2
THE ALL AMERICAN HERO
FREE! OF ALL COST AUTOGRAPHED PICTURES
HIS 3 GREATEST ADVENTURES

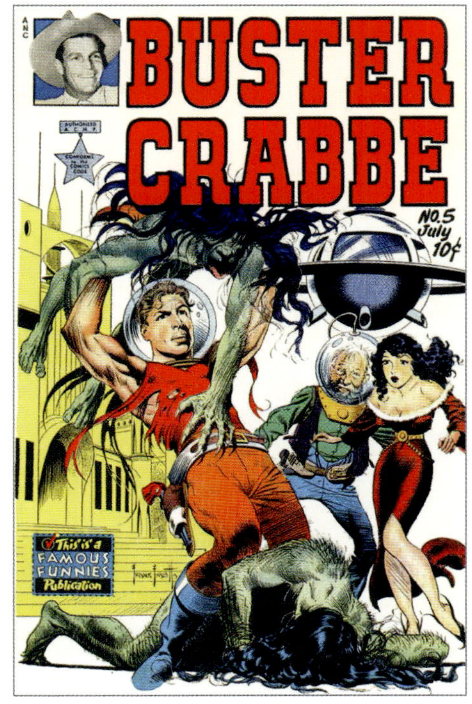

BUCK ROGERS

"Humans travel by radio! Degravity Belts! Amnesia Helmets." were just some of the sales points listed in the publicity showmanship manual for movie theaters showing the "thrill-thronged" serial *Buck Rogers* (1939). Another suggestion was to send a staff member to walk the streets dressed as a robot man: "Helmet can either be fashioned by a tinsmith or else made by your house artist of cardboard painted silver, or covered with tinfoil." They were simpler days. More ingenious marketing came in the 1950s, when the comic book industry avoided having to license the newspaper strips Flash Gordon and Buck Rogers by doing a deal with actor Larry "Buster" Crabbe instead, and then sending him on adventures in space. Issue 5 (left) featured a cover by legendary fantasy artist Frank Frazetta.

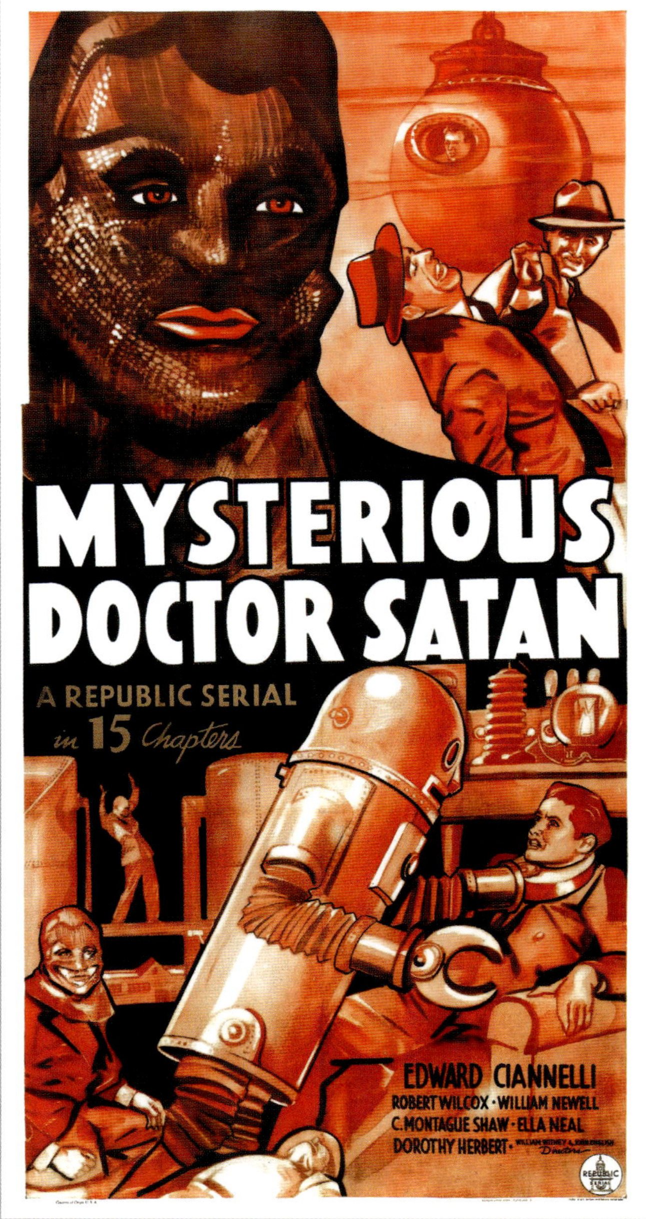

SERIAL THRILLS!

As the selection of exuberant visuals on this and the following spread show, SF flourished in the world of cinematic serials during the '30s and '40s. *The Phantom Empire* (1935) starred singing cowboy Gene Autry (playing himself) discovering an advanced subterranean civilization beneath his ranch. The posters emphasized robots and ray guns, though a fabulously inaccurate lobby card from a later Mexican release (opposite bottom left) appears to be from an entirely different "Invasion of Earth" type story, complete with UFO. *The Lost City* (1935) was a jungle-set variation on the forgotten techno-civilization theme, while *The Undersea Kingdom* (1936), Republic's response to Universal's smash hit *Flash Gordon* (1936), saw their not-dissimilar hero "Crash" Corrigan discover Atlantis, and battle the first incarnation of the cylindrical "Republic Robot" costume, later pressed into service in both *The Mysterious Doctor Satan* (1940) and *King of the Rocket Men* (1949). The latter's flying footage would go on to be endlessly recycled itself in future serials, while the character inspired Dave Stevens's 1980s comic book *The Rocketeer*, which in turn became a beloved movie in 1991.

Nat Levine presents
"THE
Phantom
Empire"
A NATION 20 000 FEET UNDERGROUND
with
Gene AUTRY
Frankie DARRO
Betsy King ROSS
"BLAZING THE TRAIL"
MASCOT SERIALS
DIRECTED BY
OTTO BROWER & B.REEVES EASON
SUPERVISED BY ARMAND SCHAEFER
A
MASCOT
MASTER SERIAL

INVASION A LA
TIERRA
La destrucción del Mundo por seres de otros PLANETAS...!
Con FRANKIE DARRO Y DOROTHY CHRISTIE
ESCALOFRIANTE REALISMO!
OPERADORA DE PELICULAS, S. A. DE C. V.

A NATION
20 000 FEET
UNDERGROUND
Nat Levine presents
GENE AUTRY
THE WORLD FAMED STAR OF
RADIO AND SCREEN
IN
"The PHANTOM EMPIRE"
with
Frankie DARRO
Betsy King ROSS
MASCOT
SERIAL in 12 SPECTACULAR FANTASTIC....EPISODES

THE PHANTOM EMPIRE
MOST SPECTACULAR SERIAL OF THE AGE
Gene AUTRY
Frankie DARRO
Betsy King ROSS
"LA REINE DE L'EMPIRE FANTOME
DE KONINGIN VAN 'T SPOOKENRIJK

NAT LEVINE Presents
Gene AUTRY
in 'THE PHANTOM EMPIRE'
"BLAZING THE TRAIL"
CHAPTER 7
FROM DEATH TO LIFE

ROBERT KENT
KAY ALDRIS
ÇELİK
BİLEK
TÜRKÇE
SERİAL
FİLM...

A REPUBLIC SERIAL in 12 AMAZING EPISODES
REPUBLIC PICTURES presents
UNDERSEA KINGDOM
with
RAY (CRASH) CORRIGAN
LOIS WILDE · MONTE BLUE · WILLIAM FARNUM
LON CHANEY JR. · LANE CHANDLER
JACK MULHALL · MALCOLM McGREGOR
PRODUCED by NAT LEVINE
DIRECTED by B. REEVES EASON — JOSEPH KANE
SCREEN PLAY by JOHN RATHMELL
MAURICE GERAGHTY—OLIVER DRAKE
ORIGINAL STORY by TRACY KNIGHT—JOHN RATHMELL
REPUBLIC PICTURES

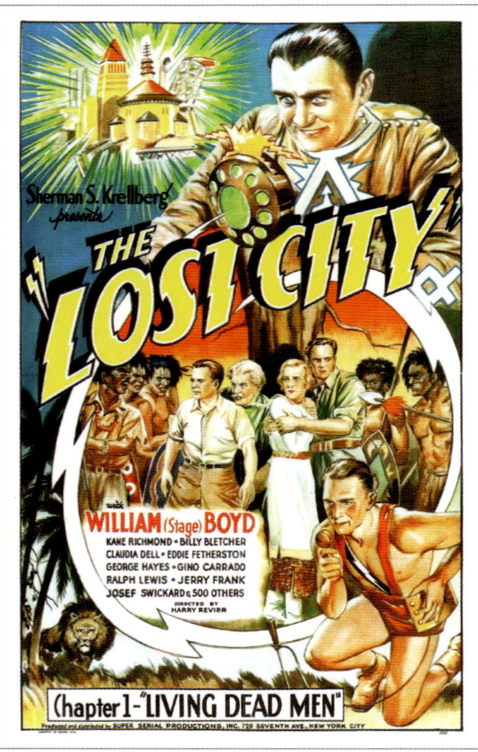
Sherman S. Krellberg presents
THE LOST CITY
WILLIAM (Stage) BOYD
KANE RICHMOND • BILLY BLETCHER
CLAUDIA DELL • EDDIE FETHERSTON
GEORGE HAYES • GINO CARRADO
RALPH LEWIS • JERRY FRANK
JOSEF SWICKARD & 500 OTHERS
DIRECTED BY HARRY REVIER
Chapter 1 - "LIVING DEAD MEN"

La INVASION de la CIUDAD PERDIDA
¡IMPRESIONANTE Y DRAMATICA LUCHA A MUERTE CON TERRIBLES SERES CREADOS PARA SEMBRAR EL TERROR Y EL PANICO!
CON
WILLIAM BOYD
KANE RICHMOND
CLAUDIA DELL
DISTRIBUIDA POR FILMS DE MEXICO, S. A. DE C. V. MONTERREY No. 101-7o. PISO MEXICO 7, D. F.

A REPUBLIC SERIAL IN 12 CHAPTERS
KING OF THE ROCKET MEN
featuring
TRISTRAM COFFIN · MAE CLARKE
HOUSE PETERS, JR. · DON HAGGERTY
I. STANFORD JOLLEY
Directed by FRED BRANNON
WRITTEN BY ROYAL K. COLE · WILLIAM LIVELY · SOL SHOR
Country of Origin U.S.A.

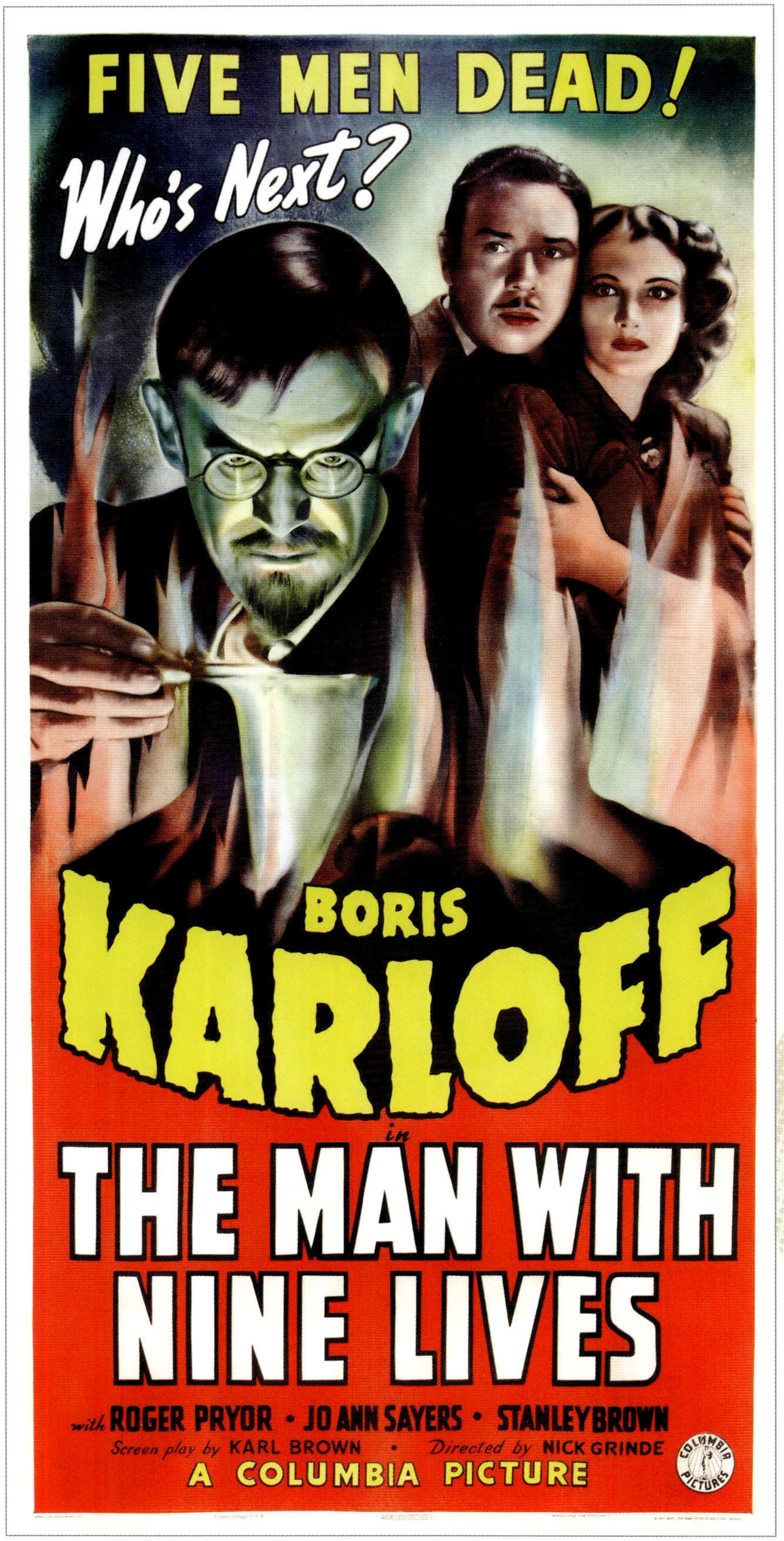
FIVE MEN DEAD!
Who's Next?
BORIS
KARLOFF
in
THE MAN WITH NINE LIVES
with ROGER PRYOR • JO ANN SAYERS • STANLEY BROWN
Screen play by KARL BROWN • Directed by NICK GRINDE
A COLUMBIA PICTURE
COLUMBIA PICTURES

INTRODUCING THE ONE MAN IN ALL THE WORLD WHO SOLVED THE RIDDLE OF ETERNAL YOUTH . . .
BORIS Karloff
The MAN WHO LIVED AGAIN
A GB Production
Karloff as a Love Crazed Scientist

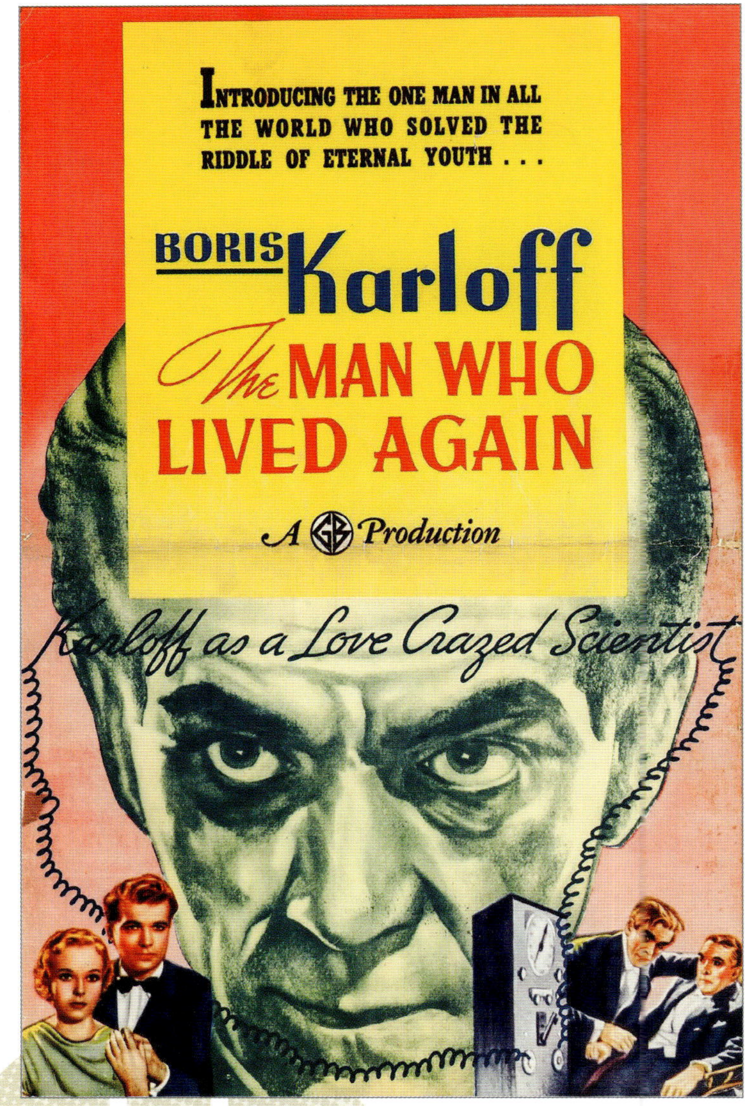

BORIS KARLOFF

"You could heave a brick out of the window and hit ten actors who could play my parts. I just happened to be on the right corner at the right time." Most filmgoers would disagree with the Englishman christened William Henry Pratt. Though forever associated with the character he fondly called "my dear old Monster," Boris Karloff's unique screen presence graced many other starring roles, often as mad scientists, or in the case of *The Walking Dead* (1936) the zombie experiment of one (a re-release half-sheet poster, opposite top left, cheekily showed him in his Frankenstein guise, nothing like his look in the film). *The Man Who Lived Again* (1936) used brain transference to avoid ageing (just like 2017's *Get Out*), while both *The Man They Could Not Hang* (1939) and *The Man With Nine Lives* (1940) were inspired by real-life scientist Robert E. Cornish, who—and this is absolutely true—reanimated two expired dogs during experiments at the University of California in the 1930s, and planned to move on to an executed convict...

KARLOFF
THE WALKING DEAD
RICARDO CORTEZ · EDMUND GWENN
MARGUERITE CHURCHILL · WARREN HULL
BARTON MacLANE · HENRY O'NEILL · JOSEPH KING
Directed by MICHAEL CURTIZ
WARNER BROS.

BORIS KARLOFF
THE WALKING DEAD
RICARDO CORTEZ

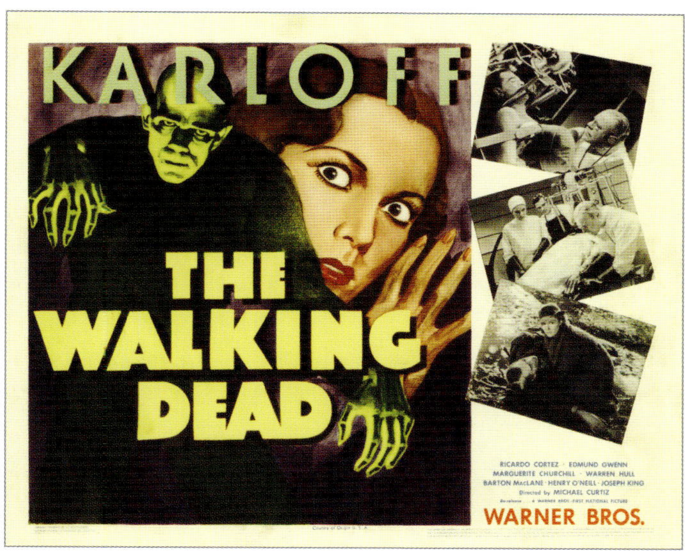

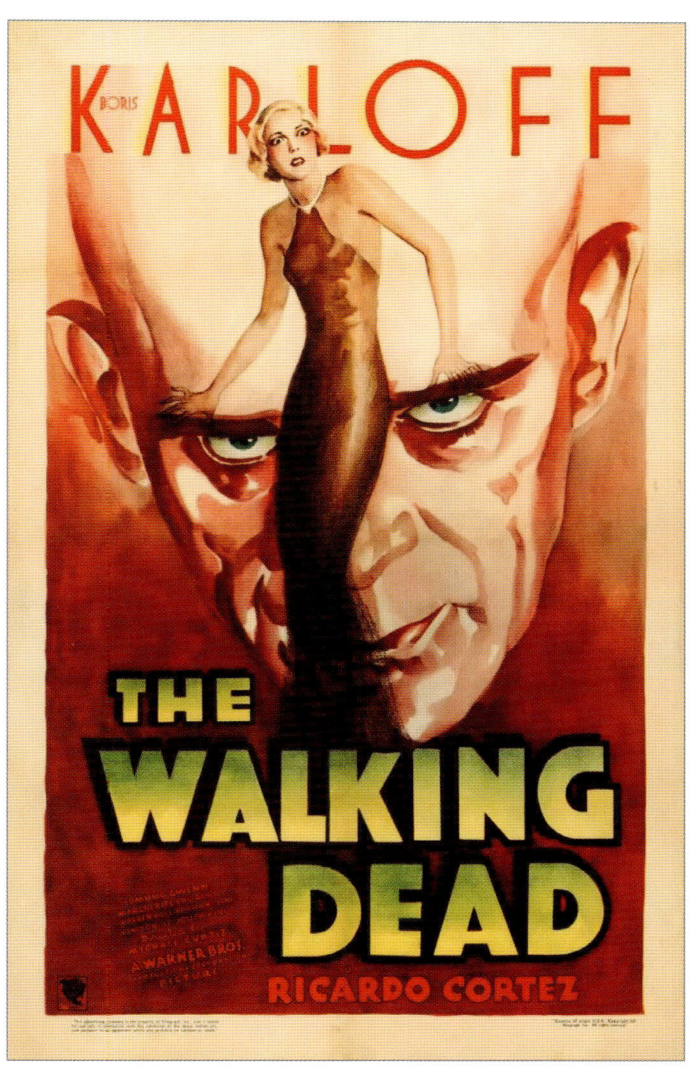

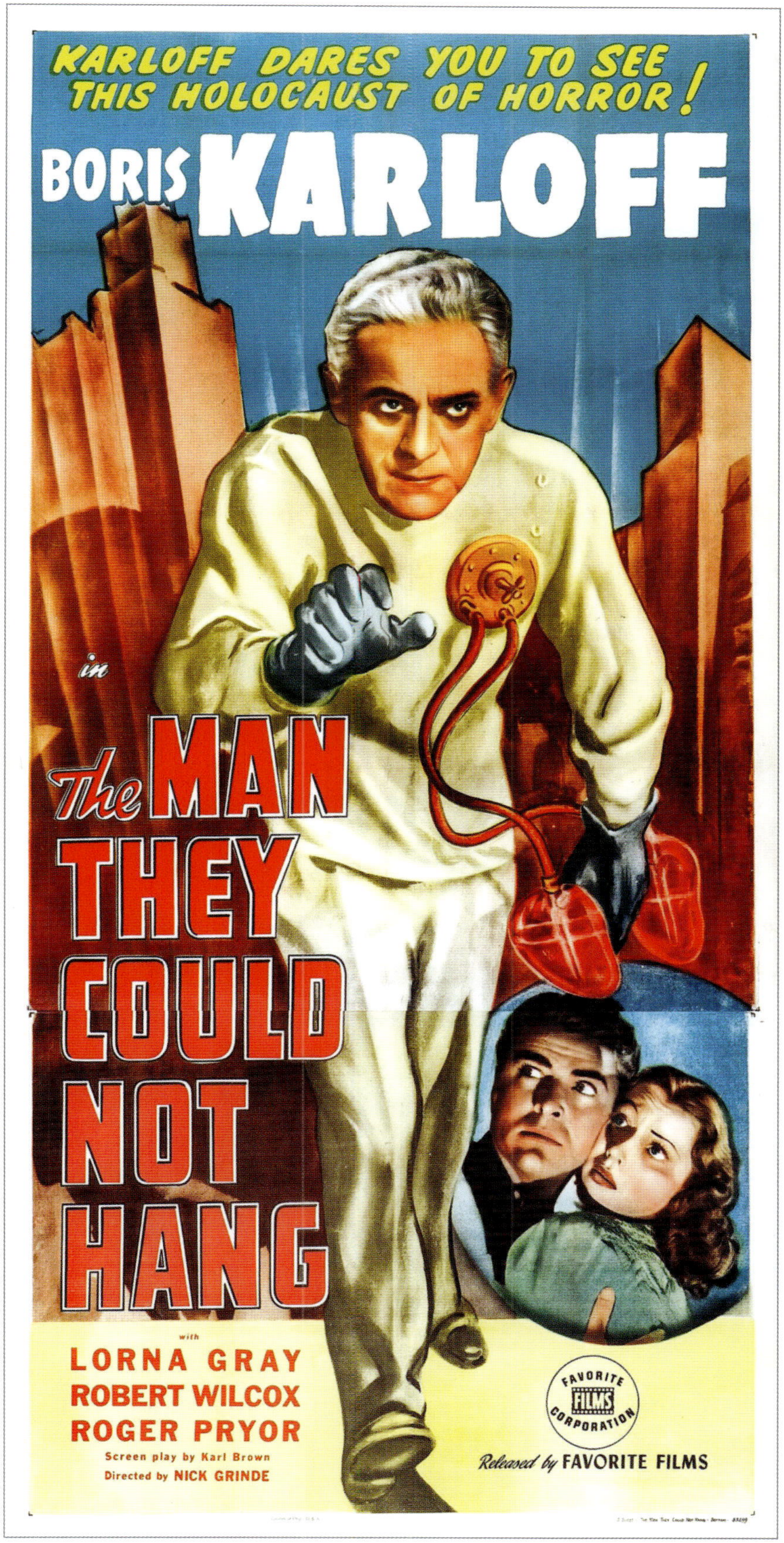

KARLOFF DARES YOU TO SEE THIS HOLOCAUST OF HORROR!
BORIS KARLOFF
in
The MAN THEY COULD NOT HANG
with
LORNA GRAY
ROBERT WILCOX
ROGER PRYOR
Screen play by Karl Brown
Directed by NICK GRINDE
FAVORITE FILMS CORPORATION
Released by FAVORITE FILMS

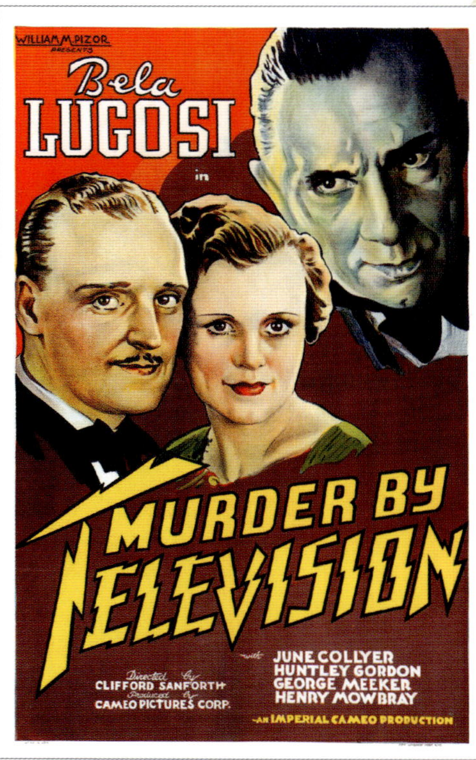

BELA LUGOSI

Asked in 1941 how he felt about being killed off in most of the films he appeared in, Bela Lugosi quipped, "It's a living." Though he never escaped a certain Count ("Dracula never ends. I don't know if I should call it a fortune or a curse, but it never ends"), the Hungarian-born actor featured in several SF-tinged horrors, often as a mad scientist—as in *The Devil Bat* (1940), *The Corpse Vanishes* (1942), and *The Ape Man* (1943)—though he played a good-guy investigator in *Murder By Television* (1935), back when television was new-fangled and slightly dangerous sounding even as a word, let alone as a device in your house. However minor the film, his hypnotic stare was always a gift to poster artists: the simple, but hugely impactful (and exceptionally rare) UK re-release poster for the sordid tale of reanimated corpses *Bowery at Midnight* (1942) being a great example.

NEW REALM PICTURES

THE MONSTER OF CRIME STREET!

Bela LUGOSI in

BOWERY AT MIDNIGHT

with John ARCHER Wanda McKAY

BRICK BRADFORD
AMAZING SOLDIER OF FORTUNE
BASED UPON THE KING FEATURES SYNDICATE'S
TREMENDOUSLY POPULAR CARTOON STRIP
with
KANE RICHMOND
(as BRICK BRADFORD)
RICK VALLIN (as SANDY)
LINDA JOHNSON (as JUNE)
PIERRE WATKIN (as SALISBURY)
Screenplay by
GEORGE H. PLYMPTON, ARTHUR HOERL and LEWIS CLAY
Directed by SPENCER BENNET · Produced by SAM KATZMAN
CHAPTER 7
INTO ANOTHER CENTURY
A COLUMBIA SERIAL

ADVENTURES IN TIME

These forgotten productions are early examples of an SF staple: what *Doctor Who* fans would call "wibbly-wobbly, timey-wimey" adventures. The star of comic strip adaptation *Brick Bradford* (1947) traveled in his "Time Top" (and looks like an inspiration for *Doctor Who*'s time agent Captain Jack). The very first time machine seen on screen (see photo above right) was in the Hungarian film *Szíriusz* (1942), followed by the time sphere in the British comedy *Time Flies* (1944, Argentinean ad image top right). *Fiddlers Three* (1944) starred English music hall comedian Tommy Trinder (catchphrase: "You lucky people!"), time warped back to ancient Rome. The *noir*-ish thriller *Repeat Performance* (1947) featured a time loop, while *Strange Holiday* (1945) had Claude Rains finding himself in an alternate US run by Nazi-style fascists, 17 years before Philip K. Dick's *The Man in the High Castle*.

MAD SCIENTISTS RETURN!

The mad doctors and evil scientists continued their experiments as the 1930s and '40s progressed, including Basil Rathbone, who was top-billed and given the lion's share of the poster art as *Son of Frankenstein* (1939), and Albert Dekker, who menaced his miniaturized victims on Carlantonio Longi's Italian poster for *Dr. Cyclops* (1940). Originally planned as a vehicle for Karloff and Lugosi, *Man-Made Monster* (1941) ended up with Lon Chaney, Jr. as an electrified zombie manipulated by Lionel Atwill's dastardly doctor. In 1953, as SF movies were booming at the dawn of a new scientific age, it was re-released with a suitably revamped title: *The Atomic Monster*.

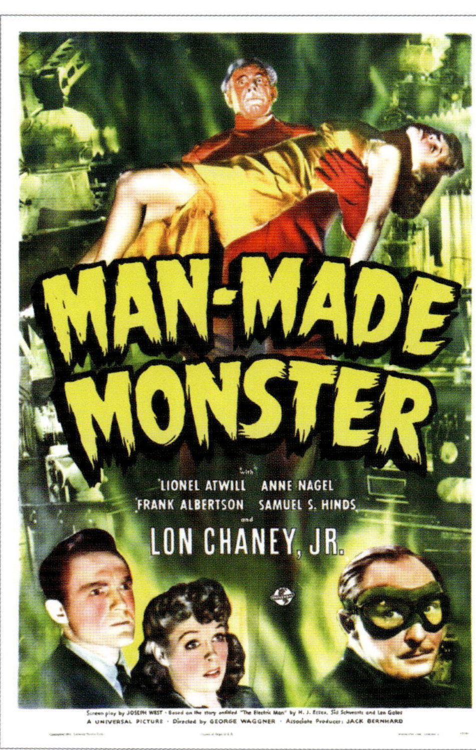

Albert
DEKKER
Janice
LOGAN
Thomas
COLEY
Regia:
ERNEST B. SCHOEDSACK
Dr. CYCLOPS
in TECHNICOLOR
ZEVS FILM
ARTERO - ROMA

THE
1950s

Margaret A. Weitekamp on *Destination Moon* and *Forbidden Planet*

In many ways, the 1950s was a decade of binaries. The geopolitical conflict of the Cold War between the United States and the Soviet Union pitted democracy against authoritarianism, and capitalism against communism on a global stage.

Within the United States, the red scare raised fears of attacks from outside as well as of subversion from within. In cities and towns across the South, the determined persistence of Civil Rights activism confronted the violence of white resistance. The pressures of conformity in newly formed suburbs contrasted with the expressiveness of the Beat movement.

Likewise, science fiction films offered visions of realistic possible futures alongside allegorical stories commenting on suburban conformity and fears of attack or subversion. Two of my favorites from the period are *Destination Moon* (1950) and *Forbidden Planet* (1956). The former, beloved by space fans, won an Academy Award for its special effects depicting a privately funded mission to the Moon. The latter became a mainstay of movie history. With a plot adapted from Shakespeare's *The Tempest*, *Forbidden Planet* introduced viewers to Robby the Robot and the memorable "monster of the Id." Like the dualities that defined the decade as a whole, these two films exemplify the divergent ways that spaceflight was depicted at the time.

Destination Moon carried the messages of "space boosters" who sought to use mass media to convince the public that spaceflight would be possible, thus building popular and political support for funding real space efforts. These realistic imaginings of possible spaceflight became known as speculative fiction. At the same time, fantastical science fiction films, such as *Forbidden Planet*, entertained audiences even as their underlying messages often grappled with serious contemporary issues. Both types of entertainment coexisted throughout the decade.

Realistic depictions of spaceflight appeared in popular culture as early as the 1940s and fantastical imagery persisted even after the launch of the first artificial satellite, *Sputnik 1*, by the Soviet Union in October 1957. For *Destination Moon* and *Forbidden Planet*, their story lines—and their posters—illustrated the two sides of how spaceflight was imagined.

PREVIOUS SPREAD: Detail from a French c1960s re-release poster for *The Day the Earth Stood Still* (1951).

BELOW: Italian poster for *Destination Moon* (1950), inspired by Chesley Bonestell's painted moon backdrops in the film.

The authenticity of *Destination Moon*, which was produced independently by George Pal and directed by Irving Pichel, started with a screenplay by Rip Van Ronkel, Robert A. Heinlein, and James O'Hanlon. Heinlein's naval and aeronautical engineering experience guided his career as a hard science fiction writer emphasizing accuracy. As much as it aimed to entertain, then, *Destination Moon* also sought to educate. In the movie's first half, a group of businessmen watch a film within the film—starring the cartoon character Woody Woodpecker—explaining how rockets function. When the mission must launch ahead of schedule, the inclusion of replacement radio operator, Joe Sweeney (Dick Wesson), serves as an audience surrogate. The underprepared ethnic character, with his pronounced Brooklyn accent, needs the astronauts to explain technical details to him, and thus also to the viewers. The movie's

ABOVE: The US half-sheet poster, emphasizing the film's long production process and Technicolor photography: this was marketed as a "prestige" project. Described by producer George Pal as "a documentary of the near future," it was the first SF film to win the Academy Award for Best Special Effects.

verisimilitude was further reinforced by the contributions of space artist Chesley Bonestell.

Destination Moon's various posters, which touted the film's use of Technicolor, used accurate speculation to generate excitement. In one version, a sleek white-silver pointed rocket zooms above a realistic lighted cityscape as seen from space (a view that had only been imagined at that point). A variation showed the spacecraft *Luna* landed vertically on the Moon's craggy surface. This scientifically based vision of the Moon was a mainstay of Bonestell's illustrations—until the Apollo lunar landings in the late 1960s revealed that the Moon really had soft hills.

For its part, *Forbidden Planet* offered a more fantastic imagining of space travel. The movie opens with a flying-saucer-shaped ship, the United Planets cruiser *C-57D*, which is a human-made spacecraft that can travel faster than the speed of light. In it, an Earth crew led by Commander John J. Adams (Leslie Nielsen) ventures to Altair IV to check on a scientific mission lost 20 years before. Their encounter with the only two survivors, Dr. Edward Morbius (Walter Pidgeon) and his daughter Altaira (Anne Francis), becomes a cautionary tale about the dangers of unfettered technology. Ironically, it is Robby the Robot, the hulking mechanical assistant that Morbius built to aid and protect them, that recognizes the threat. Morbius had been using ancient Krell technology buried deep below the planet's surface to enhance his intellectual power. But that technology also unleashed a destructive "Id Monster," which destroyed the Krell. In the film's dramatic climax, when Morbius orders Robby to kill the murderous monster, Robby goes into a self-destructive loop, recognizing the beast as Morbius's own darkest impulses. Although Morbius cannot be saved, Altaira returns to Earth in the arms of Captain Adams.

OPPOSITE: The US one-sheet for *Forbidden Planet* (1956) is arguably the most iconic SF film poster of them all. As with so many classic examples from this period, the identity of the artist has been lost to the mists of time.

BELOW: Box art for Showa's "Mechanized Robot," an unauthorized Robby toy from Japan.

Forbidden Planet used Robby the Robot as the centerpiece of a provocative movie poster. In it, Robby stands planted firmly on the planet's craggy surface, as planets swirl in a seeming mist in the background. Robby carries an unconscious Altaira; her head has lolled back, her blonde hair and limp arm hanging down, emblematic of her vulnerability. Georgia Tech film history professor J.P. Telotte has pointed out that such depictions were not uncommon in the 1950s. The poster for *The Day the Earth Stood Still* (1951), for instance, depicts the robot Gort in an aggressive pose, carrying a terrified woman. Notably, neither film includes the scenes depicted on the posters. Telotte argues that, simply, sex sells.

Focusing on Robby the Robot also tapped into the contemporary fascination with robots as emblematic of atomic-age and nascent space-age technology. In fact, the Ideal Novelty & Toy Company introduced its "Robert the Robot" toy in 1954, two years before the film character appeared. After *Forbidden Planet*, both imported and domestic imitation Robby the Robot toys found eager buyers as Robby appeared in several other films and numerous times on television.

The duality expressed in the posters for *Destination Moon* and *Forbidden Planet* reminds us of the split that also existed in how popular culture depicted spaceflight in the years before actual human missions became a reality.

M·G·M PRESENTS
FORBIDDEN PLANET
AMAZING!
STARRING WALTER PIDGEON · ANNE FRANCIS · LESLIE NIELSEN
WITH WARREN STEVENS AND INTRODUCING ROBBY, THE ROBOT
SCREEN PLAY BY CYRIL HUME
BASED ON A STORY BY IRVING BLOCK AND ALLEN ADLER
PHOTOGRAPHED IN EASTMAN COLOR
DIRECTED BY FRED McLEOD WILCOX · PRODUCED BY NICHOLAS NAYFACK
IN CINEMASCOPE AND COLOR
A METRO-GOLDWYN-MAYER PICTURE

ROCKET SHIPS

"Realistic" depictions of space travel were a key part of the boom in SF movies during the 1950s. *Rocketship X-M* (1950), a low-budget "spoiler" that beat *Destination Moon* into theaters by a month, featured a moon mission that ends up on Mars, and dealt with the dramatic possibilities of rocket fuel ratios—something that never bothered Flash Gordon. *Project Moonbase* (1953) looked forward to 1970, predicting a female astronaut in command and a female US president. Producer George Pal's *Conquest of Space* (1955) boasted real-life rocket scientist Wernher von Braun as a technical advisor, while *On the Threshold of Space* (1955) dramatized USAF tests in the run up to the space race. *First Man Into Space* (1959) was a horror-tinged tale of an experimental high altitude craft; the docudrama *X-15* (1961) featured actual NASA footage of the titular rocket plane.

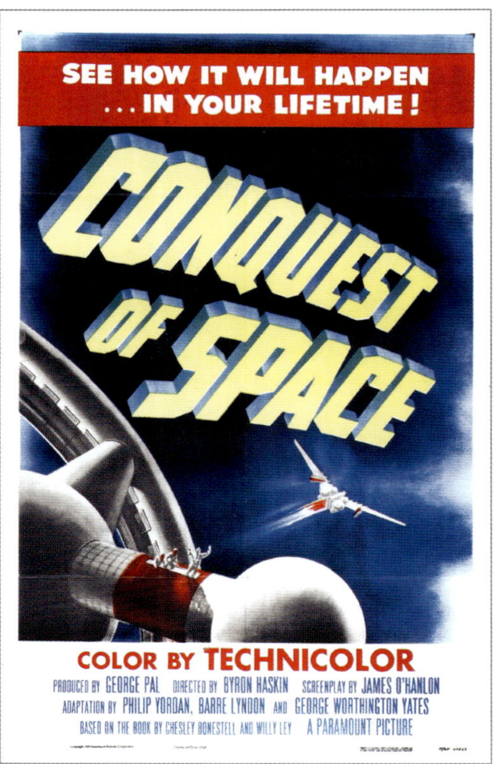

Lloyd
BRIDGES
Osa
MASSEN
RX-M
DESTINAZIONE LUNA
Regia: KURT NEUMANN
CAPITAL Pictures

THE PICTURE THAT LEAPS AHEAD OF THE HEADLINES!
M-G-M presents
FIRST MAN INTO SPACE
The most dangerous and daring mission of all time!
Starring
MARSHALL THOMPSON and MARLA LANDI
Screenplay by JOHN C. COOPER and LANCE Z. HARGREAVES
Produced by JOHN CROYDON and CHARLES F. VETTER, JR.
Directed by ROBERT DAY
AN AMALGAMATED PRODUCTION

X·15
USAF
X·15
DAVID McLEAN CHARLES BRONSON
JAMES GREGORY MARY TYLER MOORE
TONY LAZZARINO JAMES WARNER BELLAH
PANAVISION
RICHARD DONNER
UNE PRODUCTION E?G!
TECHNICOLOR
HENRY SANICOLA TONY LAZZARINO
HOWARD W. KOCH
Les Artistes Associés
UNITED ARTISTS

PARAMOUNT presenta
LA CONQUISTA DEL ESPACIO
("CONQUEST OF SPACE")
TECHNICOLOR
GEORGE PAL • BYRON HASKIN

"DESTINO, LA LUNA"
Color por TECHNICOLOR
Dist. por EAGLE LION DE MEXICO, S. A. • Paseo de la Reforma 153 México, D. F.

MARSHALL THOMPSON
MARLA LANDI en
EL PRIMER PILOTO DEL ESPACIO
con ROBERT AYRES
BILL NAGY
CARL JAFFE
BILL EDWARDS
FIRST MAN INTO SPACE
M-G-M presenta una fabulosa y aterradora historia... ¡Usted se elevará a los espacios interplanetarios!... ¡La más espectacular experiencia cinematográfica!...
Metro-Goldwyn-Mayer

PRONTO SERA POSIBLE EL PRIMER VIAJE A LA LUNA, PERO...¿LOS QUE SE ARRIESGUEN PRIMERO, SERAN CAPACES DE REGRESAR?
"PERDIDOS en la LUNA"
—PROJECT MOON BASE—
con ROSS FORD
DONNA MARTELL y
HAYDEN RORKE
DISTRIBUIDA EN 35 MM. POR: CINEMATOGRAFICA COLOSO, S. A. GUANAJUATO 219

INVASORES en la LUNA
TERROR ANTE LO DESCONOCIDO!
FANTASIA!
¡MILES DE EMOCIONES QUE LO DEJARAN EN SUSPENSO!
CUATRO HOMBRES Y UNA MUJER EN LA HAZAÑA MAS EXTRAORDINARIA DE LA HUMANIDAD!
ESTELARES:
JOHN EMERI
NOAH BERRY Jr.
y
HUGH O'BRIAN

EL AVION COHETE X-15
-X-15-
PANAVISION® y TECHNICOLOR
U.S. AIR FORCE
66670
USAF
DAVID McLEAN · CHARLES BRONSON
JAMES GREGORY · MARY TYLER MORE
UNA PRODUCCION ESSEX
Dirigida por RICHARD D. DONNER

THE DAY THE EARTH STOOD STILL

Though its box office performance was respectable rather than spectacular, *The Day the Earth Stood Still* (1951) was well reviewed as a serious, A-list picture, an SF parable (with overt biblical overtones) for the early Cold War. Its message of peace and understanding certainly continued to resonate: as President Reagan told the United Nations in 1987, "I occasionally think how quickly our differences worldwide would vanish if we were facing an alien threat from outside this world."

Studio 20th Century Fox pulled out the promotional stops with a cash prize "showmanship contest" for exhibitors and giveaway Gort masks for filmgoers. The fearsome robot bestrode the US one-sheet, and posters around the world (overleaf), though artists couldn't agree if its death ray was attacking or defending the woman in its arms. Whichever, it's not a scene in the movie. Klaatu barada nikto!

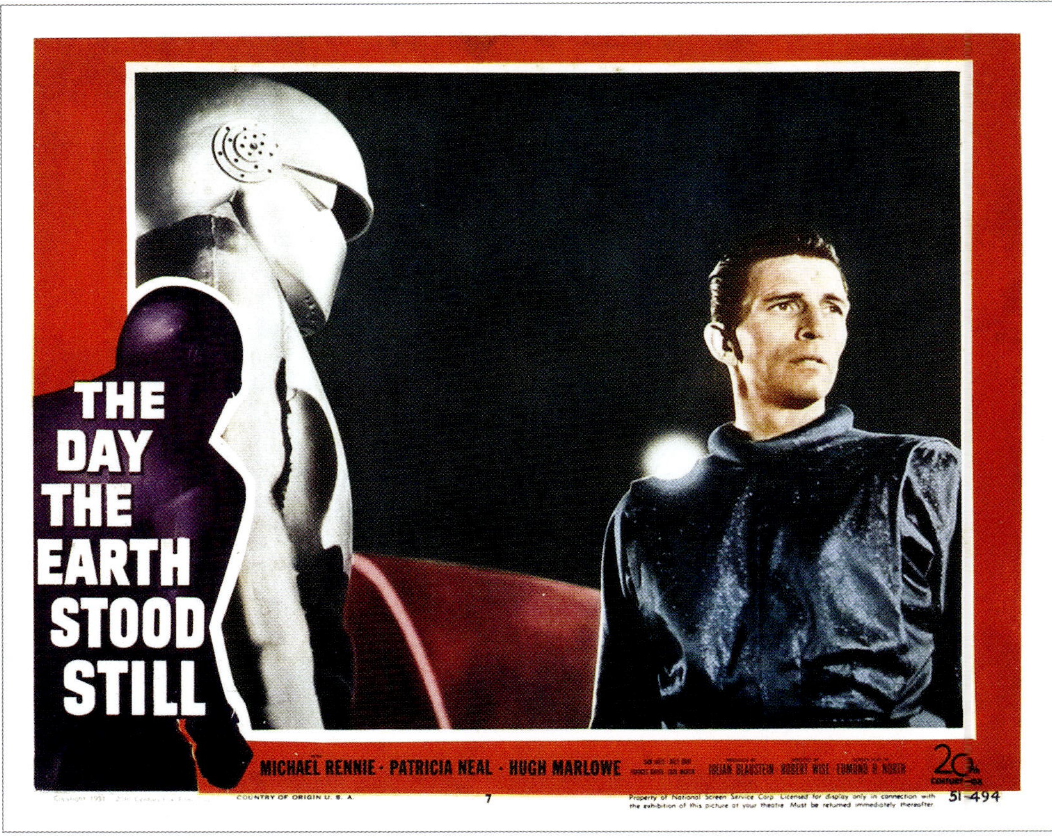

FROM OUT OF SPACE....
A WARNING AND AN ULTIMATUM!

WITH
MICHAEL RENNIE · PATRICIA NEAL · HUGH MARLOWE

SAM JAFFE · BILLY GRAY · FRANCES BAVIER · LOCK MARTIN

PRODUCED BY
JULIAN BLAUSTEIN · DIRECTED BY
ROBERT WISE · SCREEN PLAY BY
EDMUND H. NORTH

20th CENTURY-FOX

Koningin Astridplein-Antwerpen
Kinderen toegelaten
LE JOUR OU LA TERRE S'ARRETA
"THE DAY THE EARTH STOOD STILL"
avec MICHAEL RENNIE
PATRICIA NEAL
HUGH MARLOWE
20th Century-Fox
Production: JULIAN BLAUSTEIN Mise en scène ROBERT WISE Scenario EDMUND H. NORTH
DE DAG WAAROP DE AARDE STILSTOND

LE JOUR OU LA TERRE S'ARRETA...
MICHAEL RENNIE
PATRICIA NEAL
HUGH MARLOWE
SAM JAFFE·BILLY GRAY·FRANCES BAVIER·LOCK MARTIN
Producteur JULIAN BLAUSTEIN
Réalisateur ROBERT WISE
Scénario EDMUND H. NORTH
20th CENTURY-FOX
Les productions FOX-EUROPA_33, Champs Elysées_Paris.

Les Films Jacques Leitienne présentent
MISSION SPATIALE
LE JOUR OU LA TERRE S'ARRETA
AVEC MICHAEL RENNIE · PATRICIA NEAL ET HUGH MARLOWE
UN FILM DE ROBERT WISE

Michael RENNIE Patricia NEAL Hugh MARLOWE
ULTIMATUM ALLA TERRA
Sam Billy
JAFFE · GRAY
Frances Lock
BAVIER · MARTIN
20th CENTURY-FOX
Regia di: ROBERT WISE
Prod. di: JULIAN BLAUSTEIN
Sceneggiatura di: EDMUND H. NORTH
GIAM.

DEN DAG JORDEN
STOD STILLE
(THE DAY THE EARTH STOOD STILL)
MICHAEL
RENNIE
PATRICIA
NEAL
HUGH
MARLOWE
ISCENESÆTTELSE:
ROBERT WISE
20th CENTURY-FOX

WHEN WORLDS COLLIDE

Philip Wylie and Edwin Balmer's 1933 novel, originally optioned by Paramount for Cecil B. DeMille, ended up with producer George Pal, as his follow-up to *Destination Moon*. A rogue star is on a collision course with Earth, causing widespread destruction of famous landmarks as it approaches; a small band of humanity builds an "ark" rocket ship to escape… *When Worlds Collide* (1951) is practically a template for the modern-day disaster movie. As director and Pal fan Joe Dante quipped: "A terrific picture. It's been remade a number of times. Unofficially." (2021's *Don't Look Up* certainly owes it a debt of gratitude.)

The US campaign showed the flooding of New York City, with a collapsing Empire State Building. The French poster (opposite) added in the pointy-spired Chrysler Building for extra verisimilitude: artist Roger Soubie (1898–1984) began his career with travel posters.

Paramount présente:
le CHOC des MONDES
Production de
GEORGE PAL
Réalisation de
RUDOLPH MATÉ
Scénario de
SYDNEY BOEHM
d'après une nouvelle de
EDWIN BALMER et PHILIP WYLIE
Couleur de TECHNICOLOR
C'est un Film Paramount
Films Paramount
Imp. R. DELIGNE PARIS
IMPRIMÉ EN FRANCE

MORE SERIAL THRILLS!

As the resurgence in SF movies increased, old favorites returned to the big screen: *Flash Gordon's Trip to Mars* (1938) got a full-scale re-release, while the 1939 Buck Rogers serial reappeared in a cut-down feature film edit as *Planet Outlaws* (1953). "Earth Invaded in Atomic War!" promised the latter's one-sheet, using an up-to-the-minute term. In a TV-to-film first, the hit show *Captain Video* (1949–55) was adapted into the movie serial *Captain Video: Master of the Stratosphere* (1951). Star Judd Holdren continued into similar roles in *Zombies of the Stratosphere* (1952) and *Commando Cody: Sky Marshal of the Universe* (1953), both of which made plentiful use of stock footage from *King of the Rocket Men* (1949). Like much of Hollywood's '50s SF output, these and other serials were also distributed to an enthusiastic Mexican market (opposite; see also page 85).

Although he was often seen in public escorting Hollywood starlets, Holdren never married. His career soon dwindled into bit parts and he eventually became an insurance salesman, before committing suicide in 1974, aged 58. A sad tale, but to a generation of kids wearing Captain Video space helmets, he was their hero.

LOS HOMBRES RADAR DE LA LUNA
PRESENTANDO A UN NUEVO PERSONAJE
(RADAR MEN FROM THE MOON)
COMANDO CODY
EL INVENCIBLE MARISCAL DEL ESPACIO
GEORGE WALLACE · ALINE TOWNE
ROY BARCROFT · WILLIAM BAKEWELL
FRANKLIN ADREON
FRED C. BRANNON
12
SENSACIONALES EPISODIOS
DIST. POR REPUBLIC PICTURES DE MEXICO, INC. JOSE EMPARAN Nº 48 MEX. D.F.

COMANDO CODY
EL MARISCAL AEREO DEL UNIVERSO en
VENGANZA COSMICA
(COSMIC VENGEANCE)
EN FABULOSAS AVENTURAS DEL ESPACIO!
JUDD HOLDREN
ALINE TOWNE
WILLIAM SHALLERT
FRED C. BRANNON
DIST. POR REPUBLIC PICTURES DE MEXICO, INC.

EL INVASOR MARCIANO
(FLYING DISC MAN FROM MARS)
WALTER REED
LOIS COLLIER
GREGORY GAY
JAMES CRAVEN
12 AUDACES EPISODIOS DE LA GUERRA INTERPLANETARIA
UN NUEVO APOCALIPSIS
REPUBLIC PICTURES

HERBERT J. YATES presenta
MONSTRUOS DE LA ESTRATOSFERA
ZOMBIES OF THE STRATOSPHERE
PRESENTANDO A UN NUEVO PERSONAJE
"COMANDO CODY"
EL INVENCIBLE MARISCAL DEL ESPACIO
JUDD HOLDREN · ALINE TOWNE · WILSON WOOD
FRANKLIN ADREON
FRED C. BRANNON
12
SENSACIONALES EPISODIOS
ES UNA SUPERSERIE REPUBLIC JOSE EMPARAN N 48 MEXICO D.F.

JUDD HOLDREN
ALINE TOWNE
WILSON WOOD
LANE BRADFORD y
STANLEY WAXMAN
en
SATELITES SATAN
¡DOS POTENCIAS SE DISPUTAN EL ESPACIO, ASESINOS COSMICOS INVADEN Y DESTRUYEN LA TIERRA!
Una emocionante película REPUBLIK presentada por DISTRIBUIDORA SOTOMAYOR, S. A.

¡AL FIN!
EL CAPITAN VIDEO
"CAPTAIN VIDEO"
"EL AMO DE LA ESTRATOSFERA"
CINECOLOR
JUDD HOLDREN
LARRY STEWART
COLUMBIA PICTURES
15 ESCALOFRIANTES EPISODIOS!!!!

THE THING FROM ANOTHER WORLD

"What is it?" asked the press ads for *The Thing from Another World* (1951). The monster was actually 6ft 7in actor James Arness in heavy makeup, but the cagey marketing relied on a text-based approach, with the title logo design hinting at the alien's plant-based nature. ("An intellectual carrot! The mind boggles.") In Italy, the approach was far more freewheeling: the *photobusta* lobby cards (right) added a generic armed spaceman and rocket ship, while Sandro Simeoni's poster for a '60s re-release (opposite) depicted a confrontation with a creature not from the film at all, but far closer to the shape-shifting bio-stew of John W. Campbell's original source novella (and John Carpenter's 1982 remake).

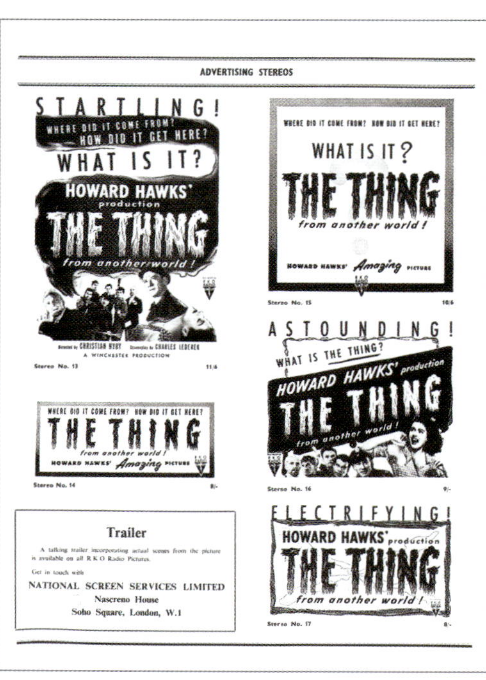
ADVERTISING STEREOS

STARTLING! WHERE DID IT COME FROM? HOW DID IT GET HERE? WHAT IS IT? HOWARD HAWKS' production THE THING from another world!

WHERE DID IT COME FROM? HOW DID IT GET HERE? WHAT IS IT? THE THING from another world! HOWARD HAWKS' Amazing PICTURE

THE THING from another world! HOWARD HAWKS' Amazing PICTURE

ASTOUNDING! WHAT IS THE THING? HOWARD HAWKS' production THE THING from another world!

ELECTRIFYING! HOWARD HAWKS' production THE THING from another world!

Trailer

NATIONAL SCREEN SERVICES LIMITED
Nascreno House
Soho Square, London, W.1

I CICLOPI DI MARTE INVADONO LA TERRA
LA COSA DA UN ALTRO MONDO
CON MARGARET SHERIDAN · KENNETH TOBEY · DEWEY MARTIN
UNA PRODUZIONE HOWARD HAWKS
REGIA DI CHRISTIAN NYBY
UNA ESCLUSIVITA' FIDA Cinematografica

AFTER THE APOCALYPSE

As nuclear tensions mounted in the real world, filmmakers began to imagine life in the aftermath of an atomic war. The small-scale, relentlessly grim drama *Five* (1951) was the first to do so, followed by the self-explanatory *1000 Years from Now* (1952, a.k.a. *Captive Women*), with its warring tribes in the ruins of New York. Producer Albert Zugsmith paired it in a double bill with his follow-up, *Invasion U.S.A.* (1952), a "red scare" tale which sees New York City hit by an A-bomb. Reynold Brown's one-sheet art for *Teenage Caveman* (1958)—very possibly painted before a frame of the film had been shot, as an image to entice potential exhibitors—promised a spectacle the film failed to deliver (see lobby card, below). On screen, it's not even a dinosaur, but an old man in the remains of a radiation suit, revealing that this prehistoric adventure has actually been set after a nuclear holocaust all along (spoiler).

PREHISTORIC REBELS against
PREHISTORIC MONSTERS!
TEENAGE
CAVEMAN
STARRING
ROBERT VAUGHN · DARRAH MARSHALL · LESLIE BRADLEY · Produced & Directed by ROGER CORMAN
Screenplay by R. WRIGHT CAMPBELL · A JAMES H. NICHOLSON and SAMUEL Z. ARKOFF Production · An AMERICAN-INTERNATIONAL Picture

INVADERS FROM MARS

Posters could show alien invaders and their spacecraft in color, but *Invaders from Mars* (1953)—rushed through production to hit the theaters before *The War of the Worlds* (1953)—was the first film to do it on screen, too. The film's carefully considered look and color palette remain highly effective, which is perhaps not surprising given that director William Cameron Menzies was also a legendary production designer, who literally invented that job title.

Renato Fratini's Italian posters (below right and opposite) take their cue from the movie's heightened dream-logic style. The prolific Fratini left his native country for higher wages in swinging '60s London, though his louche lifestyle contributed to a fatal heart attack in 1973 aged only 40. British artist Vic Fair marveled at his colleague's technique: "All that detail… Fratini could just knock it in. Look closely, and there's actually nothing there! Genius, really."

LA RANK FILM DISTRIBUTORS OF ITALY PRESENTA UNA ESCLUSIVITÀ R. K. O.
Helena CARTER · Arthur FRANZ · Jimmy HUNT
REGIA DI
WILLIAM CAMERON MENZIES
GLI INVASORI SPAZIALI
PRODUZIONE
EDWARD L. ALPERSON
EASTMANCOLOR

ALIEN INVADERS

As the following pages show, during the 1950s extraterrestrials of all shapes and sizes were queuing up to invade our planet. *The 27th Day* (1956) was a slightly more cerebral story than most, and included a happy ending where the aliens co-exist peacefully on Earth. The film's one-sheet was par for the course, though, with the archetypal visual of the female lead with skimpy clothing falling, or ripped, from her shoulder (to save you counting, there are 65 other examples of this in the book you're holding, and could have been many more).

The Crawling Eye (1958) was dismissed by *The New York Times* as doing "nothing to enhance or advance the copious genre of science fiction," but that's not entirely true: its clever concept of an alien hiding in an always stationary cloud above a mountain appears to have inspired Jordan Peele's *NOPE* (2022). It also had a memorable Italian poster by Basilio Morini (see page 103).

TERROR FROM OUTER SPACE!
MIGHTIEST SHOCKER THE SCREEN EVER HAD THE GUTS TO MAKE!
THE 27th DAY
Five people given the power to destroy nations!
WHAT WILL THEY DO? WHAT WOULD YOU DO?
starring
GENE BARRY · VALERIE FRENCH with GEORGE VOSKOVEC · ARNOLD MOSS · STEFAN SCHNABEL
Screen Play by JOHN MANTLEY · Based on His Novel · Produced by HELEN AINSWORTH
Executive Producer—LEWIS J. RACHMIL · Directed by WILLIAM ASHER · A COLUMBIA PICTURE

OUT OF THIS UNIVERSE!
The Cosmic Phantom from Time and Space!
"We could feel hypnotic eyes roving over our bodies ...watching...spying!"
THE Cosmic Man
Starring
BRUCE BENNETT
JOHN CARRADINE
ANGELA GREENE
SCOTTY MORROW
AN ALLIED ARTISTS PICTURE
PRODUCED BY ROBERT A. TERRY
DIRECTED BY HERBERT GREENE
ORIGINAL STORY AND SCREENPLAY BY ARTHUR C. PIERCE

EVERY SECOND YOUR PULSE POUNDS
THEY GROW FOOT BY INCREDIBLE FOOT!
Shock by Incredible shock this ravaging death overruns the earth... menacing mankind with overwhelming chaos!
When men of different planets unite to combat the most loathesome peril the universe has ever known!
COSMIC MONSTERS
FORREST TUCKER · GABY ANDRE · MARTIN BENSON
Produced by GEORGE MAYNARD · Directed by GILBERT DUNN
A DCA Release

MASS INVASION OF THE WORLD!
an unearthly enemy defying modern science in a war to-the-death!
INVISIBLE INVADERS
Co-starring
JOHN AGAR · JEAN BYRON
with PHILIP TONGE · ROBERT HUTTON · JOHN CARRADINE
Written by SAMUEL NEWMAN · Directed by EDWARD L. CAHN · Produced by ROBERT E. KENT
A PREMIUM PICTURES, INC. Presentation · Released thru UNITED UA ARTISTS

The nightmare terror of the slithering eye that unleashed agonizing horror on a screaming world!
WARNING
If you've ever been hypnotized do not come alone.
A man dissolves... and out of the oozing mist comes the hungry eye, slave to the demon brain!
THE CRAWLING EYE
FORREST TUCKER · LAURENCE PAYNE · JENNIFER JAYNE
Directed by ROBERT S. BAKER, MONTY BERMAN · Produced by QUENTIN LAWRENCE
a DCA release
the company that brought you "RODAN"

FORREST TUCKER
JANET MUNRO
LAURENCE PAYNE
JENNIFER JAYNE
REGIA
QUENTIN LAWRENCE
MORINI
I MOSTRI DELLE ROCCE ATOMICHE
Distribuzione
EURO INTERNATIONAL FILMS
Produzione ROBERT S.BAKER - MONTY BERMAN

THE WAR OF THE WORLDS

A big-budget Technicolor extravaganza that duly became a box office smash, producer George Pal's *The War of the Worlds* (1953) was the first screen adaptation of H.G. Wells's 1898 novel. The updated storyline made chilling use of new technology: not even an atomic bomb can stop these aliens.

The descending Martian hand on the initial US one-sheet (opposite) soon made way for posters featuring their now-iconic war machines. In 2000, art director Albert Nozaki (1912–2003) remembered coming up with the manta ray-like look: "In the script, the three legs of the ship were extended, based on the ideas in Wells's work. But I realized there was an impracticality of the design, given that it was the 1950s and significant technological changes had taken place… I took the initiative to make it another shape, and in July 1951 on a Sunday afternoon at home, the shape of a sea creature flashed across my mind… The film looks as futuristic now as it did back then."

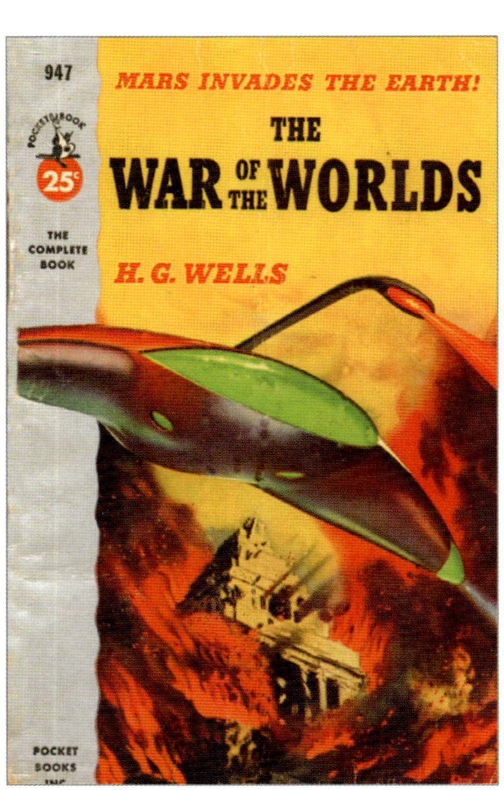

H·G·WELLS'
THE War OF THE Worlds
COLOR BY TECHNICOLOR
PRODUCED BY
GEORGE PAL
DIRECTED BY
BYRON HASKIN
SCREEN PLAY BY
BARRE LYNDON
A PARAMOUNT PICTURE

PARAMOUNT présente
LE CHEF D'OEUVRE DE
H.G.WELLS
LA GUERRE
DES MONDES
THE WAR OF THE WORLDS
avec
GENE BARRY
et
ANN ROBINSON
Couleurs par
Technicolor
Production
GEORGE PAL
Regie
BYRON HASKIN
C'est un Film Paramount
OORLOG DER WERELDEN

H. G. WELLS'
KLODERNES
KAMP
‹The WAR OF THE WORLDS›
GENE BARRY
ANN ROBINSON · TECHNICOLOR
Produceret af GEORGE PAL · Iscenesat af BYRON HASKIN
Manuskript BARRÉ LYNDON · EFTER EN ROMAN AF H.G.WELLS

宇宙戦争
最高の原作、最高の製作者が遂に
完成した宇宙科学映画の驚異的巨篇!!
英文豪 H・G・ウエルズ原作
科学映画の才一人者 ジョージ・パル製作
バイロン・ハスキン監督
パラマウント超特作
総天然色
THE WAR OF THE WORLDS

COLORE DELLA
TECHNICOLOR
LA
GUERRA DEI MONDI
(THE WAR OF THE WORLDS)
Prodotto da . . . GEORGE PAL
Diretto da . . . BYRON HASKIN
Sceneggiatura di BARRE' LYNDON
E' un film Paramount
TRATTO DAL ROMANZO DI
H. G. WELLS
"IL TERRORE VIENE DA MARTE"
PUBBLICATO IN ITALIA
DALL EDITORE ELMO

Les MARTIENS
ont envahi la Terre...
un spectacle inimaginable
d'après le célèbre roman de
H. G. WELLS

Couleur de
TECHNICOLOR

HOTEL

la Guerre des Mondes

Les parents sont informés que certaines scènes de la "Guerre des Mondes" risquent d'impressionner les enfants nerveux et sensibles.

Production de
GEORGE PAL

Réalisation de
BYRON HASKIN

Scénario de
BARRE LYNDON

C'est un Film Paramount

C. VENIN

CINÉMATO

IMPRIMÉ EN FRANCE

FLYING SAUCERS

In June 1947 pilot Kenneth Arnold saw nine objects flying impossibly fast across the Oregon sky. They moved, he later told a reporter, "like a saucer if you skip it across the water." Arnold never actually described the craft as saucer-*shaped*, but the press coined the term "flying saucers" nevertheless, and sightings of strange airborne discs soon proliferated.

Director Mikel Conrad was quick off the mark with *The Flying Saucer* (1950), a ripped-from-the-headlines low-budget production that he also co-wrote, produced, and starred in. "Invasion!" promised the film's Mexican lobby card (below), but there were no aliens: the saucer turned out to be an Earth scientist's invention. Using the preferred US Air Force term, *UFO* (1956) was a drama–documentary that trumpeted its actual footage of unidentified flying objects; *Earth vs. the Flying Saucers* (1956), though "suggested" by Major Donald E. Keyhoe's non-fiction book, relied on Ray Harryhausen's fanciful stop-motion effects.

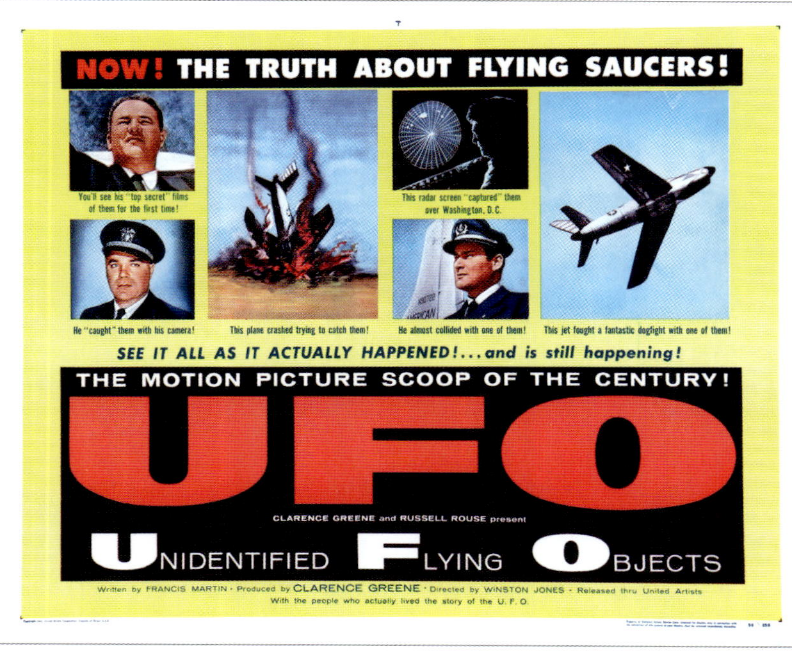

"TRUE"
Magazine says:
"THE FLYING SAUCERS ARE REAL!"
OUT OF THE UNKNOWN COMES A STRANGE NEW TERROR!
THE FLYING SAUCER
Starring
Mikel Conrad
Pat Garrison
Hantz Von Teuffen
Lester Sharpe · Russell Hicks
Frank Darien
Produced and Directed By MIKEL CONRAD
Associated Producer MORRIS M. WEIN
Original Story By MIKEL CONRAD
Screen Adaptation By HOWARD IRVING YOUNG
A COLONIAL PRODUCTIONS PICTURE
Released by FILM CLASSICS, INC.

ATTENTION EARTH-PEOPLE!
THIS IS AN INVASION BY FLYING SAUCERS!
THIS IS IT!
The battle that may be waged in your lifetime!
EARTH VS. THE FLYING SAUCERS
starring
HUGH MARLOWE · JOAN TAYLOR with DONALD CURTIS
Screen Play by GEORGE WORTHING YATES and RAYMOND T. MARCUS
Screen Story by CURT SIODMAK · Technical Effects by RAY HARRYHAUSEN
Produced by CHARLES H. SCHNEER · Executive Producer: SAM KATZMAN
Directed by FRED F. SEARS · A COLUMBIA PICTURE
PRINTED IN U.S.A.

ATOMIC MONSTERS

Director Ishiro Honda was clear about his intentions: "The creation of the atomic bomb had become a universal problem. I felt this atomic fear would hang around our necks for eternity… Having seen the terror of the atomic bomb in real life, it is most important to weave this element into the film well, so that everyone will understand." The stomping star of *Godzilla* (1954) was indeed immediately seen as a metaphor for the destructive force of the bomb, with the ruins of Tokyo unavoidably bringing to mind the devastation at Hiroshima and Nagasaki. The film still packs a punch, especially in the somber original version, not widely available outside Japan until the film's 50th anniversary. Until then, most international audiences knew only the more bombastic "Americanization" *Godzilla, King of the Monsters* (1956), which trimmed the original's quieter moments, and added footage of Raymond Burr as a US reporter witnessing the mounting chaos.

Overleaf: Many irradiated and/or giant monsters followed in the Big G's wake. As is often the case in the SF genre, the Italian posters were a cut above their US equivalents (see key on p313 for details).

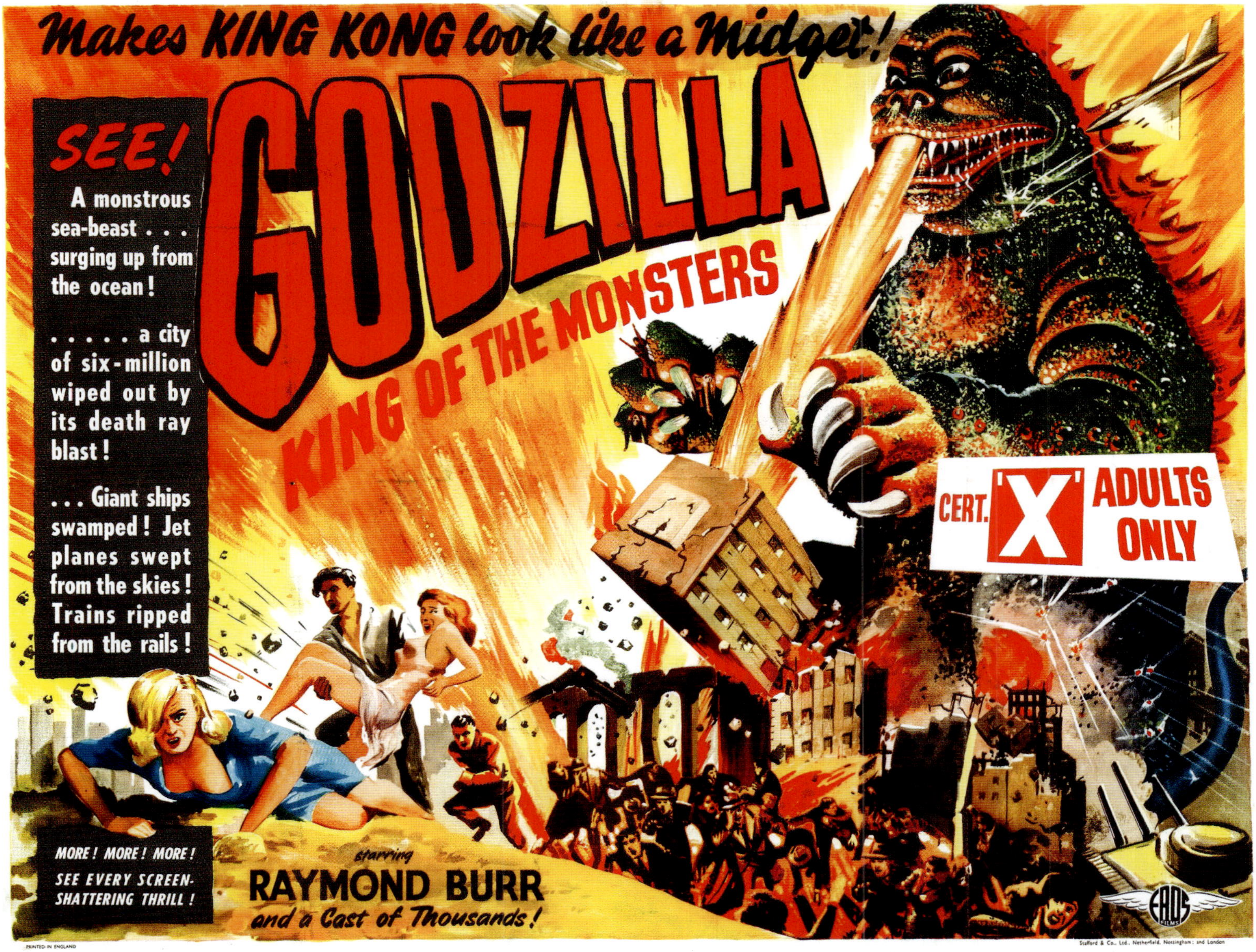

Makes KING KONG look like a Midget!
GODZILLA
KING OF THE MONSTERS
SEE!
A monstrous sea-beast . . . surging up from the ocean!
. . . . . . a city of six-million wiped out by its death ray blast!
. . . Giant ships swamped! Jet planes swept from the skies! Trains ripped from the rails!
CERT. 'X' ADULTS ONLY
MORE! MORE! MORE!
SEE EVERY SCREEN-SHATTERING THRILL!
starring
RAYMOND BURR
and a Cast of Thousands!
PRINTED IN ENGLAND

GODZILLA
LE MONSTRE DE L'OCEAN PACIFIQUE

ЯПОНСКИ ИГРАЛЕН ФИЛМ
ГОДЗИЛА

PROBUZENÁ ZKÁZA

GODZILLA
film produkcji japonskiej

DISTRIBUZIONE
IL
MOSTRO
DEI CIELI
JEFF MORROW · MARA CORDAY EDGAR BARRIER LOUIS MERRILL REGIA FRED F. SEARS

RODAN, il mostro alato
CON
KENJI SAWARA
YUMI SHIRAKAWA
AKIHIKO HIRATA
REGIA:
INOSHIRO HONDA
DISTRIBUZIONE
R K O RADIO FILMS
STAMPATO DALLA TECHNICOLOR
UNA PRODUZIONE TOHO PRESENTATA DAI KING BROTHERS

IL MOSTRO
CHE SFIDO' IL MONDO
TIM HOLT · AUDREY DALTON HANS CONRIED · BARBARA DARROW
Regia ARNOLD LAVEN

IL
MOSTRO
CHE
SFIDO' il MONDO
TIM HOLT · AUDREY DALTON
HANS CONRIED · BARBARA DARROW
REGIA di ARNOLD LAVEN

TUTTO IL MONDO IN ALLARME CONTRO I DIABOLICI MOSTRI NUCLEARI
NEL PIU' ALLUCINANTE FILM DI FANTASCIENZA
JACK WALLACE
FRED KASAY
SUSY SETSUKO
Y. KASAMA
M. KOIZUMI
BEN YAMA
IL RE DEI mostri
REGIA: M. ODA
ESCLUSIVITA': CESTIA FILM
DIRETTORE FOTOGRAFIA: SEY EUDO
Vecchioni & Guadagno Via Casal de Merode, 8 Roma Luglio 1957

CRAWLING TERROR

Critic Katy Waldman's 2013 take for *Slate* on '50s nuclear monster movies is an interesting one: "Who exactly are the enemies poised to dismantle the American dream? Women? Soviets? Heedless scientists? Somehow all three converge in images of irradiated, unknowable creatures eager to reproduce throughout the United States." Back in 1954, the brass at Warner Bros. probably hadn't given that much thought, but they knew that *Them*, with its giant ants mutated by an atomic bomb test, had made $2 million at the box office—more "big bug" movies soon followed. *The Deadly Mantis* (1957) was technically a non-radioactive prehistoric creature, though it did want to destroy the seat of US government in Washington, D.C. The arachnid star of *Tarantula!* (1955) grew to 100ft thanks to an irradiated food supplement, but it never attacked a woman, as in Reynold Brown's six-sheet (that's not its only inaccuracy: count the legs).

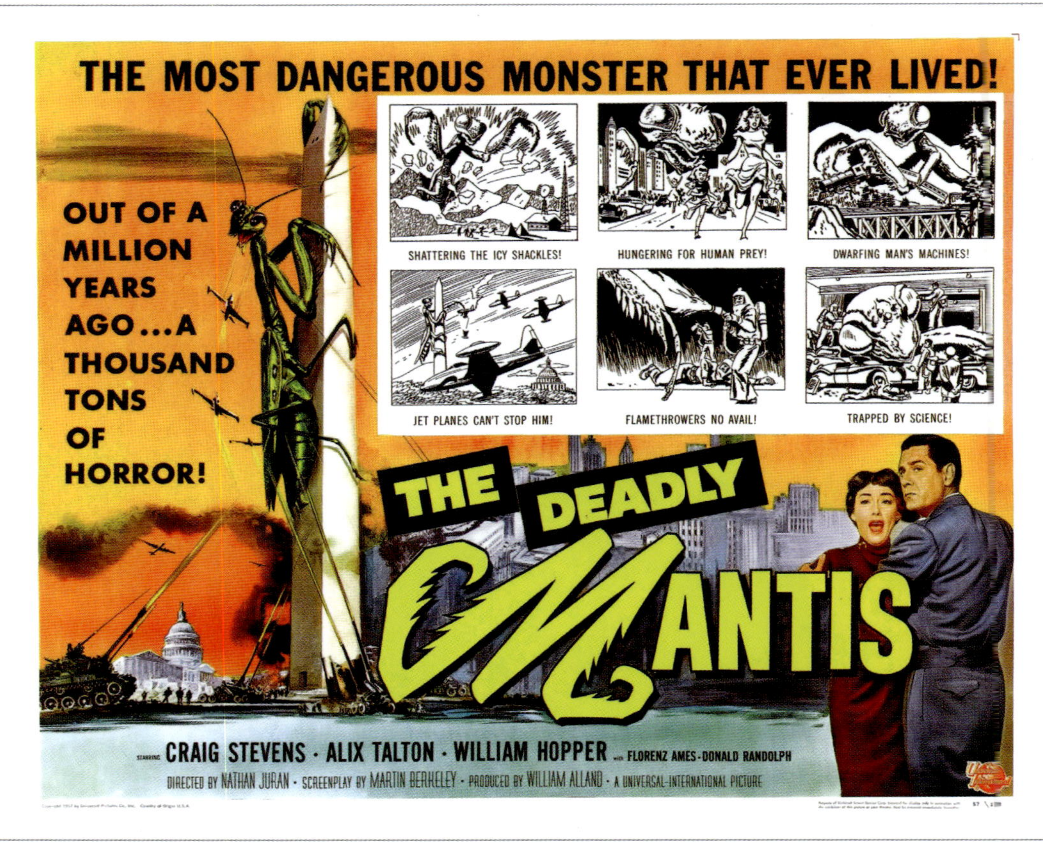

TARANTULA!
MONSTER SPIDER
100 FEET HIGH!
A Universal-International Picture starring
JOHN AGAR · MARA CORDAY
LEO G. CARROLL
with NESTOR PAIVA · ROSS ELLIOTT
DIRECTED BY JACK ARNOLD · SCREENPLAY BY ROBERT M. FRESCO AND MARTIN BERKELEY · PRODUCED BY WILLIAM ALLAND
Universal International

The story of four people who probed deeper into Science's greatest mystery—only to become trapped in a forbidden valley of pre-historic monsters!

LOST WORLDS OF THE '50s

The prehistoric-meets-modern-day subgenre continued into the '50s, though the films were often disappointing. Reynold Brown's breathtaking gouache-on-board one-sheet art (above) for *The Land Unknown* (1957) only heightened the dismay of filmgoers seeing the motley collection of men in suits, puppets, and disconsolate monitor lizards on screen. The Belgian posters (opposite top and bottom right) for *The Beast of Hollow Mountain* (1956) and *Two Lost Worlds* (1951) over-promise wildly: in the latter's case, the dinosaur action consists of a few seconds recycled from *One Million B.C.* (1940). That same stock footage is also seen in *Untamed Women* (1952); fittingly, the film's rather uncouth Mexican lobby card (opposite, middle left) "quotes" the dinosaur art from *Two Lost Worlds*. The Mexican lobby card (opposite, bottom left) for *The Monster of Piedras Blancas* (1959) shows the prehistoric "diplovertebron," made by thrifty producer Jack Kevan recycling molds from the *Forbidden Planet* mutant's feet, and hands from *The Mole People* (1956).

LES ARTISTES ASSOCIÉS
présentent
Couleurs par
DE LUXE
CINEMASCOPE
LA
MONTAGNE
MYSTERIEUSE
"THE BEAST
OF HOLLOW
MOUNTAIN"
Guy
MADISON
Patricia
MEDINA
REGISCOPE
UNITED
ARTISTS
Prod.: WILLIAM et EDWARD NASSOUR
Mise en scène: EDWARD NASSOUR
Het GEHEIMZINNIG GEBERGTE

El VALLE de los
DINOSAUROS

UN MONSTRUO SALIDO DE LAS
PROFUNDIDADES DEL MAR...
SENSACIONAL AVENTURA
DE TERROR Y SUSPENSO
QUE HIELA LA SANGRE
JEANNE CARMEN
LES TREMAYNE
JOHN HARMON
DON SULLIVAN
el MONSTRUO
NECESITABA SANGRE HUMANA
PARA VIVIR

Le
MONDE
PERDU
"TWO LOST WORLDS"
LAURA ELLIOTT
JIM ARNESS · GLORIA PETROFF · BILL KENNEDY
Regie: NORMAN DAWN · Production: BORIS PETROFF
UNITED
ARTISTS
DE VERLOREN WERELD

RAY HARRYHAUSEN

After serving an apprenticeship with Willis O'Brien, Ray Harryhausen (1920–2013) was ready to take a step up. His first film in charge of creature effects was *The Beast From 20,000 Fathoms* (1953), an early atomic monster tale which influenced *Godzilla* (1954); "the *Godzilla* stuff was a direct… filch," as Harryhausen himself put it. Stop-motion effects for other SF movies followed, including *It Came From Beneath the Sea* (1955), *Earth vs. the Flying Saucers* (1956), and *20 Million Miles to Earth* (1957). "They were considered B pictures because they were made on a tight budget," he recalled in a 2005 interview, "but we outlived many of the A pictures made at the same time." Eventually Harryhausen moved on to Greek mythology as a backdrop to his films: "I'd got tired of destroying cities, you know?"

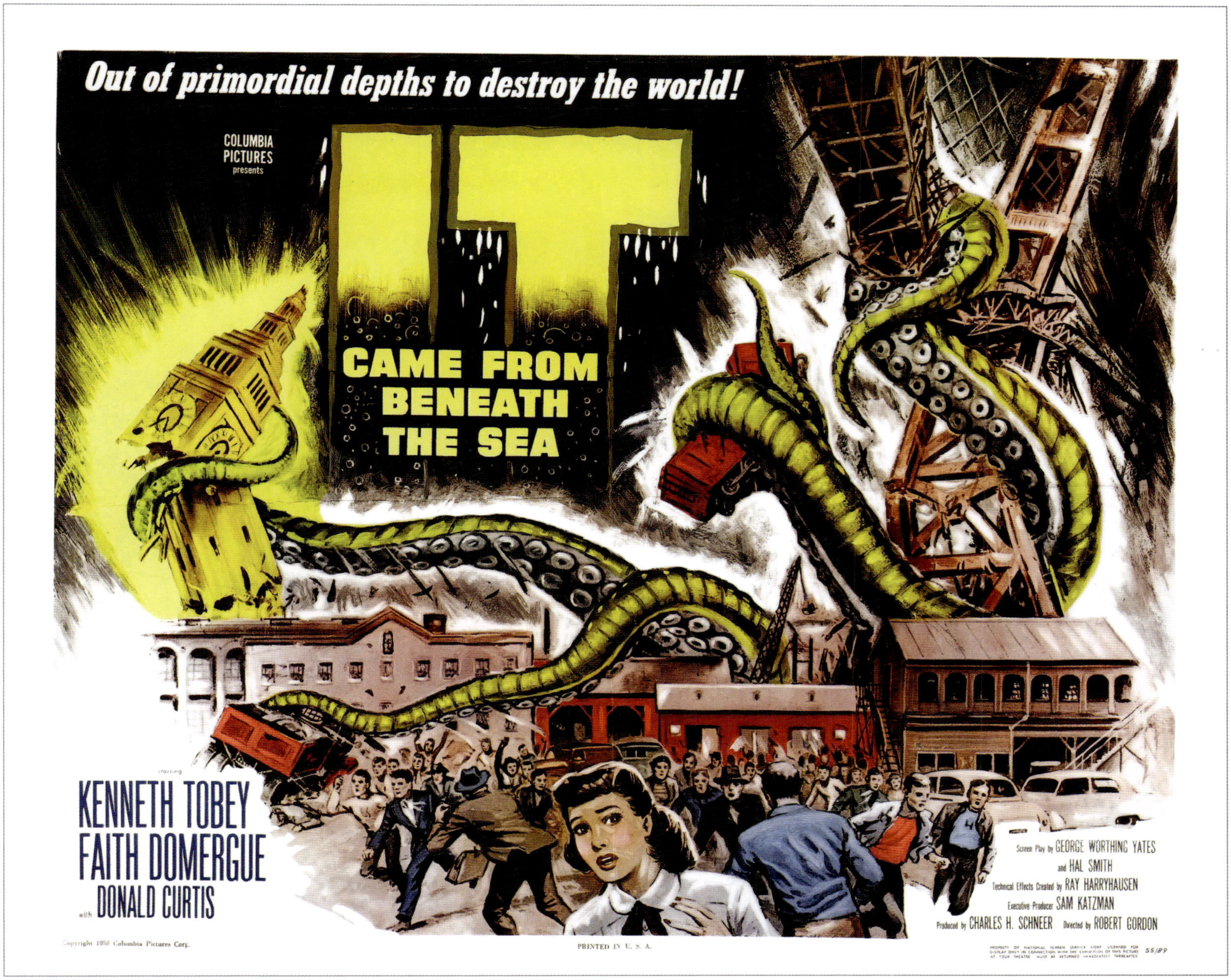
Out of primordial depths to destroy the world!
COLUMBIA PICTURES presents
IT
CAME FROM BENEATH THE SEA
starring
KENNETH TOBEY
FAITH DOMERGUE
with DONALD CURTIS
Screen Play by GEORGE WORTHING YATES
and HAL SMITH
Technical Effects Created by RAY HARRYHAUSEN
Executive Producer SAM KATZMAN
Produced by CHARLES H. SCHNEER Directed by ROBERT GORDON
Copyright 1955 Columbia Pictures Corp.
PRINTED IN U. S. A.
PROPERTY OF NATIONAL SCREEN SERVICE CORP. LICENSED FOR DISPLAY ONLY IN CONNECTION WITH THE EXHIBITION OF THIS PICTURE AT YOUR THEATRE. MUST BE RETURNED IMMEDIATELY THEREAFTER
55/89

Il Mostro dei Mari
KENNETH TOBEY · FAITH DOMERGUE · DONALD CURTIS
COLUMBIA
CEIAD
GEORGE WORTHING YATES : HAL SMITH
RAY HARRYHAUSEN
Produzione: CHARLES E. SCHNEER ·
Regia di ROBERT GORDON

Primordial monster attacks the world!
IT
CAME FROM BENEATH THE SEA
COLUMBIA
KENNETH TOBEY · FAITH DOMERGUE
DONALD CURTIS
FOR GENERAL EXHIBITION
PRINTED BY W. E. SMITH LIMITED SYDNEY

COLUMBIA PICTURES presents
IT
CAME FROM BENEATH THE SEA
starring
KENNETH TOBEY · FAITH DOMERGUE
with DONALD CURTIS
Screen Play by GEORGE WORTHING YATES and HAL SMITH · Technical Effects Created by RAY HARRYHAUSEN
Executive Producer SAM KATZMAN · Produced by CHARLES H. SCHNEER · Directed by ROBERT GORDON
Copyright 1955 Columbia Pictures Corp.
PRINTED IN U. S. A.
PROPERTY OF NATIONAL SCREEN SERVICE CORP. LICENSED FOR DISPLAY IN CONNECTION WITH THE EXHIBITION OF THIS PICTURE AT YOUR THEATRE. MUST BE RETURNED IMMEDIATELY THEREAFTER.
55/89

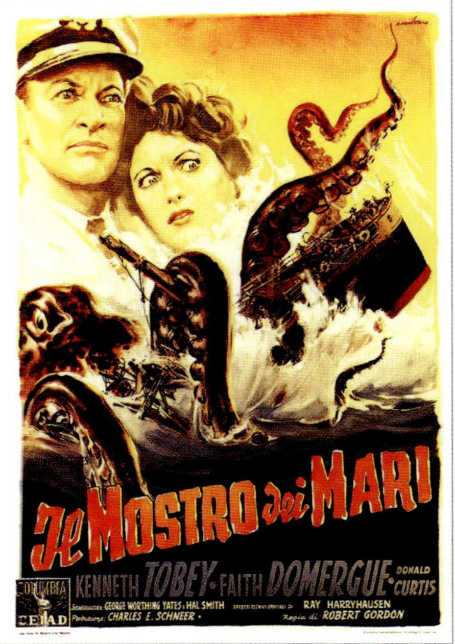

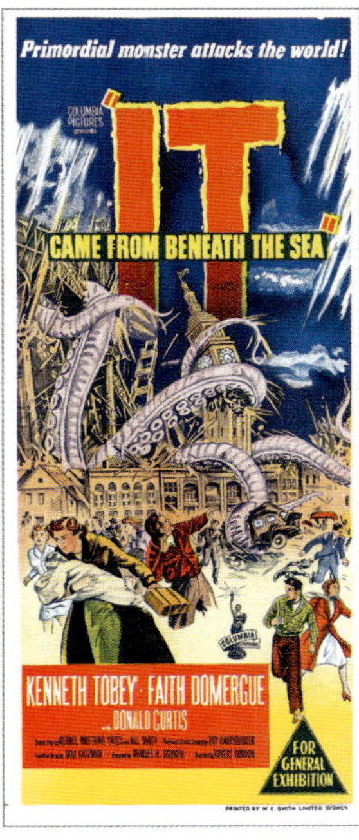

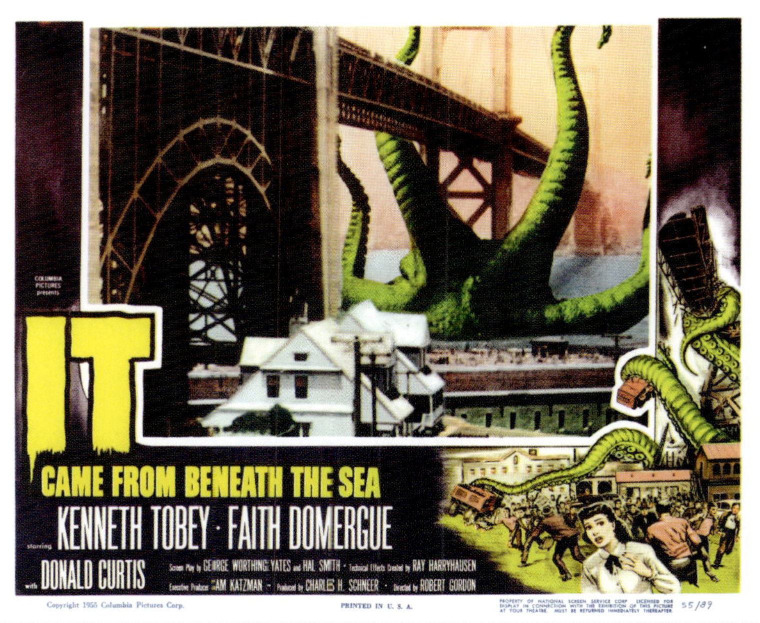

EARTH vs. THE FLYING SAUCERS
A COLUMBIA PICTURE

CALLING ALL FLYING SAUCERS!
THIS IS A SPACE MESSAGE! TO FLYING SAUCERS WHERE EVER YOU ARE!
"...WE ARE PREPARED TO RESIST YOUR ATTACK! ..FOR THE FIRST TIME OUR WORLD IS UNITED. WE WILL NOT SURRENDER!"
EARTH vs. THE FLYING SAUCERS
HUGH MARLOWE · JOAN TAYLOR with DONALD CURTIS

LA COLUMBIA PICTURES PRESENTA
LA TERRA contro i DISCHI VOLANTI
con HUGH MARLOWE · JOAN TAYLOR e DONALD CURTIS
SCENEGGIATURA DI GEORGE WORTHING YATES e RAYMOND T. MARCUS. SOGGETTO DI CURT SIODMAK
EFFETTI TECNICI DI RAY HARRYHAUSEN. UNA PRODUZIONE DI CHARLES H. SCHNEER
REALIZZATA DA SAM KATZMAN. REGIA DI FRED F. SEARS
COLUMBIA CEIAD

LA COLUMBIA PICTURES PRESENTA
LA TERRA contro i DISCHI VOLANTI
con HUGH MARLOWE · JOAN TAYLOR e DONALD CURTIS
SCENEGGIATURA DI GEORGE WORTHING YATES e RAYMOND T. MARCUS. SOGGETTO DI CURT SIODMAK
EFFETTI TECNICI DI RAY HARRYHAUSEN. UNA PRODUZIONE DI CHARLES H. SCHNEER
REALIZZATA DA SAM KATZMAN. REGIA DI FRED F. SEARS
COLUMBIA CEIAD

OUT-OF-SPACE CREATURE
INVADES THE EARTH!
20 MILLION MILES TO EARTH
WILLIAM HOPPER · JOAN TAYLOR
Screen Play by BOB WILLIAMS and CHRISTOPHER KNOPF · Story by CHARLOTT KNIGHT
Technical Effects Created by RAY HARRYHAUSEN
Produced by CHARLES H. SCHNEER · Directed by NATHAN JURAN
A MORNINGSIDE PRODUCTION · A COLUMBIA PICTURE

AMAZING STORIES
SCIENCE FICTION NOVEL
20 MILLION MILES TO EARTH
35¢
BY HENRY SLESAR—
Based on
Columbia Pictures'
Shock-Thriller
This Outerspace Monster Leveled Cities—Ravaged Earth

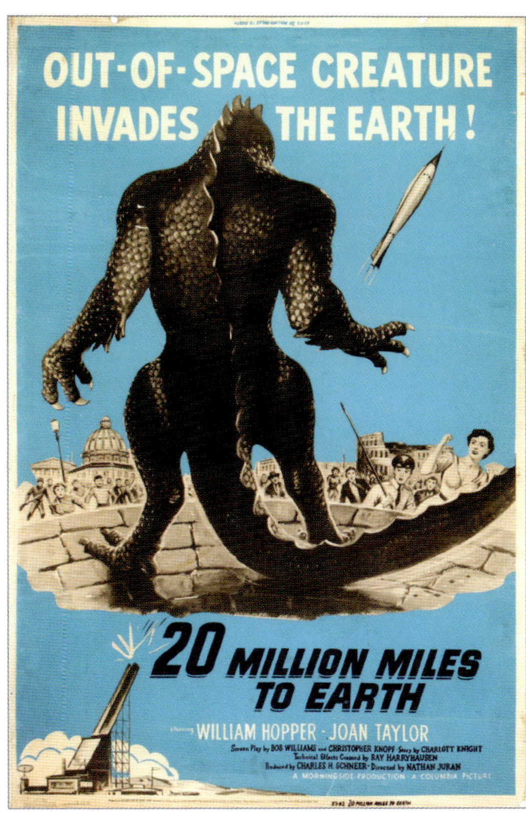

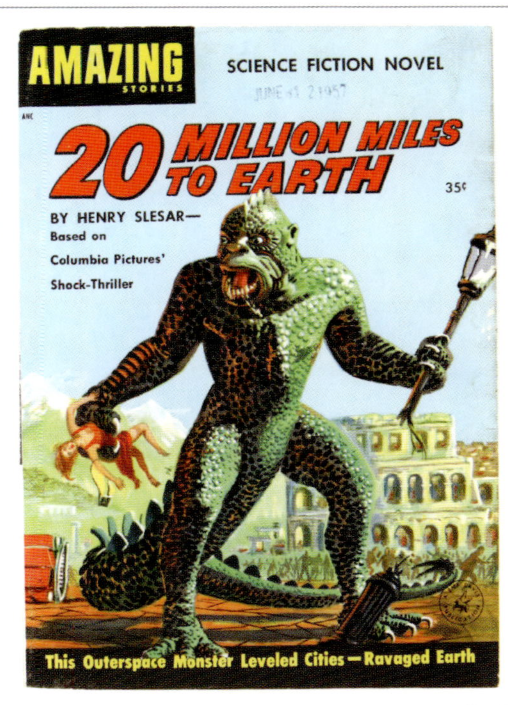

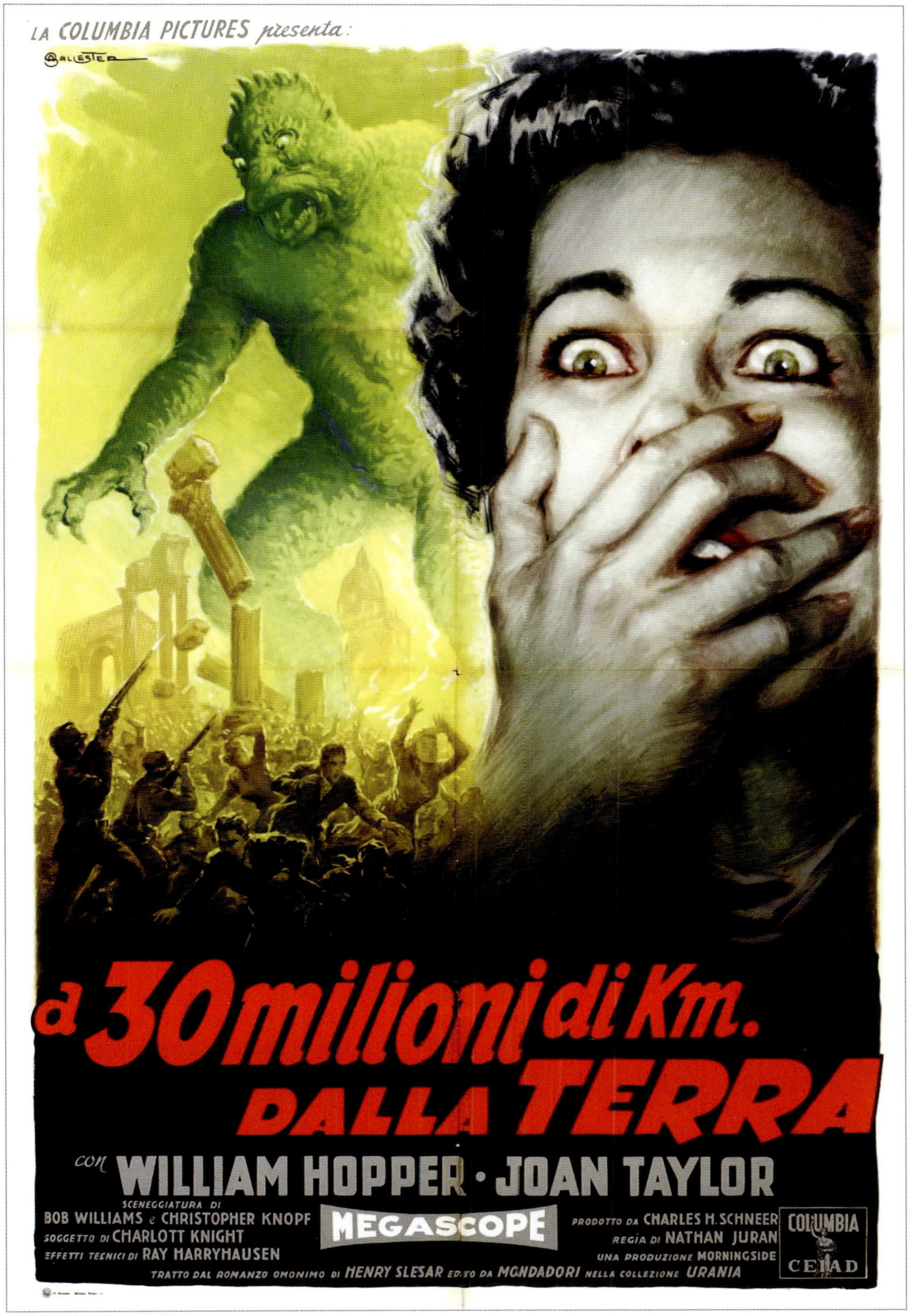

LA COLUMBIA PICTURES presenta:
a 30 milioni di Km. DALLA TERRA
con WILLIAM HOPPER · JOAN TAYLOR
SCENEGGIATURA DI
BOB WILLIAMS e CHRISTOPHER KNOPF
SOGGETTO DI CHARLOTT KNIGHT
EFFETTI TECNICI DI RAY HARRYHAUSEN
MEGASCOPE
PRODOTTO DA CHARLES H. SCHNEER
REGIA DI NATHAN JURAN
UNA PRODUZIONE MORNINGSIDE
COLUMBIA
CEIAD
TRATTO DAL ROMANZO OMONIMO DI HENRY SLESAR EDITO DA MONDADORI NELLA COLLEZIONE URANIA

SF 3D

"From Ray Bradbury's great science fiction story!" declared the US window card (opposite) for *It Came From Outer Space* (1953), but only in tiny letters. The main promotional push was for 3D, the cinematic innovation that had the first of its several short-lived crazes in the early '50s. The promise of "an avalanche in your lap!" was from a major studio film; decidedly more basic were *Robot Monster* and *Cat-Women of the Moon*, two 1953 movies that could boast an Elmer Bernstein score, though the latter misspelled his name "Bernstien" on the credits, and also swiped art from *Destination Moon* for its poster (compare with page 78).

3-DIMENSION
EXCITEMENT THAT CAN
ALMOST TOUCH YOU!
IT
CAME
FROM
OUTER
SPACE
From Ray Bradbury's
great science fiction story!
AN AVALANCHE
IN YOUR LAP!
A HELICOPTER
OVER YOUR HEAD!
A SPACE SHIP
ZOOMS AT YOU!
Starring
RICHARD CARLSON · BARBARA RUSH
with CHARLES DRAKE · RUSSELL JOHNSON · KATHLEEN HUGHES · JOE SAWYER
Universal International
Directed by JACK ARNOLD - Screenplay by HARRY ESSEX Produced by WILLIAM ALLAND - A UNIVERSAL-INTERNATIONAL PICTURE
Copyright 1953 by Universal Pictures Co., Inc.
Country of Origin U. S. A.
Printed in U. S. A.
Property of National Screen Service Corp. Licensed for display only in connection with the exhibition of this picture at your theater. Must be returned immediately thereafter.
53/351-30

QUATERMASS

The adventures of Professor Bernard Quatermass battling extraterrestrial threats moved quickly from empty-the-streets appointment television on the BBC to Hammer Films' cinematic adaptations. Creator Nigel Kneale (1922–2006) was unimpressed: "They just wanted the poster… it didn't matter about the script," he despaired of *The Quatermass Xperiment* (1955), which was retitled *The Creeping Unknown* for the US market, "the most awful title visited on any piece of work." Hammer did at least employ Kneale to help script *Quatermass 2* (1957, a.k.a. *Enemy From Space*), but the writer avoided getting involved with promotion: "I just didn't want to know. I could guess all too well the sort of horrors: the screaming blonde on the poster, with the people ogling, distraught, as things fell over. Posters for horror films, they'd actually been quite intelligent at one stage, but reduced to screaming blondes. It was not what I ever set out to do. It was very sad."

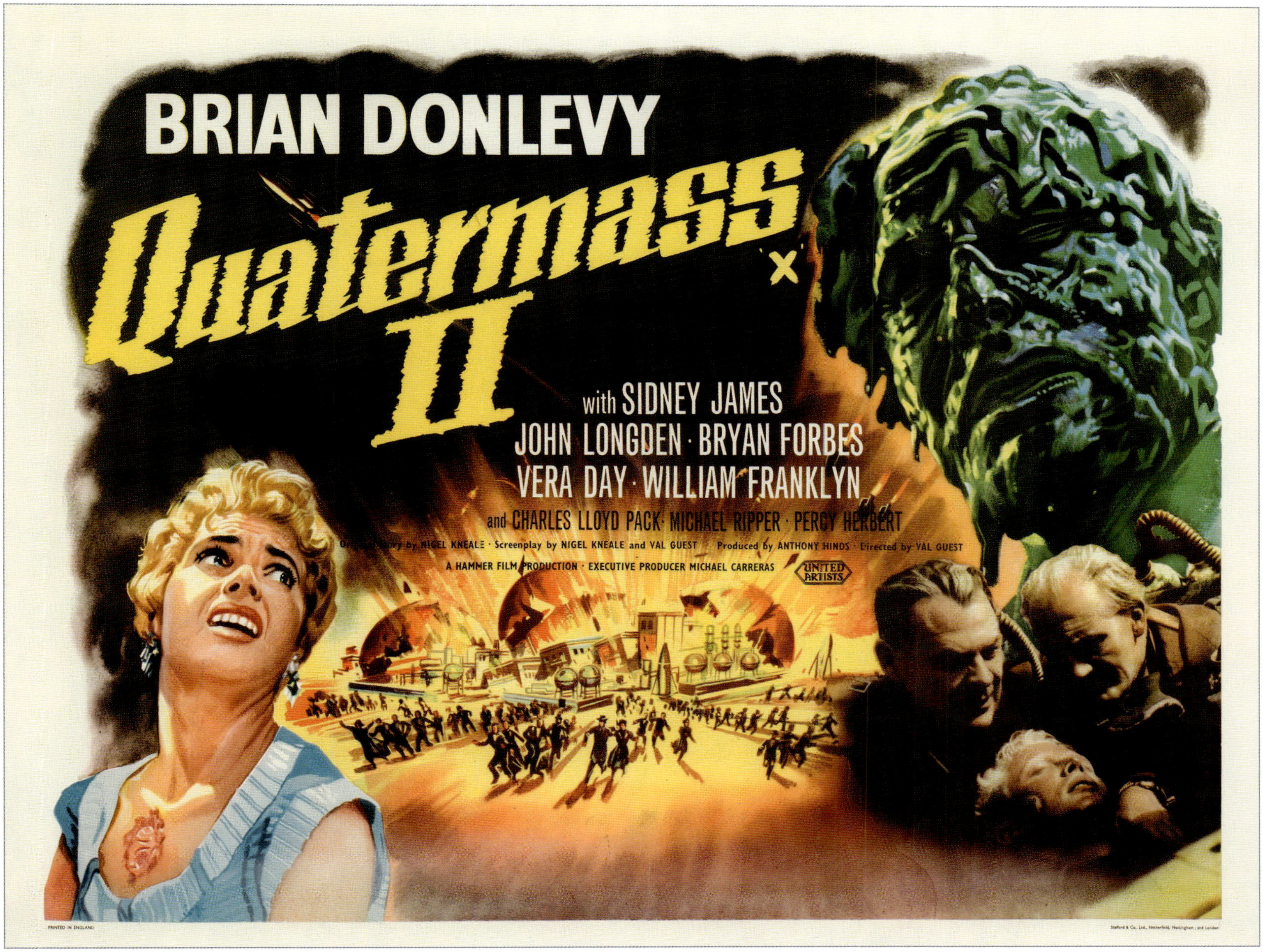
BRIAN DONLEVY
Quatermass II
X
with SIDNEY JAMES
JOHN LONGDEN · BRYAN FORBES
VERA DAY · WILLIAM FRANKLYN
and CHARLES LLOYD PACK · MICHAEL RIPPER · PERCY HERBERT
Screenplay by NIGEL KNEALE and VAL GUEST · Produced by ANTHONY HINDS · Directed by VAL GUEST
A HAMMER FILM PRODUCTION · EXECUTIVE PRODUCER MICHAEL CARRERAS
UNITED ARTISTS
PRINTED IN ENGLAND
Stafford & Co., Ltd., Netherfield, Nottingham ; and London

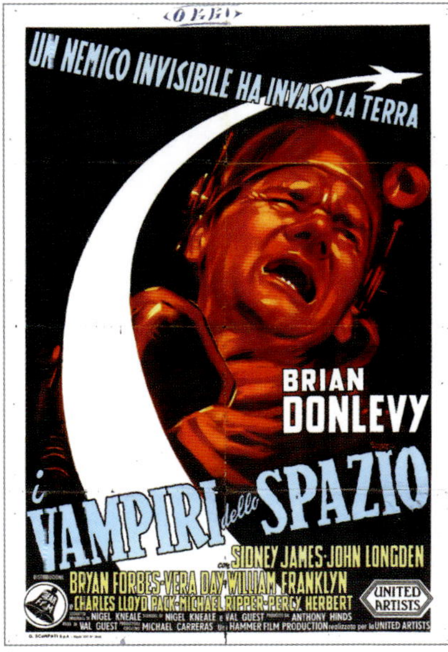

UN NEMICO INVISIBILE HA INVASO LA TERRA
BRIAN DONLEVY
i VAMPIRI dello SPAZIO
con SIDNEY JAMES · JOHN LONGDEN
BRYAN FORBES · VERA DAY · WILLIAM FRANKLYN
e CHARLES LLOYD PACK · MICHAEL RIPPER · PERCY HERBERT
NIGEL KNEALE · NIGEL KNEALE e VAL GUEST · ANTHONY HINDS
VAL GUEST · MICHAEL CARRERAS · Una HAMMER FILM PRODUCTION realizzata per la UNITED ARTISTS
UNITED ARTISTS

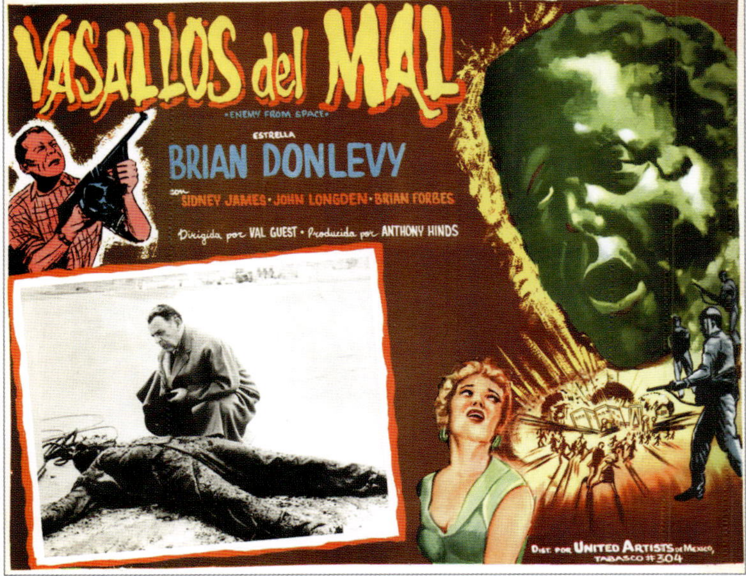

VASALLOS del MAL
"ENEMY FROM SPACE"
ESTRELLA
BRIAN DONLEVY
con
SIDNEY JAMES · JOHN LONGDEN · BRIAN FORBES
Dirigida por VAL GUEST · Producida por ANTHONY HINDS
DIST. POR UNITED ARTISTS DE MEXICO, TABASCO # 304

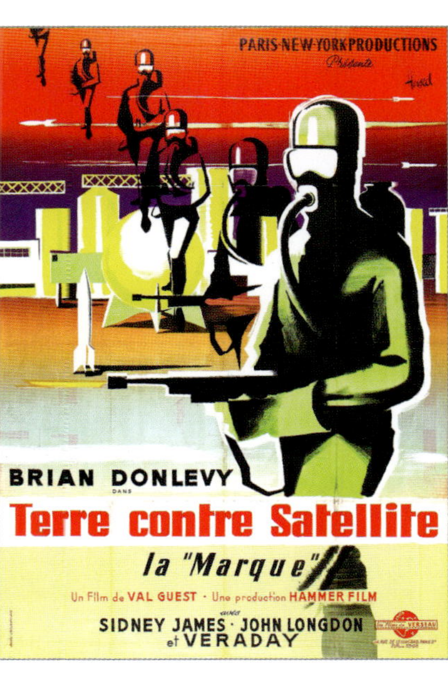

PARIS-NEW-YORK PRODUCTIONS
Présente
BRIAN DONLEVY
DANS
Terre contre Satellite
la "Marque"
Un Film de VAL GUEST · Une production HAMMER FILM
avec
SIDNEY JAMES · JOHN LONGDON
et VERADAY

Missions to Mars

SF filmmakers were soon looking for destinations beyond the Moon. *Red Planet Mars* (1952), despite the promise of "Out-Of-This-World EXCITEMENT" and an approaching fireball on the poster, is actually an Earthbound drama about faked (or are they?) radio broadcasts from Mars causing havoc with Western civilization. *Flight to Mars* (1951), which *is* about the first manned mission to the planet, was shot in five days using recycled sets, props, and costumes from the previous year's *Destination Moon* and *Rocketship X-M*. Director Ib Melchior had a comparatively luxurious nine days for *The Angry Red Planet* (1959) but conceded, "It's not a great, artistic effort. But it is visually interesting and fun and entertaining… It may not have been Shakespeare, but it serves its purpose."

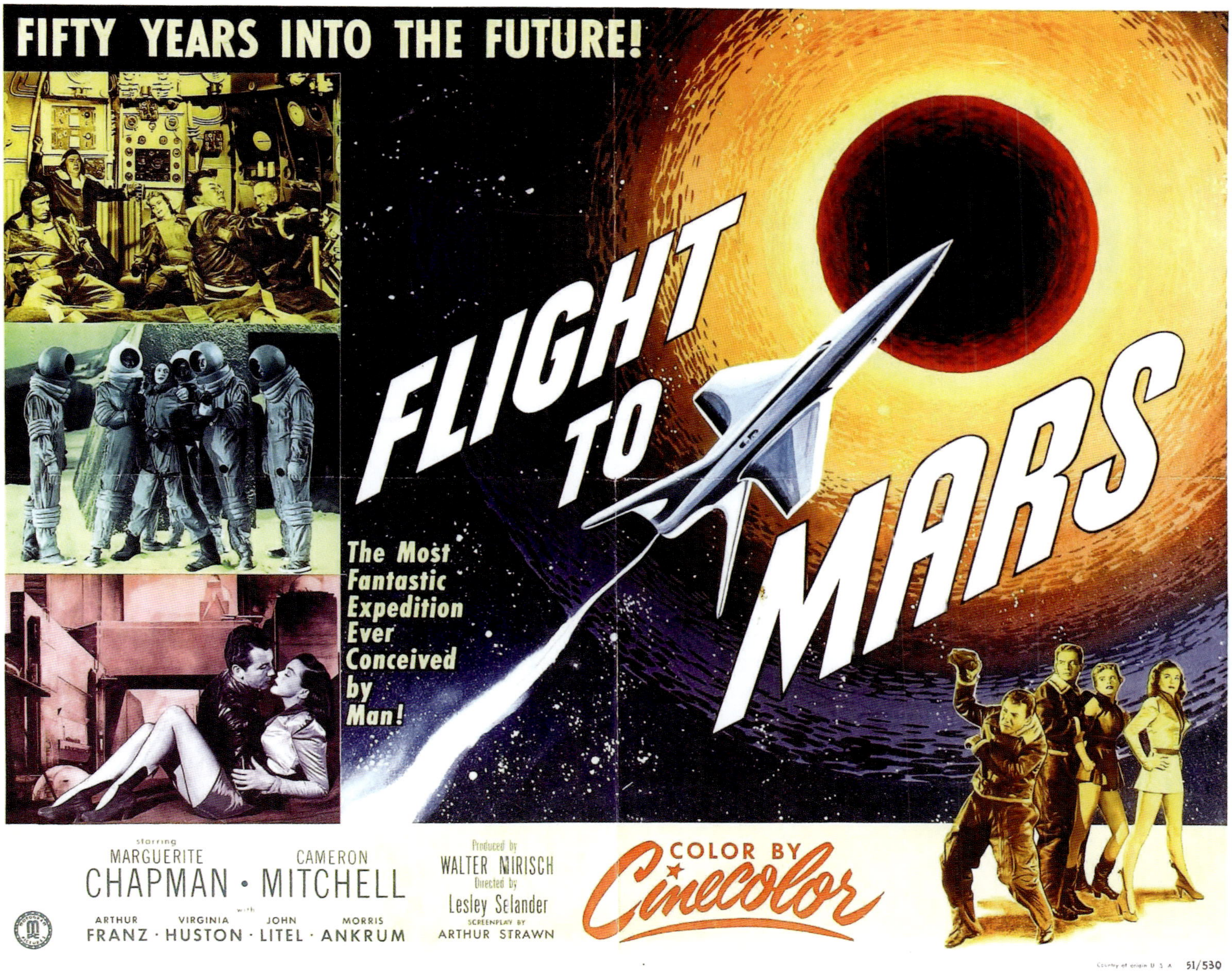
FIFTY YEARS INTO THE FUTURE!
FLIGHT TO MARS
The Most Fantastic Expedition Ever Conceived by Man!
starring
MARGUERITE CHAPMAN · CAMERON MITCHELL
with
ARTHUR FRANZ · VIRGINIA HUSTON · JOHN LITEL · MORRIS ANKRUM
Produced by WALTER MIRISCH
Directed by Lesley Selander
SCREENPLAY BY ARTHUR STRAWN
COLOR BY Cinecolor
51/530

SPECTACULAR ADVENTURE BEYOND TIME AND SPACE...
AS cinemagic TAKES YOU TO
THE ANGRY RED PLANET
IN MAGNIFICENT COLOR
AN AMERICAN-INTERNATIONAL PICTURE
Starring
Gerald Mohr · Nora Hayden · Les Tremayne · Jack Kruschen ·
Directed by Ib Melchior · Produced by Sid Pink and Norman Maurer
Screenplay by Sid Pink and Ib Melchior · A Sino Production

LOS INCREIBLES SECRETOS DE MARTE DESCUBIERTOS EN LA TIERRA.
DONALD HYDE Y ANTHONY VEILLER Presentan
EL MILAGRO DE MARTE
·RED PLANET MARS·
con PETER GRAVES · ANDREA KING · HERBERT BERGHOF
y WALTER SANDE · MARVIN MILLER · WILLIS BOUCHEY · MORRIS ANKRUM
Productor ANTHONY VEILLER Director HARRY HORNER
UNA PELICULA DE ARTISTAS UNIDOS DIST. POR EAGLE LION DE MEXICO, S.A. P. REFORMA 153 MEX.

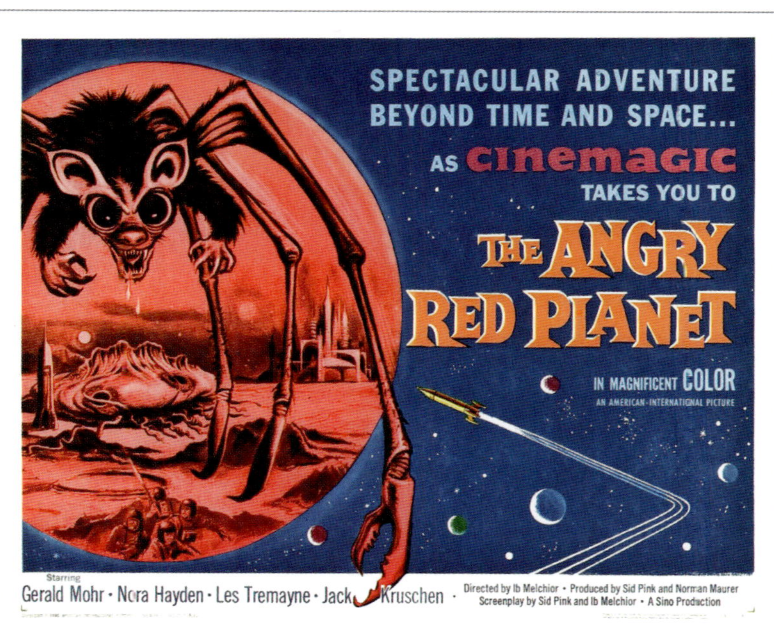

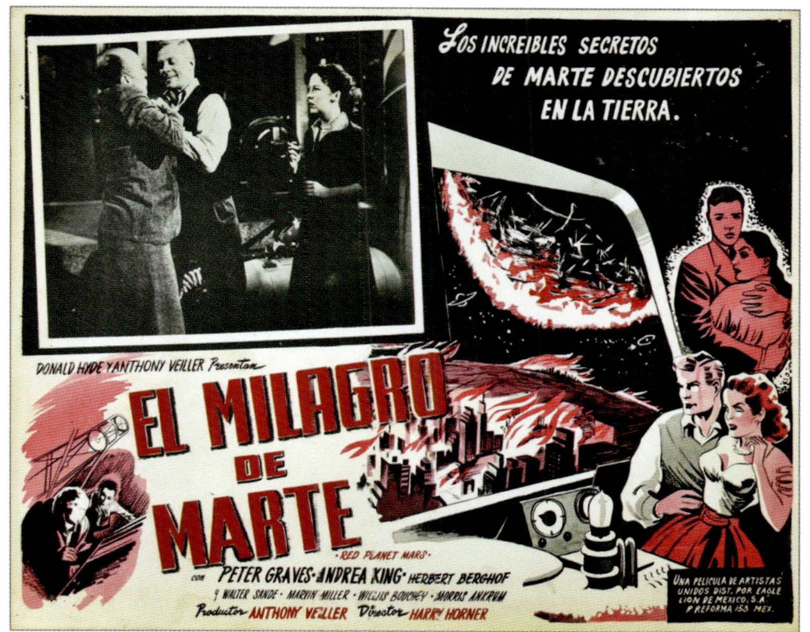

THIS ISLAND EARTH

This Island Earth, released in June 1955, was Universal's first color SF film, which they were keen to stress had been "2 ½ years in the making!" Indeed, back in March 1954 the studio publicity machine was already teasing that Faith Domergue would be sharing a love scene with an extraterrestrial creature in their forthcoming epic. "The guy's half human and half insect," reported Erskine Johnson, duly picking up the story in his syndicated Hollywood gossip column. "This will be no novelty, though, to a lot of US women who say they've been married to insects for years."

The Metaluna Mutant went without a romantic interlude in the final movie, but became an icon nevertheless. Reynold Brown's US one-sheet (opposite) shows several mutants—the film only has one—with legs that don't look like the on-screen mutant's hastily donned slacks (a last resort when the SFX team could not get the original costume to work). Arnaldo De Amicis's Italian poster art (overleaf) chooses to emphasize Jeff Morrow, as cerebral alien scientist Exeter.

THE SUPREME EXCITEMENT
OF OUR TIME!
IN COLOR BY
TECHNICOLOR
THIS
ISLAND
EARTH
2½
YEARS
IN THE
MAKING
!
THIS ISLAND EARTH
Universal International
starring
JEFF MORROW · FAITH DOMERGUE · REX REASON with LANCE FULLER · RUSSELL JOHNSON
DIRECTED BY JOSEPH NEWMAN · SCREENPLAY BY FRANKLIN COEN AND EDWARD G. O'CALLAGHAN · PRODUCED BY WILLIAM ALLAND · A UNIVERSAL-INTERNATIONAL PICTURE
Copyright 1955 by Universal Pictures Co., Inc.
Litho. in U.S.A.
55/214

SCIENCE FICTION
THIS ISLAND EARTH
A NOVEL BY
RAYMOND F. JONES
THIS EXCITING NEW BOOK NOW A
UNIVERSAL-INTERNATIONAL
TECHNICOLOR FILM
The Most Startling Adventure in the History of Tomorrow!

Due anni e mezzo di lavorazione!
Jeff
MORROW
Faith
DOMERGUE
Rex
REASON
Lance
FULLER
Russel
JOHNSON
Regia:
JOSEPH NEWMAN
Prodotto da
WILLIAN ALLAND
Universal International
TECHNICOLOR
CITTADINO dello SPAZIO
Dal capolavoro di R. JONES pubblicato nei «ROMANZI DI URANIA» di Mondadori

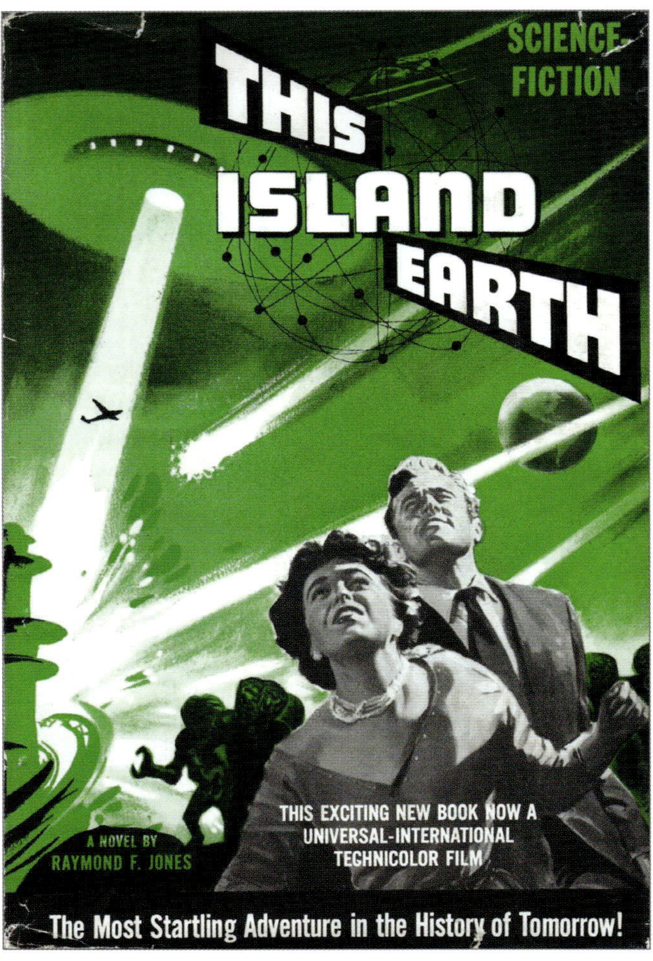

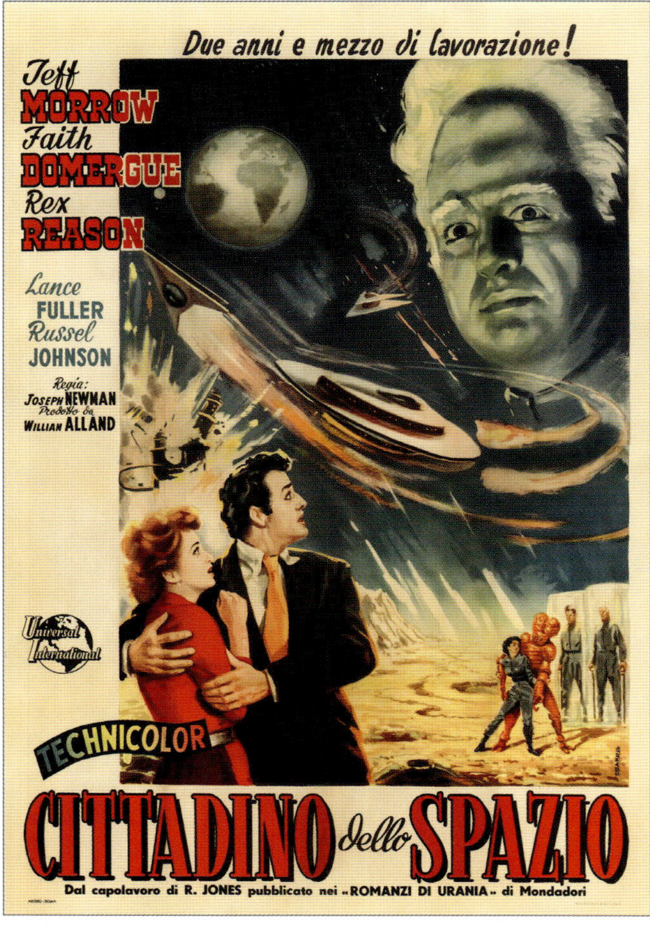

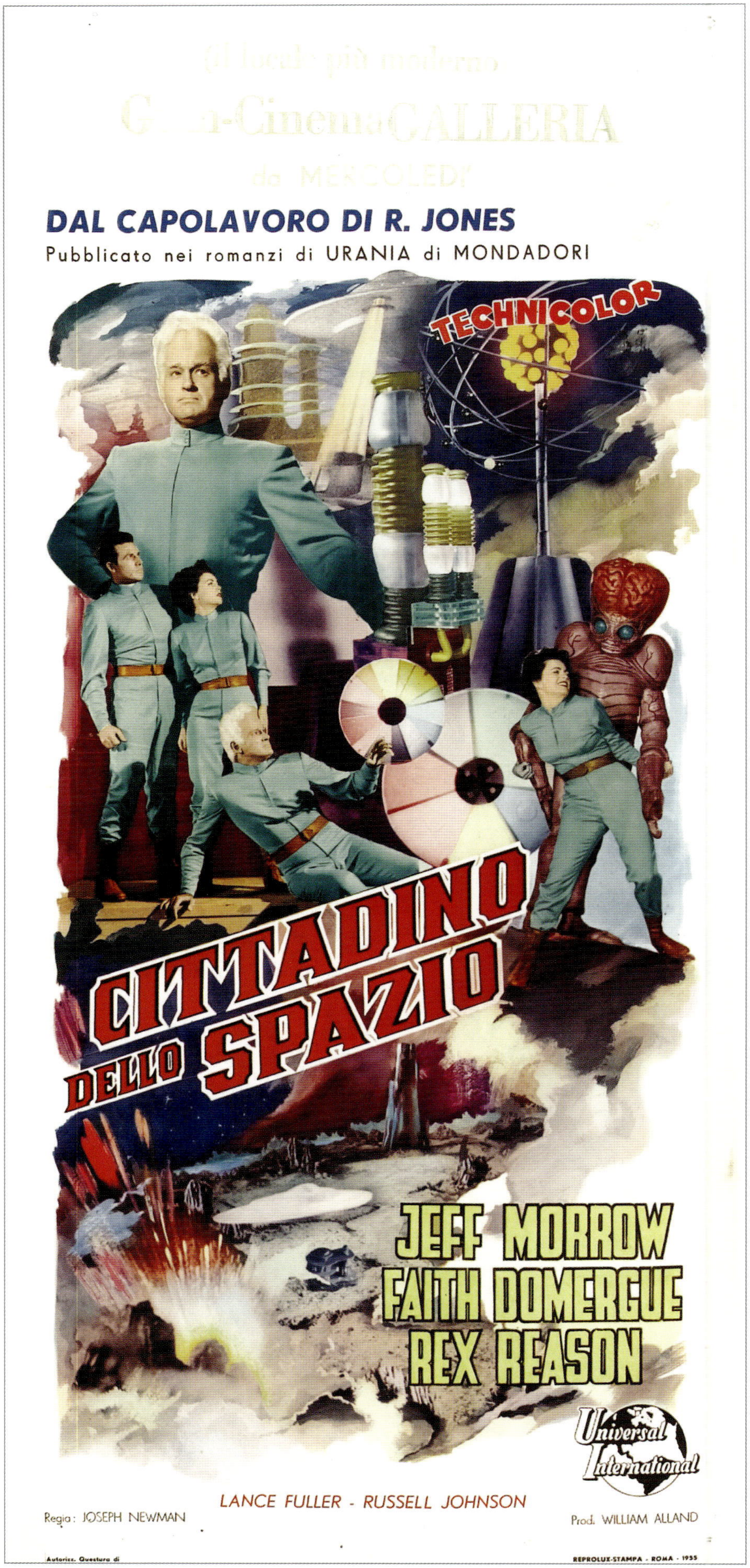
DAL CAPOLAVORO DI R. JONES
Pubblicato nei romanzi di URANIA di MONDADORI
TECHNICOLOR
CITTADINO DELLO SPAZIO
JEFF MORROW
FAITH DOMERGUE
REX REASON
Universal International
LANCE FULLER - RUSSELL JOHNSON
Regia: JOSEPH NEWMAN
Prod. WILLIAM ALLAND
Autorizz. Questura di
REPROLUX-STAMPA - ROMA - 1955

Universal International
TECHNICOLOR
DE AMICIS
CITTADINO DELLO SPAZIO
JEFF MORROW · FAITH DOMERGUE · REX REASON · LANCE FULLER · RUSSELL JOHNSON
Regia di JOSEPH NEWMAN Prod. WILLIAM ALLAND

ROGER CORMAN

As befits such a titan of cinema, the career of writer–director–producer Roger Corman has been exhaustively chronicled, not least by the man himself in his entertaining autobiography *How I Made 100 Movies in Hollywood and Never Lost a Dime* (1990; he's made quite a few more since then). Though his work spans various genres, he often found success with SF projects, including his very first film as producer, *Monster from the Ocean Floor* (1954). Made for $12,000 in six days, Corman recalled that, "I was surprisingly confident. I think if I were to do it now, I would be very worried that I couldn't do it. But at the age of 25 or whatever, I had ambition and confidence. You do things that, when you're older and smarter, you wouldn't do." That confidence led to a partnership with James H. Nicholson and Samuel Z. Arkoff's American Releasing Corporation, which became American International Pictures (AIP). A stream of hits followed, including *The Beast with a Million Eyes* (1955), *Day the World Ended* (1955), *It Conquered the World* (1956), and *Not of this Earth* (1957).

Corman knew how important the advertising visuals were when it came to converting his tight budgets into maximum box office returns: "I'm not aware that the function of any poster for any picture has ever been anything than to sell tickets… We were probably a little more overt in what we were doing than the major studios, but what we were trying to do was to entice the audience, to show to the audience that this was a film they wanted to see. A film should be exciting, just that. You can do almost anything to an audience except bore them. And the advertising campaign should be even more exciting than the film." The Italian poster for *Day the World Ended* (opposite) certainly lives up to that dictum, and also follows another of Corman's rules: "In science fiction films, the monster should always be bigger than the leading lady."

RICHARD DENNING · LORI NELSON
ADELE JERGENS
REGIA:
ROGER CORMAN
IL MOSTRO
DEL PIANETA PERDUTO

ALBERT KALLIS

Albert Kallis, a second-generation movie marketer (his father Mischa ran Paramount and then Universal's publicity art departments), was working with top-flight designer Saul Bass on major studio films when a 29-year-old Roger Corman cheekily asked, "What would it take to get you?" "'If, after a general conversation about the film you'd leave all the decisions to me, I might be interested,'" Kallis later recalled telling him, "'*and* I'll give you a fixed price.' That appealed to Roger greatly!" The handshake deal lasted 17 years, with Kallis working as a one-man art department, and later, as AIP's output increased, handing off concepts to other artists, including Reynold Brown.

"At AIP, the ads always came first," Kallis admitted. "What was important was the thrust, the sense of what you were selling and how it would appeal... Our problem was to make the artwork leap off the newspaper page or poster, to create that compelling sense, 'I've gotta see it *now*!'" Ad campaigns for non-existent movies were created, and if exhibitors liked the look of them, only then would the cameras roll: "Invariably, I never saw an AIP movie before I did the advertising." As one theater owner told him, "If we could put sprocket holes on your ad campaigns, then we'd really have something!" Kallis's eye-popping compositions, usually painted in gouache on Whatman artboard, have become a cornerstone of SF poster art.

Not content with leaving his stamp on just one area of American culture, Kallis, a true Renaissance man, went on to write for the stage, and co-found The International House of Pancakes restaurant chain.

EVERY MAN ITS PRISONER...EVERY WOMAN ITS SLAVE!
IT CONQUERED THE WORLD
PETER GRAVES · BEVERLY GARLAND · LEE VAN CLEEF

INVASION OF THE SAUCER-MEN
See TEENAGERS vs. THE SAUCER-MEN!
See DISEMBODIED HAND THAT CRAWLS...!
See NIGHT THE WORLD NEARLY ENDED...!
See EARTH ATTACKED BY FLYING SAUCERS!
STEVE TERRELL · GLORIA CASTILLO · FRANK GORSHIN

HUMAN EMOTIONS STRIPPED RAW!
The terrifying story that COULD COME TRUE!
DAY THE WORLD ENDED
ATTACKED ...by a creature from hell!
SUPERSCOPE
RICHARD DENNING
LORI NELSON · ADELE JERGENS

A CREATURE FROM
BEYOND THE STARS
EVIL...BEAUTIFUL...DEADLY...!
THE ASTOUNDING
SHE MONSTER
ROBERT CLARKE · KENNE DUNCAN · MARILYN HARVEY
with JEANNE TATUM · SHIRLEY KILPATRICK · EWING BROWN
Story and Screenplay by FRANK HALL · Produced and Directed by RONNIE ASHCROFT
A HOLLYWOOD INTERNATIONAL Production
An AMERICAN INTERNATIONAL Release

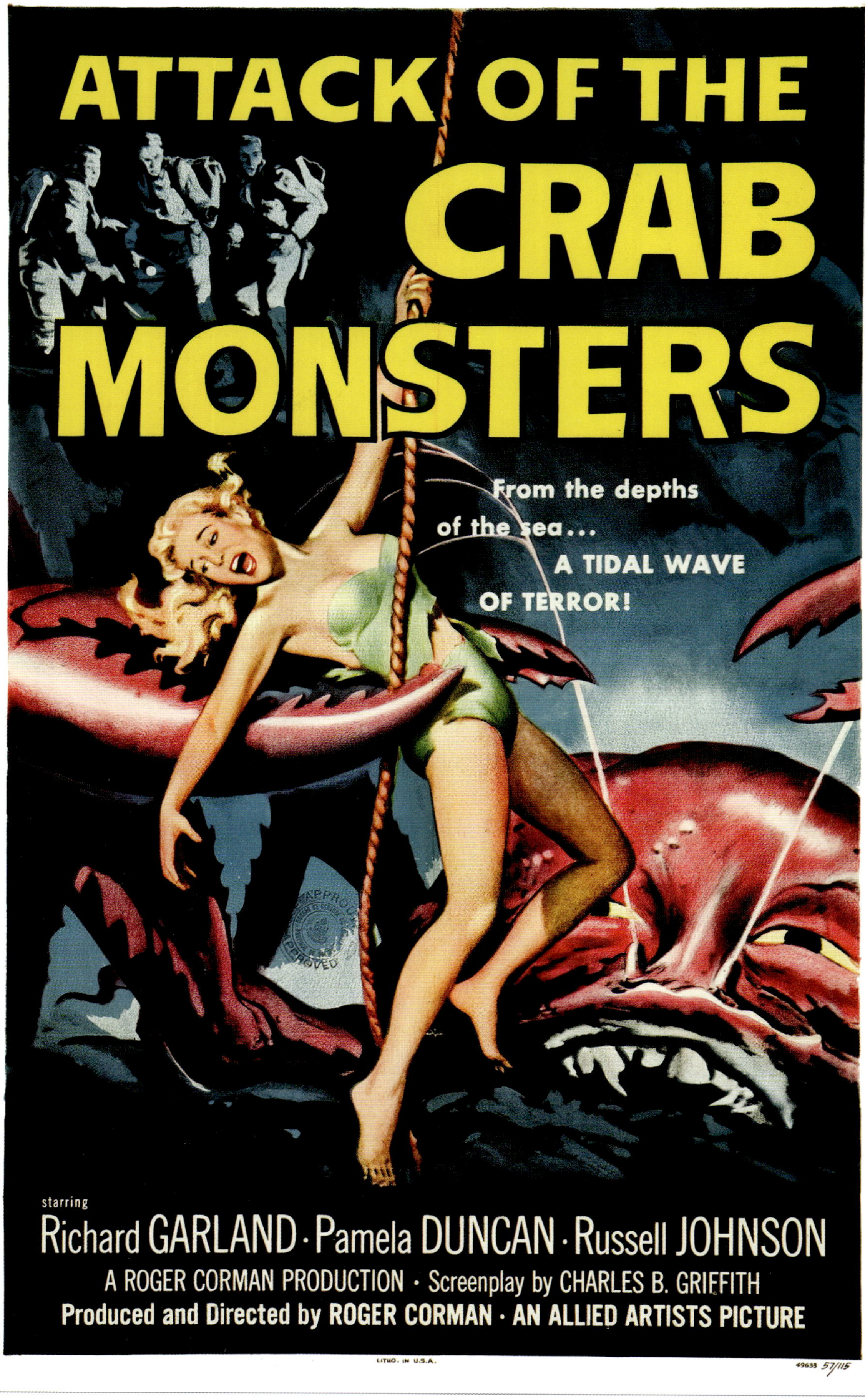

ATTACK OF THE
CRAB
MONSTERS
From the depths
of the sea...
A TIDAL WAVE
OF TERROR!
starring
Richard GARLAND · Pamela DUNCAN · Russell JOHNSON
A ROGER CORMAN PRODUCTION · Screenplay by CHARLES B. GRIFFITH
Produced and Directed by ROGER CORMAN · AN ALLIED ARTISTS PICTURE
LITHO. IN U.S.A.
49633 57/115

FREEZING HORROR!
...as a living nightmare strikes from the depths of the sea!
THE PHANTOM FROM 10,000 LEAGUES
Starring
KENT TAYLOR · CATHY DOWNS · MICHAEL WHALEN
A MILNER BROS. PRODUCTION

Out of This World
SHOCK SENSATION!
ANTHONY DEXTER
SUSAN SHAW
PAUL CARPENTER
FIRE MAIDENS of OUTER SPACE
SEE
SEE
SEE
And introducing JACQUELINE CURTIS
A Saturn Films Presentation of a Cy Roth Production · Distributed by TOPAZ FILM CO.

FROM TIME UNBORN...A HIDEOUS SHE-THING!
TERROR
FROM THE YEAR
5,000
starring
JOYCE HOLDEN · WARD COSTELLO · FREDERIC DOWNS

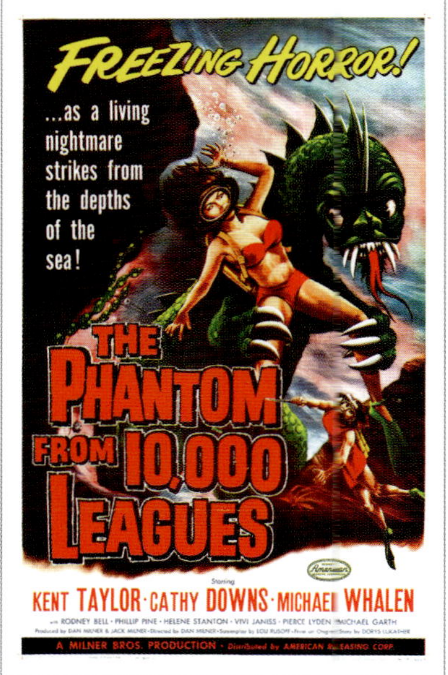

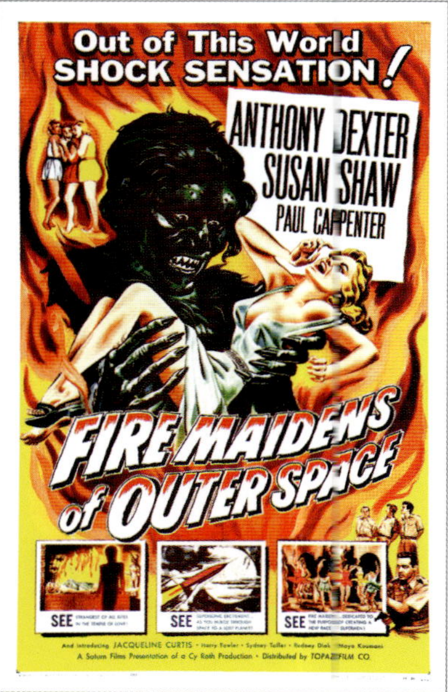

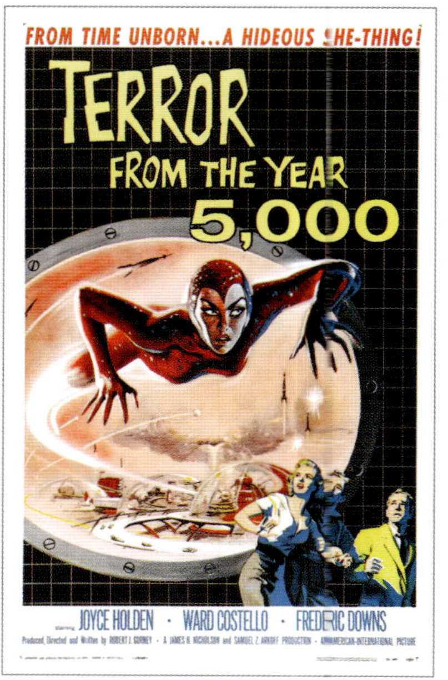

AMAZING...COLOSSAL.....!
GROWING...!
GROWING...!
GROWING...!
TO A GIANT...!
TO A MONSTER...!
TO A BEHEMOTH...!
WHEN WILL IT STOP...??
AMERICAN - INTERNATIONAL presents
THE AMAZING COLOSSAL MAN
starring
GLENN LANGAN
CATHY DOWNS
WILLIAM HUDSON
Produced & directed by
BERT I. GORDON
Screenplay by
MARK HANNA & BERT I. GORDON
A
JAMES H. NICHOLSON
SAMUEL Z. ARKOFF
Production

Screaming Terror!
THE BEAST WITH 1,000,000 EYES!
filmed for WIDE SCREEN in TERROR-SCOPE
with Paul BIRCH · Lorna THAYER · Dona COLE and the BEAST
Produced & Directed by DAVID KRAMARSKY · Screenplay by TOM FILER
A SAN MATEO PICTURE · Presented by PALO ALTO PRODUCTIONS
American

BERT I. GORDON

A writer, producer, and director who also created his own special effects, Bert I. Gordon (1922–2023) started young: "My aunt gave me a camera when I was about eight or nine years old, and I would do tricks with it. Like have someone standing in the scene and then stop the camera and have them walk out so they'd 'pop' off." That technical know-how got him a head start in Hollywood, where he became known for a series of giant monster movies that earned him the nickname Mr. B.I.G. *King Dinosaur* (1955), *The Cyclops* (1957), *The Amazing Colossal Man* (1957), its sequel *War of the Colossal Beast* (1958), and *Earth vs. the Spider* (1958, a.k.a. *The Spider*) all used back projection and other methods of camera trickery to create oversized adversaries, as did *Beginning of the End* (1957), which featured footage of grasshoppers crawling over photographs of buildings. "With insects, you waste a lot of film," Gordon admitted. "You hope they'll do what you want. Sometimes you have to improvise and say, 'Oh, they did that. I'll change the script.'"

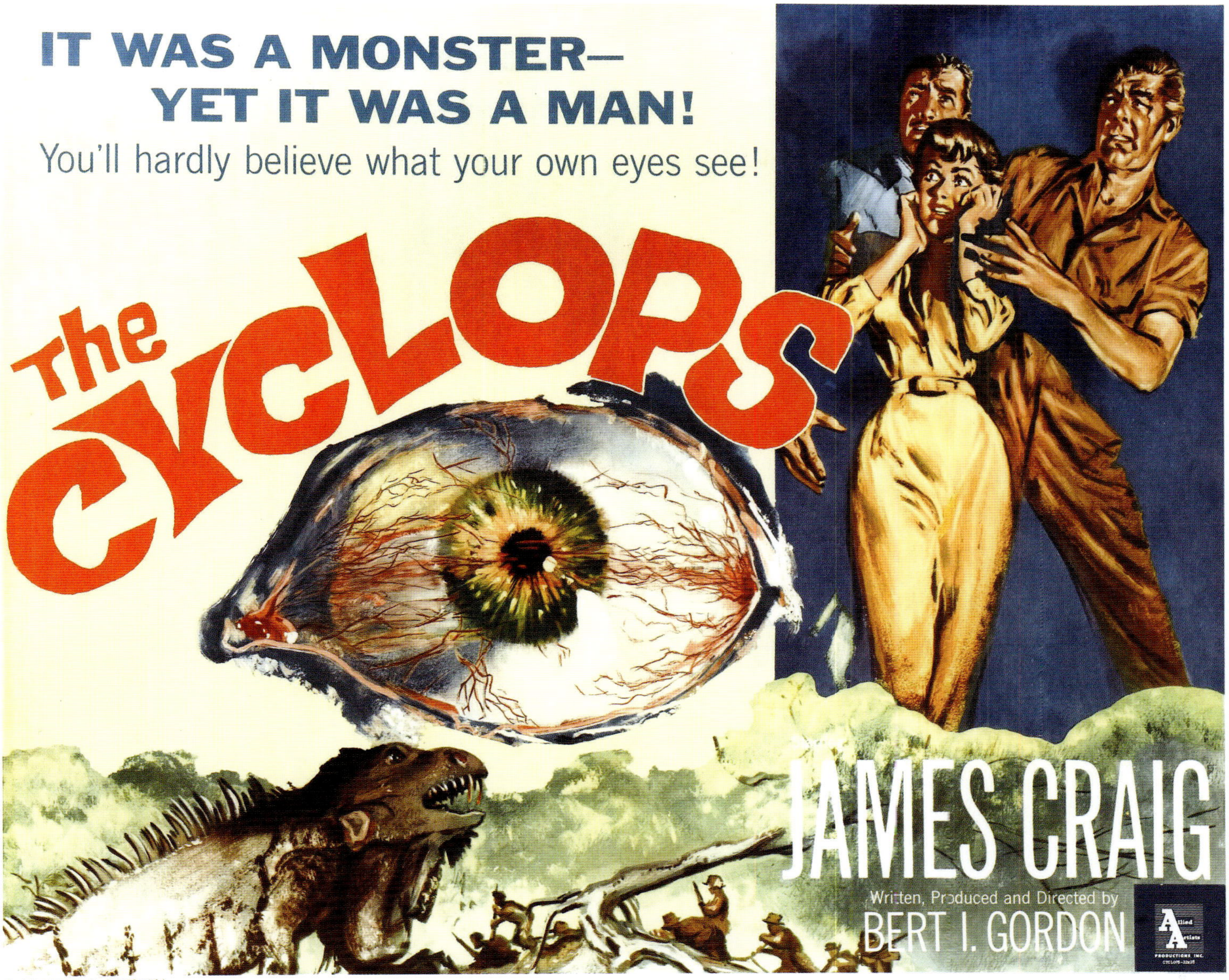

IT WAS A MONSTER—
YET IT WAS A MAN!
You'll hardly believe what your own eyes see!

The CYCLOPS

JAMES CRAIG

Written, Produced and Directed by
BERT I. GORDON

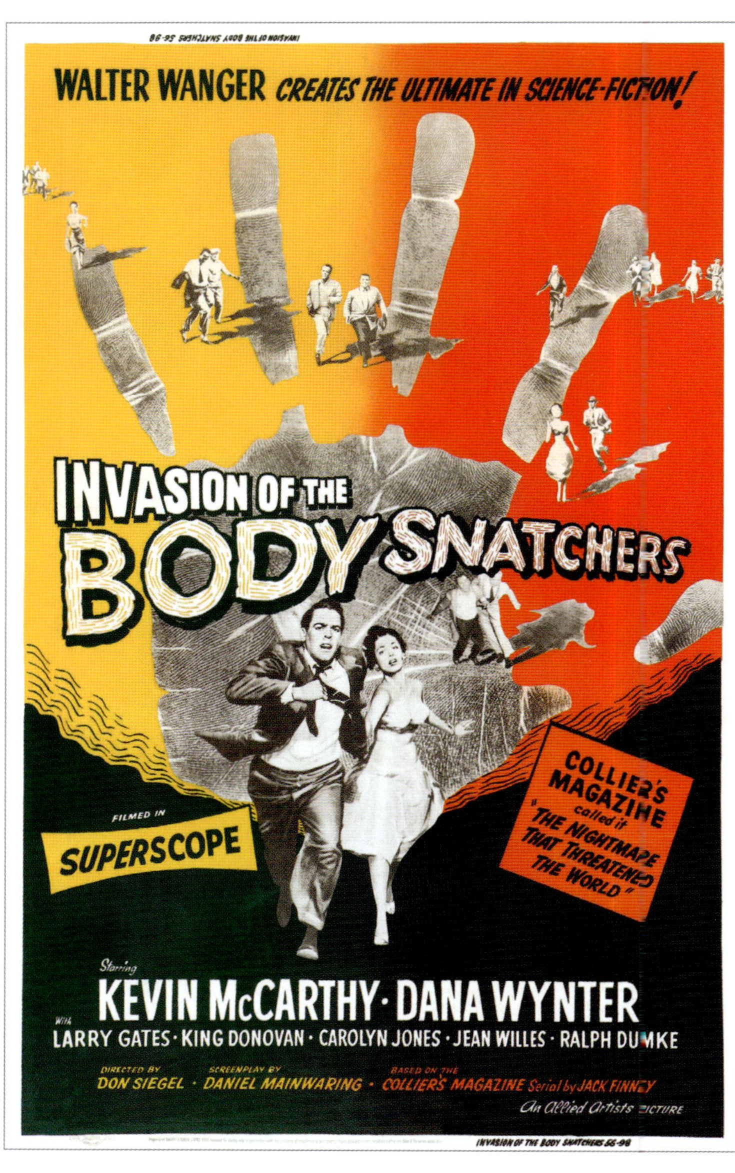

INVASION OF THE BODY SNATCHERS

Executive producer Walter Mirisch claimed that *Invasion of the Body Snatchers* (1956) was never meant to be "anything other than a thriller, pure and simple," but this tale of a quiet invasion of small town Americans being replaced with emotionless alien duplicates was immediately seen as an allegory of (take your pick!) the McCarthy era, communism, totalitarianism, or the increasing depersonalization of modern times: "pod people" remains a disparaging term to this day.

The Italian poster (opposite) developed the handprint/alien claw motif from the US campaign to great effect. Artist Alessandro Biffignandi (1935–2017), best known for his sex and horror comic book covers, began his career as a student of fellow Italian poster designer Averardo Ciriello.

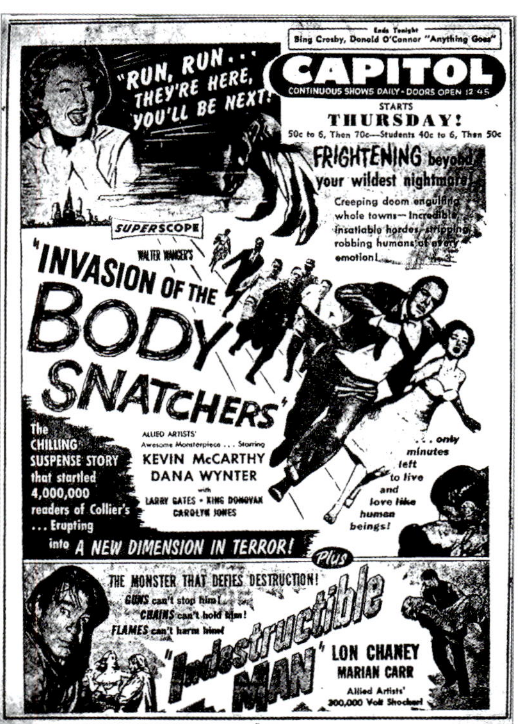

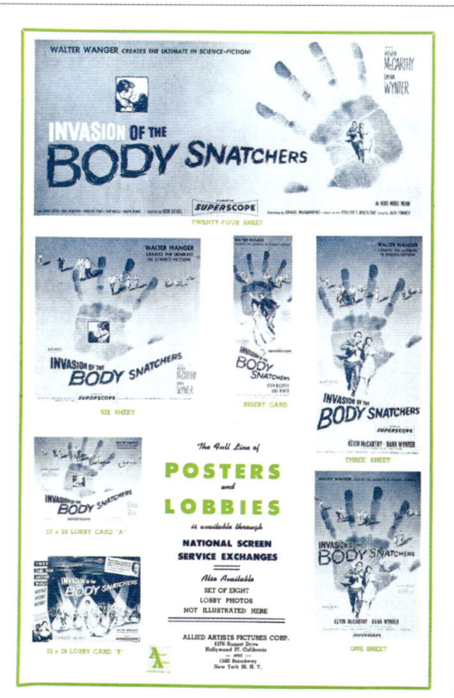

UN FILM
Allied Artists
PRODOTTO DA
WALTER WANGER
DISTRIBUZIONE
lux film
KEVIN McCARTHY
DANA WYNTER
con
LARRY GATES · KING DONOVAN
CAROLYN JONES · JEAN WILLES
RALPH DUMKE
REGIA DI
DON SIEGEL
INVASIONE degli ULTRACORPI
Scritto da
DANIEL MAINWARING
Tratto da un romanzo di
JACK FINNEY
pubblicato dal
COLLIER'S MAGAZINE
STUDIO FAVALLI
G. SCARPATI S.p.A. - Napoli 1957

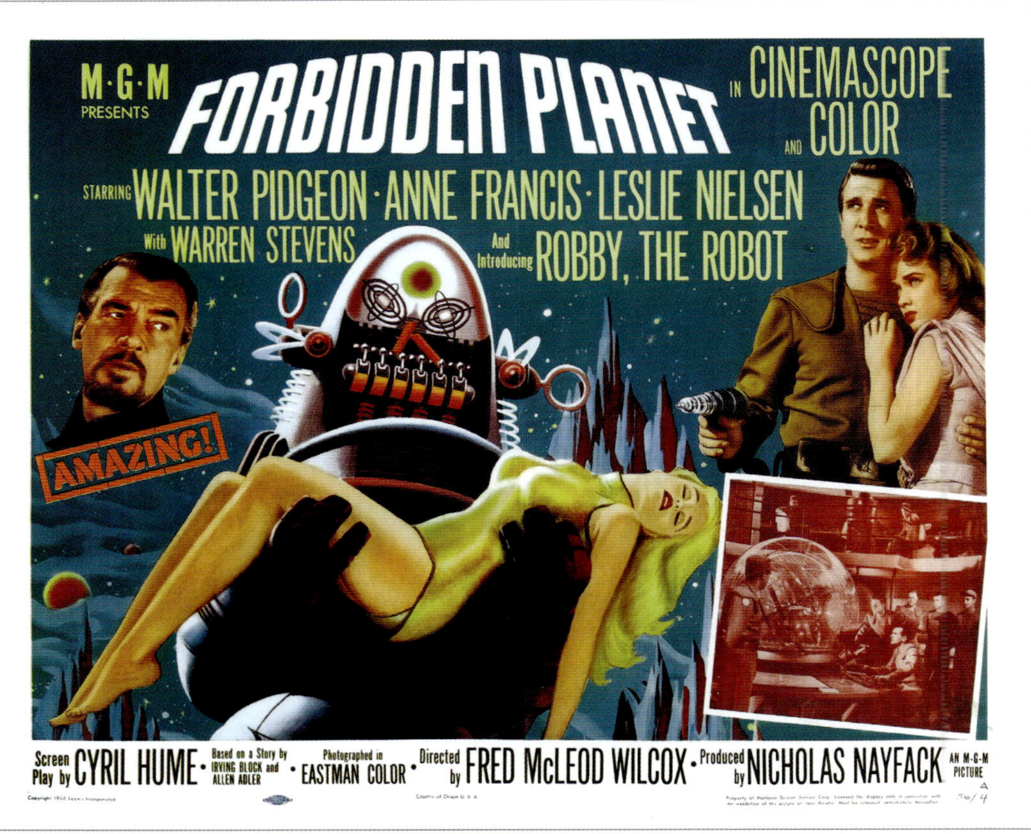

FORBIDDEN PLANET

A critical and box office hit on its release in 1956, *Forbidden Planet* quickly became an influential classic of the genre, not least on the adventures of another interstellar crew: Gene Roddenberry later screened the film to help "stimulate our own thinking" as he developed *Star Trek*.

Robby the Robot was the focus of the marketing imagery, including Bantam's tie-in novel cover (above), one of the few pieces of art not to show him carrying Altaira (Anne Francis), the iconic pose which was used, though flipped, on the silk screen-style US poster (opposite). The Italian two-*fogli* (overleaf, top right) was the only poster to show Doc Ostrow (Warren Stevens) being carried, a scene that actually *is* in the movie. The Italian four-*fogli* (see page 145) opted for a haunting portrait of Walter Pidgeon as Morbius. Both were painted by Averardo Ciriello (1918–2016), who created over 3,000 film posters, though was best known for his erotic comic book covers.

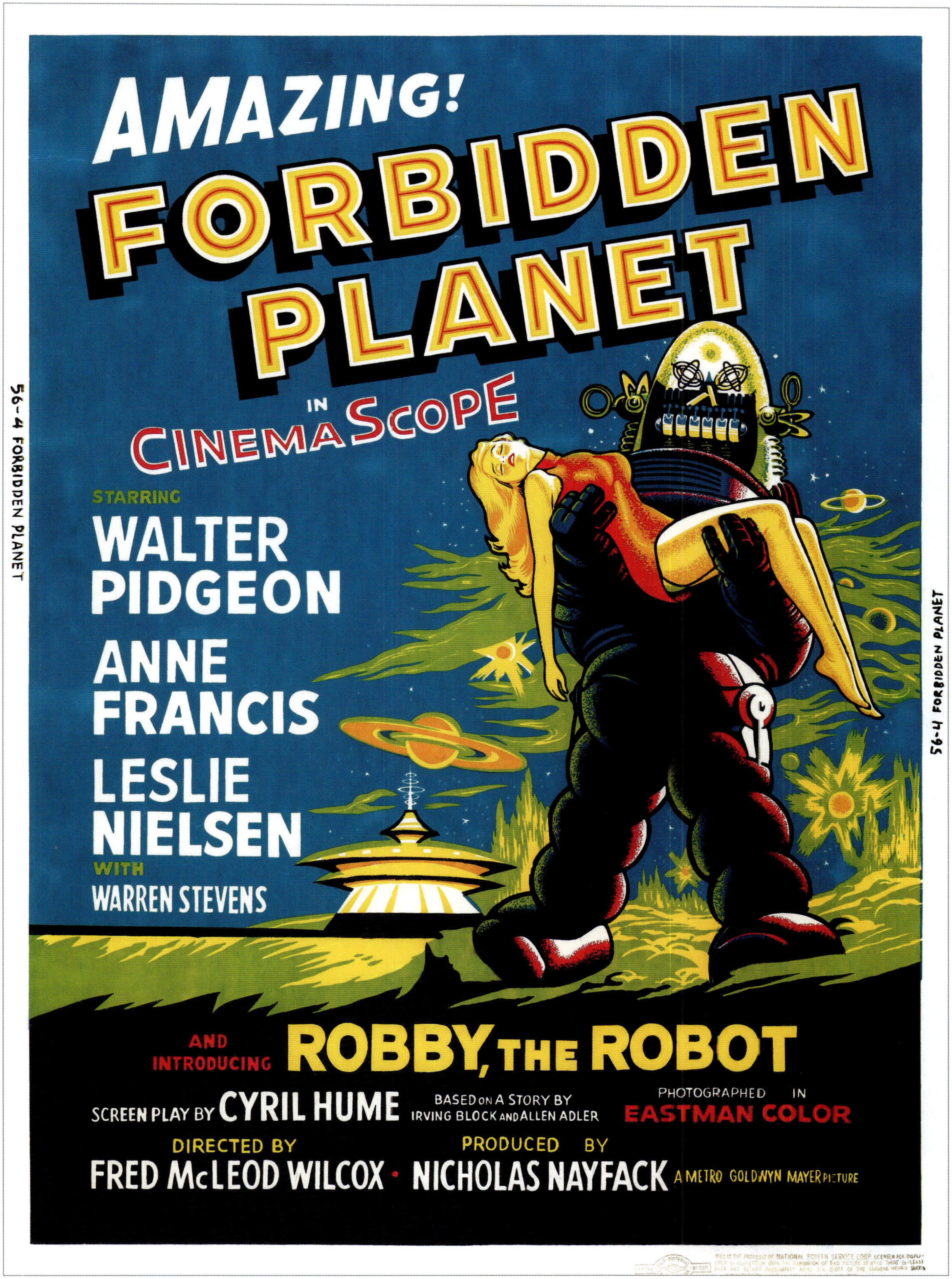

AMAZING!

FORBIDDEN PLANET

IN CINEMASCOPE

STARRING
WALTER PIDGEON
ANNE FRANCIS
LESLIE NIELSEN
WITH
WARREN STEVENS

AND INTRODUCING ROBBY, THE ROBOT

SCREEN PLAY BY CYRIL HUME
BASED ON A STORY BY IRVING BLOCK AND ALLEN ADLER
PHOTOGRAPHED IN EASTMAN COLOR

DIRECTED BY FRED McLEOD WILCOX · PRODUCED BY NICHOLAS NAYFACK
A METRO GOLDWYN MAYER PICTURE

56-4 FORBIDDEN PLANET

56-4 FORBIDDEN PLANET

EL PLANETA DESCONOCIDO
«FORBIDDEN PLANET»
ARTISTAS
WALTER PIDGEON ANNE FRANCIS
LESLIE NIELSEN PRESENTANDO ROBBY, THE ROBOT
en COLOR y CINEMASCOPE
con sonido estereofónico perspecta
DIRECTOR: FRED McLEOD WILCOX
PRODUCTOR: NICHOLAS NAYFACK
Metro-Goldwyn-Mayer

WALTER PIDGEON · ANNE FRANCIS
LESLIE NIELSEN CON WARREN STEVENS
E PER LA PRIMA VOLTA SULLO SCHERMO
ROBBY, IL ROBOT
M-G-M
IL PIANETA PROIBITO
(FORBIDDEN PLANET)
DIRETTO DA FRED McLEOD WILCOX
PRODOTTO DA NICHOLAS NAYFACK
CINEMASCOPE
CON SUONO STEREOFONICO PERSPECTA
SCENEGGIATURA CYRIL HUME
FOTOGRAFATO IN EASTMAN COLOR

FORBIDDEN PLANET
M-G-M Press-Sheet
IT'S OUT OF THIS WORLD!
AMAZING!
M-G-M PRESENTS IN COLOR AND CINEMASCOPE
FORBIDDEN PLANET
WALTER PIDGEON · ANNE FRANCIS · LESLIE NIELSEN ROBBY, THE ROBOT
禁断の惑星

M-G-M
CINEMASCOPE
WALTER PIDGEON
ANNE FRANCIS
LESLIE NIELSEN
IL PIANETA PROIBITO
(FORBIDDEN PLANET)
CON WARREN STEVENS
ROBBY IL ROBOT
Diretto da FRED McLEOD WILCOX
Prodotto da NICHOLAS NAYFACK
Sceneggiatura di CYRIL HUME
EASTMAN COLOR

WALTER PIDGEON · LESLIE NIELSEN · ANNE FRANCIS
CINEMASCOPE
EASTMANCOLOR
IL PIANETA PROIBITO
REGIA: FRED MAC LEOD WILCOX
UNA ESCLUSIVITA' SUPERCINEMATOGRAFICA

SILK SCREEN STYLE

Originating in China during the Song dynasty over 1,000 years ago, screen printing is a technique that forces inks or dyes through a mesh or screen (originally made of silk) onto a substrate. Using stencils to block certain areas, an image can be built up using several screens, color by color. As the following selection shows, in the 1950s especially, silk screen-style posters and banners were sometimes produced in addition to the standard one-sheets. Though many were printed via the usual offset lithography process (using photographic plates), the few that were actually screen-printed are most prized today. While the designs were usually simplified, the blocks of bright color "popped" in a way sure to catch the eye of filmgoers, and the posters were often used at outdoor drive-in theaters.

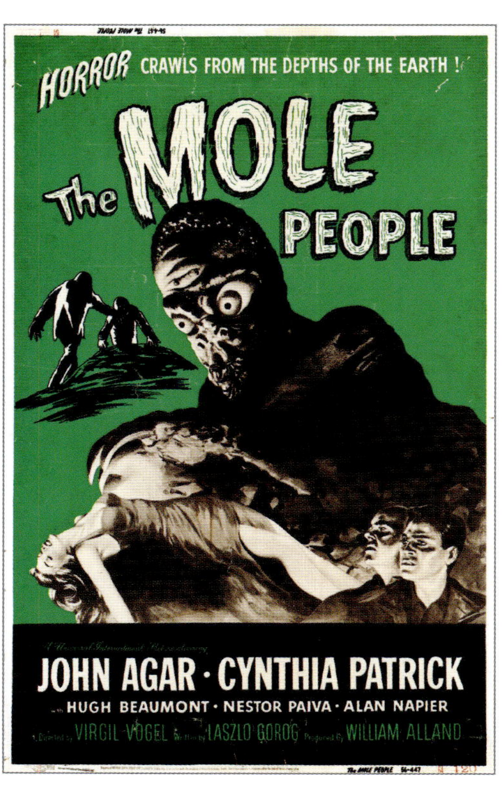

Universal-International presents
MONSTER ESCAPES!
CITY FLEES IN TERROR!
REVENGE OF THE CREATURE
starring JOHN AGAR LORI NELSON JOHN BROMFIELD NESTOR PAIVA
Directed By JACK ARNOLD · Screenplay By MARTIN BERKELEY · Story By WILLIAM ALLAND · Produced By WILLIAM ALLAND

MANKIND'S FIRST FANTASTIC FLIGHT TO VENUS–
The Female Planet!
QUEEN OF OUTER SPACE
COLOR BY DELUXE CINEMASCOPE
An ALLIED ARTISTS Picture
Starring ZSA ZSA GABOR
ERIC FLEMING · LAURIE MITCHELL · LISA DAVIS
From a Story by BEN HECHT · Produced by BEN SCHWALB · Directed by EDWARD BERNDS · Screenplay by CHARLES BEAUMONT

THE SUPREME EXCITEMENT OF OUR TIME!
2½ YEARS IN THE MAKING
Universal-International presents
THIS ISLAND EARTH
IN COLOR BY TECHNICOLOR
JEFF MORROW · FAITH DOMERGUE · REX REASON
LANCE FULLER · RUSSELL JOHNSON
JOSEPH NEWMAN · FRANKLIN COEN and EDWARD G. O'CALLAGHAN · WILLIAM ALLAND

CONQUEST OF SPACE
COLOR BY TECHNICOLOR
PRODUCED BY GEORGE PAL · DIRECTED BY BYRON HASKIN
SCREENPLAY BY JAMES O'HANLON
ADAPTATION BY PHILIP YORDAN, BARRE LYNDON AND GEORGE WORTHINGTON YATES
Based on the Book by CHESLEY BONESTELL AND WILLY LEY
A PARAMOUNT PICTURE

The Weirdest Visitor The Earth Has Ever Seen!
Sherrill Corwin presents
THE MAN FROM PLANET X
Starring
ROBERT CLARKE · MARGARET FIELD · RAYMOND BOND
Directed by EDGAR G. ULMER
Written and Produced by AUBREY WISBERG and JACK POLLEXFEN
Released Thru UNITED ARTISTS

HOWLING
For All The Flesh And Blood On Earth!
VOGUE PICTURES, INC. presents
"IT! THE TERROR FROM BEYOND SPACE"
Starring MARSHALL THOMPSON · SHAWN SMITH · KIM SPALDING
with ANN DORAN · DABBS GREER · PAUL LANGTON · ROBERT BICE
Written by JEROME BIXBY · Directed by EDWARD L. CAHN · Produced by ROBERT E. KENT
Released thru UNITED ARTISTS

TARANTULA!
GIANT SPIDER STRIKES!
Starring
JOHN AGAR
MARA CORDAY
LEO G. CARROLL
with
NESTOR PAIVA
ROSS ELLIOTT
Directed by
JACK ARNOLD
Screenplay by
ROBERT M. FRESCO
MARTIN BERKELEY
Produced by
WILLIAM ALLAND
A Universal-International Picture
TARANTULA 55-390

A FASCINATING ADVENTURE INTO THE UNKNOWN
THE INCREDIBLE
SHRINKING MAN
Starring
Grant WILLIAMS · Randy STUART
APRIL KENT · PAUL LANGTON · RAYMOND BAILEY
Directed by
JACK ARNOLD
Screen Play by
RICHARD MATHESON
Produced by
ALBERT ZUGSMITH
A UNIVERSAL-INTERNATIONAL PICTURE

A CREATURE FROM BEYOND THE STARS!
THE ASTOUNDING SHE MONSTER
ROBERT CLARKE · KENNE DUNCAN · MARILYN HARVEY
JEANNE TATUM · SHIRLEY KILPATRICK · EWING BROWN
FRANK HALL
RONNIE ASHCROFT
A HOLLYWOOD INTERNATIONAL Production
An AMERICAN INTERNATIONAL Release

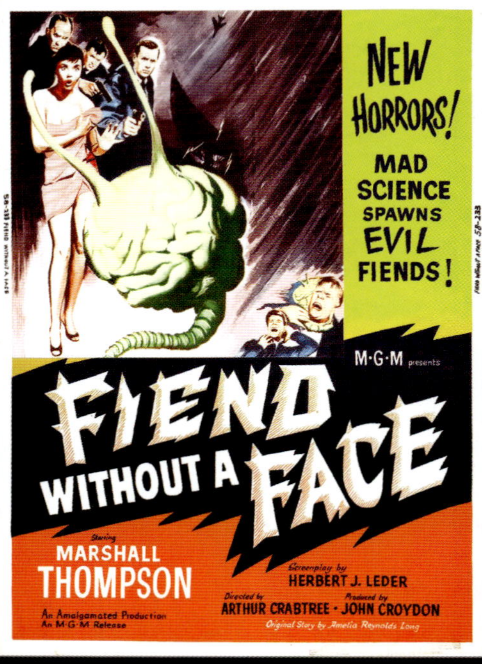
NEW HORRORS!
MAD SCIENCE SPAWNS EVIL FIENDS!
M·G·M presents
FIEND WITHOUT A FACE
Starring
MARSHALL THOMPSON
Screenplay by
HERBERT J. LEDER
Directed by
ARTHUR CRABTREE
Produced by
JOHN CROYDON
An Amalgamated Production
An M·G·M Release

WATCH OUT! THE Beast IS COMING!
WARNER BROS. present
The Beast From 20,000 Fathoms
PAUL CHRISTIAN · PAULA RAYMOND
CECIL KELLAWAY · KENNETH TOBEY
DONALD WOODS · JACK PENNICK · LEE VAN CLEEF · STEVE BRODIE · ROSS ELLIOTT
RAY HARRYHAUSEN
EUGENE LOURIE
WARNER BROS.

HOWARD DUFF EVA BARTOK
SPACEWAYS
A Lippert Pictures Presentation

THE SHE-CREATURE
STARRING CHESTER MORRIS · MARLA ENGLISH · TOM CONWAY
Distributed by AMERICAN INTERNATIONAL PICTURES

ROBOT MONSTER
3 DIMENSION IN TRU-STEREO
with GEORGE NADER CLAUDIA BARRETT
RELEASED THRU ASTOR PICTURES CORP.

THE MONOLITH MONSTERS
STARRING
GRANT WILLIAMS · LOLA ALBRIGHT
A UNIVERSAL-INTERNATIONAL PICTURE

THEM
"THEM" starring JAMES WHITMORE · EDMUND GWENN · JOAN WELDON · JAMES ARNESS
Presented By WARNER BROS.

IT CAME FROM OUTER SPACE
3-DIMENSION
Starring RICHARD CARLSON BARBARA RUSH
A UNIVERSAL-INTERNATIONAL PICTURE
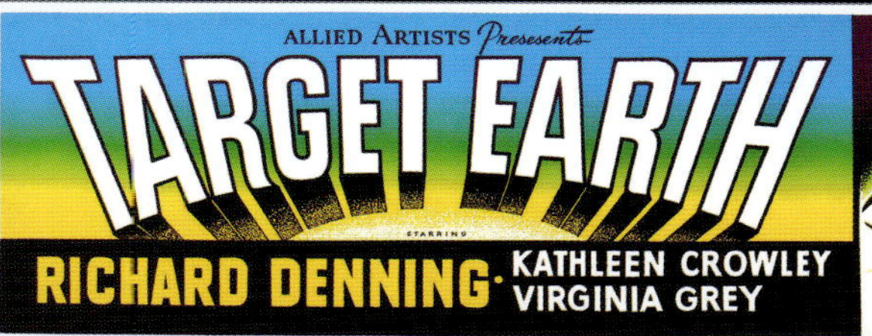
ALLIED ARTISTS Presents
TARGET EARTH
STARRING
RICHARD DENNING · KATHLEEN CROWLEY VIRGINIA GREY

INVADERS FROM MARS
PHOTOGRAPHED IN COLOR
STARRING
HELENA CARTER · ARTHUR FRANZ · JIMMY HUNT

THE DAY THE EARTH STOOD STILL
WITH
MICHAEL RENNIE · PATRICIA NEAL
HUGH MARLOWE
20th CENTURY-FOX

PHANTOM FROM SPACE
Released Thru UNITED ARTISTS

HOWARD HAWKS'
THE THING
from another world !
DISTRIBUTED BY RKO RADIO

5798
SIGNET
A Startling View of Life in 1984
1984
A Novel by GEORGE ORWELL
FREEDOM IS SLAVERY
IGNORANCE IS STRENGTH
IS WATCHING YOU!
ANTI SEX LEAGUE
Also a film, starring Edmond O'Brien, Michael Redgrave and Jan Sterling: a Columbia Pictures release.
A SIGNET BOOK Complete and Unabridged

1984
A FILM OF TOMORROW TO SHOCK YOU TODAY!
An ASSOCIATED BRITISH Presentation
CAMPAIGN SHEET

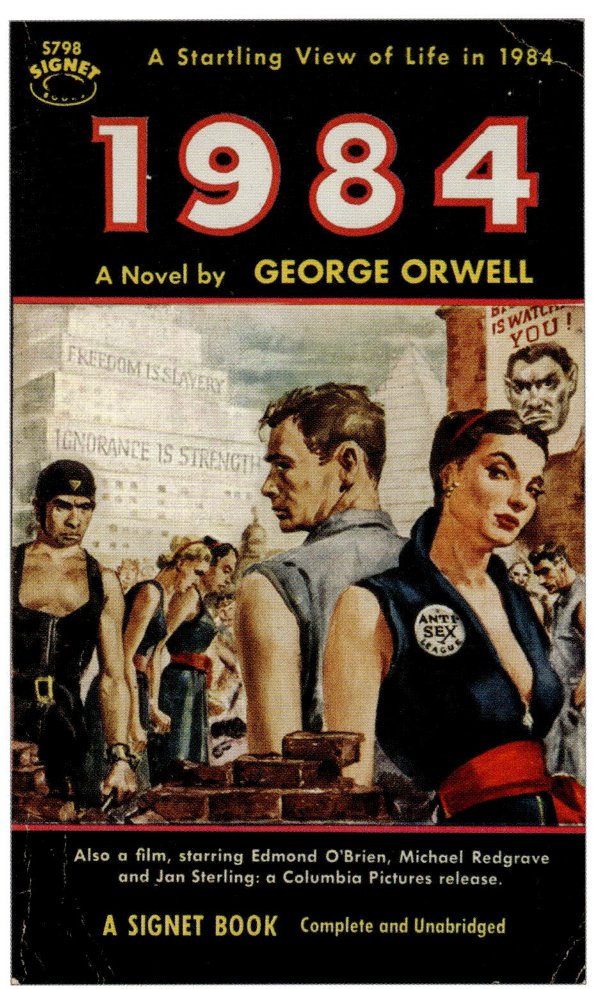

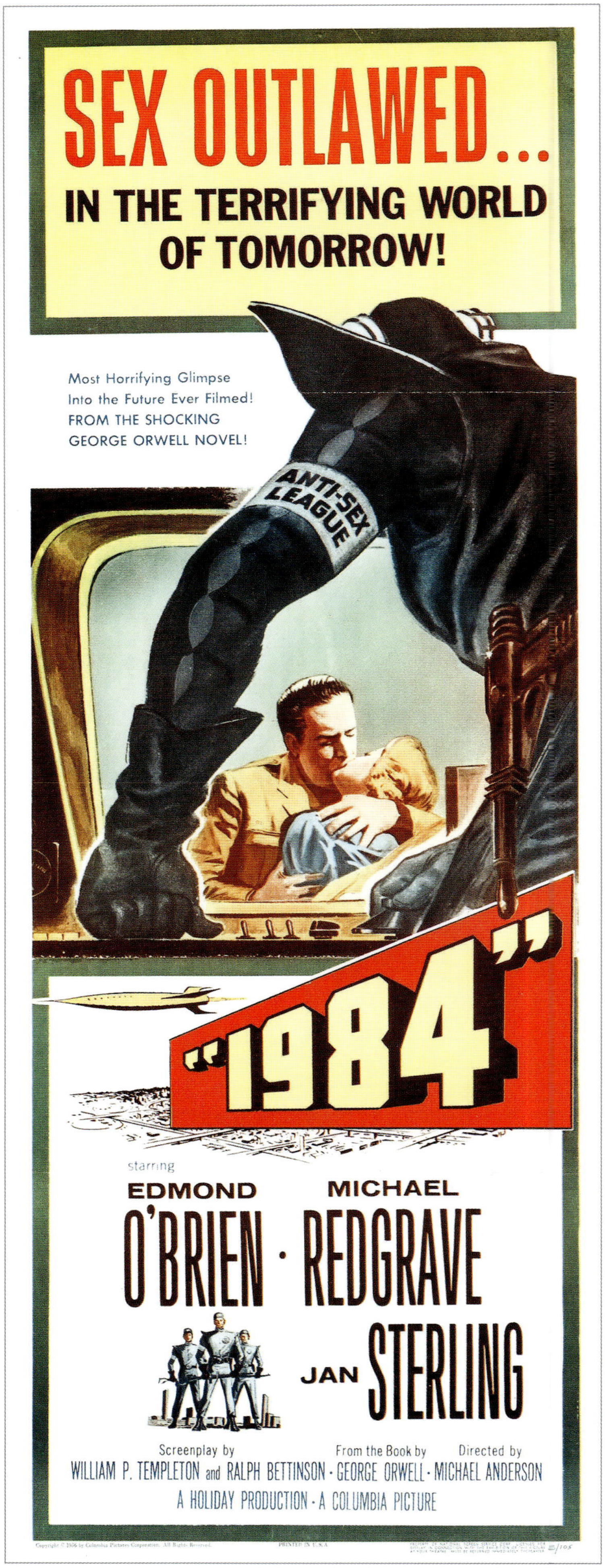

SEX OUTLAWED...
IN THE TERRIFYING WORLD OF TOMORROW!
Most Horrifying Glimpse
Into the Future Ever Filmed!
FROM THE SHOCKING
GEORGE ORWELL NOVEL!
ANTI-SEX LEAGUE
"1984"
starring
EDMOND O'BRIEN · MICHAEL REDGRAVE
JAN STERLING
Screenplay by WILLIAM P. TEMPLETON and RALPH BETTINSON · From the Book by GEORGE ORWELL · Directed by MICHAEL ANDERSON
A HOLIDAY PRODUCTION · A COLUMBIA PICTURE

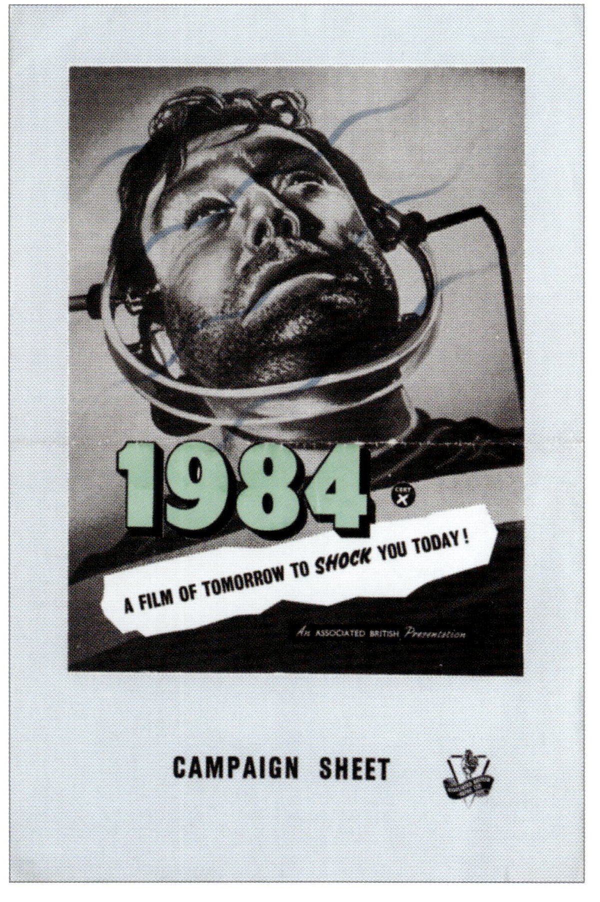

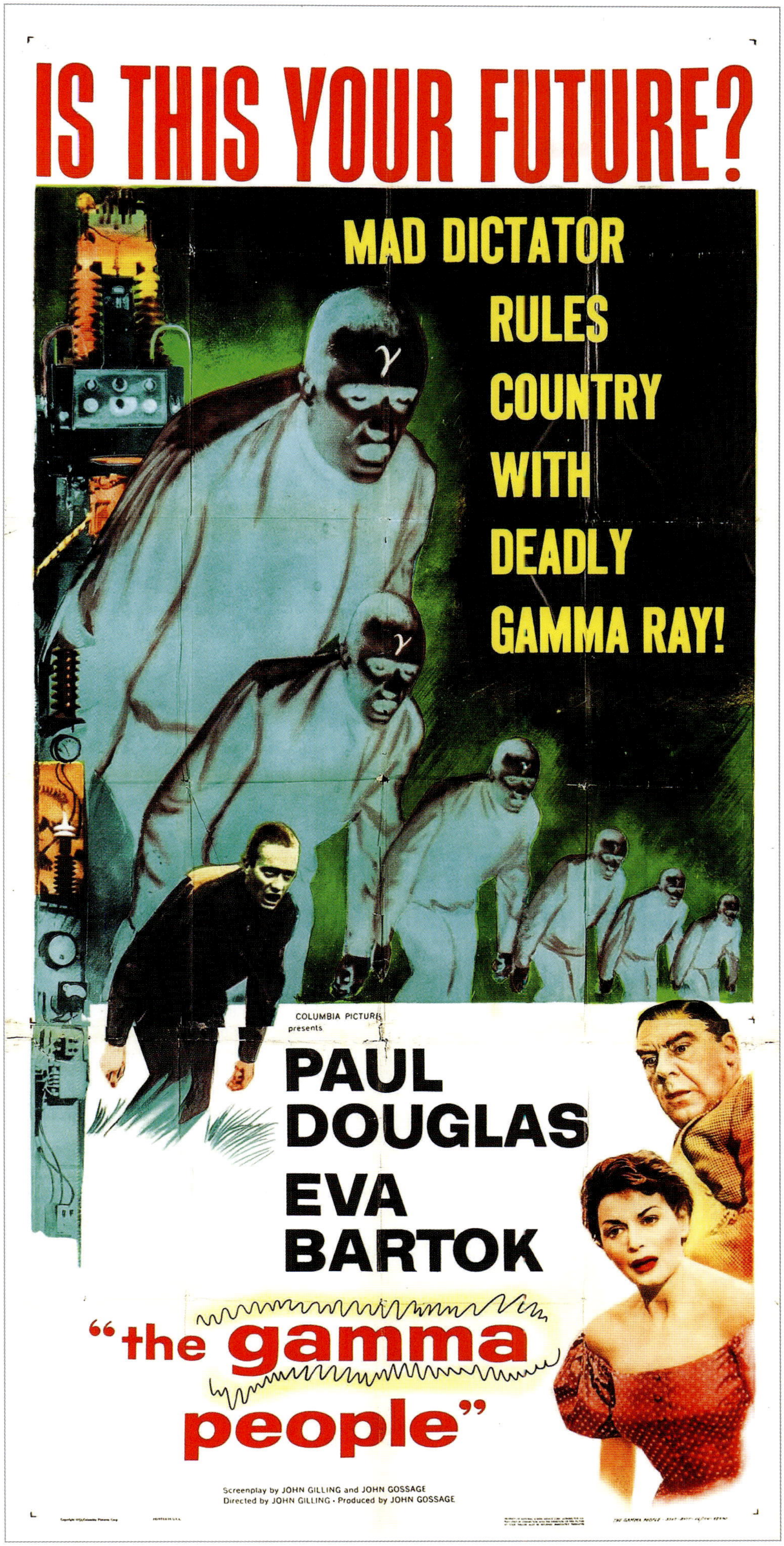

A DYSTOPIAN DOUBLE BILL

1956 saw a double bill of British-made SF films released in US movie theaters. The B picture was *The Gamma People*, featuring a mad scientist experimenting on the youth of an isolated Eastern Bloc dictatorship; top of the bill was *1984*, a prestige adaptation of George Orwell's 1949 novel about a totalitarian future. Marketing (including a pulpy Signet tie-in paperback) emphasized the sex, melodrama, and futuristic trappings rather than the biting political satire of the book.

Though made in Britain, the film's leads Edmond O'Brien and Jan Sterling came from America, as did a chunk of the budget, direct from the government in the form of the US Information Agency, who saw a chance to make the "the most devastating anti-Communist film of all time." Additional support came from the American Committee for Cultural Freedom, an innocent-sounding organization that was actually a CIA front.

SCIENCE FICTION DOUBLE FEATURE

Especially at the low-budget end of the market, many SF films were made to be initially released as part of a double bill, as in the "All new! Monster vs. Monster!" twin terror show of *It Conquered the World* and *The She-Creature* in 1956. Sometimes, the pairing was a second bite of the cherry, as with the UK re-release of *The Fly* (1958) and its sequel *Return of the Fly* (1959), complete with a new quad poster design, and the excellent tagline, "See them together but don't see them alone!" Equally memorable was the promise that "Maddened Mastodons fight for savage women" in the "All time thrill show" of *Two Lost Worlds* (1951) and *Unknown Island* (1948), though sadly this proved to be entirely inaccurate.

GRAND NATIONAL PICTURES present
THE DOUBLE HORROR SENSATION OF THE YEAR!
BEAST FROM HAUNTED CAVE
SCREAMING YOUNG GIRLS SUCKED INTO A LABYRINTH OF HORROR BY A BLOOD-STARVED GHOUL FROM HELL.
The WASP WOMAN
A BEAUTIFUL WOMAN BY DAY - A LUSTING QUEEN WASP BY NIGHT.
MICHAEL FOREST SHEILA CAROL FRANK WOLFF
starring SUSAN CABOT · FRED EISLEY · BARBOURA MORRIS
Produced and Directed by ROGER CORMAN · Written by LEO GORDON

PREHISTORIC, PRIMITIVE, PRIMEVAL MONSTERS OF 100,000,000 YEARS AGO... Alive AGAIN TODAY!
MADDENED MASTODONS FIGHT FOR SAVAGE WOMEN
TWO LOST WORLDS
ALL TIME THRILL SHOW
UNKNOWN ISLAND
IN COLOR

SEE THEM TOGETHER BUT DON'T SEE THEM ALONE!
VINCENT PRICE
The Fly
PATRICIA OWENS HERBERT MARSHALL
RETURN OF THE FLY
BRETT HALSEY JOHN SUTTON
COLOR
TERRIFYING! NERVE SHATTERING! BLOODCURDLING!

MEET THE MONSTERS FACE-TO-FACE!
...TWIN TERRIFYING TERRORS IN ONE TOWERING THRILL SHOW!
1400 POUNDS OF FROZEN FURY that moves like man!
THE MAMMOTH MONSTER THAT TERRORIZED THE EARTH!
MONSTER FROM GREEN HELL
JIM DAVIS · BARBARA TURNER
ROBERT E. GRIFFIN
HALF HUMAN
JOHN CARRADINE
HALF-MAN, HALF-BEAST but ALL MONSTER!

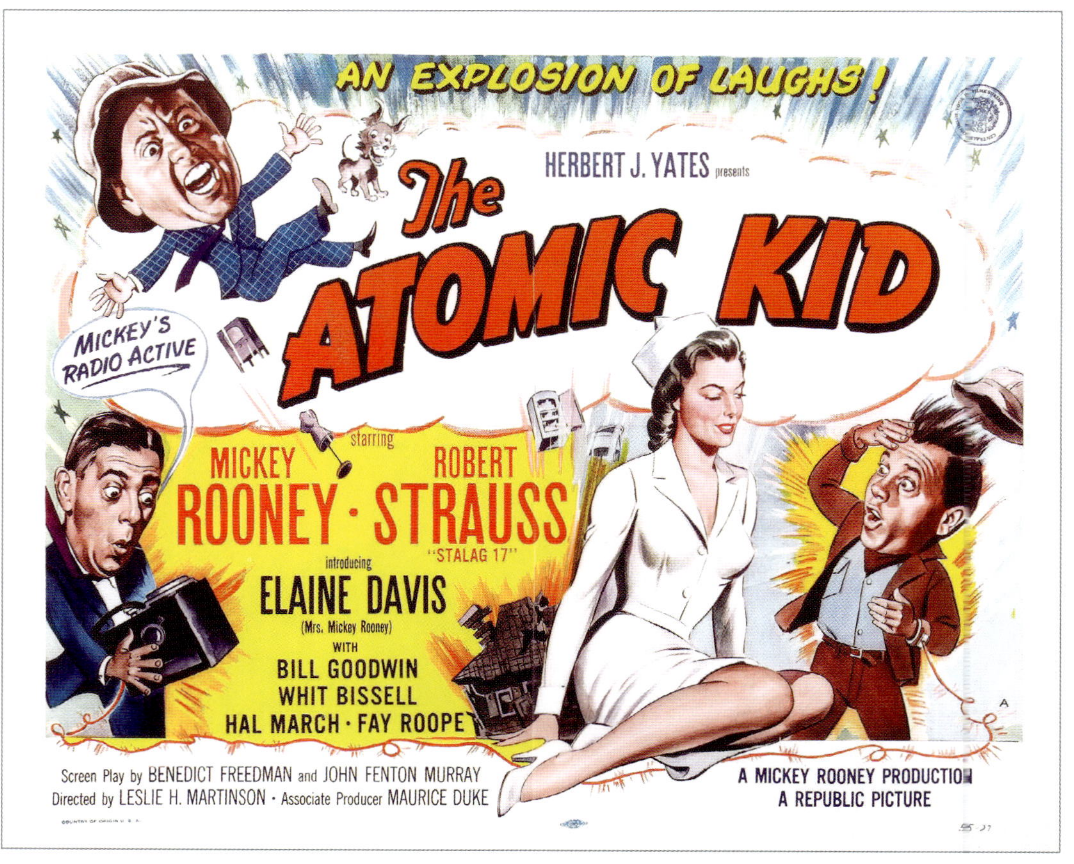

SF COMEDY

Perhaps due to the lingering memory of *Just Imagine* (1930) as a box office failure, SF movies played for laughs remained rare, even as the genre was gaining in popularity. Bud and Lou saw some success with *Abbott and Costello Go to Mars* (1953)—best joke? They don't go to Mars—but hopes for the sentient TV fable *The Twonky* (1953) were so low that the producer reportedly sighed, "That's alright. I need a tax write-off this year anyway." (It duly flopped.) Mickey Rooney provided "an explosion of laughs" as a uranium prospector turned radioactive FBI agent in *The Atomic Kid* (1954), a film given a respectful nod in *the* SF comedy classic: it's playing at Hill Valley's movie theater in *Back to the Future* (1985). *Boom in the Moon* (1946), Buster Keaton's last starring role, isn't a classic, but Carlantonio Longi's poster for its 1950s Italian release (opposite) most certainly is.

CÆSAR FILM
PRESENTA
Longi
BUSTER KEATON
nella.... LUNA!
Produzione
SALKIND

COSMIC FRANKENSTEIN TERRORIZES EARTH!

Already one whole city has been devoured...and still it grows, minute by minute, reaching out with countless invisible mouths to swallow the earth!

THE MAGNETIC MONSTER

The astounding story of the "thing" that came alive!

IVAN TORS presents

"THE MAGNETIC MONSTER" starring RICHARD CARLSON

featuring King Donovan · Jean Byron · Jarma Lewis · Screenplay by Curt Siodmak and Ivan Tors · Produced by IVAN TORS · Directed by CURT SIODMAK · An A-Men Production · Released thru United Artists

THE OSI TRILOGY

In the age of the modern blockbuster, interwoven "universes" of films are all the rage, with the Marvel Cinematic Universe (MCU) being perhaps the most high-profile example. Though Universal had already pioneered the idea with its stable of battling horror monsters, Hungarian-born producer Ivan Tors created an early SF version in his loosely linked trilogy of films featuring agents from the Office of Scientific Investigation (OSI). The plots veered towards speculative science "fact" rather than fantasy. *The Magnetic Monster* (1953) was a radioactive isotope that escaped its lab and threatened to destroy the world; *Riders to the Stars* (1954) featured astronauts prospecting for meteors; *Gog* (1954) was a deadly proto-Terminator robot. Tors's TV series *Science Fiction Theater* (1955–57) went on to explore similar stories, sometimes re-using props from the OSI films.

The Magnetic Monster was a product of recycling itself, as its writer and director Curt Siodmak recalled: "The story was that Andrew Marton, the best second-unit director in America, returned from Berlin with ten minutes of special effects from a German film called *Gold* [1934, see page 38], which must have cost millions. He and Tors came to me to write a screenplay around those shots, which were of a gigantic atom smasher which at the end exploded. We shot the film for $105,000! We made very little money on that film. My ideas, as usual, were premature. *The Andromeda Strain* [1971] had the same idea twenty years later. It made millions. Also, our title was silly."

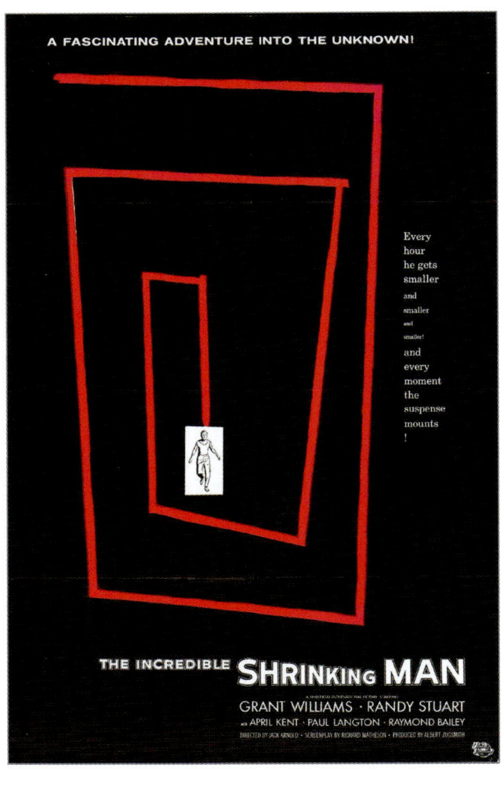

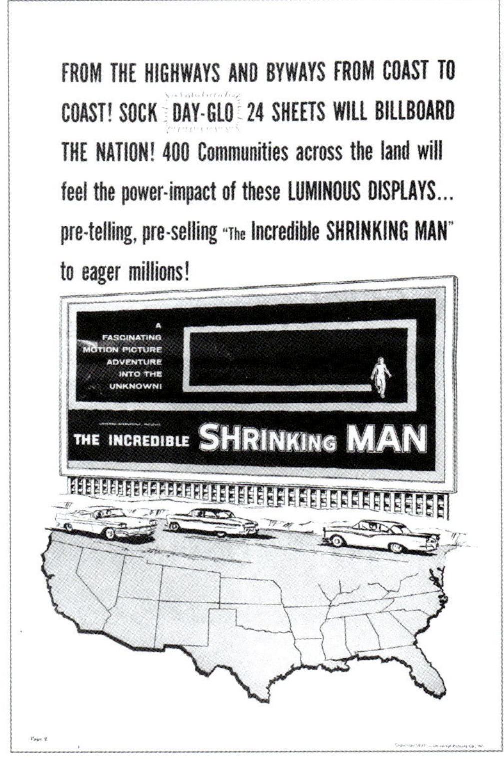

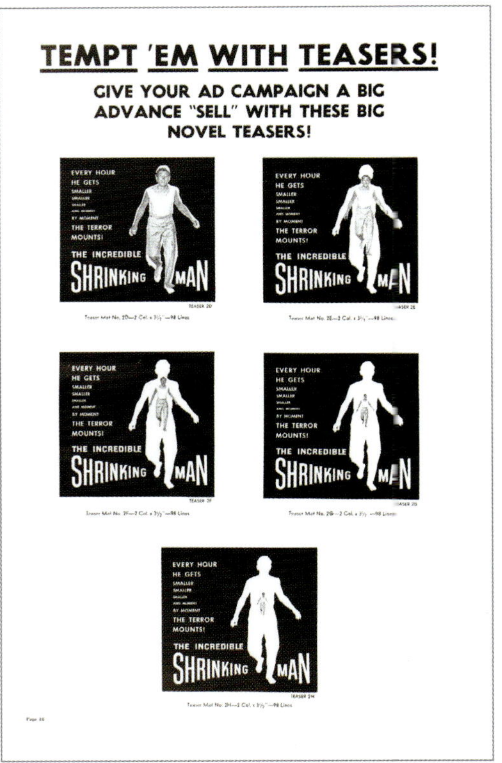

THE INCREDIBLE SHRINKING MAN

Universal knew a great SF movie high concept when it saw one: the studio bought the rights to Richard Matheson's novel *The Shrinking Man* before he'd even finished writing it. Producer Albert Zugsmith added the "Incredible" to the title, and the marketing department set about selling the film with a full media blitz that included radio ads narrated by the King of voiceover artists, Orson Welles. Posters also played their part, of course, including with an advance "teaser" campaign (above) with a strikingly simple graphic approach that was well ahead of its time. The main US one-sheet (opposite) was more traditional, with forced perspective art by Reynold Brown, who remembered, "It was an extremely difficult job, but a challenge I liked. The effect of the screen across the cat's face was also tough because I painted it with very great detail. First, I painted the cat, then I laid-over this cross-hatching."

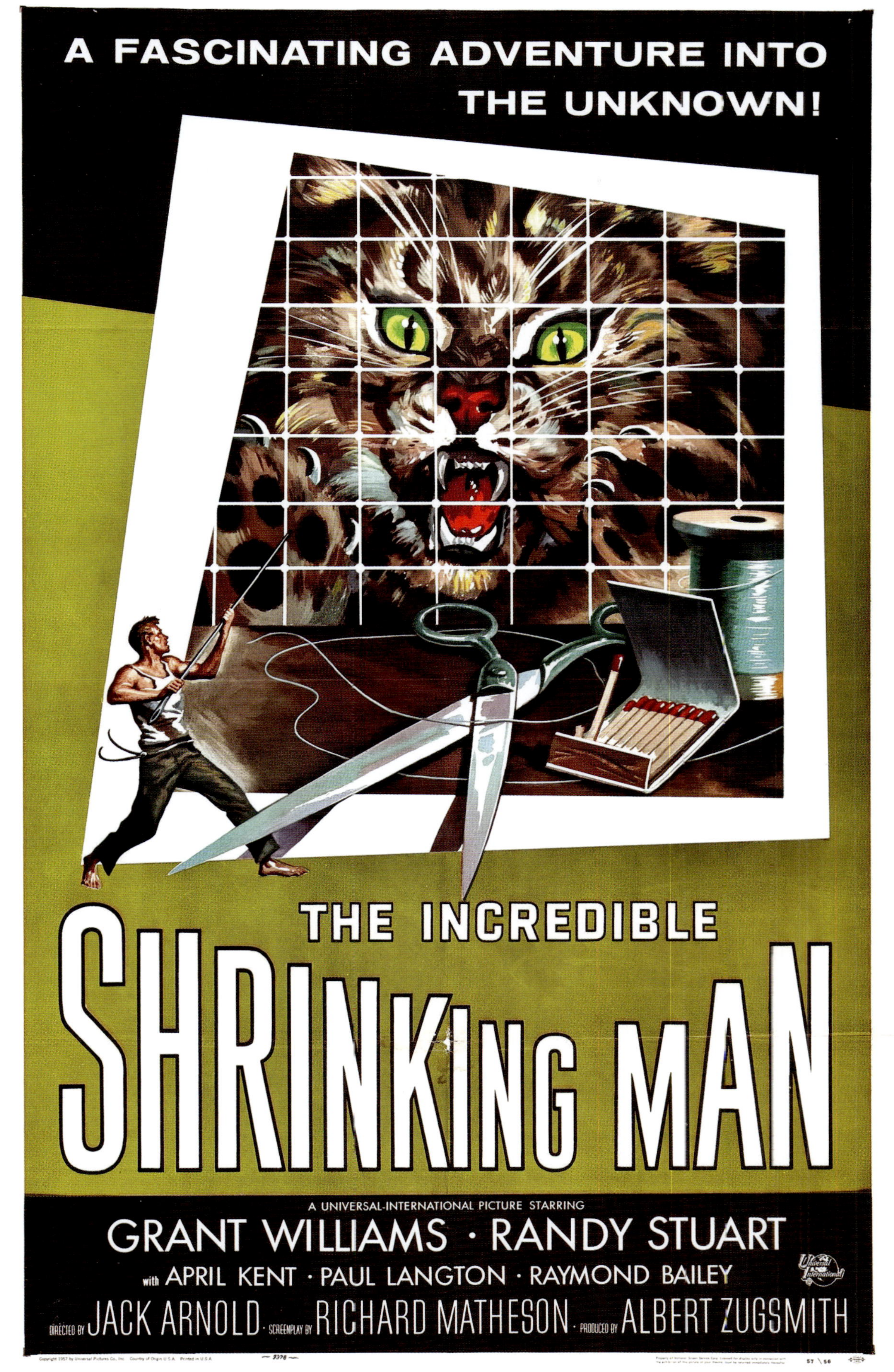
A FASCINATING ADVENTURE INTO THE UNKNOWN!
THE INCREDIBLE
SHRINKING MAN
A UNIVERSAL-INTERNATIONAL PICTURE STARRING
GRANT WILLIAMS · RANDY STUART
with APRIL KENT · PAUL LANGTON · RAYMOND BAILEY
DIRECTED BY JACK ARNOLD · SCREENPLAY BY RICHARD MATHESON · PRODUCED BY ALBERT ZUGSMITH

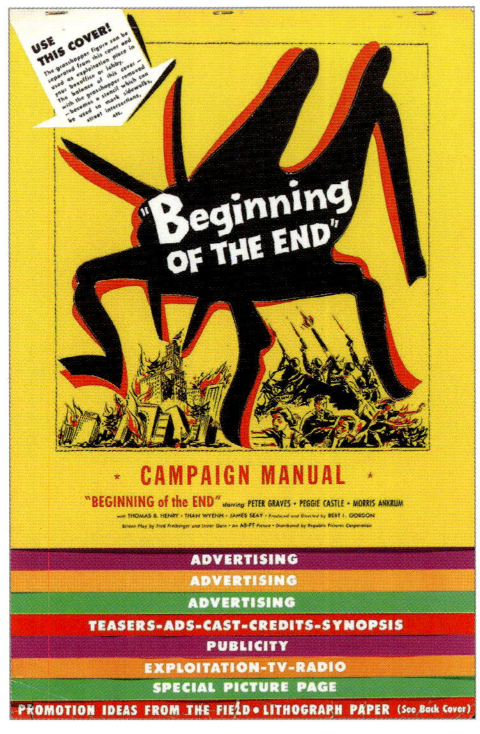

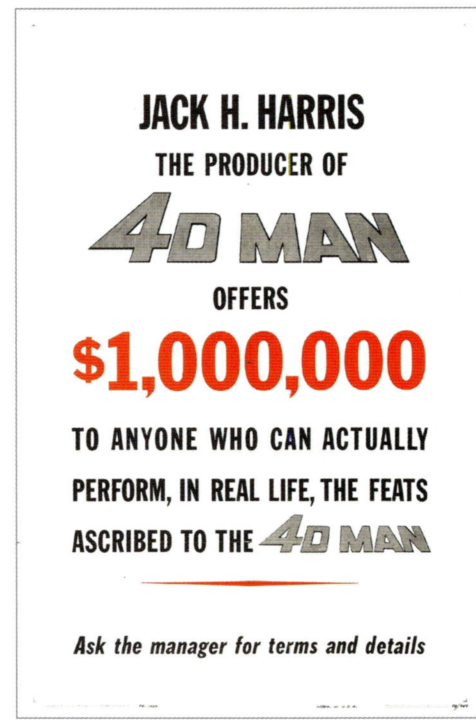

BALLYHOO!

Publicity gimmicks ranged from the sublime to the ridiculous in the 1950s. In an early example of what's now known as "in universe" marketing, newspaper-style brochures, or "heralds" (opposite), were an eye-catching way of promoting forthcoming attractions, though a "mask for the kids" of Christopher Lee's Creature from Hammer's decidedly non-kid-friendly reboot *The Curse of Frankenstein* (1957) was a rather odd choice. Dangling a cash prize was popular: *4D Man* (1959) producer Jack H. Harris's million dollars was safe, as someone who could pass through solid matter was unlikely to materialize, but lazily worded ad copy for teleportation head-swap drama *The Fly* (1958)—"$100 if you prove it can't happen!"—was rapidly changed to "$100 *to the first person* who can prove it can't happen!" presumably as a queue of scientists started to form.

IT'S TERRORIFIC*!

A MONSTER MASK FOR THE KIDS!

* It's full of terror and terrific showmanship! You order the mat at National Screen Service, print it locally and give it to the kids. They'll do the rest! Every mask is a walking ad! AND IT CAN DO A GREAT JOB IN YOUR TV EXPLOITATION! JUST SEND A MASK TO EACH TV COMEDIAN OR DISK JOCKEY AT THE LOCAL STATION!

The mat is 4-columns wide and measures 7½" x 10". Mask shown here greatly reduced. Print title, theatre, playdate on reverse side.

ORDER: MAT F-401X At NSS

EXTRA **WORLD NEWS** EXTRA

★★★★★ SPECIAL EDITION FINAL

WORLD THREATENED WITH DESTRUCTION BY DISTANT PLANET

Story Inside

Army Meets Strange Foe! Machine guns and tanks make no impression on 9-foot indestructible robot on a death-dealing rampage in Washington, D. C. Menacing visitor arrives in weird space ship accompanied by strange companion. Demands audience with the President. Threatens to destroy universe if we don't see things his way.

INVASION FROM SPACE

EXTRA!  **EXTRA!**

Vol. 1. No. 1 Planet X

'THE MAN FROM PLANET X'

The Weirdest Visitor The Earth Has Ever Seen!

EXPLAINS EARTH INVASION FROM DOOMED PLANET

FEARSOME INVADER FROM OUTER SPACE

An Astounding Motion Picture Reveals What Might Happen If Earth Is Invaded By Eeric "X-Men"

A FACE TO HAUNT THE EARTH FOREVER: Here is the strange and startling Man From Planet X, who appeared on Earth like a bolt from the blue—which, in fact, is how it was. From the ice-bound and decaying Planet X, home of a superior and scientific, but dying, people, he had been dispatched to Earth as a one-man reconnaissance mission. His task was to survey the terrain and transmit his information via special beams to Planet X, which was hurtling toward a directed collision with Earth. His plan was frustrated, however, by the alertness of a reporter, a scientist, a local Scottish constable and the organization of Scotland Yard. Army bullets averted the full-scale assault from Planet X. What that assault might have meant remains a mystery, but no human who saw the single Man From Planet X will ever forget him.

OPEN 1:30

Starts Tomorrow

Air Conditioned

Civic THEATRE

THE WORLD'S MOST TITANIC KILLERS!

SPECIAL: Pacific island ravaged by giant Decapods! Entire Navy expedition reported wiped out! Scientists say "too big to kill . . . too monstrous to escape"!

Photo News Flash

CRAB MONSTERS!

CLAWING, CRUSHING TERRORS BIGGER THAN A BUILDING!

STORY ON PAGE 2

VAMPIRE CREATURES FROM MYSTERY PLANET ATTACK EARTH!
Science Tells of Fiendish Plan to Drain World of Human Blood!

STORY ON PAGE 3

EXTRA **The Chicago Press News** EXTRA

CHICAGO EVACUATED!

GIANT CREATURES INVADE CITY! TERRORIZE ENTIRE POPULATION!

U. S. ARMY PREPARES TO USE "A" BOMB

By Staff Correspondent

CHICAGO-This entire city, the second largest in the United States, is a ghost town today! Every human being—except a certain few Army Personnel and civilian experts—is gone! All that remains is grasshoppers—thousands of them—giant grasshoppers ten to twelve feet tall! The mains and ... one is ... respo...

Is This The "BEGINNING of the END"?

"I AM SURE THE FIRE-BALL IS A SPACE SHIP. MY FATHER, AN ENGINEER AT THE CORAL BLUFFS HUSH-HUSH ATOMIC PROJECT, LAUGHS, BUT GOES TO INVESTIGATE."

BUT IT **DID** HAPPEN OFFICERS! MY HUSBAND WALKED OUT THERE AND VANISHED!! IF YOU'LL ONLY LOOK AROUND...

SURE-LADY-BUT IT'S CRAZY.!!

FOR THE TENSE AND GRIPPING UNDERGROUND BATTLE BETWEEN MEN OF EARTH AND THE HORRENDOUS CREATURES FROM OUTER SPACE...FOR THE DARING RESCUES OF PAT AND ME...FOR THE FATE OF THE SPACE SHIP AND IT'S FRIGHTFUL PASSENGERS-- SEE **"INVADERS FROM MARS"** COMING SOON TO YOUR LOCAL NEIGHBORHOOD MOVIE THEATRE-

- HOLLYWOOD 28 - FOR 20th CENTURY-FOX

PRINTED IN U.S.A.

SPONSORED COMICS

The "funny pages" comics section was usually one of the most-thumbed of any newspaper, so disguising an ad as a comic strip was an obvious choice, especially for those films aiming at a teen audience. The strips seen here for *Gog* (1954) and *Earth vs. the Flying Saucers* (1956) came as studio-supplied "ad mats," which could be supplied to local newspapers by exhibitors. The full color pages for *Invaders from Mars* (1953) and *How to Make a Monster* (1958) were printed as giveaway heralds, and are the work of Sponsored Comics Inc., who produced uncredited, work-for-hire strips for movie ads, but also for brands (McDonalds, Kirkby's Shoes) and even political campaigns (including an "I Like Ike" comic book for Eisenhower's 1952 Presidential run). The strips work as trailers for the film, though in the case of *How to Make a Monster*, it's a somewhat meta, fourth-wall-breaking side story to the plot of the movie.

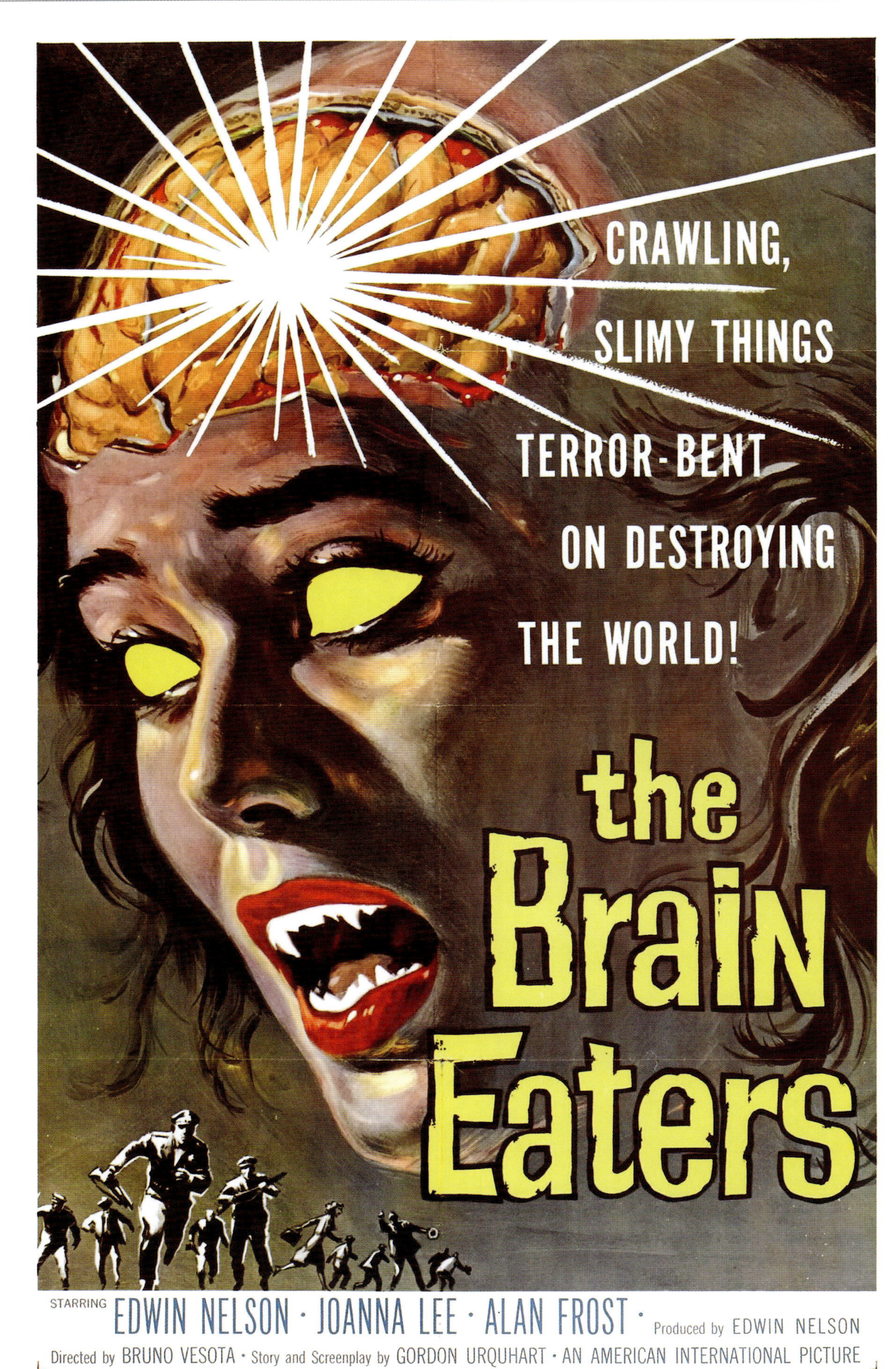

CRAWLING, SLIMY THINGS TERROR-BENT ON DESTROYING THE WORLD!
the Brain Eaters
STARRING EDWIN NELSON · JOANNA LEE · ALAN FROST · Produced by EDWIN NELSON
Directed by BRUNO VESOTA · Story and Screenplay by GORDON URQUHART · AN AMERICAN INTERNATIONAL PICTURE

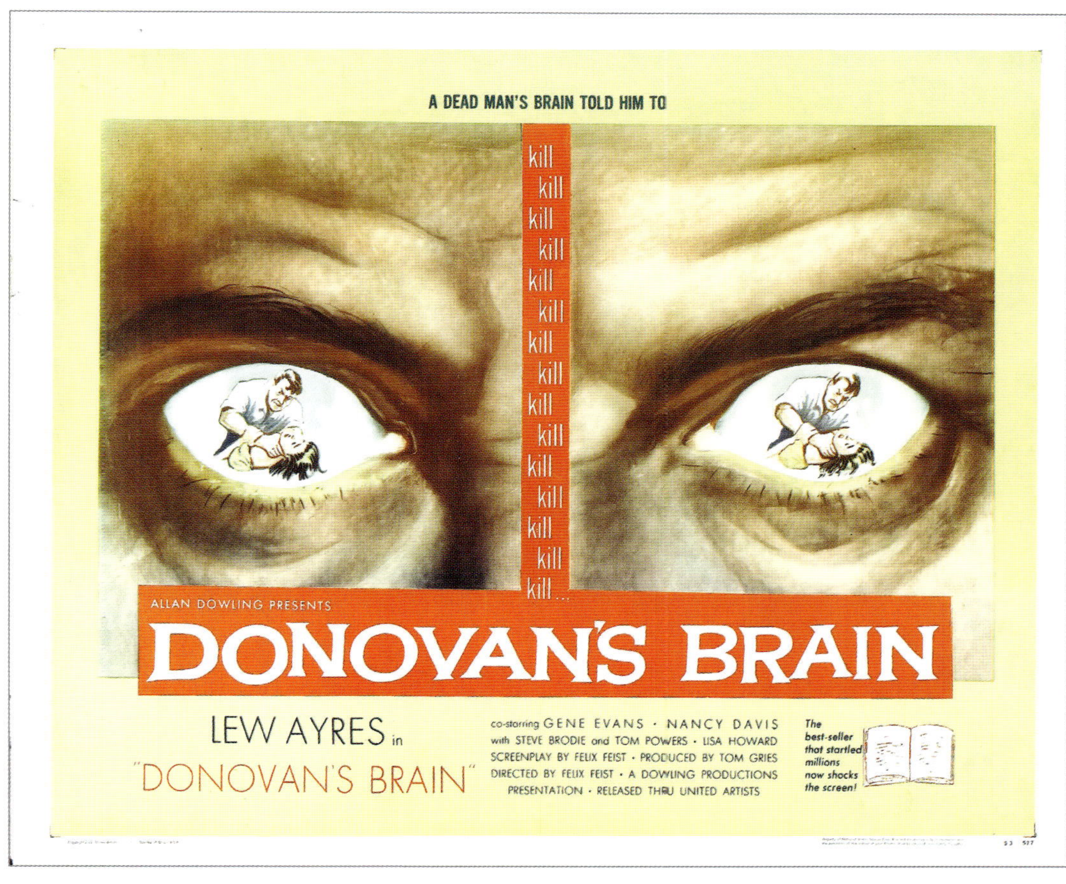

BRAINS!

The visceral appeal of the word "brain," let alone an image of the exposed organ, was not lost on filmmakers. "The best-seller that startled millions now shocks the screen!" declared the half-sheet for *Donovan's Brain* (1953), complete with a helpful little drawing of a book. Not that he merited a mention on the poster, but the author of the original 1942 novel was at least approached to adapt his work; although, as Curt Siodmak wearily recounted, "They didn't like my screenplay, which was the novel just broken down. They wrote a new one, in a week! In it God destroys the brain with a thunderbolt. That's where I left the projection room."

Albert Kallis's arresting one-sheet for *The Brain Eaters* (1958) promised an image found nowhere in the movie. Though not based on a novel, Robert Heinlein thought it close enough to his book *The Puppet Masters* to sue. He didn't want a credit though, as he found the film "wanting."

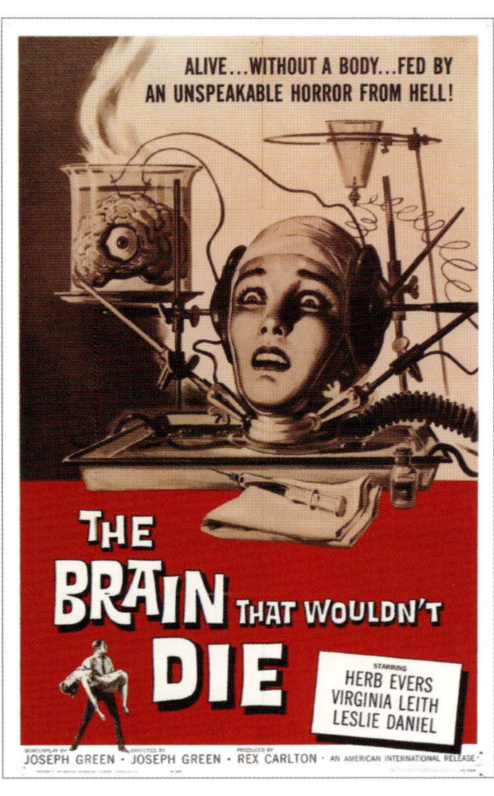

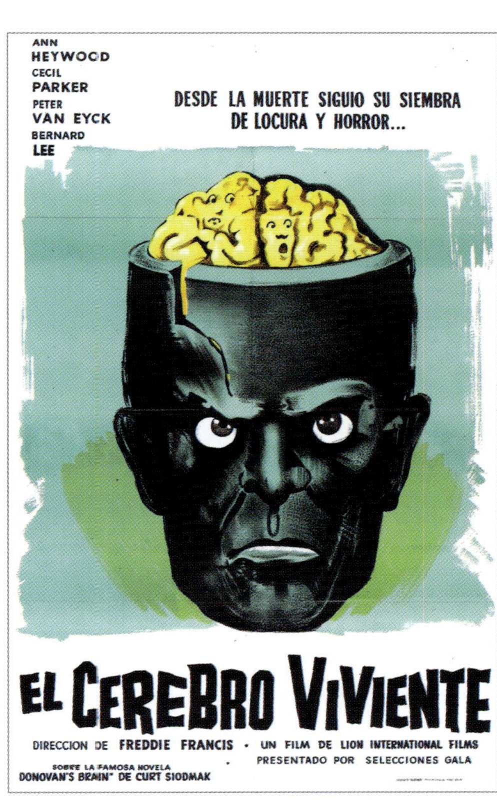

SUPER GIANT

Before Ultraman and Kamen Rider there was Super Giant, Japan's first cinematic superhero, in a series of films released from 1957–59. Ken Utsui starred as a Man of Steel from the Emerald Planet, who comes to Earth to fight crime (sound familiar?), and while the films were eventually re-edited for US TV in the '60s, before that they received theatrical releases in Europe. The glorious two-*fogli* (opposite) for *Super Giant* (1957) was by Arnaldo (Aldo) De Amicis (1904–78), an Italian poster artist also known for his comics work, especially historical adventure strips for the Catholic Church-approved magazine *Il Vittorioso*.

DAL MISTERO DELLO SPAZIO UN UOMO INVINCIBILE PER LA SALVEZZA DELLA TERRA
DISTRIBUZIONE
FILMAR
DEAMICIS
GLI INVASORI della BASE SPAZIALE
CON
WILLIAM COORES · KEN UTSUI · STEVE MILLER · JIUKO JKENCHI · JACK LEWIS
REGIA: BEN ISHUI
WIDESCREEN
PRODUZIONE: TOHO FILM

REYNOLD BROWN

In the opinion of his fellow poster artist Joseph Smith, "He was a great classical illustrator, a quiet genius. Any painting he ever made you could look at and say Reynold Brown. That's why studios used him: he captured something that they didn't have in photographs… he captured his own imagination and put it down on paper." For film historian Stephen Rebello, "His images grab the eye and don't let go… he had a natural instinct for selling what Hollywood had to offer."

After an early career as a cartoonist, William Reynold Brown (1917–91) was a technical artist during World War II for North American Aviation—producing some of the first "cutaway" drawings showing the inner workings of aircraft—before becoming a prolific magazine and book cover illustrator. He went on to create over 300 film posters across all genres, but his SF work, as the many examples in this book attest, is among his finest and best loved.

For Brown, there was no great mystery to his technique: "My job was to make a movie seem better than it was… to make people think a movie was really going to be good. Sometimes I wasn't even told the name of the movie I was working on. I'd see from the script where the action scenes were and take off from there. Sometimes, it had to come from my imagination or I'd be given stills to let me know what a monster or set looked like. Once my color pencil 'comp' [comprehensive: a preliminary drawing showing the complete intended design] was approved I'd do a black ink drawing which was sometimes photographed and made into newspaper ads. If they wanted an exact likeness of a star, I got photos of them. To construct a head, I did a likeness in brown India ink. Then, I'd layer-on water colors, which really work best because if I didn't like it, I could wash the whole thing off and re-do it."

A devout Catholic, who grew uneasy with the increasingly graphic sex and violence in movies, Brown retired from Hollywood to paint scenes of the American West. Though not the household name he deserves to be, as Professor of Art History Karal Ann Marling pointed out, "Brown was seen by more people than saw, to this day, any piece of fine art in America… isn't that enough?"

ATTACK
OF THE 50 FT.
WOMAN
starring ALLISON HAYES · WILLIAM HUDSON · YVETTE VICKERS · PRODUCED BY BERNARD WOOLNER
DIRECTED BY NATHAN HERTZ · WRITTEN BY MARK HANNA · AN ALLIED ARTISTS PICTURE
58 \223

CENTURIES OF PASSION
PENT UP IN HIS SAVAGE HEART!
CREATURE FROM THE BLACK LAGOON
Starring
RICHARD CARLSON
JULIA ADAMS
with RICHARD DENNING · ANTONIO MORENO · NESTOR PAIVA · WHIT BISSELL

Universal International presents
REVENGE OF THE CREATURE
ALL NEW
THRILLS! SHOCK! SUSPENSE!
STARRING
JOHN AGAR · LORI NELSON
JOHN BROMFIELD with NESTOR PAIVA
Directed by JACK ARNOLD · Screenplay by MARTIN BERKELEY · Produced by WILLIAM ALLAND

Beauty AND THE MAN-BEAST FROM A LOST WORLD!
TERROR runs rampant
on the city streets...
as the Monster strikes AGAIN!
THE CREATURE WALKS AMONG US
STARRING
JEFF MORROW · REX REASON · LEIGH SNOWDEN
with GREGG PALMER · MAURICE MANSON
Directed by JOHN SHERWOOD · Story and Screenplay by ARTHUR ROSS · Produced by WILLIAM ALLAND · A Universal-International Picture

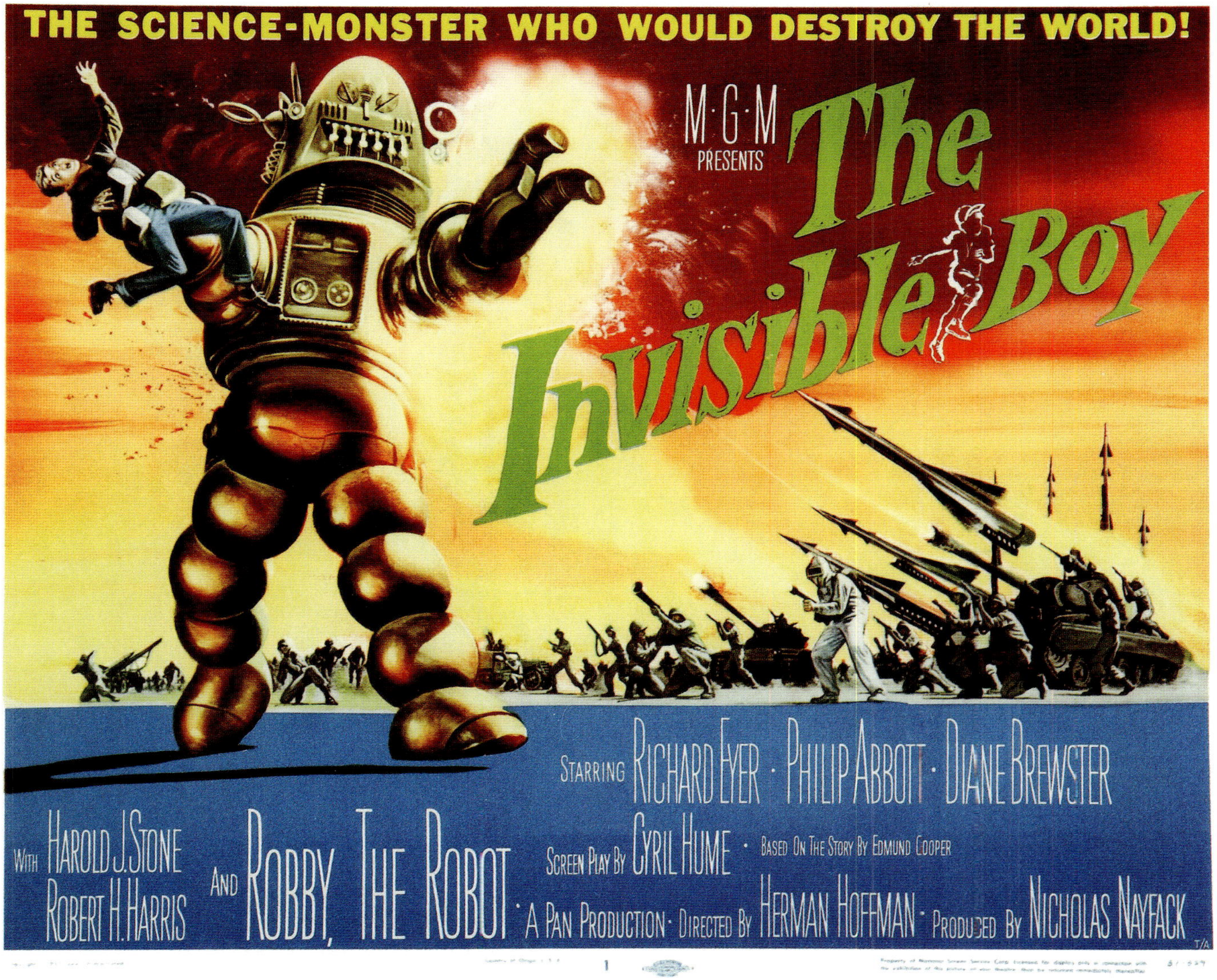
THE SCIENCE-MONSTER WHO WOULD DESTROY THE WORLD!
M·G·M PRESENTS
The Invisible Boy
STARRING RICHARD EYER · PHILIP ABBOTT · DIANE BREWSTER
WITH HAROLD J. STONE ROBERT H. HARRIS AND ROBBY, THE ROBOT
SCREEN PLAY BY CYRIL HUME · BASED ON THE STORY BY EDMUND COOPER
A PAN PRODUCTION · DIRECTED BY HERMAN HOFFMAN · PRODUCED BY NICHOLAS NAYFACK

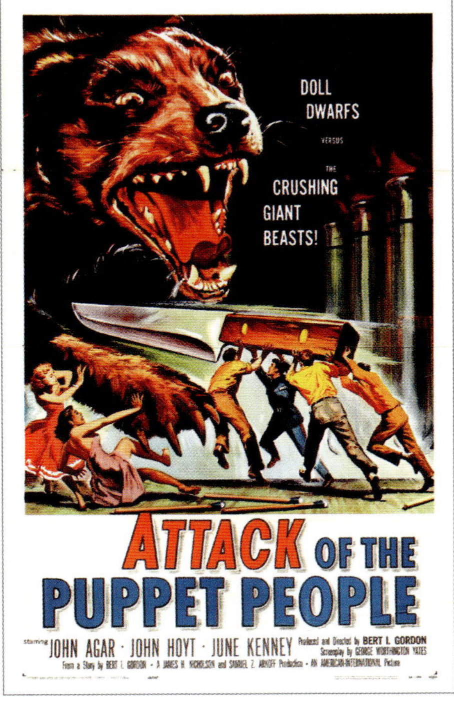

DOLL DWARFS
VERSUS
THE CRUSHING GIANT BEASTS!
ATTACK OF THE PUPPET PEOPLE
starring JOHN AGAR · JOHN HOYT · JUNE KENNEY
Produced and Directed by BERT I. GORDON
Screenplay by GEORGE WORTHINGTON YATES
From a Story by BERT I. GORDON · A JAMES H. NICHOLSON and SAMUEL Z. ARKOFF Production · AN AMERICAN-INTERNATIONAL Picture

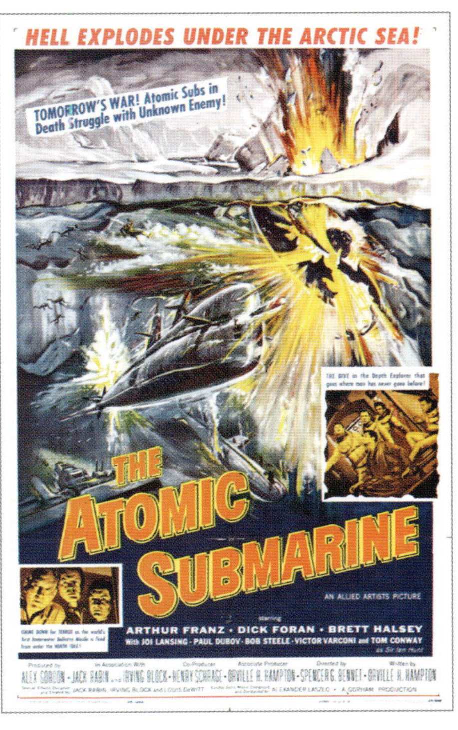

HELL EXPLODES UNDER THE ARCTIC SEA!
TOMORROW'S WAR! Atomic Subs in Death Struggle with Unknown Enemy!
THE ATOMIC SUBMARINE
AN ALLIED ARTISTS PICTURE
starring
ARTHUR FRANZ · DICK FORAN · BRETT HALSEY
with JOI LANSING · PAUL DUBOV · BOB STEELE · VICTOR VARCONI and TOM CONWAY

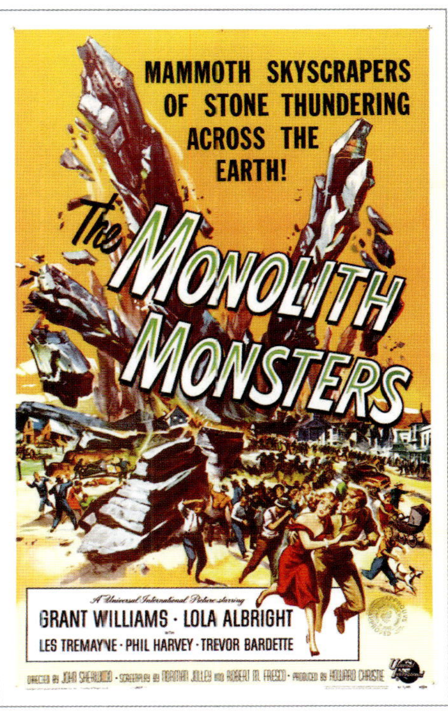

MAMMOTH SKYSCRAPERS OF STONE THUNDERING ACROSS THE EARTH!
The MONOLITH MONSTERS
A Universal International Picture starring
GRANT WILLIAMS · LOLA ALBRIGHT
with
LES TREMAYNE · PHIL HARVEY · TREVOR BARDETTE

STEVEN'S BLOB

"I was a late bloomer in the acting world," Steve McQueen once admitted in a rare interview. As 28-year-old "Steven" he got $3,000 for his first movie lead, playing a teenager in *The Blob* (1958). It was a huge hit, though not one he enjoyed remembering: "I don't want to talk about that movie. Next question… No, I wasn't the blob." The titular creature (Neil deGrasse Tyson's favorite Hollywood alien) oozes across a US poster that, like the one-sheet of its double-bill partner *I Married a Monster From Outer Space*, is utterly outclassed by its Italian equivalent. The stunning four-*fogli* for *Fluido mortale* (Deadly Fluid), as *The Blob* became, is by Sandro Simeoni (1928–2008). After starting out as a police sketch artist, he soon unleashed his fervent creativity painting posters that, as the official Simeoni Archive sheepishly accepts, sometimes feature "images that while fully representing the film in question, don't actually appear in the scenes of the movie itself."

STEVEN McQUEEN · ANETA CORSEAU · EARL ROWE
FLUIDO MORTALE
PRODOTTO DA
JACK H. HARRIS
DIRETTO DA
IRVIN S. YEAWORTH, Jr.
COLORE DE LUXE
Paramount Films
SCENEGGIATURA DI
THEODORE SIMONSON E KATE PHILLIPS
DA UN'IDEA DI
IRVINE H. MILLGATE
UNA PRODUZIONE
TONYLYN

ATTACK OF THE Bs!

Whether they were technically released on the bottom half of a double bill or not, the catch-all term "B-movie" covers all those films which couldn't claim to have big stars or budgets, but were packed with thrills nevertheless—or at least, so the posters promised. It helped if your promotional efforts had A-list visuals, like Albert Kallis's key art for *Night of the Blood Beast* (1959), or the uncredited artist who provided the surprisingly elegant one-sheet for *The Killer Shrews* (1959). Often, taglines had to do the heavy lifting. *The Black Scorpion* (1957) one-sheet (overleaf) was particularly strident: "The management reserves the right to put up the lights any time the audience becomes too emotionally disturbed! We urge you not to panic or bolt from your seats!"

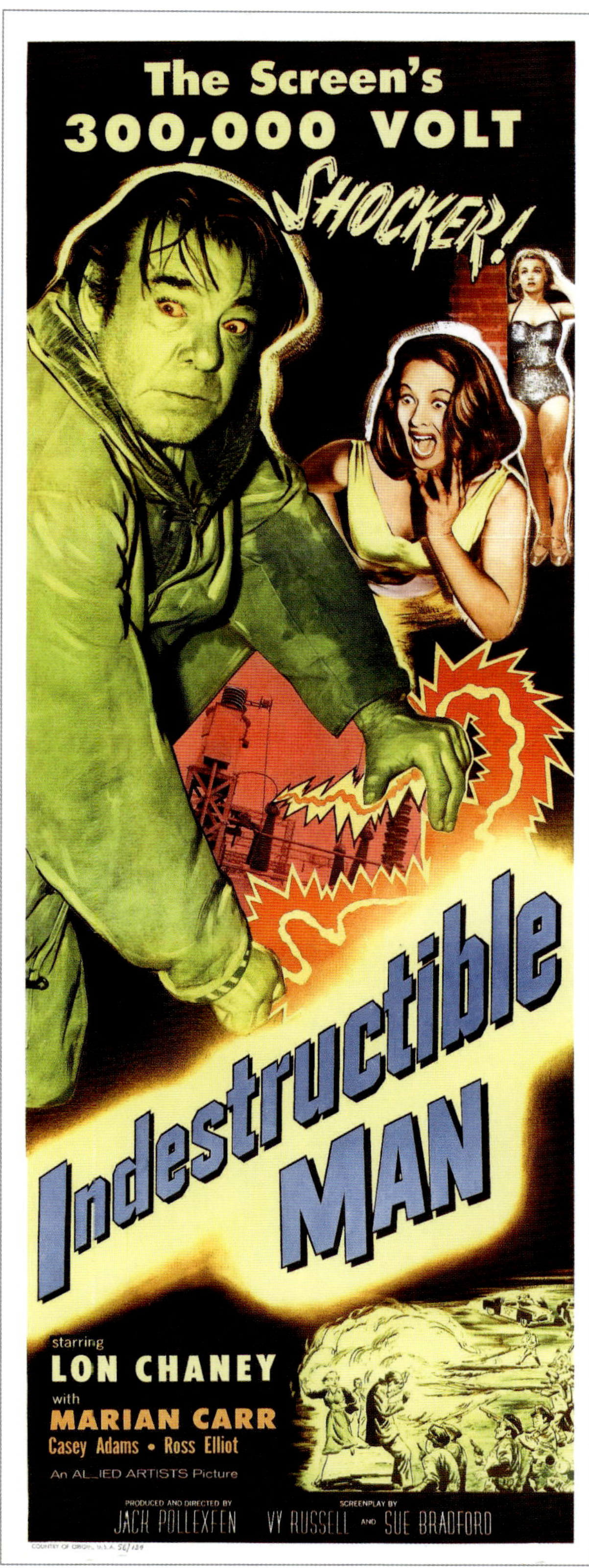
The Screen's
300,000 VOLT
SHOCKER!
Indestructible
MAN
starring
LON CHANEY
with
MARIAN CARR
Casey Adams • Ross Elliot
An ALLIED ARTISTS Picture
PRODUCED AND DIRECTED BY
JACK POLLEXFEN
SCREENPLAY BY
VY RUSSELL AND SUE BRADFORD

No girl was safe
as long as this
HEAD HUNTING THING
roamed the land!
NIGHT
OF THE
BLOOD
BEAST
Starring
MICHAEL EMMET · ANGELA GREENE · JOHN BAER · Executive Producer ROGER CORMAN · Produced by GENE CORMAN · Directed by BERNARD L. KOWALSKI · Screenplay by MARTIN VARNO · AN AMERICAN-INTERNATIONAL PICTURE

El MONSTRUO de MARTE
"ROBOT MONSTER"
MONSTRUOS INVASORES DE OTRO PLANETA INMUNES AL FUEGO Y A LAS BALAS, LUCHAN POR DESTRUIR AL GENERO HUMANO!
con GEORGE
NADER
y CLAUDIA
BARRET
BESTIAS FEROCES ATACAN LA TIERRA!
TERROR...SUSPENSO...AVENTURA!
DISTRIBUIDA POR: • PELICULAS COMERCIALES DE MEXICO, S.A. • GUANAJUATO 239-A • MEXICO, D.F.

EVERY HORROR YOU'VE SEEN ON THE SCREEN GROWS PALE BESIDE THE HORROR OF
"THE BLACK SCORPION"
SHOWN UNCUT! Every terror exactly as filmed!
NOTE: The management reserves the right to put up the lights any time the audience becomes too emotionally disturbed!
WE URGE YOU NOT TO PANIC OR BOLT FROM YOUR SEATS!
RICHARD DENNING · MARA CORDAY

UNSPEAKABLE HORRORS FROM OUTER SPACE PARALYZE THE LIVING AND RESURRECT THE DEAD!
PLAN 9 FROM OUTER SPACE
with BELA LUGOSI VAMPIRA LYLE TALBOT
A J. Edward Reynolds Production
Produced and Directed by Edward D. Wood, Jr.

Paramount présente
LES ENFANTS DE L'ESPACE
SPACE CHILDREN
MICHEL RAY · ADAM WILLIAMS · PEGGY WEBBER
Une Production WILLIAM ALLAND Mise en scène JACK ARNOLD
DE KINDEREN VAN DE RUIMTE

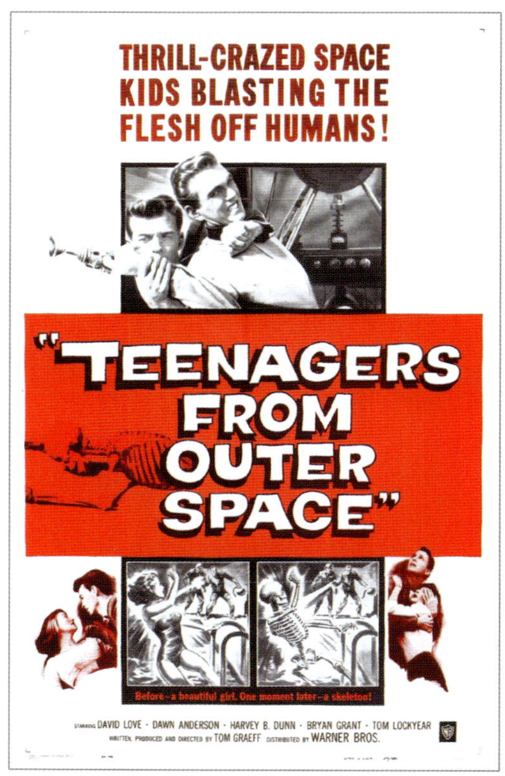
THRILL-CRAZED SPACE KIDS BLASTING THE FLESH OFF HUMANS!
"TEENAGERS FROM OUTER SPACE"
Before—a beautiful girl. One moment later—a skeleton!
DAVID LOVE · DAWN ANDERSON · HARVEY B. DUNN · BRYAN GRANT · TOM LOCKYEAR
WRITTEN, PRODUCED AND DIRECTED BY TOM GRAEFF DISTRIBUTED BY WARNER BROS.

ONE DAY AFTER A MILLION YEARS
IT CAME OUT OF HIDING TO...
KILL! KILL! KILL!
GUY MADISON · PATRICIA MEDINA
in
"THE BEAST OF HOLLOW MOUNTAIN"
And introducing the new REGISCOPE Process
Screenplay by ROBERT HILL · From an original story by WILLIS O'BRIEN
Produced by WILLIAM and EDWARD NASSOUR
Directed by EDWARD NASSOUR
CINEMASCOPE · COLOR by DE LUXE
Released thru UNITED ARTISTS

The screen's master of the WEIRD...
IN HIS NEWEST and MOST DARING
SHOCKER!
BELA LUGOSI
More horrifying than "DRACULA"-"FRANKENSTEIN"
IT'LL MAKE YOUR SKIN CRAWL!
BRIDE OF THE MONSTER
co-starring TOR JOHNSON · TONY McCOY
with LORETTA KING · HARVEY DUNN
Produced and Directed by EDWARD D. WOOD, Jr.
Screenplay by EDWARD D. WOOD, Jr. and ALEX GORDON
Executive Producer DONALD McCOY · Associate Producer TONY McCOY

Vargas
Vargas
Vargas
Vargas Interprets the Women of the Future for the Screen's Science-Fiction Sensation . . .
WORLD Without END
AN ALLIED ARTISTS PICTURE starring HUGH MARLOWE · NANCY GATES PRODUCED BY RICHARD HEERMANCE WRITTEN AND DIRECTED BY EDWARD BERNDS
FILMED IN CINEMASCOPE PRINT BY TECHNICOLOR

QUEENS OF OUTER SPACE

As every filmmaker knows, one of the first rules of promotion is that "sex sells." Patricia Laffan as the *Devil Girl from Mars* (1954) and Zsa Zsa Gabor as the *Queen of Outer Space* (1958) were nicely portrayed by comparatively little known Mexican illustrator Rodolfo Aguirre Tinoco (left) and German painter Ernst Litter (below left) respectively, but B-movie *World Without End* (1956) hired a big A-list name, as the pressbook was eager to point out: "Vargas, internationally known painter of curvaceous femininity, was commissioned by Allied Artists to do the art for a special six-sheet." Peruvian–American pin-up artist Alberto Vargas (1896–1982) was paid $1,500, way above average at the time for poster work. Remaining copies of the fabulous result (opposite) are rare, perhaps because the pressbook suggested cutting out the figures to display around the lobby.

VARGAS, WORLD FAMOUS ILLUSTRATOR, INTERPRETS 'WOMEN OF THE FUTURE' FOR 'WORLD WITHOUT END.' SPECIAL SIX SHEET AVAILABLE!

Vargas, internationally-known painter of curvaceous femininity, was commissioned by Allied Artists to do the art for a special six sheet interpreting the three beautiful stars who appear in "World Without End." The poster, illustrated right, has been designed in a manner that enables you to use it as a lobby setpiece, cutting out the figures or, if you wish, you can cut out each figure individually as shown on left and spot them in various parts of your lobby, theatre front or in store windows. [The figures are 5' 6" in height.]

Downtown department stores may be willing to use these cutouts in their windows to merchandise "Styles of the Future." Another angle would be to spot individual cutouts along side of new cars advertising "The Forward Look," or "The Car of the Future." Tie in "World Without End" by adding picture title, theatre and playdate and be sure to mention Vargas.

Vargas Interprets the Women of the Future for the Screen's Science-Fiction Sensation... WORLD Without END

PLEASE NOTE: ORDER SPECIAL "WOMEN OF THE FUTURE" SIX SHEET FROM YOUR NEAREST ALLIED ARTISTS EXCHANGE

FOR SCIENCE-FICTION FANS

[illegible]

ELECTRICAL APPLIANCES TIE IN

Electrical appliances, manufactured by the Landers Frary and Clark Company of New Britain, Connecticut, are carried by appliance and department stores all over the nation. Shown here are two specially posed stills in which Lisa Montell, featured starlet in "World Without End" is pictured in one with a Universal Coffeemaker, and in the other with a Universal Electric blanket. Use the stills as they are, or blow them up for special window displays. Both stills are available FREE by writing direct to Allied Artists Exploitation Dept., 4376 Sunset Drive, Hollywood 27, Calif. Ask for stills A-WWE.

News Photos

Back your campaign on "World Without End" by ordering a supply of News Photos, an exclusive Allied Artists accessory. These newslike bulletins contain the film's dramatic highlights. Space is left on the bottom for your theatre imprint. A limited quantity of News Photo bulletins may be obtained, at no cost, from your NEAREST ALLIED ARTISTS EXCHANGE.

'Space O'Rain' Waterproof Suits For Contests, Giveaways, Etc.

Here's an offer you shouldn't pass up if you want to get plenty of extra dollars into your box office. And it's inexpensive.

A nation-wide tie up has been consummated with the Double-Jay Company, manufacturers of Space O'Rain waterproof suits for children to plug and promote "World Without End," a picture with a terrific kid appeal.

A Space O'Rain suit is the ideal giveaway as it will appeal to both parents and kids, and is perfect for special kiddie shows or for your regular Saturday matinee. Thousands of these suits have been sold at $4.95 each. The Double-Jay Company has agreed to supply the suits to exhibitors at the factory price of $1.58 each, complete with Matching Space Helmet, Style No. 612-C, individually packed, postage or freight PAID. The suits come in three sizes. (Small 4-6, Medium 7-9, Large 10-12).

Order direct from Double-Jay Company, 332 West 9th Street, Kansas City, Missouri. Send check with order.

RADIO TRANSCRIPTIONS

Six seat-selling radio spots, recorded by one of Hollywood's ace announcers are contained on one platter. This record is available to you at no cost.

There are 2 one-minute spots, 2 twenty-second spots and 2 ten-second spots. The two longer spots have ten seconds open on the end to permit announcer to come in with local tie-in copy. These announcements, properly scheduled, are bound to create a potential audience that will wend its way to your box office.

TELEVISION TRAILERS

Reach the television viewers in your area with the specially prepared television trailers on "World Without End." Fully aware of the fact that these trailers will be seen by viewers of all age brackets, they have been carefully designed for general appeal. The trailers have silent action footage on the ends which allows time enough for mention of theatre and playdate by your station announcer. The trailers are yours free on request.

Order TV Trailers and/or Radio Transcriptions from Allied Artists Exploitation Dept., 4376 Sunset Drive, Hollywood 27, Calif., or Allied Artists Publicity Dept., 1560 Broadway, New York 36, N.Y.

TELEVISION SLIDE

Television slides are available at $4.00 each, including imprinting and postage. These slides have been prepared so that they can be used with or without station ID. Sufficient space has been left open for this purpose. (See illustration). All orders must be accompanied by check or money order. Order direct from: CHATIS ART DISPLAYS, 6453 Sunset Blvd., Hollywood, California.

FROM BELGIUM, WITH LOVE

As the following selection shows, posters produced for the Belgian market sometimes featured art markedly different from their US equivalents, often playing up the romance angle by giving female characters weight equal to or even greater than their male counterparts. This may have been because the local artists were able to ignore the contract-related stipulations regarding the size actors had to be depicted, under which American artists usually worked. This still applies today: the relative size of the heads on the poster for an ensemble film like *Avengers: Endgame* (2019) is a good guide to the relative size of the stars' paychecks.

Universal Film S.A. présente
LA CITÉ PÉTRIFIÉE
"THE MONOLITH MONSTERS"
Grant WILLIAMS · Lola ALBRIGHT
Regie JOHN SHERWOOD
DE VERSTEENDE STAD
Universal International
IMPRIMÉ EN BELGIQUE
EDICOLOR _ Bruxelles _ Tél. : 54.78.71

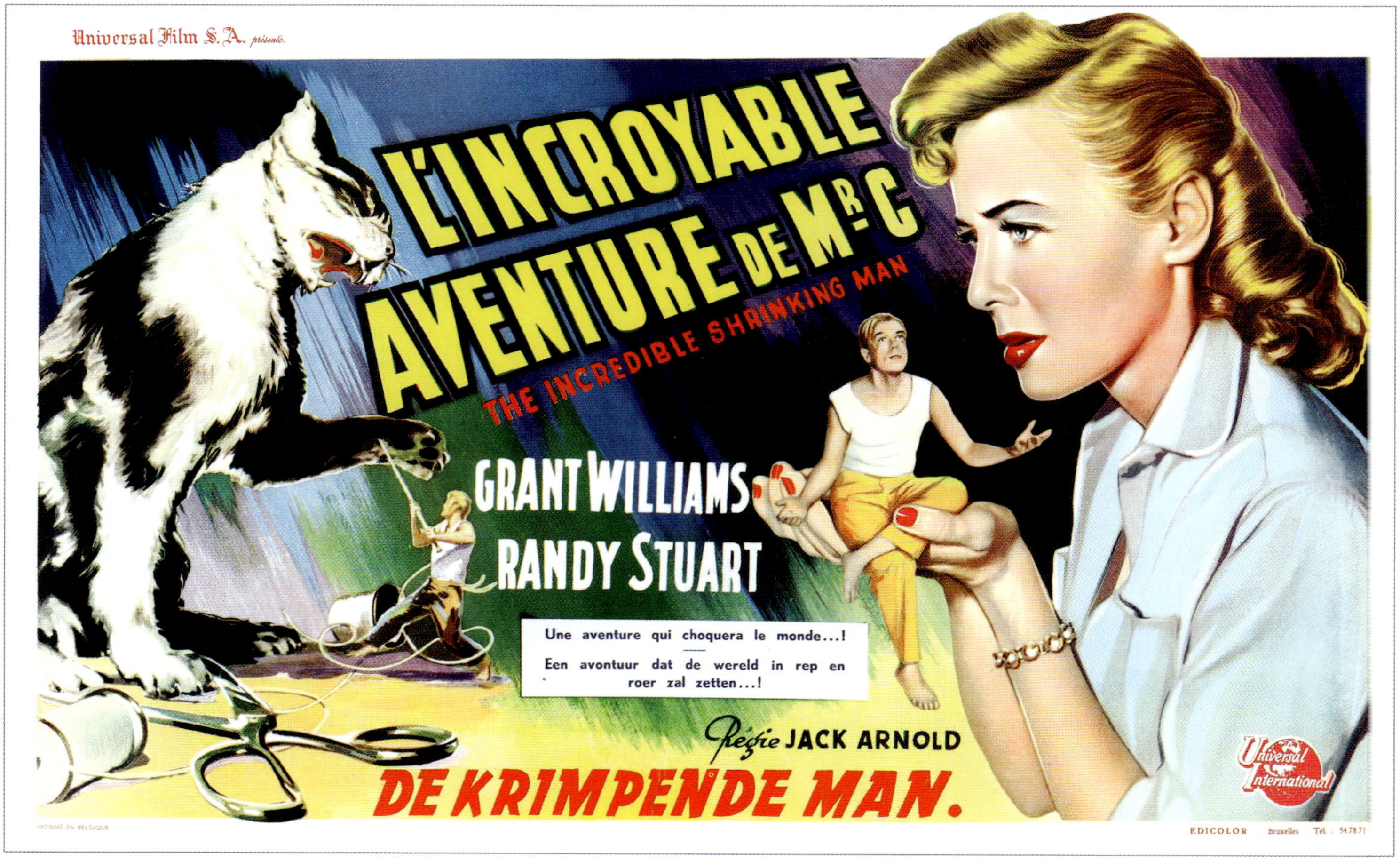

Universal Film S.A. présente
L'INCROYABLE AVENTURE DE Mr C
THE INCREDIBLE SHRINKING MAN
GRANT WILLIAMS
RANDY STUART
Une aventure qui choquera le monde...!
Een avontuur dat de wereld in rep en roer zal zetten...!
Régie JACK ARNOLD
Universal International
DE KRIMPENDE MAN.
IMPRIMÉ EN BELGIQUE
EDICOLOR Bruxelles Tél.: 54.78.71

WARNER BROS présente :
Le Monstre aux abois
(4 D MAN)
ROBERT
LANSING
LEE
MERIWETHER
JAMES
CONGDON
WARNER COLOR
Production Fairview
Distribuée par
WB
MONSTER OP LOER
IMPRIMÉ EN BELGIQUE
IMPR. L.F. DE VOS & Cº S.A. ANVERS

BRITISH QUADS

Since the 1930s, the standard film poster size in the UK has been the 30-by-40-inch "quad" (short for quadruple crown, based on the original, but now long-discontinued 15-by-20-inch crown format). The landscape orientation meant that British posters were adjusted, or more often completely redesigned versions of the portrait-shaped US one-sheets. Sometimes the art eclipsed the originals, as with Jock Hinchcliffe's quads for *The Fly* (1958) and its sequel (above and overleaf). More common was a somewhat simplified approach, often with a more limited color palette, but no less effective for that—the unusual hues of the quad for *The Beast From 20,000 Fathoms* (1953) being a good example (see page 187).

SCIENCE'S DEADLIEST ACCIDENT

TARANTULA!

"X"

STARRING JOHN AGAR · MARA CORDAY
LEO G. CARROLL WITH NESTOR PAIVA · ROSS ELLIOTT

A UNIVERSAL-INTERNATIONAL PICTURE
DIRECTED BY JACK ARNOLD · SCREENPLAY BY ROBERT M. FRESCO AND MARTIN BERKELEY
PRODUCED BY WILLIAM ALLAND

THEY'RE OUT OF THIS WORLD... ON A MISGUIDED MISSILE
MARS THATAWAY
BUD ABBOTT and LOU COSTELLO
GO TO MARS
WITH MARI BLANCHARD
ROBERT PAIGE · HORACE McMAHON and the MISS UNIVERSE BEAUTIES
DIRECTED BY CHARLES LAMONT · SCREENPLAY BY D.D. BEAUCHAMP and JOHN GRANT · PRODUCED BY HOWARD CHRISTIE
A UNIVERSAL-INTERNATIONAL PICTURE
G.F.D. RELEASE

CRAWLING, CREEPING, UNBELIEVABLE TERROR!
INVASION OF THE HELL CREATURES
CERT X ADULTS ONLY
SEE... THE NIGHT OF THE GREEN HORROR!
SEE... THE DISEMBODIED HAND THAT CRAWLS!
SEE... THE EARTH INVADED BY CREATURES FROM HELL!
with
STEVE TERRELL · GLORIA CASTILLO · FRANK GORSHIN
Distributed by ANGLO AMALGAMATED FILM DISTRIBUTORS LTD.

ALL NEW and MORE HORRIFIC THAN BEFORE!
RETURN OF THE FLY
CERT. "X" ADULTS ONLY
CINEMASCOPE PICTURE
STARRING VINCENT PRICE
AND BRETT HALSEY · JOHN SUTTON DAVID FRANKHAM · DAN SEYMOUR
PRODUCED BY BERNARD GLASSER · DIRECTED FROM HIS SCREENPLAY BY EDWARD L. BERNDS
BASED UPON GEORGE LANGELAAN'S SHORT STORY "THE FLY"
PRODUCED BY ASSOCIATED PRODUCERS, INC. · RELEASED BY 20th CENTURY-FOX

THE DEADLY MANTIS
CRAIG STEVENS · ALIX TALTON · WILLIAM HOPPER
FLORENZ AMES · DONALD RANDOLPH
A UNIVERSAL-INTERNATIONAL PICTURE
RANK FILM DISTRIBUTORS LTD.

ITS EXCLUSIVE!
The MOST AMAZING STORY EVER FILMED
THE SCREENS FIRST STORY OF MANS CONQUEST OF SPACE
ROCKETSHIP X-M
U
EXPEDITION MOON!
LLOYD BRIDGES · OSA MASSEN
JOHN EMERY · NOAH BEERY Jr. · HUGH O'BRIEN
MORRIS ANKRUM

THE SUPREME EXCITEMENT OF OUR TIME NOW ON THE SCREEN AFTER 2½ YEARS IN THE MAKING
THIS ISLAND EARTH
JEFF MORROW
FAITH DOMERGUE
REX REASON
with LANCE FULLER · RUSSELL JOHNSON
Colour by TECHNICOLOR
A UNIVERSAL-INTERNATIONAL PICTURE

RAGING UP FROM THE BOTTOM OF TIME TO LOOSE ITS CRUSHING FURY ON A CITY!

Sensation from Warner Bros.

The Beast From 20,000 Fathoms

THE STORY OF THE SEA'S MASTER BEAST

CAST OF THOUSANDS! OVER A YEAR IN THE MAKING! "X" CERT ADULTS ONLY

Starring

PAUL CHRISTIAN • PAULA RAYMOND • CECIL KELLAWAY • KENNETH TOBEY • JACK PENNICK

Directed by EUGENE LOURIE

Produced by HAL CHESTER & JACK DIETZ

R.K.O. Radio Pictures Presents

THE MYSTERIANS

SEE THE FANTASTIC FOREST FIRE

SEE A COMPLETE VILLAGE DISAPPEAR

SEE THE INCREDIBLE MONSTER ROBOT

SEE THE WORLD'S FORCES MOBILIZED AGAINST INVADERS FROM ANOTHER PLANET

SEE AN ARMY COMPLETELY DESTROYED

SEE THE EERIE BATTLE OF DEATH RAYS!

RKO RADIO PICTURES

Produced by TOMOYUKI TANAKA
Directed by INOSHIRO HONDA
Director of Special Photographic Effects EIJI TSUBURAYA

PUBLICITY POSES

As the avid readers of magazines like *Famous Monsters* knew, studio publicity stills were often the best chance to get a proper look at a creature that is perhaps only glimpsed, or kept largely in shadow on screen, like Ray "Crash" Corrigan as *It! The Terror From Beyond Space* (1958), or Marla English's monstrous alter ego in *Voodoo Woman* (1957), gamely posing with its co-star (below right). Such photos were also useful reference for artists: the frankly unsavory still (below center) for *The Monster that Challenged the World* (1957) obviously inspired the film's Belgian poster (see p182), though the latter did not include the crates Audrey Dalton is balancing on.

VOS-(18-6)-21
VOGUE PICTURES, Inc. Presents "IT! THE TERROR FROM BEYOND SPACE"
Co-Starring MARSHALL THOMPSON • SHAWN SMITH • KIM SPALDING
Directed by EDWARD L. CAHN — Produced by ROBERT E. KENT — Released thru UNITED ARTISTS
Copyright 1958, United Artists Corp. Permission granted for Newspaper and Magazine reproduction. (Made in U.S.A.)
"Property of National Screen Service Corp. Licensed for display only in connection with the exhibition of this picture at your theatre. Must be returned immediately thereafter."
58/340

ROBOTS!

"Fantastic science fiction… that may soon become science fact" announced the trailer for *The Colossus of New York* (1958), one of several '50s SF movies to deal with robot technology—though the eponymous star with its human brain was technically a cyborg, and was nowhere near as colossal on screen as the posters suggested. *Target Earth* (1954) aimed for the "Raw Panic" of an invasion by a metallic alien army, but the budget only stretched to one rather disappointing robot costume. More memorable were *Tobor the Great* (1954), an early example of a robot with emotions, and the return of *Forbidden Planet*'s Robby the Robot in *The Invisible Boy* (1957), retitled *Il Robot e la Sputnik* in Italy to cash in on the Russian satellite then in the headlines.

HERBERT J. YATES PRESENTA
TOBOR
CHARLES DRAKE
KARIN BOOTH
BILLY CHAPIN
REGIA DI
LEE SHOLEM

JOHN BARAGREY
MALA POWERS
OTTO KRUGER
ROBERT HUTTON
ROSS MARTIN
IL COLOSSO DI NEW YORK
(THE COLOSSUS OF NEW YORK)
PRODOTTO DA
WILLIAM ALLAND
DIRETTO DA
EUGENE LOURIE
È un film Paramount
SCENEGGIATO DA
THELMA SCHNEE
BASATO SU DI UN RACCONTO DI
WILLIS GOLDBECK

REPUBLIC PICTURES PRESENTA:
TOBOR EL MAGNIFICO
(TOBOR THE GREAT)
¡TODOS SE CONMOVERAN CONOCIENDO A TOBOR... EL MONSTRUO MECANICO QUE PERCIBE COMO USTED TODAS LAS EMOCIONES HUMANAS!
CHARLES DRAKE · KARIN BOOTH
BILLY CHAPIN · TAYLOR HOLMES · STEVEN GERAY
DIRECTOR LEE SHOLEM
UNA PRODUCCION DUDLEY PICTURES CORPORATION

PARAMOUNT presenta
CEREBRO DIABOLICO
"THE COLOSSUS OF NEW YORK"
JOHN BARAGREY · MALA POWERS · OTTO KRUGER
ROBERT HUTTON · ROSS MARTIN
ES UN FILM PARAMOUNT
WILLIAM ALLAND
EUGENE LOURIE

獣人雪男

あッ！驚愕の一瞬！忽然アルプスの雪を蹴って巨獣人雪男人間に迫る！

製作 田中友幸　脚本 村田武雄
原作 香山滋　特殊技術 円谷英二

監督 本多猪四郎

宝田明　河内桃子　根岸明美　中村伸郎　堺左千夫　山本廉　笠原健司　大村千吉　相良三四郎　堤康久　瀬良明　谷晃　高堂国典　小杉義男

東宝

東宝株式会社製作・配給

監督・本多猪四郎

東宝

地に熱震を呼び、水は龍巻と化す大猛威！
紅蓮の炎に包まれ天翔る世紀の怪鳥ラドン！

イーストマンカラー
総天然色

空の大怪獣
ラドン

撮影 芦田勇・美術 北辰雄・録音 宮崎正信・照明 森茂・音楽 伊福部昭

製作 田中友幸
原作 黒沼健
脚本 村田武雄
〃 木村武
特技監督 円谷英二
特殊技術 渡辺明
〃 城田正雄
〃 向山宏

佐原健二　白川由美（石原忠改め）　平田昭彦　山田巳之助　大仲清治（新人）　田島義文　中田康子　小堀明男

東宝株式会社　製作・配給

ISHIRO HONDA

Though best remembered for his first SF feature, which launched the longest-running film franchise in history, director Ishiro Honda (1911–93) returned to the genre many times after *Godzilla* (1954), as this selection of '50s posters shows (see key on p314 for details). The son of a Buddhist monk, Honda tried to bring a humanist message of cooperation and understanding into his films, which he hoped would have lasting value: "It was definitely my pleasure that I was able to make something that people can remember. If I had not made *Godzilla* or *The Mysterians*… it wouldn't be the same. There is nothing like the happiness I get from those [movies]."

The alien invasion epic *The Mysterians* (1957) was promoted on its 1959 release in the West with some unusual visuals by Lt. Colonel Robert B. Rigg of the US Army (see p194, top). Rigg, who in a storied career had evaded imprisonment by both Soviet and Chinese security forces, witnessed atomic bomb tests, and written a book on future war technology, was also an accomplished artist. He was drafted in to create what the pressbook described as a "special series of paintings depicting the Mysterians, and the fantastic equipment used by them in invading the earth."

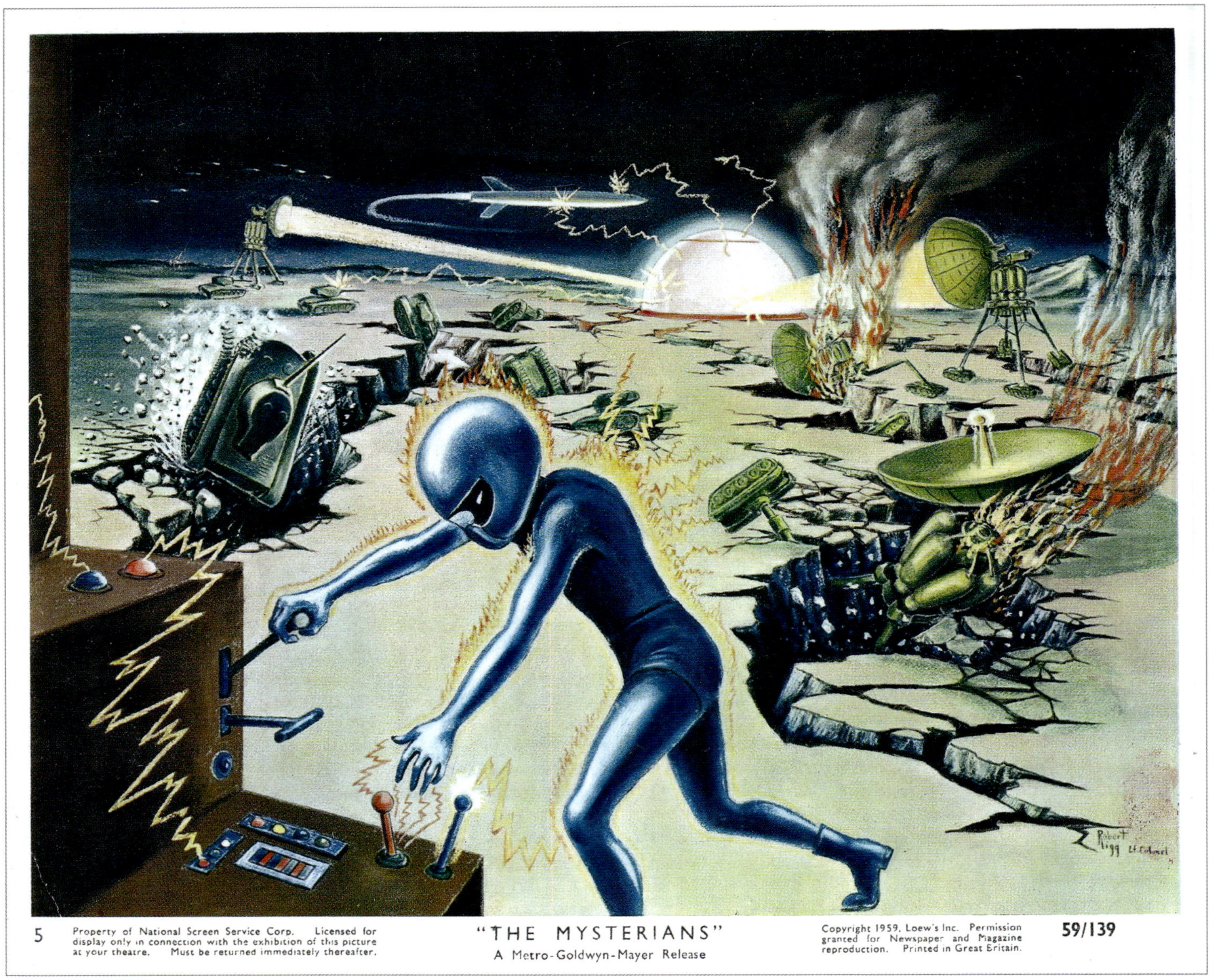
5
Property of National Screen Service Corp. Licensed for display only in connection with the exhibition of this picture at your theatre. Must be returned immediately thereafter.
"THE MYSTERIANS"
A Metro-Goldwyn-Mayer Release
Copyright 1959, Loew's Inc. Permission granted for Newspaper and Magazine reproduction. Printed in Great Britain.
59/139

1400 POUNDS OF FROZEN FURY that moves like man!
HALF HUMAN
HALF-MAN, HALF-BEAST but ALL MONSTER!
starring
JOHN CARRADINE
with RUSS THORSON · ROBERT KARNES · MORRIS ANKRUM
A dca RELEASE

MOLECULAR MAN TERRIFIES THE WORLD!
THE H MAN
IN EASTMAN COLOR
A COLUMBIA PICTURE

RANK PRÉSENTE UNE SÉLECTION RKO
PRISONNIÈRES DES MARTIENS
GRAND ECRAN - COULEURS

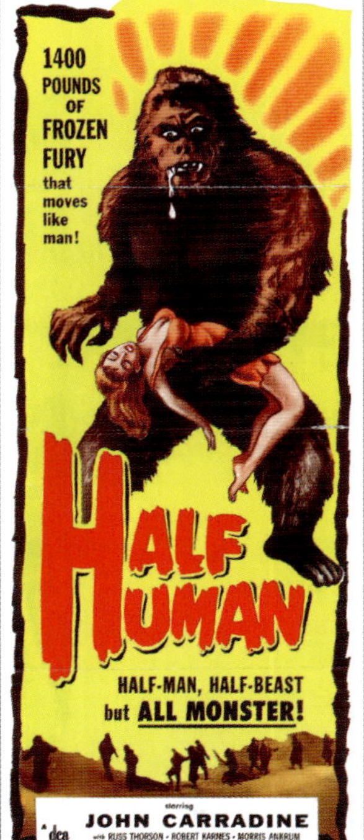

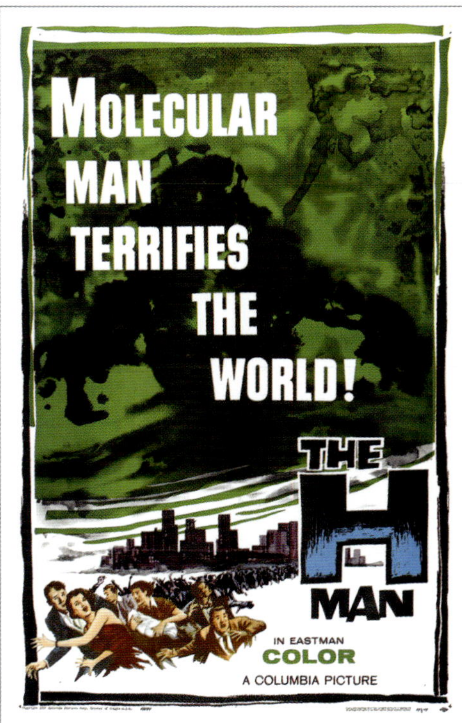

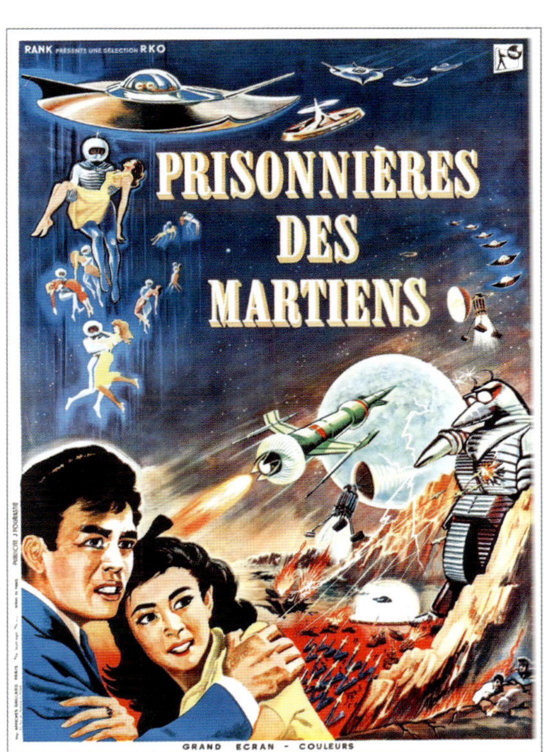

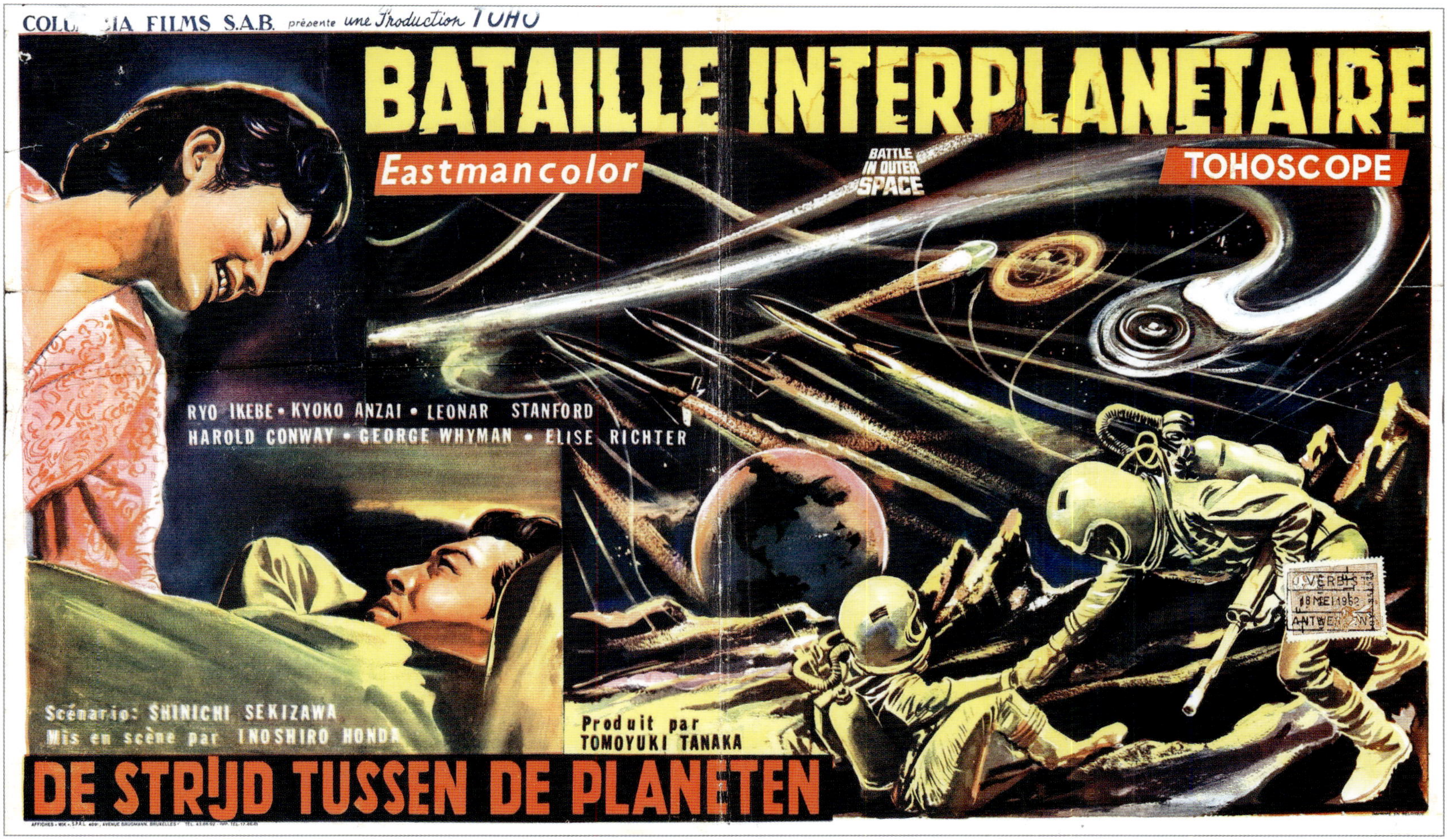
COLUMBIA FILMS S.A.B. présente une Production TOHO
BATAILLE INTERPLANETAIRE
Eastmancolor
BATTLE IN OUTER SPACE
TOHOSCOPE
RYO IKEBE • KYOKO ANZAI • LEONAR STANFORD
HAROLD CONWAY • GEORGE WHYMAN • ELISE RICHTER
Scénario: SHINICHI SEKIZAWA
Mis en scène par INOSHIRO HONDA
Produit par
TOMOYUKI TANAKA
DE STRIJD TUSSEN DE PLANETEN

VARAN
The Unbelievable
FROM A WORLD BELOW, IT CAME TO TERRORIZE TO DESTROY TO REVENGE!
A CROWN INTERNATIONAL RELEASE
MYRON HEALY • TSURUKO KOBAYASHI and a cast of thousands
62/380

FROM A WORLD BELOW, IT CAME TO TERRORIZE-
TO DESTROY-
TO REVENGE!
VARAN
The Unbelievable
FOR CENTURIES IT SLEPT FAR BELOW THE SEA UNTIL MODERN MAN... EVER SEARCHING... EVER PROBING DEEPER INTO THE UNKNOWN... DISTURBED ITS PEACE... THEN IT ROSE... FROM THE DEPTHS... SLOWLY... SURELY ... UNRELENTINGLY... TO WREAK ITS VENGEANCE... TO KILL... TO DESTROY A CIVILIZATION THAT WANTED TO KNOW TOO MUCH!
A CROWN INTERNATIONAL RELEASE
MYRON HEALY • TSURUKO KOBAYASHI and a cast of thousands
Produced and Directed by JERRY A. BAERWITZ • Screenplay by SID HARRIS • Filmed in WIDE SCREEN

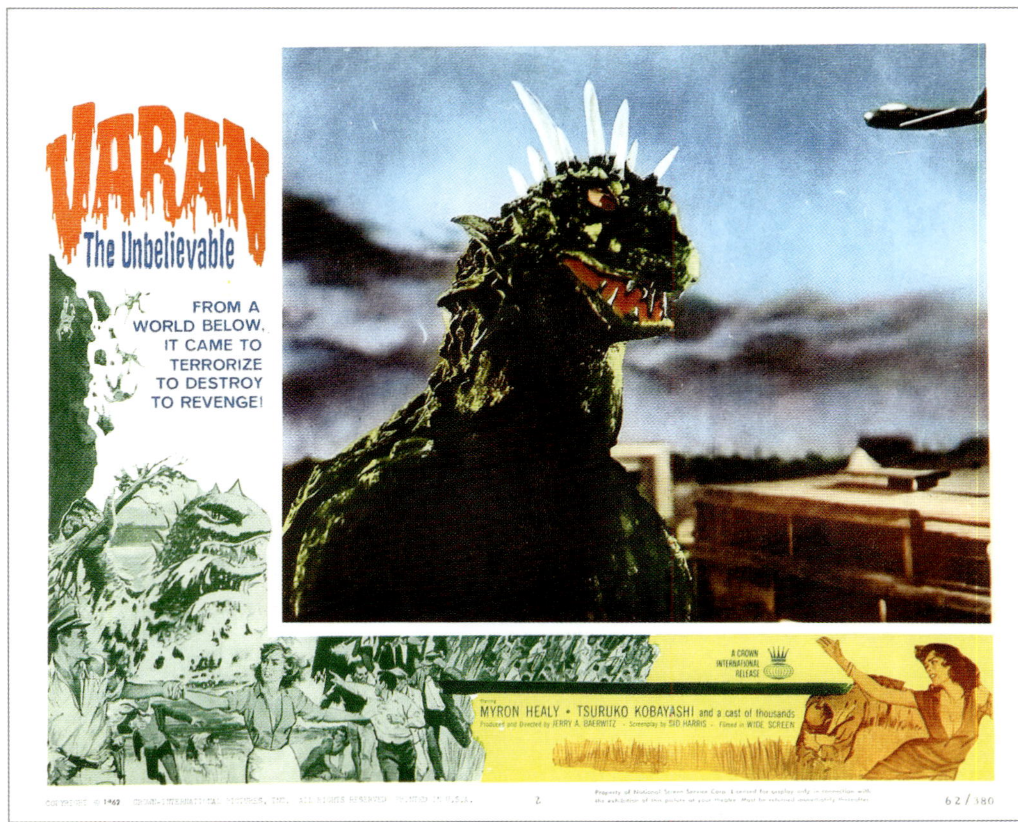

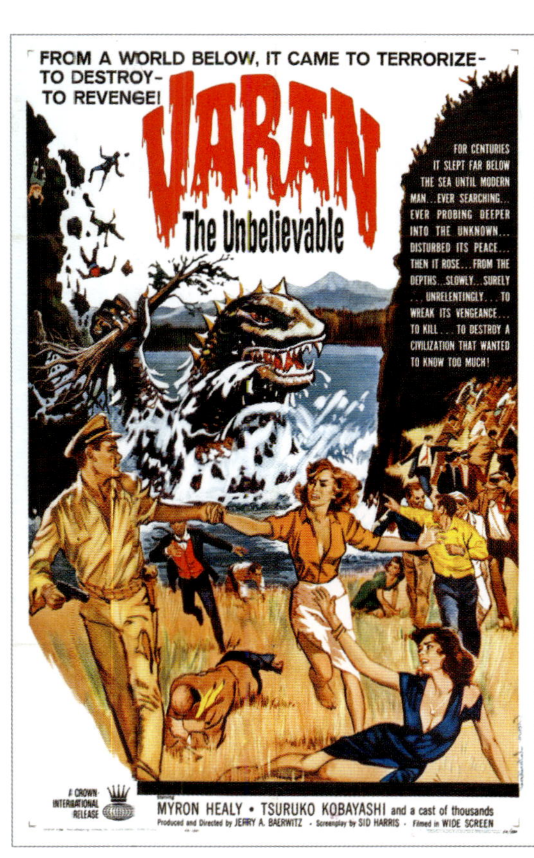

AT THE END OF THE WORLD

1959 saw the decade closing with two films depicting the aftermath of a radioactive Armageddon. "The biggest story of our time… If you never see another motion picture in your life you must see *On the Beach*" insisted the press ads for what was very much an A-list picture, with four big star names, adapting Nevil Shute's novel. The US one-sheet (below) was by the Italian artist Nicola Simbari (1927–2012), a rare example of a painter who mixed commercial advertising work with a thriving career in "fine art." His poster suggested the lurking threat of radiation, rather than the on-the-nose mushroom cloud of the tie-in novel cover (right). Harry Belafonte produced and starred in *The World, the Flesh and the Devil*, featuring an interracial love triangle in a deserted New York. The ending, featuring the three characters hand-in-hand as "The Beginning" appears on screen, was meant to imply racial and sexual harmony, but ended up confusing audiences and satisfied no one, including the cast.

WHEN NEW YORK BECOMES A GHOST TOWN AND THREE SURVIVORS TAKE OVER

IT WILL GRIP YOUR IMAGINATION AS NO FILM HAS EVER DONE BEFORE!

Talk about something **NEW** on the screen. It's the most unusual story ever told. What would **YOU** do if **YOU** were this girl, alone with two men? Who wins when these two stalk each other through empty streets, over roof-tops with rifles in hand and lust in their hearts?

NEVER ANYTHING LIKE IT!

The biggest city in the world deserted, not a thing in motion, empty buildings, empty streets. You'll marvel how it's done, because it was actually filmed here.

M-G-M Presents A SOL C. SIEGEL Production Starring

HARRY BELAFONTE / INGER STEVENS / MEL FERRER

THE WORLD, THE FLESH and THE DEVIL

Screen Play by RANALD MacDOUGALL • Screen Story by FERDINAND REYHER • in CinemaScope • Made by Siegel-HarBel Productions

Directed by RANALD MacDOUGALL • Produced by GEORGE ENGLUND

MGM présente

UNE PRODUCTION SOL C. SIEGEL - HARBEL

HARRY BELAFONTE

INGER STEVENS

MEL FERRER

CINEMASCOPE

le MONDE, la CHAIR et le DIABLE

RANALD MacDOUGALL GEORGE ENGLUND

THE WORLD, THE FLESH AND THE DEVIL

de wereld, de vrouw en de duivel.

THE
1960s

Nick Jones on *Alphaville* and *2001: A Space Odyssey*

If the science fiction films of the 1950s demonstrated a preoccupation with the external—monstrous invasions and threats both alien and man-made—the SF flicks of the 1960s took an increasingly cerebral turn, looking inwards as much as outwards; literally, in the case of Richard Fleischer's *Fantastic Voyage* (1966), in which a submarine and its crew are shrunk to microscopic size and injected into the body of a Soviet defector.

PREVIOUS SPREAD: Detail from a French poster for *Destroy All Monsters* (1968), art by Constantin Belinsky.

BELOW: "Exciting! Witty! Fast moving!" US lobby card for *Alphaville* (1965), featuring a positive quote from the formidable *New York Times* reviewer Bosley Crowther, who was not always well disposed towards SF. He dismissed *Godzilla* as "an incredibly awful film" and *When Worlds Collide* as "anticlimactic."

OPPOSITE: Colorful 4 *fogli* for *Alphaville*'s Italian release, with art by Averardo Ciriello, who used a similar style on his posters for the 1960s James Bond movies.

Which isn't to say there wasn't room for bombast and spectacle too. While the decade began with two films based on introspective British novels—George Pal's 1960 adaptation of H.G. Wells's *The Time Machine*, and Wolf Rilla's *Village of the Damned* (1960), based on John Wyndham's *The Midwich Cuckoos*—some of the best SF films of the decade found novel ways to navigate between the two poles. B-movie maestro Roger Corman's *X: The Man with the X-ray Eyes* (1963) took its preposterous conceit to sublimely absurd extremes, with Ray Milland's Dr. James Xavier developing eye drops that grant him x-ray vision, only to find himself by film's end able to see to the center of the universe, where resides "the eye that sees us all." As madness consumes him, his only recourse is to tear out his own eyes. Bigger of budget, but no less willing to push its ideas to the limit, Franklin J. Schaffner's *Planet of the Apes* (1968) transformed Pierre Boulle's 1963 novel into a cinematic masterpiece, with an iconic final shot that ranks among the greatest ever twist endings.

Two 1960s films in particular exemplify the forging of the cerebral and the otherworldly into visionary wholes, and symbolize the propensity for looking inwards, most obviously in the shape of the computer minds at the core of their plots.

Directed by French New Wave filmmaker Jean-Luc Godard, *Alphaville* (1965) brilliantly blends science fiction with hard-boiled film noir. Aptly shot in stark black-and-white—something it shares in common with some other more cerebral 1960s SF movies, including *Village of the Damned* and

UN FILM DI JEAN-LUC GODARD
AGENTE
LEMMY CAUTION:
MISSIONE
ALPHAVILLE
EDDIE CONSTANTINE · ANNA KARINA
AKIM TAMIROFF
HOWARD VERNON
UNA COPRODUZIONE FILMSTUDIO S.p.A., Roma - CHAUMIANE PRODUCTION, Paris

Chris Marker's influential short *La Jetée* (1962)—the film follows secret agent Lemmy Caution as he travels to Alphaville, a city on another planet, to assassinate Professor von Braun, inventor of Alpha 60, the despotic sentient computer which rules the city. Caution, the creation of British thriller writer Peter Cheyney, featured in 11 novels (1936–46) and at least as many French movies, played in most by American expat singer and actor Eddie Constantine, *Alphaville* included.

Writing on the BFI website on the occasion of *Alphaville*'s 50th anniversary in 2015, film critic Barry Keith Grant noted that where Godard's fellow New Wave auteur François Truffaut struggled to successfully adapt Ray Bradbury's *Fahrenheit 451* in 1966, Godard made a more effective stab at science fiction the year before, albeit a form of SF more concerned with art, ideology, and culture than the more typical preoccupations of the genre. Certainly Godard seems unmoved by the trappings of SF; *Alphaville* was shot by cinematographer Raoul Coutard entirely on location in Paris, the film's dystopian setting conjured from everyday locales like hotel lobbies and swimming pools, sans special effects—"a fable on a realistic ground," as Godard put it.

By contrast, Stanley Kubrick and Arthur C. Clarke, the director and writer of *2001: A Space Odyssey* (1968), were deeply concerned with the hows and wherefores of their story, not least the journeying to other worlds. Where Lemmy Caution's method of travel to Alphaville is barely acknowledged—he simply arrives there in his car—Kubrick and Clarke researched and extrapolated every aspect of their milieu in an effort to make their film as plausible as possible. Kubrick had first approached Clarke in 1964 with a notion of making the "proverbial good science fiction movie." By that point the director had already absorbed enormous amounts of science fiction and fact, and while he was clear about his destination—a film about man's relation to the universe—he needed Clarke's help in achieving something never before attempted in cinema.

Over the next four years, the pair set about realizing that vision. At Kubrick's behest Clarke began writing a novel rather than a screenplay, in order to give full rein to their imaginations, with the screenplay to be based on that book (eventually published two months after the release of the film). In the event, the novel and the screenplay were written simultaneously, one feeding into the other, back and forth symbiotically. Based on Clarke's 1951 short story "The Sentinel," the film developed into much more than the discovery of an alien artifact, encompassing the dawn of man, the flourishing of the space age—encapsulated by a three-million year jump cut from a prehistoric bone flung in the air to an orbital weapons platform—and humanity's eventual evolution, accomplished through peerless production design and revolutionary effects. Among these, *Discovery One*—the ship transporting Drs. Dave Bowman (Keir Dullea) and Frank Poole (Gary Lockwood) and their team to Jupiter on the trail of a radio signal transmitted by an alien monolith found buried on the moon—with its centrifugal living quarters, and the psychedelic rush of Bowman's "ultimate trip," as some later promotional posters put it, through the Star Gate.

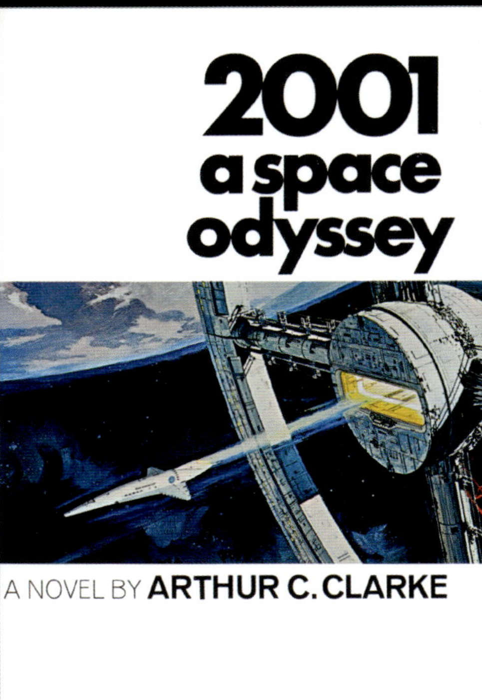

TOP: Cover of the US first edition hardback of the novel that Clarke wrote in tandem with the screenplay.

ABOVE: A UK quad from 1969, one of the earliest posters to use the "ultimate trip" tagline.

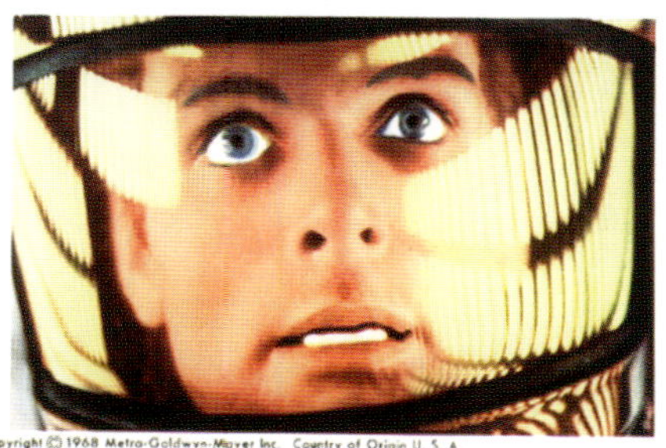

Driving the second half of the narrative is HAL 9000, the AI which controls *Discovery*, and which bears some comparison to Alpha 60. Where Alpha 60 is authoritarian and controlling, with a grating, gargling voice—performed by an anonymous actor with throat cancer utilizing a voice box—HAL is on first inspection subservient and soothing, as voiced by Canadian actor Douglas Rain, whom Kubrick had heard narrating the 1960 animated documentary *Universe*. In his own way, however, HAL proves almost as malevolent as Alpha 60, murdering most of the *Discovery* crew and having to be disabled by the surviving Bowman, just as Alpha 60 is incapacitated by Lemmy Caution, in both cases prompting philosophical exchanges on the nature of existence: the external threat looking inwards for answers to eternal questions.

ABOVE: US half-sheet by renowned space artist Robert McCall, who also worked extensively with NASA, both documenting the space race, and designing mission patches, including for the Apollo 17 moon landing.

THE TIME MACHINE

After *The Conquest of Space* (1955) failed at the box office, producer George Pal took until the next decade before he could mount his adaptation of H.G. Wells's 1895 novella, but it was worth the wait: the 1960 film was a hit and won an Academy Award for its special effects. The US poster art was by Reynold Brown, who said that "George Pal gave me a lot of freedom" when it came to the work, though his paintings' ultimate fate was not a fond memory: "Pal kept all my original artwork for *The Time Machine* in his house in Hollywood. It all burned up in a fire." Pal had considered the urbane James Mason or David Niven for the lead, but instead chose strapping young Australian actor Rod Taylor, seen staring out of the Italian two-*fogli* (opposite). The art was by Silvano "Nano" Campeggi (1923–2018), who created more than 3,000 movie posters during a long career, which ultimately won him the prestigious Fiorino D'Oro award from his home city of Florence.

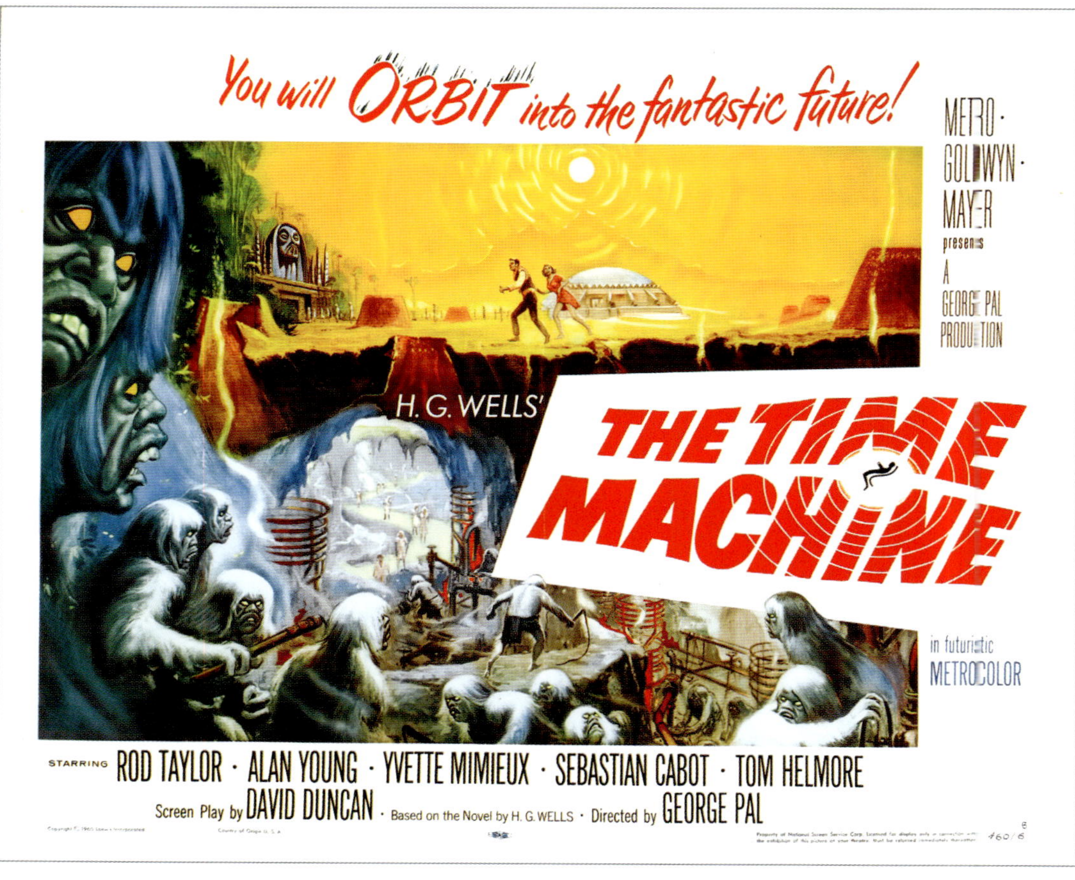

Metro Goldwyn Mayer
Una produzione GEORGE PAL
L'UOMO CHE VISSE
(THE TIME MACHINE)
NEL FUTURO
di H. G. WELLS
ROD TAYLOR · ALAN YOUNG · YVETTE MIMIEUX · SEBASTIAN CABOT · TOM HELMORE
Diretto da GEORGE PAL · Sceneggiatura di DAVID DUNCAN
Dal romanzo di H. G. WELLS
METROCOLOR
Zincografica Fiorentina
AVVERTENZA

LOST WORLDS OF THE 60S

The decade began with more trips to the well of Verne and Conan Doyle, with the Christmas 1959 release *Journey to the Center of the Earth* followed that summer by *The Lost World* (1960): both featured "dinosaurs" which were actually lizards with stuck-on fins, though at least the posters, such as Boris Grinsson's French *grande* (opposite bottom left), didn't give that away. *The Mysterious Island* (1961) benefitted from Ray Harryhausen's bravura stop-motion effects, but the most memorable thing about Hammer Films' *The Lost Continent* (1968) was its taglines: "SACRIFICE to giant jaw-snapping mollusks! HELPLESS BEAUTIES attacked by crazed kelp-monsters!" Reynold Brown provided a typically dynamic US one-sheet for Ishiro Honda's *Latitude Zero* (1969); the gnomic Polish poster (bottom right) was by Andrzej Bertrandt and Marian Stachurski.

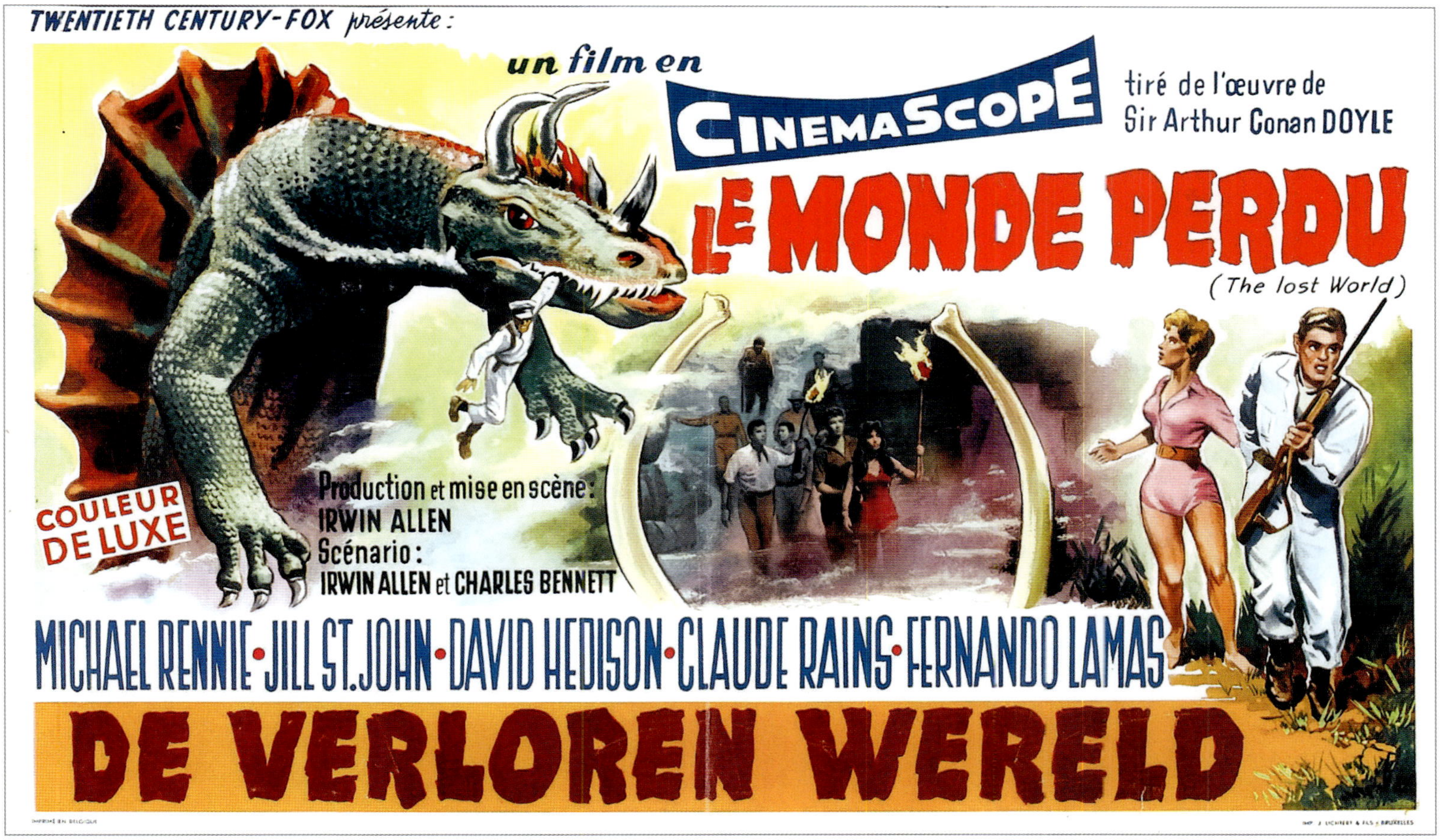
TWENTIETH CENTURY-FOX présente :
un film en
CINEMASCOPE
tiré de l'œuvre de
Sir Arthur Conan DOYLE
LE MONDE PERDU
(The lost World)
COULEUR DE LUXE
Production et mise en scène:
IRWIN ALLEN
Scénario:
IRWIN ALLEN et CHARLES BENNETT
MICHAEL RENNIE · JILL ST. JOHN · DAVID HEDISON · CLAUDE RAINS · FERNANDO LAMAS
DE VERLOREN WERELD

Le monde magique de
JULES VERNE
VOYAGE AU CENTRE DE LA TERRE
PAT BOONE · JAMES MASON · ARLENE DAHL · DIANE BAKER
COULEURS PAR DELUXE CINEMASCOPE
Prod. CHARLES BRACKETT · Réal. HENRY LEVIN · Scen. WALTER REISCH et CHARLES BRACKETT

20th Century Fox présente
LE PEUPLE DES ABIMES
ERIC PORTER · HILDEGARD KNEF · SUZANNA LEIGH · TONY BECKLEY · NIGEL STOCK · NEIL McCALLUM · BENITO CARRUTHERS · JIMMY HANLEY
Couleurs par DeLuxe

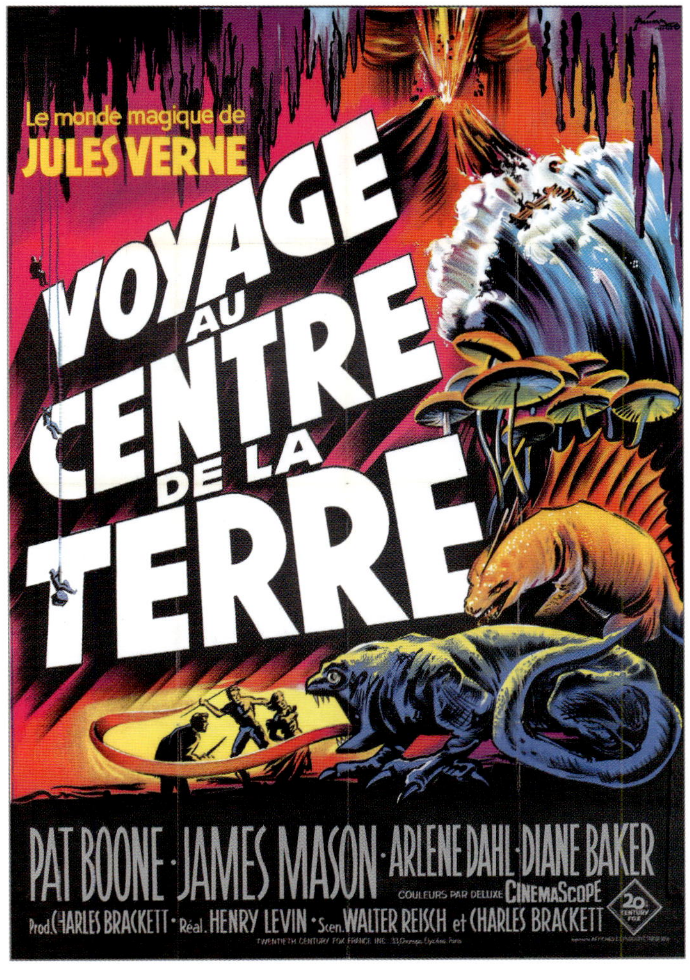

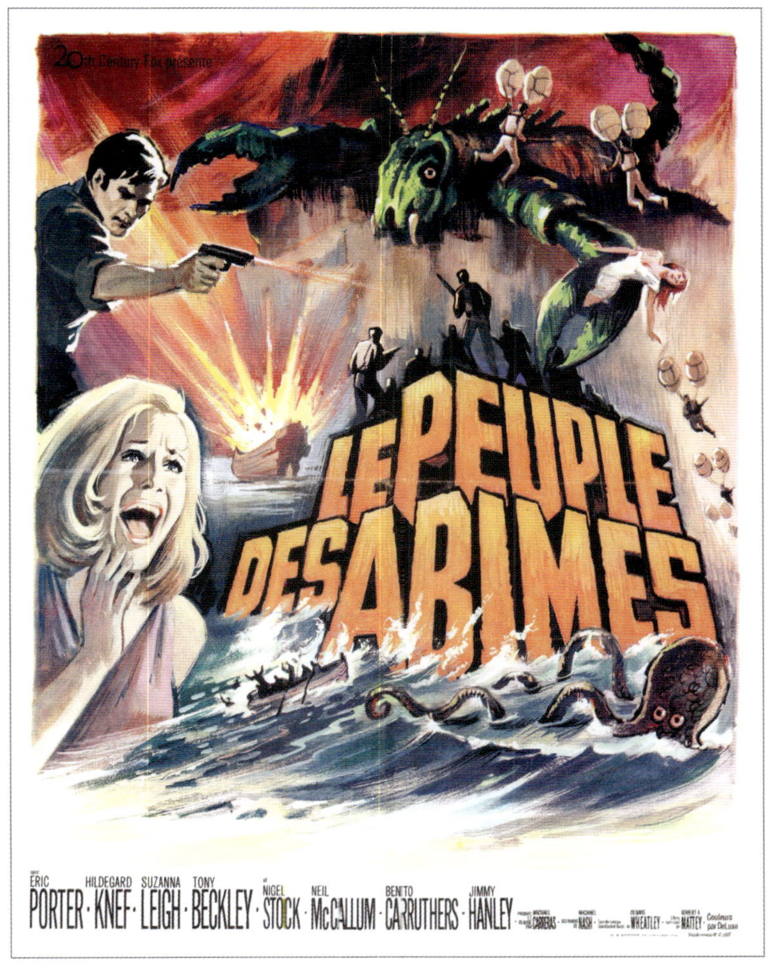

GIANT MONSTERS

As the following pages of images from around the world show (see key on page 314 for details), colossal creatures continued their crusade of chaos throughout the 1960s. *Gorgo*, *Konga*, and *Reptilicus* all appeared in 1961; the first two were shot in England, the third was, and is, the only giant monster movie from Denmark. All three received spin-off comics in the US from publisher Charlton, where artists included Steve Ditko, who drew the cover for *Konga* #4 (below center) a few months before he co-created Spider-Man. The US one-sheet for *Gorgo* (see page 210, bottom right) was by Joseph [Joe] Smith, who didn't even get to complete a proper painting: MGM art director Paul Brewer liked Smith's rough so much that he just used that. Spanish artist "Jano" did finish his Gorgo art (see page 210, bottom left), but painted the Japanese *kaiju* Gamera by mistake!

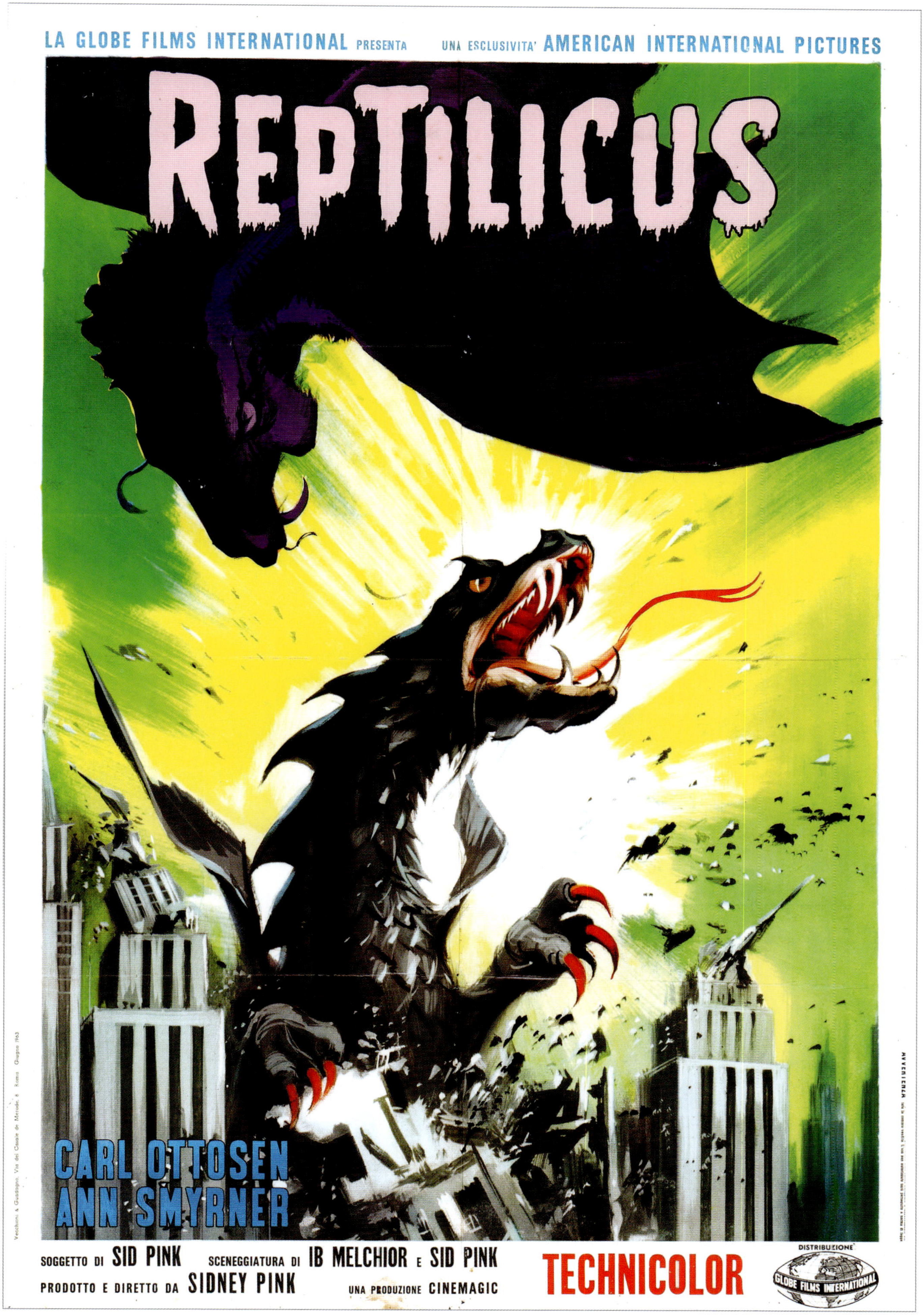

LA GLOBE FILMS INTERNATIONAL PRESENTA UNA ESCLUSIVITA' AMERICAN INTERNATIONAL PICTURES

REPTILICUS

CARL OTTOSEN
ANN SMYRNER

SOGGETTO DI SID PINK SCENEGGIATURA DI IB MELCHIOR E SID PINK
PRODOTTO E DIRETTO DA SIDNEY PINK UNA PRODUZIONE CINEMAGIC

TECHNICOLOR

DISTRIBUZIONE

THE BIGGEST THING SINCE CREATION!
The GIANT
BEHEMOTH
An ALLIED ARTISTS Picture
starring GENE EVANS · ANDRE MORELL · JOHN TURNER · A DAVID DIAMOND PRODUCTION
Directed by EUGENE LOURIE · Screenplay by EUGENE LOURIE · Special Effects Designed and Created by JACK RABIN · IRVING BLOCK · LOUIS DE WITT

LA GLOBE FILMS INTERNATIONAL PRESENTA UNA ESCLUSIVITA' EROS FILMS
il DRAGO degli ABISSI
CON
GENE EVANS · ANDRE MORELL · JOHN TURNER · LEIGH MADISON
REGIA DI
DOUGLAS HICKOX E EUGENE LOURIE
PRODUZIONE
DAVID DIAMOND

JANO.
GORGO
EL MONSTRUO
BILL TRAVERS · WILLIAM SYLVESTER · VINCENT WINTER
COLOR

LIKE NOTHING YOU'VE EVER SEEN BEFORE!
METRO-GOLDWYN-MAYER Presents
A KING BROTHERS Production
GORGO
Starring
BILL TRAVERS · WILLIAM SYLVESTER
With
Vincent Winter · Bruce Seton · Joseph O'Conor · Martin Benson · Barry Keegan · Dervis Ward · Christopher Rhodes
Screen Play by JOHN LORING and DANIEL HYATT · Original Story by EUGENE LOURIE and DANIEL HYATT
Directed by EUGENE LOURIE · Produced by FRANK KING and MAURICE KING
TECHNICOLOR

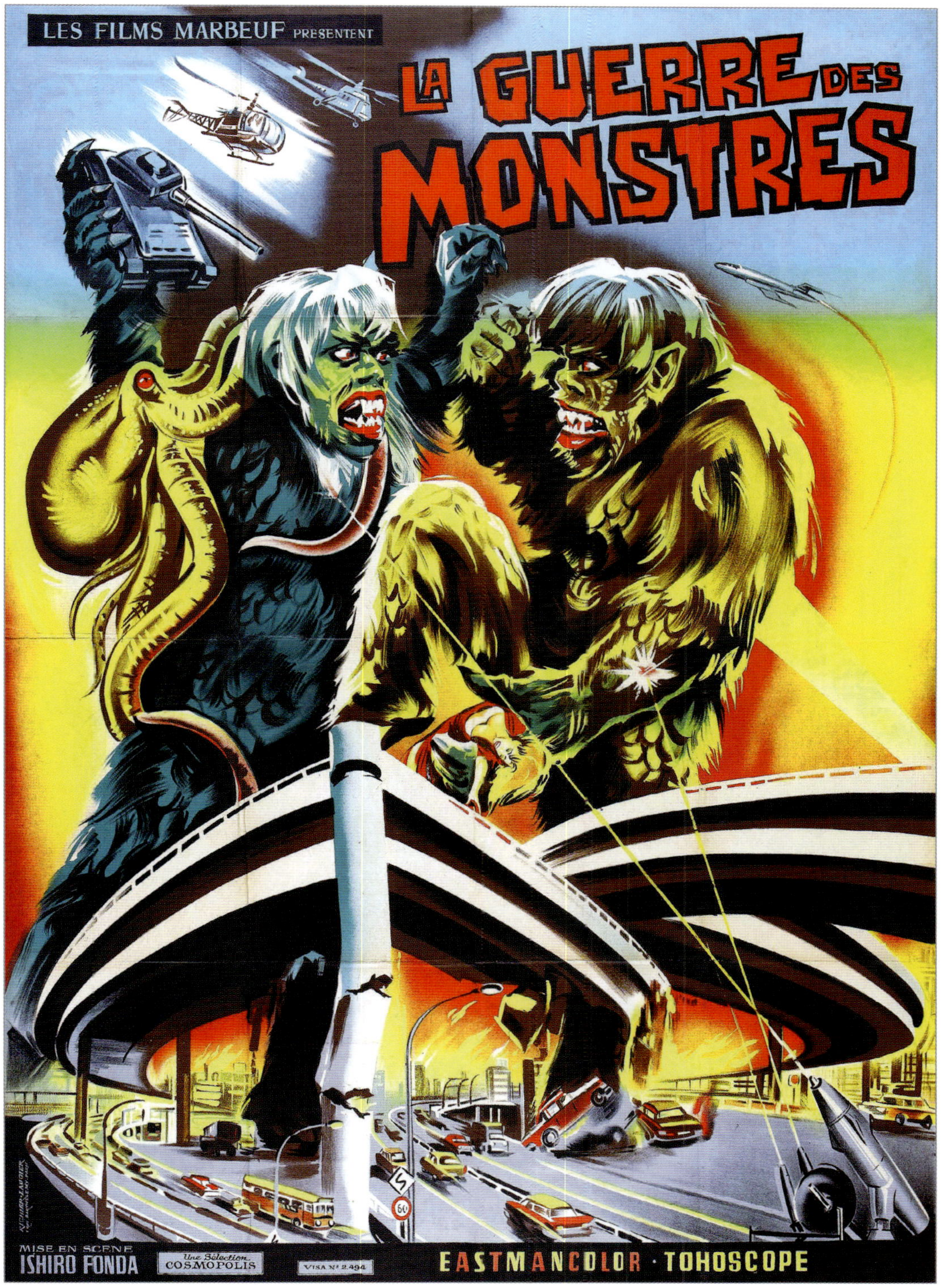

LES FILMS MARBEUF PRESENTENT

LA GUERRE DES MONSTRES

MISE EN SCENE ISHIRO FONDA

Une Sélection COSMOPOLIS

VISA N° 2.494

EASTMANCOLOR · TOHOSCOPE

THE EYES HAVE IT

English SF writer John Wyndham's 1957 novel *The Midwich Cuckoos* was given the punchier title *Village of the Damned* for its 1960 movie adaptation. Posters (apart from Roger Soubie's French *grande*, opposite top right) highlighted the staring eyes of the unearthly, telekinetic children—the glowing eye effects used in the film were removed from the UK print by spooked censors. *Children of the Damned* (1964) was a thematic rather than direct sequel, with somewhat more sympathetic young mutants—but the posters once again focused on the eyes, and the kids once again all died horribly at the end.

GEORGE
SANDERS · BARBARA
SHELLEY
MICHAEL
GWYNN
DIRETTO DA
WOLF RILLA
PRODOTTO DA
RONALD
KINNOCK
SCENEGGIATURA DI
STIRLING SILLIPHANT
WOLF RILLA
GEORGE BARCLAY
IL
VILLAGGIO
DEI DANNATI
(VILLAGE OF THE DAMNED)
Dal romanzo "The Midwich Cuckoos"
di JOHN WYNDHAM

Metro-Goldwyn-Mayer
PRESENTE
GEORGE SANDERS
BARBARA SHELLEY
le
Village
des
Damnés
d'après le roman de
JOHN WYNDHAM
avec
MICHAEL GWYNN
INTERDIT AUX
MOINS DE 18 ANS
Réalisation de
WOLF RILLA
Production de
RONALD KINNOCH

THEY COME TO CONQUER THE WORLD...
METRO · GOLDWYN · MAYER
presents
A LAWRENCE P. BACHMANN
production
Starring
IAN HENDRY
CHILDREN
OF THE
DAMNED
X
...so young,
so innocent,
so utterly
deadly!
With ALAN BADEL · BARBARA FERRIS · Screenplay by JOHN BRILEY · Produced by BEN ARBEID · Directed by ANTON M. LEADER

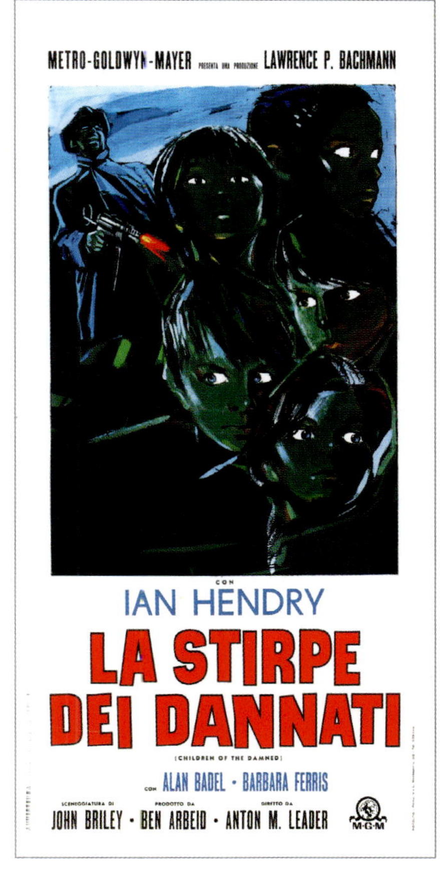
METRO-GOLDWYN-MAYER
LAWRENCE P. BACHMANN
CON
IAN HENDRY
LA STIRPE
DEI DANNATI
(CHILDREN OF THE DAMNED)
CON ALAN BADEL · BARBARA FERRIS
JOHN BRILEY · BEN ARBEID · ANTON M. LEADER
M-G-M

THE DAY OF THE TRIFFIDS

A British production starring imported Hollywood actor Howard Keel, *The Day of the Triffids* (1962) was only loosely based on John Wyndham's 1951 novel of a world threatened by carnivorous plants. In the UK, the quad poster (right) by Bill Wiggins was the main promotional image; the US had a more scattergun approach, evolving from an early image (possibly by Reynold Brown) on the cover of the pressbook, through a fun "Darwin's Stranger Than Fiction" advance one-sheet, to the final one-sheet by Joe Smith (below, left to right). "The few stills they sent made the monsters look like big rubber mats," Smith remembered. "I got $350 for that. Silly, isn't it?" The Italian four-*fogli* (opposite) is unsigned, but has the hallmarks of the "why let what's actually in the film get in the way of a good poster?" approach of Sandro Simeoni.

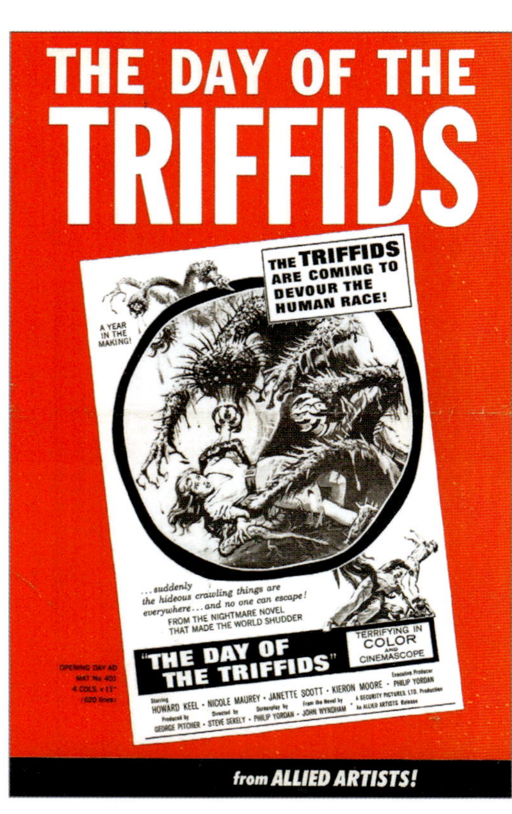

THE RANK ORGANISATION PRESENTA
L'INVASIONE DEI MOSTRI VERDI
(THE DAY OF THE TRIFFIDS)
HOWARD KEEL
NICOLE MAUREY
EASTMAN COLOUR
CINEMASCOPE
BASATO SUL ROMANZO DI JOHN WYNDHAM
SCENEGGIATURA PHILIP YORDAN
DIRETTO DA STEVE SEKELY
PRODOTTO DA GEORGE PITCHER
PRODUTTORE ESECUTIVO PHILIP YORDAN

東宝
マタンゴ
総天然色
吸血の魔手で人間を襲う"第三の生物"マタンゴの恐怖！
監督・本多猪四郎
特技監督・円谷英二
製作・田中友幸
久保明
佐原健二
太刀川寛
土屋嘉男
小泉博
八代美紀
水野久美
原作・星新一
福島正実
脚本・木村武
撮影・小泉一
美術・育野重一
録音・矢野口文雄
照明・小島正七
音楽・別宮貞雄
整音・下永尚
特殊スタッフ
撮影・有川貞昌
富岡素敬
美術・渡辺明
照明・岸田九一郎
合成・向山宏
東宝株式会社製作・配給
Printed in Japan © TOHO Co., Ltd 1963

THE NAVY VS NIGHT MONSTERS
ALL NEW! in Terrifying COLOR
VAN DOREN EISLEY MASON GRAY VAN
SANDE FAULKNER TERRY
Copyright 1966 Standard Club of California All Rights Reserved Printed in U.S.A.

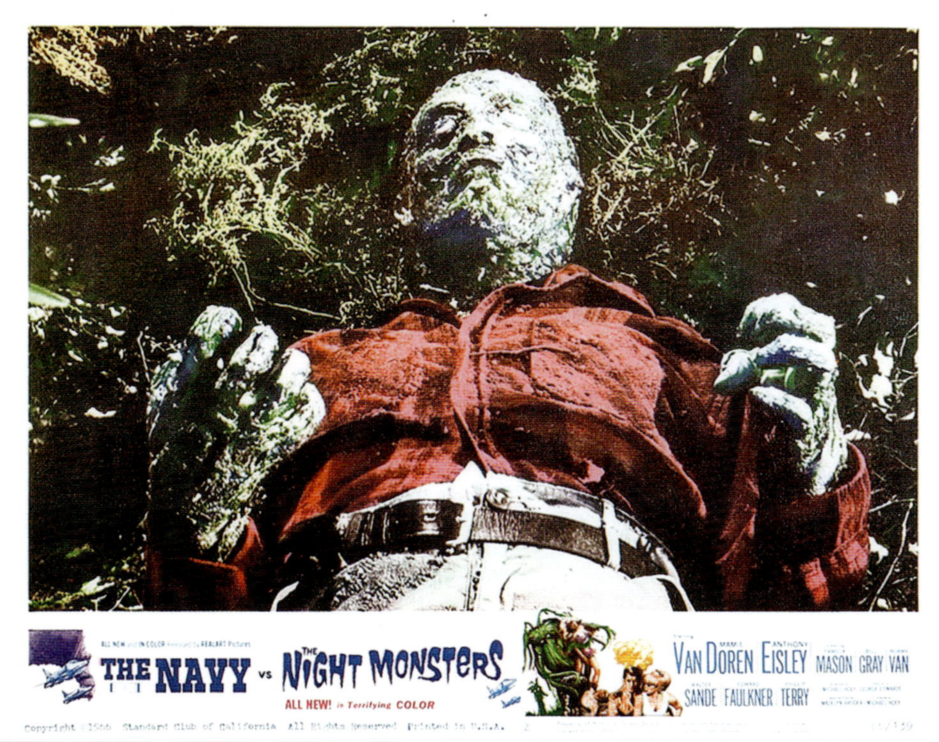

PLANT-BASED TERROR

"Blood-sucking creatures attack humans. Fear the 'Third Life-form!'" announces the domestic poster for Ishiro Honda's Japanese SF/horror hybrid *Matango* (1963). In contrast to Honda's *kaiju* films, this story of a mutant mushroom infection was a much darker, intimate, and disturbing tale, one which the director pointed out to his actors was "a serious drama picture, so please keep this in mind and work accordingly." The result was, as Honda conceded, not "a typical Japanese mainstream movie at all. When critics saw it [they] didn't like it, so that was pretty much the end of that film."

As for *The Navy vs. the Night Monsters* (1966), the poster looks great, but let Leonard Maltin's mini-review be your guide: '1) Look at the title. 2) Examine the cast. 3) Be aware that the plot involves omnivorous trees. 4) Don't say you weren't warned."

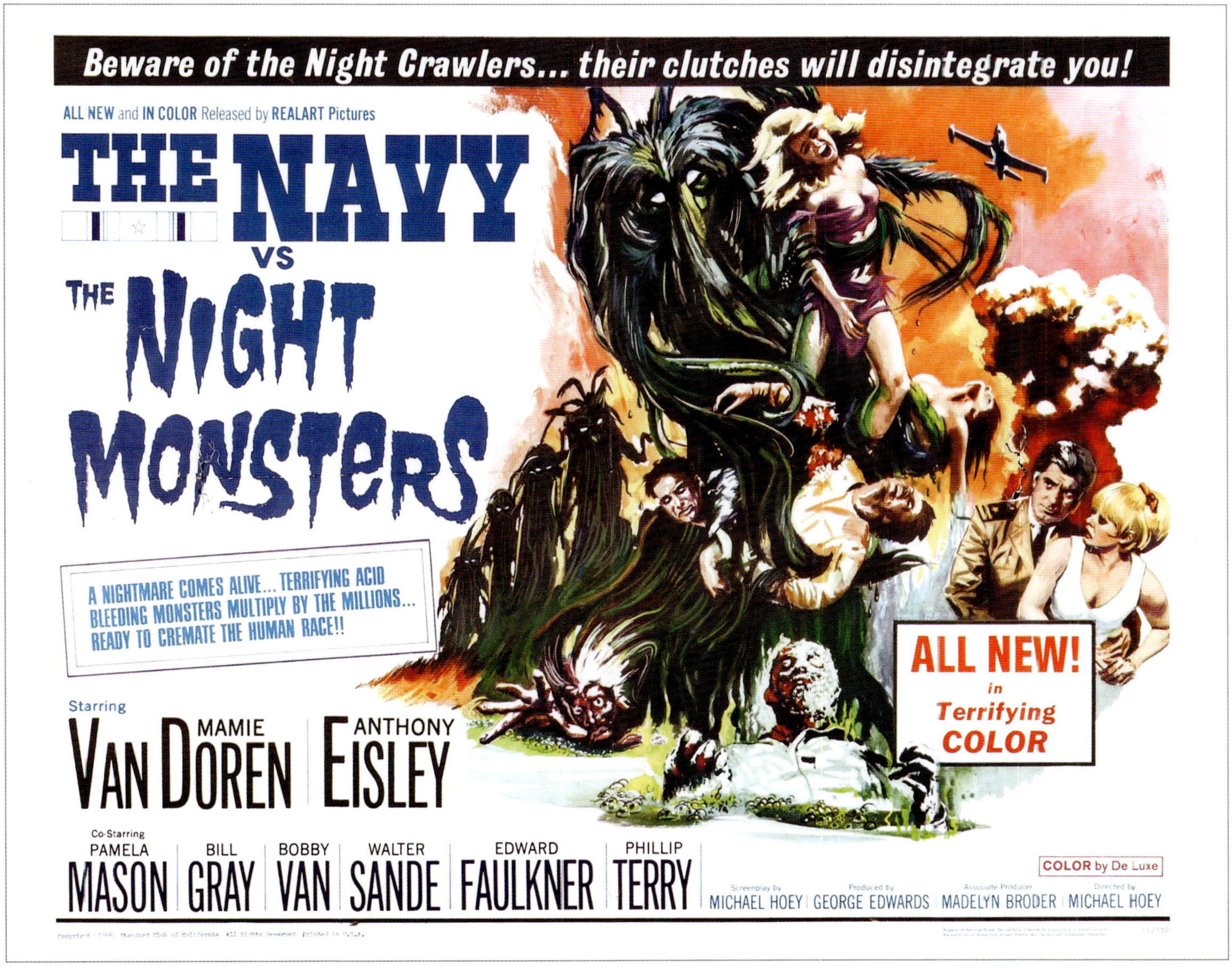
Beware of the Night Crawlers... their clutches will disintegrate you!
ALL NEW and IN COLOR Released by REALART Pictures
THE NAVY
VS
THE NIGHT MONSTERS
A NIGHTMARE COMES ALIVE... TERRIFYING ACID BLEEDING MONSTERS MULTIPLY BY THE MILLIONS... READY TO CREMATE THE HUMAN RACE!!
ALL NEW! in Terrifying COLOR
Starring
MAMIE VAN DOREN
ANTHONY EISLEY
Co-Starring
PAMELA MASON
BILL GRAY
BOBBY VAN
WALTER SANDE
EDWARD FAULKNER
PHILLIP TERRY
COLOR by De Luxe
Screenplay by MICHAEL HOEY
Produced by GEORGE EDWARDS
Associate Producer MADELYN BRODER
Directed by MICHAEL HOEY

YOU ARE THERE IN SPACE BEYOND SPACE!
You will probe the unknown... beyond the mysteries of the sixth sense...Your deepest, gravest fears dug up and pitted against you...Travel X times faster than imagination and...
journey to the seventh planet
in color
STARRING JOHN AGAR · GRETA THYSSEN · ANN SMYRNER · MIMI HEINRICH · screenplay by SIDNEY PINK and IB MELCHOIR • produced and directed by SIDNEY PINK • a CINEMAGIC production • an AMERICAN INTERNATIONAL PICTURE

PARAMOUNT presenta
ROBINSON CRUSOE EN MARTE
TECHNICOLOR
LA EPOPEYA DE LA ERA DEL ESPACIO: UN ASTRONAUTA SOLITARIO LLEGA A MARTE Y LUCHA ARDUAMENTE PARA SOBREVIVIR SIN OXIGENO, COMIDA NI AGUA

A lone U.S. astronaut
pitted against all the odds beyond this earth!
ROBINSON CRUSOE ON MARS
TECHNICOLOR
THIS FILM IS SCIENTIFICALLY AUTHENTIC ...IT IS ONLY ONE STEP AHEAD OF PRESENT REALITY!
SPACE-SHIP WRECKED IN THE SKY! ONLY HIS NERVE AND KNOW-HOW TO SAVE HIM!
Laser-beam Gun at the Ready for Any Weird Space Visitors That Come!
Angry Martian Fireballs Pursue Him Fiercely across Awesome Craters!
Trapped by Strange Volcanos under Deep, Dangerous Martian Canals!
Gasping His Last Oxygen Till He Stumbles on Life-giving Bloodstones!
TECHNISCOPE PAUL MANTEE · VICTOR LUNDIN and MONA, THE WOOLLY MONKEY · AUBREY SCHENCK · BYRON HASKIN · IB MELCHIOR and JOHN HIGGINS

YOU are in the FUTURE before it happens!
AMERICAN INTERNATIONAL presents
THE TIME TRAVELERS COLOR

IB MELCHIOR

Surely the only film director to have co-authored a book on Californian swimming pool design, the multitalented Ib Melchior (1917–2015) arrived in New York from his native Denmark in 1938. Awarded the Bronze Star for his service with US Army Counterintelligence in World War II, he became a fiction writer (his 1956 short story "The Racer" became the 1975 movie *Death Race 2000*), and film director, producer and screenwriter, with credits including *The Angry Red Planet* (1959), *Journey to the Seventh Planet* (1962), and *Robinson Crusoe on Mars* (1964). He also had a hand in creating *Lost in Space* (1965–68).

The Time Travelers (1964), a solid B-movie that he wrote and directed and which went on to inspire the TV series *The Time Tunnel* (1966), was an early credit for celebrated cinematographer Vilmos Zsigmond, and had a US one-sheet from Reynold Brown at the height of his powers, but is perhaps most notable for the story Melchior, ever the showman, was still telling well into his retirement: "In *The Time Travelers*, I explain how time travel could happen. I made it all up, but I thought it was plausible. One day, in the midst of the shooting, two gentlemen come, and say, 'We want to talk to you. Who told you about how time travel can be made?' I said, 'Nobody! I made it up.' Well it turned out that they were doing something called Predictor Instruments for the United States military, and the way that I explained my time travel was *exactly* what they were doing, so I had to take it out because of national security."

APOCALYPSE THEN

Filmgoers had a variety of apocalypses to choose from in the 1960s, including straight-up nuclear war in *Panic in the Year Zero!* (1962) and Toho's chilling *The Last War* (1961), and atomic tests sending the planet spiraling toward the sun in *The Day the Earth Caught Fire* (1961). Life after the end of civilization also continued to fascinate filmmakers: Roger Corman's *Last Woman on Earth* (1960) was self-explanatory, while the British absurdist fable *The Bed Sitting Room* (1969) defied easy summary. *The Last Man on Earth* (1964) was the first adaptation of Richard Matheson's 1954 novel of a vampiric plague, *I Am Legend*. Reynold Brown's one-sheet featured a rare use of a cross-hatching effect on its portrait of star Vincent Price. The gothic mansion added atmosphere, but was not in the film.

DO YOU DARE IMAGINE WHAT IT WOULD BE LIKE TO BE
...THE LAST MAN ON EARTH...OR THE LAST WOMAN?
Alive among the lifeless...alone among the crawling creatures
of evil that make the night hideous with their inhuman craving!
VINCENT PRICE
STARRING AS
The Last Man on Earth
CO-STARRING
FRANCA BETTOIA · EMMA DANIELI · GIACOMO ROSSI-STUART
Directed by
SIDNEY SALKOW
Produced by
ROBERT L. LIPPERT
Screenplay by
LOGAN SWANSON & WILLIAM F. LEICESTER
From the novel "I AM LEGEND" by
RICHARD MATHESON
AN AMERICAN INTERNATIONAL PICTURE

Nigel Kneale and Tom Chantrell

Though he had had great success adapting John Osborne's kitchen-sink dramas *Look Back in Anger* and *The Entertainer* for their film versions in 1958 and 1960 respectively, Nigel Kneale knew he was still typecast as a certain kind of writer when he was offered the chance to adapt H.G. Wells for *First Men in the Moon* (1964): "It wasn't that long since the last of the Quatermass things on television, so I suppose they thought, 'It's science fiction, get Kneale.'" The resulting movie was presented as a grand adventure, complete with stop-motion effects from Ray Harryhausen, but Kneale, whose script was rewritten by Jan Read, thought it was an opportunity missed: "They wanted to jazz it up, make it funnier than I had imagined… The saddest thing in any kind of fantasy film is if it drops from a sense of wonder… to a kind of comedy, knockabout, tongue-in-cheek thing. It's much harder to make something wonderful, and very often impossible; you get people going around in rubber suits looking important and pointing."

Kneale's own SF hero returned to the big screen in Hammer Films' *Quatermass and the Pit* (1967, a.k.a. *Five Million Years to Earth*). The UK quad (opposite top) was by Hammer's regular artist, the prolific Tom Chantrell (1916–2001). British film poster historian Sim Branaghan summarized Chantrell's skill: "Tom rarely saw the films he was paid to illustrate, considering this a waste of time. All he required was a synopsis and a handful of stills. He had a tremendous technical ability, and an instinctive feel for an eye-catching image. His best posters are a riot of brilliantly deployed color across epic, wonderfully composed canvases." Chantrell rarely spoke about his work, but once recalled: "I worked next door to Hammer and got on very well, it was a busy time and did a lot of work for them. I was sometimes working on five posters at one time." Though Kneale disapproved of screaming women on posters, Chantrell was unapologetic: "To be honest I'd rather draw the ladies, I was always better at drawing women, just loved them."

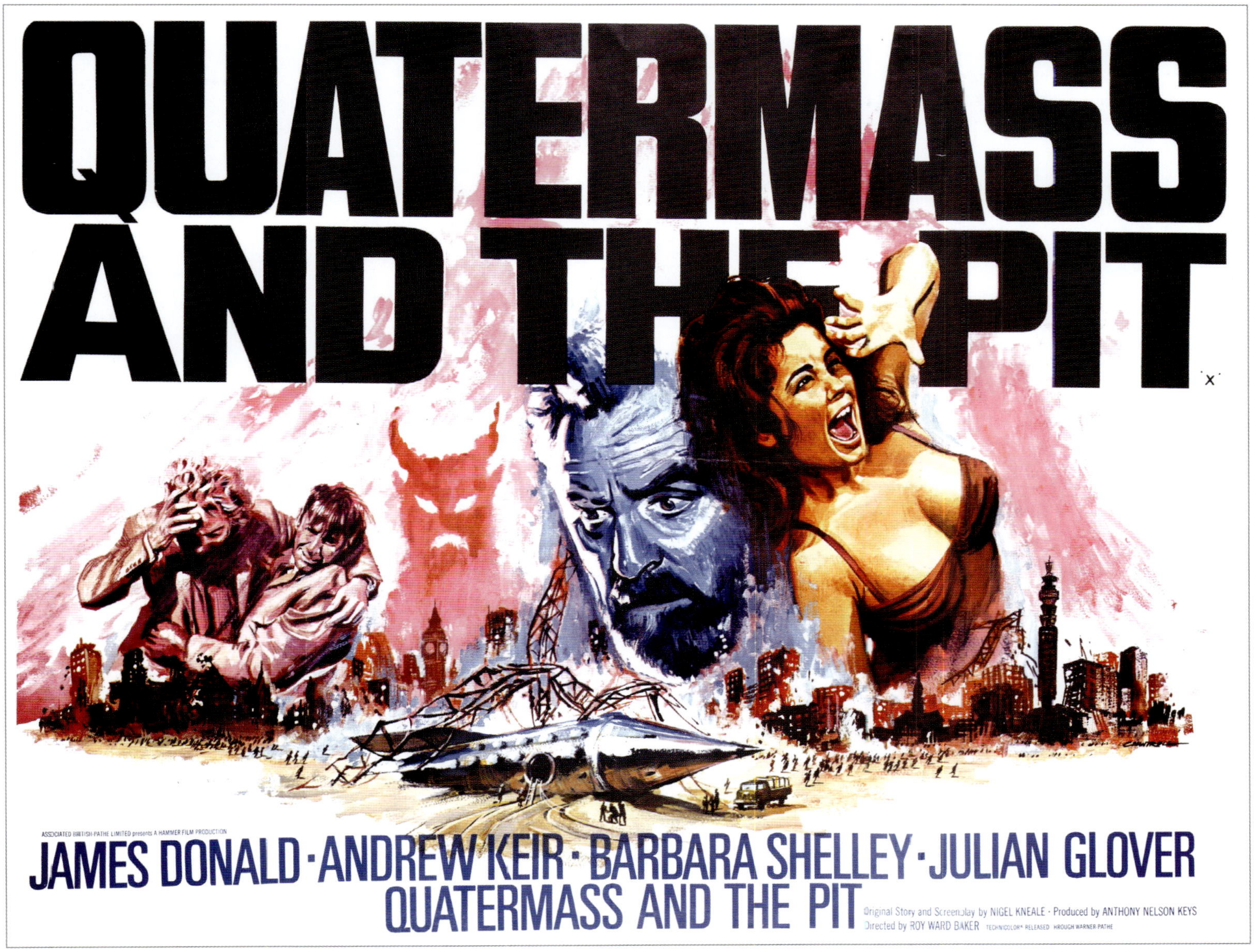

QUATERMASS AND THE PIT

X

ASSOCIATED BRITISH-PATHE LIMITED presents A HAMMER FILM PRODUCTION

JAMES DONALD · ANDREW KEIR · BARBARA SHELLEY · JULIAN GLOVER

QUATERMASS AND THE PIT

Original Story and Screenplay by NIGEL KNEALE · Produced by ANTHONY NELSON KEYS

Directed by ROY WARD BAKER TECHNICOLOR® RELEASED THROUGH WARNER PATHE

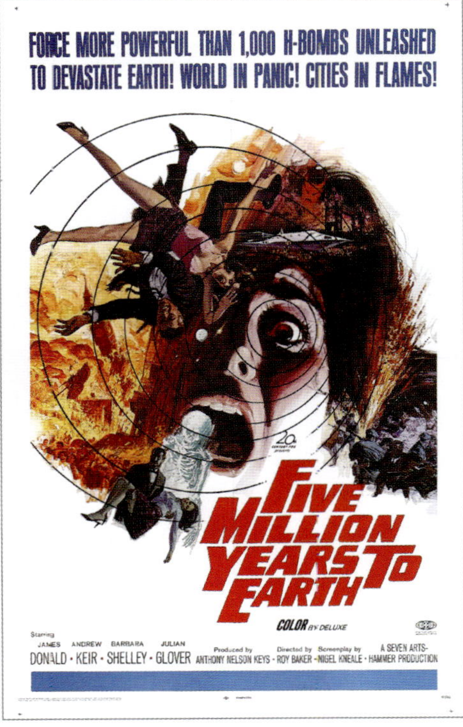

PERVERTED...SOULLESS! THE MOST DANGEROUS AND DIFFERENT MOTION PICTURE EVER BROUGHT TO THE SCREEN!
MICHAEL RELPH and BASIL DEARDEN'S
THE MIND BENDERS
STARRING
DIRK BOGARDE · MARY URE · JOHN CLEMENTS
Produced by MICHAEL RELPH · Directed by BASIL DEARDEN
Original Screenplay by JAMES KENNAWAY
AN AMERICAN INTERNATIONAL PICTURE

TERRIFYING WEIRD...MACABRE! Unseen things out of Time and Space!
UNEARTHLY STRANGER
AN AMERICAN INTERNATIONAL PICTURE
Starring
JOHN NEVILLE · GABRIELLA LICUDI · PHILIP STONE
Produced by ALBERT FENNELL · Directed by JOHN KRISH · Screenplay by REX CARLTON · A JULIAN WINTLE-LESLIE PARKYN PRODUCTION

LA GLOBE FILMS INTERNATIONAL PRESENTA
ANGLO AMALGAMATED FILM DISTRIBUTORS LTD
DIRK BOGARDE
MARY URE · JOHN CLEMENTS
IL CRANIO E IL CORVO
PRODOTTO DA MICHAEL RELPH
REGIA DI BASIL DEARDEN
SOGGETTO E SCENEGGIATURA DI JAMES KENNAWAY

EDWARD JUDD in
INVASION
'U'
YOKO TANI
VALERIE GEARON · LYNDON BROOK · TSAI CHIN · ERIC YOUNG

BRITISH Bs

The UK produced its fair share of SF B-movies, some of them unjustly forgotten. "When science is powerless and emotion takes control" was a surprisingly restrained "Catchline" suggested in the pressbook for *Unearthly Stranger* (1963), an unsettling drama featuring John Neville as a scientist who suspects his new wife is an alien. The suave Dirk Bogarde starred in the "Perverted... Soulless!" *The Mind Benders* (1963), a dour tale of sensory deprivation experiments (making it a direct forerunner of 1980's *Altered States*) that must have made a very odd double bill when AIP paired it in the US with *Operation Bikini* (1963). The alien incursion in *Invasion* (1965) was a low-budget affair, though the distributor paid extra for pink day-glo ink on the UK quad.

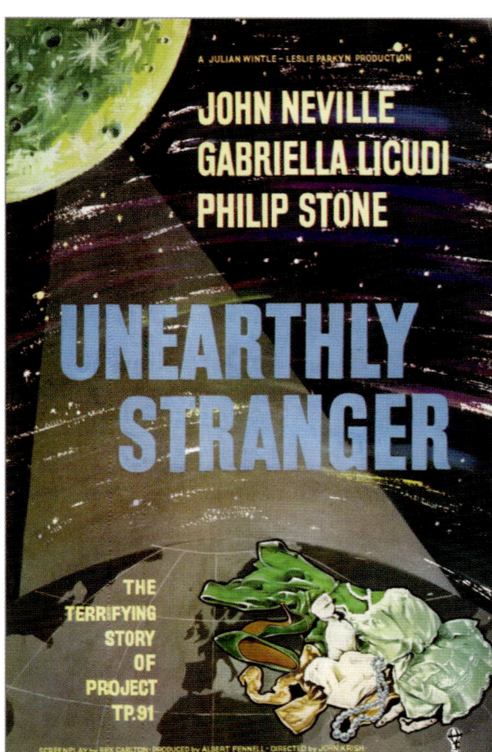

JOHN NEVILLE
GABRIELLA LICUDI
PHILIP STONE
UNEARTHLY
STRANGER
THE TERRIFYING STORY OF PROJECT TP.91

5 in. x 3 col. Price 14/6

JOHN NEVILLE
GABRIELLA LICUDI
PHILIP STONE
UNEARTHLY
STRANGER

6 in. x 1 col. Price 12/-

2 in. x 2 col. Price 8/-

2 in. x 1 col.
Price 7/-

CATCHLINES

A TENSE DRAMA OF HORRORS FROM THE UNKNOWN.

BEINGS FROM ANOTHER PLANET SENT TO DESTROY !

WHEN SCIENCE IS POWERLESS AND EMOTION TAKES CONTROL

A MASS MURDER OF SCIENTISTS WAS THEIR FIENDISH PLAN

WHAT UNEARTHLY AND FIENDISH FORCE CAN DRIVE A MAN TO THE VERY BRINK OF INSANITY ?

THE TERRIFYING STORY OF A POWER BEYOND SPACE THAT CAN CONTROL A HUMAN BRAIN

4 in. x 2 col. Price 11/6

PAGE SEVEN

SUSPENSE BEYOND ENDURANCE

What terrible sequence of events can destroy a respectable scientist at the very moment he completes his most important experiment ? The answer can be found in an astonishing new British suspense drama UNEARTHLY STRANGER now showing at the . . . . .

John Neville, one of Britain's leading stage actors, stars as a scientist who tries to unravel the mysterious death of his colleague engaged on Project TP 91—an experiment whereby man will be able to project himself through Time and Space. But because of his discoveries his life becomes a nightmare existence.

Exotic beauty Gabriella Licudi stars as his wife—a woman who becomes a stranger to him . . almost an unearthly stranger, when he discovers that she does not blink her eyelids, has no pulse, and can handle red hot metal with her bare hands.

Could there be a power beyond time and space that can control a human brain ? The Julian Wintle-Leslie Parkyn production UNEARTHLY STRANGER provides an answer in a film that carries suspense almost to the limit of human endurance. Also starring Philip Stone. UNEARTHLY STRANGER is produced by Albert Fennell, directed by John Krish and distributed by Anglo Amalgamated.

To reveal too much of the story would spoil audiences' enjoyment of this tension packed film.

PRESS ADS

JOHN NEVILLE
GABRIELLA LICUDI
PHILIP STONE
UNEARTHLY
STRANGER
THE TERRIFYING STORY OF PROJECT TP.91

6 in. x 2 col. Price 14/6

JOHN NEVILLE
GABRIELLA LICUDI
PHILIP STONE
UNEARTHLY
STRANGER

3 in. x 2 col. Price 10/6

PRICES QUOTED ARE FOR MATS, BUT BLOCKS CAN ALSO BE SUPPLIED.

PLEASE STATE CLEARLY WHEN ORDERING WHETHER MATS OR BLOCKS ARE REQUIRED.

PAGE SIX

DALEKS!

As the UK quad (above) by Bill Wiggins emphasizes, the evil denizens of Skaro triumphantly escaped the confines of black-and-white television in *Dr. Who and the Daleks* (1965), swiftly returning in *Daleks' Invasion Earth 2150 A.D.* (1966), this time accompanied by their grim-faced Robomen minions (Wiggins's stunning UK quad design was, not surprisingly, copied on the international posters).

The Daleks were originally created for TV's *Doctor Who* (1963–) by writer Terry Nation, who became a royalties millionaire when "Dalekmania" merchandising took off. The actual design came from BBC staff member Raymond Cusick, who was begrudgingly awarded an ex-gratia payment of £100. Mind you, he wouldn't even have got that had he not been covering for the designer originally scheduled for the job: a young fella named Ridley Scott.

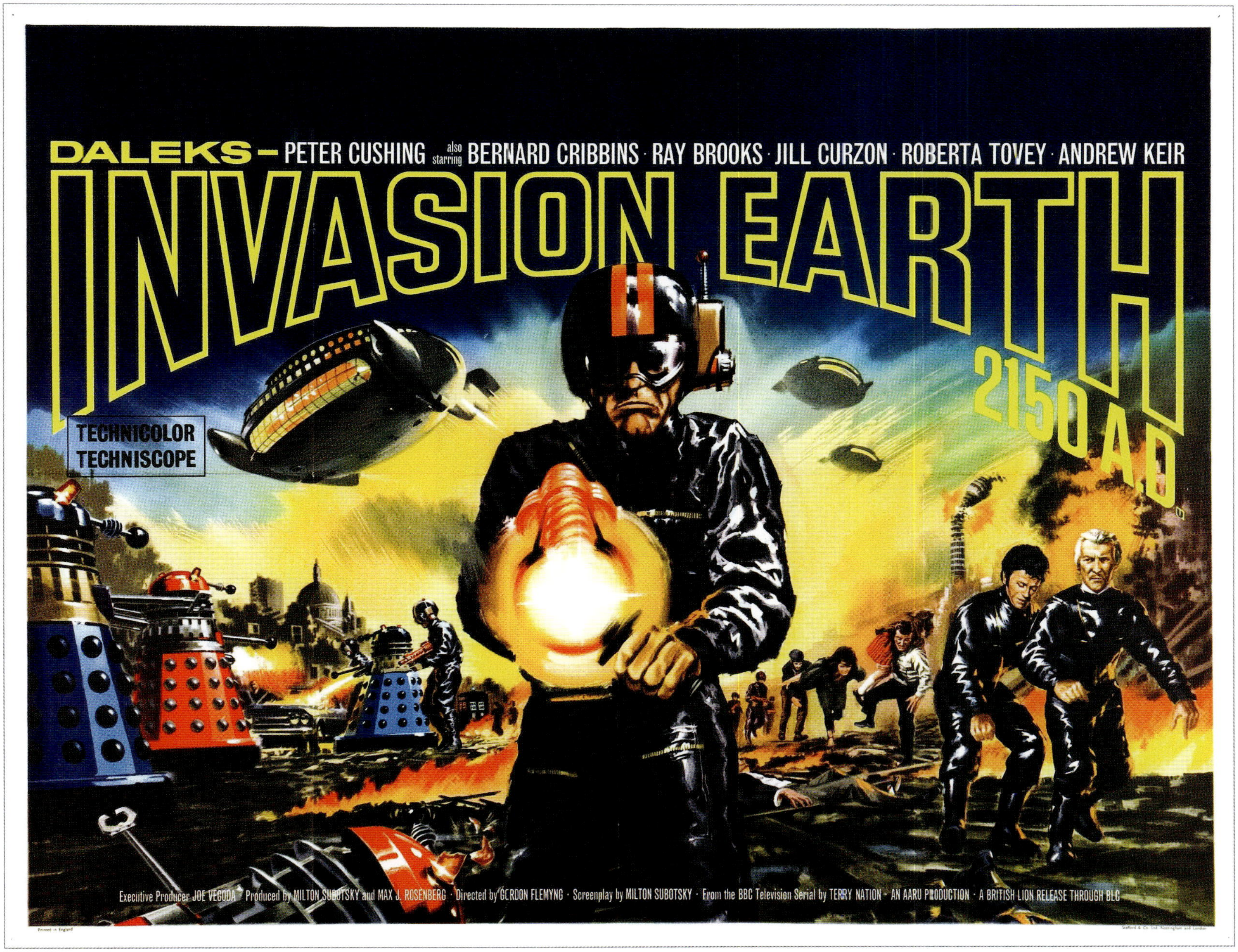
DALEKS – PETER CUSHING also starring BERNARD CRIBBINS · RAY BROOKS · JILL CURZON · ROBERTA TOVEY · ANDREW KEIR
INVASION EARTH
2150 A.D.
TECHNICOLOR
TECHNISCOPE
Executive Producer JOE VEGODA · Produced by MILTON SUBOTSKY and MAX J. ROSENBERG · Directed by GORDON FLEMYNG · Screenplay by MILTON SUBOTSKY · From the BBC Television Serial by TERRY NATION · AN AARU PRODUCTION · A BRITISH LION RELEASE THROUGH BLC

LES DALEKS
ENVAHISSENT LA TERRE
(Daleks · Invasion Earth 2150 A.D.)
TECHNICOLOR
TECHNISCOPE
PETER CUSHING
BERNARD CRIBBINS · RAY BROOKS · JILL CURZON · ROBERTA TOVEY · ANDREW KEIR

WHO WERE THESE DEMONS FROM ANOTHER WORLD??
PETER CUSHING also starring BERNARD CRIBBINS · RAY BROOKS
JILL CURZON · ROBERTA TOVEY · ANDREW KEIR
DALEKS -
INVASION
EARTH
2150 A.D.
TECHNICOLOR
TECHNISCOPE
FOR GENERAL EXHIBITION

DALEKS
IL FUTURO FRA UN MILIONE DI ANNI
New Arts Associates Inc. s.r.l. presenta
PETER CUSHING nel film
con BERNARD CRIBBINS - RAY BROOKS
JILL CURZON - ROBERTA TOVEY - ANDREW KEIR
REGIA: GORDON FLEMYNG
TECHNICOLOR - TECHNISCOPE

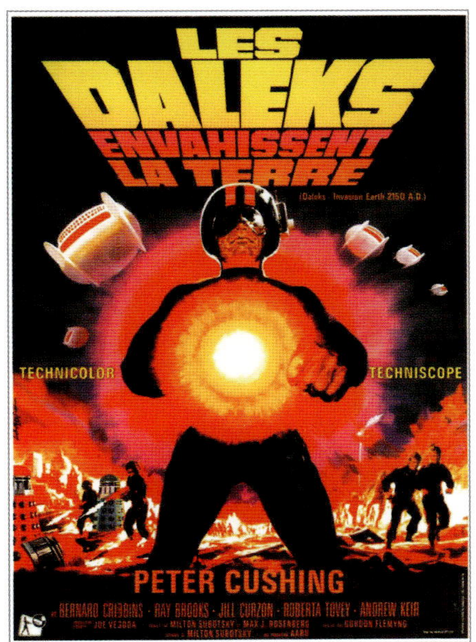

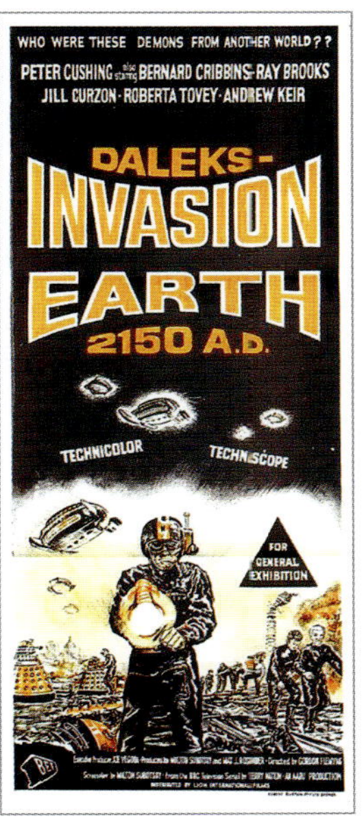

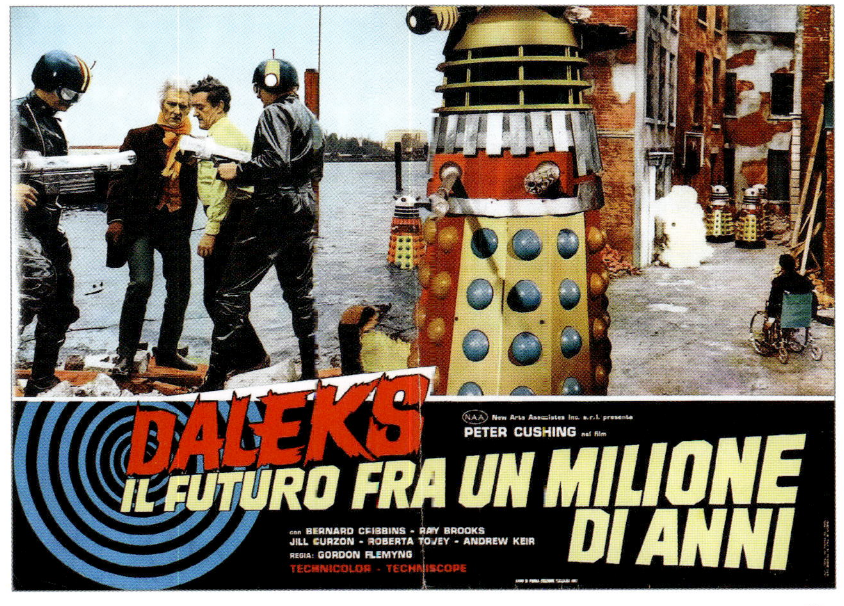

ALPHAVILLE

Jean-Luc Godard's *Alphaville* (1965) was shot in black and white, as befits a film which mixes the iconography of *film noir* with an SF story. Though Kiroku Higaki's Japanese poster (above center), Andrzej Krajewski in Poland (above right), and the unsigned Danish poster (bottom right) introduced color, the French *grande* (opposite) unapologetically embraced the monochrome aesthetic. Artist Jean Mascii (1926–2003) created over 1,500 film posters from the 1950s to the '80s. His home country's newspaper *Libération* described him as an artist who helped forge "the classic 'grammar' of posters: the hero's face stands out against a series of sketches illustrating the twists and turns of the plot." Mascii himself noted, "I worked in gouache, perfectly suited to reproduction in lithography. I was given a synopsis or photo sets and I would get to it."

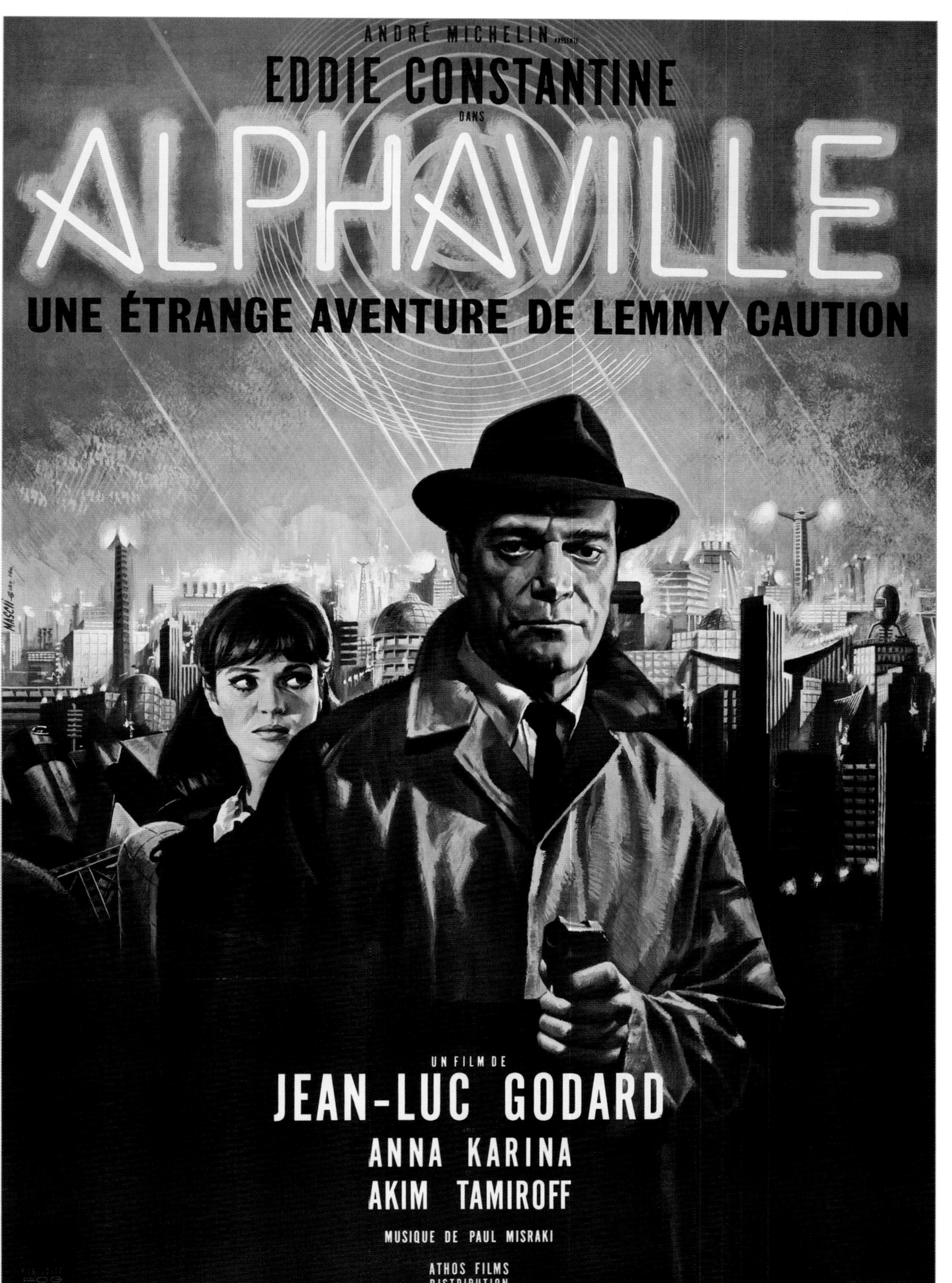
ANDRÉ MICHELIN PRÉSENTE
EDDIE CONSTANTINE
DANS
ALPHAVILLE
UNE ÉTRANGE AVENTURE DE LEMMY CAUTION
UN FILM DE
JEAN-LUC GODARD
ANNA KARINA
AKIM TAMIROFF
MUSIQUE DE PAUL MISRAKI
ATHOS FILMS
DISTRIBUTION

Frankenheimer's Identity Crisis

John Frankenheimer directed two films in the '60s that dealt with identity and self-determination, both mental and physical. In *The Manchurian Candidate* (1962), a US soldier doesn't realize he's been reprogrammed as an assassin by an international communist conspiracy—it didn't hurt the box office that the film opened at the height of Cuban missile crisis. *Seconds* (1966), described by *Time Out New York* as "easily one of the most subversive films ever to have come out of Hollywood," featured an unfulfilled banker paying "The Company" to receive a new identity, complete with surgically altered face, teeth, and fingerprints. What could possibly go wrong? In Japan, Hiroshi Teshigahara's contemporaneous *The Face of Another* (1966) featured a burn victim receiving a lifelike prosthetic mask rather than plastic surgery, but the narrative themes were similar, as was the poster (opposite bottom right).

ROCK HUDSON
IN THE JOHN FRANKENHEIMER FILM
SECONDS
'X'

A telephone connected to the grave told him a sweet and terrible secret.

A JOEL PRODUCTIONS INC. PRESENTATION
CO-STARRING
SALOME JENS / WILL GEER / SCREENPLAY BY LEWIS JOHN CARLINO
BASED ON A NOVEL BY DAVID ELY / PRODUCED BY EDWARD LEWIS / DIRECTED BY JOHN FRANKENHEIMER
PRODUCED IN ASSOCIATION WITH GIBRALTAR PRODUCTIONS INC.

Printed in England
S. & D. S. Ltd.

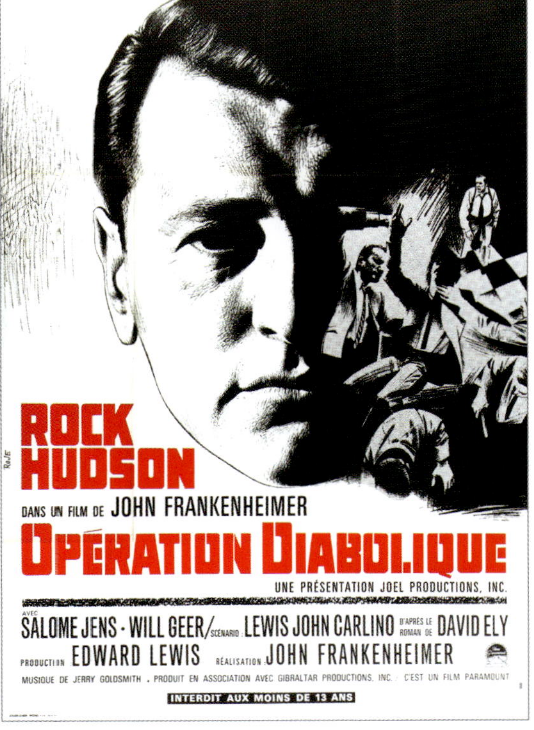

FAHRENHEIT 451

French New Wave director François Truffaut spent years trying to film Ray Bradbury's 1953 novel of a book-burning future. Paul Newman, Jean-Paul Belmondo, and Peter O'Toole all came and went. Terence Stamp was cast, but dropped out when he feared being upstaged by Julie Christie in a dual role (see tie-in book cover, left). Eventual lead actor Oskar Werner was argumentative during the shoot, and when *Fahrenheit 451* finally came out in 1966, its dystopian thunder had been stolen by *Alphaville* (1965). Truffaut called it the "saddest and most difficult" experience of his career. Plus, he'd turned down *Bonnie and Clyde* (1967) to make it.

By minimizing the obvious flames motif, two international poster designs stood out: Kemény György's pop art approach in Hungary (above right), and Kiroku Higaki's photo montage for Japan (opposite), which focused on the film's fashionable young stars, also picturing its equally cool director.

もし、この世界から文字が抹殺されたら？
FRANCOIS TRUFFAUT
極度に発達した物質文明の未来社会を鋭く描いた問題作！
フランソワ・トリュフォー監督作品
華氏451
テクニカラー
JULIE CHRISTIE OSKAR WERNER
"fahrenheit 451"
TECHNICOLOR
From the world famed novel by
RAY BRADBURY
Directed by
FRANCOIS TRUFFAUT
ジュリー・クリスティ
オスカー・ウェルナー
シリル・キューサック
アントン・ディフリング
ジェレミー・スペンサー
アレックス・スコット
文部省選定
ユニヴァーサル映画
映倫

QUEEN OF BLOOD

When he acquired the US distribution rights to the Soviet SF film *Nebo Zovyot* (1959), producer Roger Corman made sure he got his money's worth. An Americanized redub/re-edit, overseen by a young film school student called Francis Ford Coppola, was released as *Battle Beyond the Sun* in 1962. He then tasked writer/director Curtis Harrington to make a new film using chunks of special effects footage from it, which became *Queen of Blood* (1966). Shot in just six days, it's an SF/horror tale that has been seen as a precursor to *Alien* (1979). Harrington certainly thought so: "Ridley's film is like a greatly enhanced, expensive and elaborated version of *Queen of Blood*." As Kim Newman has pointed out, though, the scenario of a crew confined on a ship with a monster picking them off in turn can be traced back to the *Demeter* episode in Bram Stoker's *Dracula*.

HIDEOUS BEYOND BELIEF...
with an INHUMAN CRAVING!
AMERICAN INTERNATIONAL'S
QUEEN OF BLOOD
IN PATHÉCOLOR
STARRING
JOHN SAXON · BASIL RATHBONE · JUDI MEREDITH
CO-STARRING
DENNIS HOPPER · Written and Directed by CURTIS HARRINGTON · Produced by GEORGE EDWARDS · AN AMERICAN INTERNATIONAL PICTURE

Constantin Belinsky

Like many European movie poster artists from the last century, the available biographical details are thin: Ukrainian-born Constantin Belinsky (1904–99) arrived in Paris in 1925 and became a sculptor of female nudes, but is best known for his work from 1930 into the '70s painting thousands of film posters across all genres (often signed simply "CB"). As this small SF selection shows, his style was instantly recognizable—expressive, immediate, and always with the brightest of color palettes.

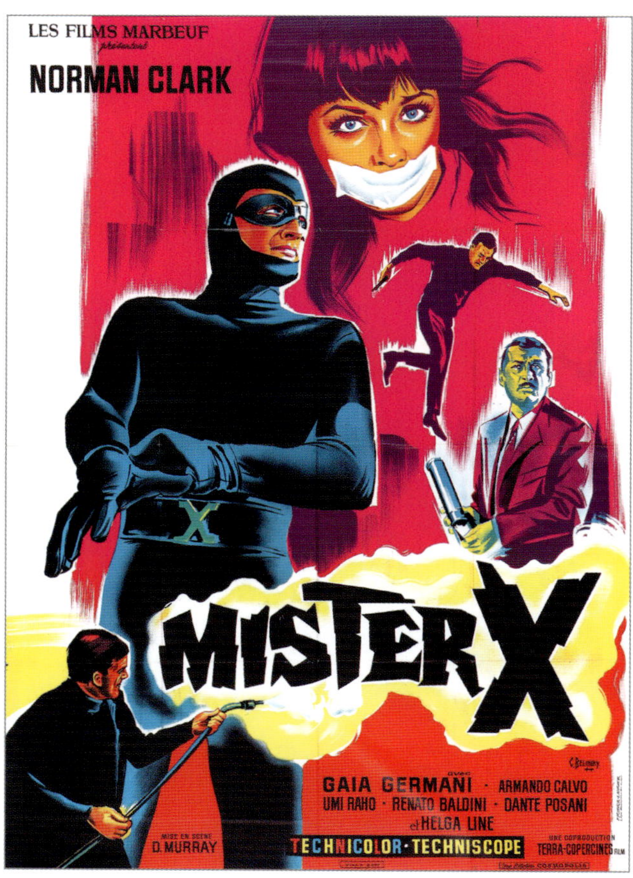

LES FILMS MARBEUF
présentent
LES
ENVAHISSEURS
ATTAQUENT
AKIRA KUBO · JUN TAZAKI · ANDREW HUGHS · YUKIKO KOBAYASHI
MISE EN SCENE
I. HONDA
Une Sélection COSMOPOLIS
EASTMANCOLOR - CINEMASCOPE
VISA N° 5830
PRODUCTION
TOHO COMPANY LIT.

FANTASTIC FOGLIO

Italian film poster design arguably reached its apotheosis in the 1960s. Whether produced for initial releases, or as new campaigns for re-releases of older movies (as with 1951's *The Lost Continent*, above left, and *This Island Earth*, above right), the artwork at its best combined supreme technical skill with a level of imagination and visual impact that the films themselves often struggled to match. Sometimes this involved playing fast and loose with the actual content of the plot, whether ignoring it entirely (the *This Island Earth* poster has very little to do with the film), or "enhancing" it: Sandro Simeoni's art (opposite) for the early '60s release of *4D Man* (1959) suggests that Robert Lansing's character has fangs, which he doesn't onscreen, though to be fair the fourth-dimensional scientist does become an energy vampire of sorts.

The popular formats of the 39-by-55-inch two-*fogli* (sheet) and 55-by-78-inch four-*fogli* were dramatically larger than the standard 27-by-41-inch US one-sheet, and as an added bonus for collectors, each usually featured entirely different artwork, as with Mario Piovano's posters (overleaf and page 241, top left) for the 1968 re-release of *Rodan* (1957).

WARNER BROS.
COLOR DELUXE
DELITTO IN
4ª DIMENSIONE
ROBERT LANSING · LEE MERIWETHER · JAMES CONGDON
REGIA DI IRVIN SHORTESS YEAWORTH, Jr.
SCENEGGIATURA DI THEODORE SIMONSON E CY CHERMAK
PRODOTTO DA JACK H. HARRIS · UNA PRODUZIONE FAIRVIEW

ESCLUSIVITA' ARDIN CINEMATOGRAFICA
RODAN
IL MOSTRO
ALATO
KENYI SAWARA
WILLIAM SCOTTY
RICHARD HIRATA
JOHN GARRY
REGIA: I. HONDA
SCHERMO PANORAMICO
TECHNICOLOR

ARDIN
CINEMATOGRAFICA
RODAN
IL MOSTRO
ALATO
KENYI SAWARA
WILLIAM SCOTTY
RICHARD HIRATA
JOHN GARRY
REGIA: I. HONDA
SCHERMO PANORAMICO
TECHNICOLOR

ALBERT DEKKER · JANICE LOGAN · THOMAS COLEY · CHARLES HALTON
nel film IL Dr. CYCLOPS:
IL MOSTRO ATOMICO
REGIA DI ERNEST SCHOEDSACK

LASER X: OPERAZIONE UOMO
MARY PEACH · BRYANT HALIDAY · NORMAN WOOLAND
RONALD ALLEN · DEREK FARR · TRACEY CRISP
LADY FILM
VINOD PATHAK
IAN CURTEIS
EASTMANCOLOR
TECHNISCOPE

LUCAS FILM
LE DONNE DEL PIANETA PREISTORICO
WENDELL COREY
KEITH LARSEN · JOHN AGAR · PAUL GILBERT
MERRY ANDERS · IRENE TSU
ARTHUR PIERRE
Colore de Luxe

LA VENDETTA DEL RAGNO NERO
ED KEMMER
JANE KENNEY
GENE PERSSON
REGIA
BERT I. GORDON

ANTONIO MARGHERITI

The SF films of Italian director Antonio Margheriti (1930–2002, a.k.a. Anthony Dawson) are practically their own subgenre, and have certainly been deemed worthy of academic attention. UK-based Professor of Continental Philosophy Patricia MacCormack described them as "extraordinarily odd without being laughable… Blow-up women, karate-expert alien bikini-girls, dwarves, disembodied sentient organs (specifically lungs), and op-art sets juxtaposed with environments which look as if they are being strangled by tentacles, are some of the ingeniously weird features of these films." *Battle of the Worlds* (1961) led to the space station "Gamma One" quartet, shot back-to-back with the same sets and actors: *The Wild, Wild Planet* (1966), *War of the Planets* (1966), *War Between the Planets* (1966), and *Snow Devils* (1967). Though Margheriti didn't direct, *The Green Slime* (1968) was a semi-sequel with the same deranged vibe, as seen in G.D. Stefano's Italian poster (opposite).

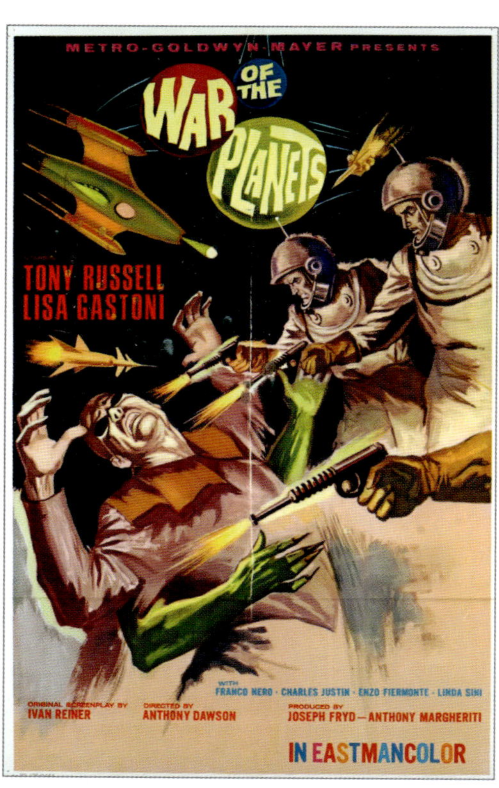

METRO GOLDWYN MAYER PRESENTA

il Fango Verde

(THE GREEN SLIME)

ROBERT HORTON · LUCIANA PALUZZI · RICHARD JAECKEL

SCENEGGIATURA DI CHARLES SINCLAIR, WILLIAM FINGER & TOM ROWE

PRODOTTO DA IVAN REINER & WALTER H. MANLEY DIRETTO DA KINJI FUKASAKU A COLORI

RETURN OF THE Bs

The cavalcade of cheap and cheerful SF B-movies continued into the '60s. Hammer Films' "space western" *Moon Zero Two* (1969) had posters with varied design approaches (opposite) but still flopped. As director Roy Ward Baker conceded, "It was undercut by the fact that you could turn on the television and see Neil Armstrong jumping about on the real moon." Sometimes the posters frankly looked as cheap as the movies: *The Beast of Yucca Flats* (1961) and *Monster A Go-Go!* (1965) had especially lamentable one-sheets (see page 247).

All the films in this selection (and indeed all the '50s B-movies on pages 174–77) have at least enjoyed a second lease of life, as the subjects of relentless mockery on the TV show *Mystery Science Theater 3000* (1988–).

WARNER BROS. présente

ALERTE SATELLITE 02

MOON ZERO TWO

JAMES OLSON
CATHERINA VON SCHELL
WARREN MITCHELL
ADRIENNE CORRI
ORI LEVY
DUDLEY FOSTER
BERNARD BRESSLAW

ALARM SATELIET 02

Régie ROY WARD BAKER
TECHNICOLOR

IMP. WAGRAM BRUXELLES tel. 17.48.81

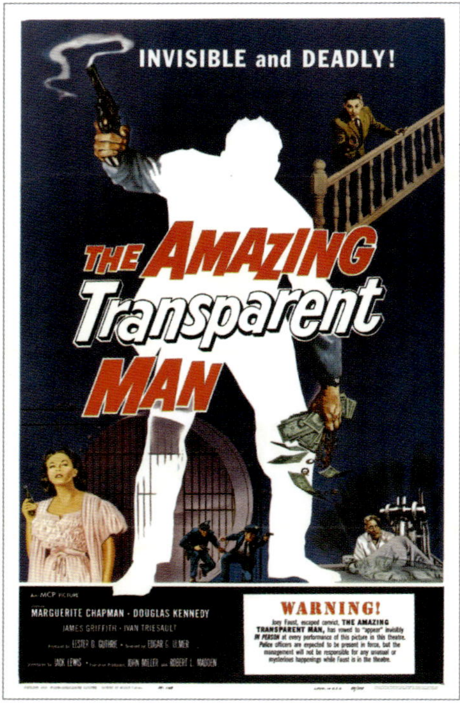

INVISIBLE and DEADLY!
THE AMAZING Transparent MAN
An MCP PICTURE
MARGUERITE CHAPMAN · DOUGLAS KENNEDY
JAMES GRIFFITH · IVAN TRIESAULT
WARNING!
Joey Faust, escaped convict, THE AMAZING TRANSPARENT MAN, has vowed to "appear" invisibly IN PERSON at every performance of this picture in this theatre. Police officers are expected to be present in force, but the management will not be responsible for any unusual or mysterious happenings while Faust is in the theatre.

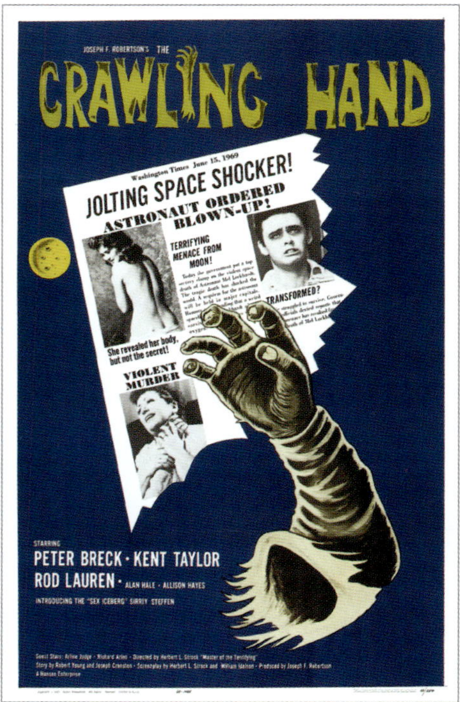

JOSEPH F. ROBERTSON'S THE
CRAWLING HAND
JOLTING SPACE SHOCKER!
ASTRONAUT ORDERED BLOWN-UP!
TERRIFYING MENACE FROM MOON!
TRANSFORMED?
She revealed her body, but not the secret!
VIOLENT MURDER
STARRING
PETER BRECK · KENT TAYLOR
ROD LAUREN · ALAN HALE · ALLISON HAYES
INTRODUCING THE "SEX ICEBERG" SIRRY STEFFEN

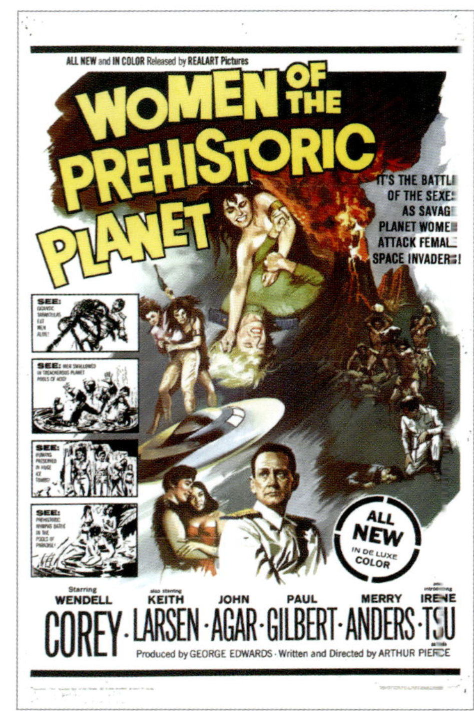

ALL NEW and IN COLOR Released by REALART Pictures
WOMEN OF THE PREHISTORIC PLANET
IT'S THE BATTL
OF THE SEXE
AS SAVAG
PLANET WOME
ATTACK FEMAL
SPACE INVADER
SEE:
SEE:
SEE:
SEE:
ALL NEW IN DE LUXE COLOR
Starring WENDELL COREY · also starring KEITH LARSEN · JOHN AGAR · PAUL GILBERT · MERRY ANDERS · IRENE TSU
Produced by GEORGE EDWARDS · Written and Directed by ARTHUR PIERCE

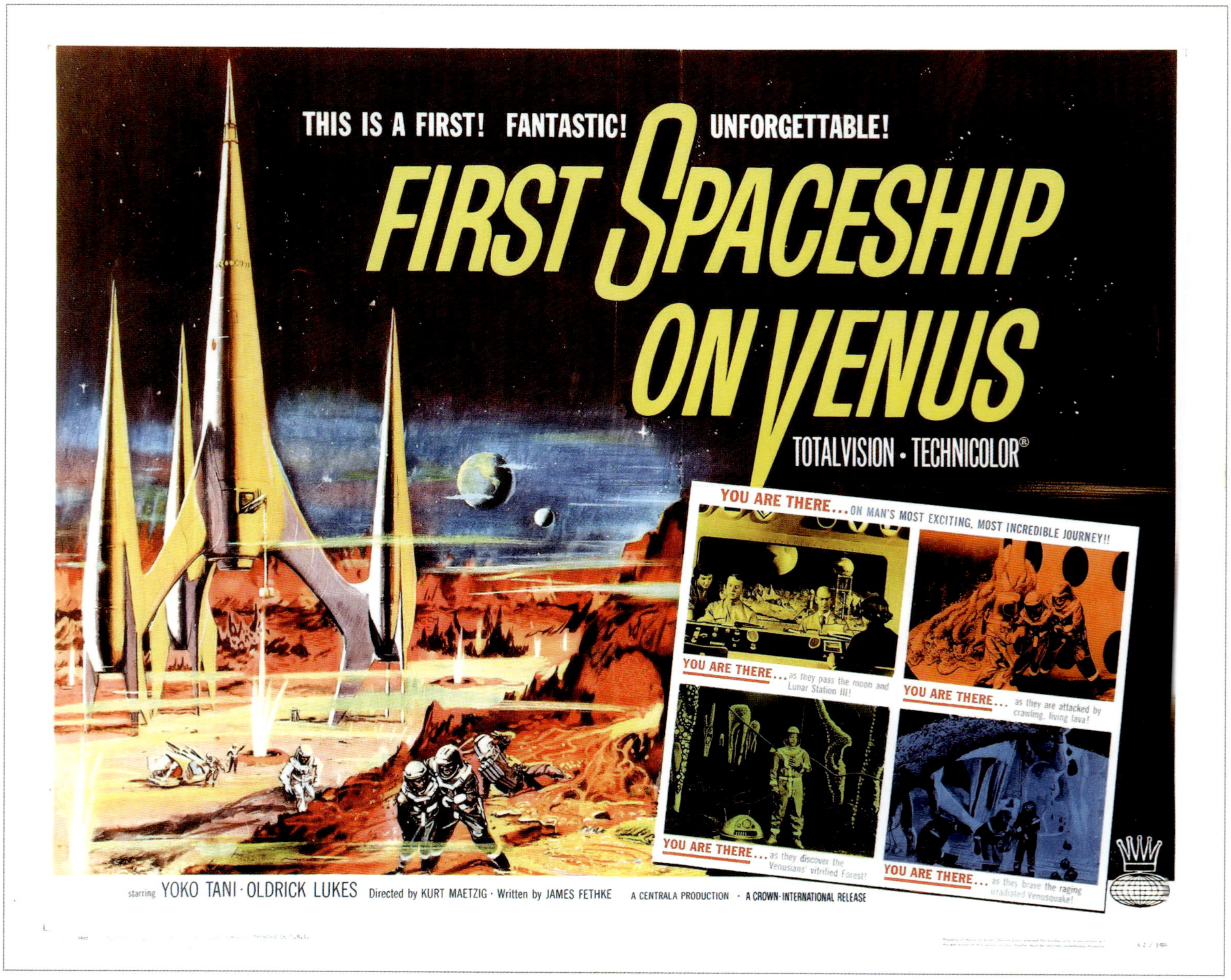
THIS IS A FIRST! FANTASTIC! UNFORGETTABLE!
FIRST SPACESHIP ON VENUS
TOTALVISION · TECHNICOLOR®
YOU ARE THERE... ON MAN'S MOST EXCITING, MOST INCREDIBLE JOURNEY!!
YOU ARE THERE... as they pass the moon and Lunar Station III!
YOU ARE THERE... as they are attacked by crawling, living lava!
YOU ARE THERE... as they discover the Venusians' vitrified Forest!
YOU ARE THERE... as they brave the raging irradiated Venusquake!
starring YOKO TANI · OLDRICK LUKES Directed by KURT MAETZIG · Written by JAMES FETHKE A CENTRALA PRODUCTION · A CROWN-INTERNATIONAL RELEASE

THE FANTASTIC SPACE-AGE SHOCK SHOW
NEW! NOT 3-D
THE FIRST PICTURE PROJECTED IN
ULTRA-DEPTH
NEW! UNLIKE ANYTHING BEFORE!
WE DARE YOU TO REMAIN SEATED AS GIGANTIC MARTIAN FIREBALLS CRASH OUT OF THE SCREEN AND EXPLODE OVER YOUR HEAD!
WE DOUBLE DARE YOU TO REMAIN IN THE THEATRE AS A TITANIC MARTIAN ELECTRICAL STORM CRASHES OUT INTO THE AUDIENCE!
WE TRIPLE DARE YOU TO RETAIN CONTROL OF YOUR MIND AS SCREECHING CREATURES ATTACK YOUR BRAIN!
K&H ORGANIZATION PRESENTS
A GIRL AND 3 MEN FACE HORRORS OF MARS!
2000 YEAR OLD CREATURES REFUSE TO DIE!
HAUNTED CITY OF THE DEAD!
THE WIZARD OF MARS
SPIKED PENDULUM OF DEATH AT THE CENTER OF TIME!
STARRING JOHN CARRADINE AS THE "WIZARD"
COLOR BY DE LUXE
ALSO STARRING ROGER GENTRY VIC McGEE and JERRY RANNOW AS CHARLIE with EVE BERNHARDT
STORY by DAVID L. HEWITT AND ARMANDO BUSICK WRITTEN-PRODUCED-DIRECTED by DAVID L. HEWITT

CARDOZA-FRANCIS "PRESENTS"
"THE BEAST OF YUCCA FLATS"
Starring
DOUGLAS MELLOR
BARBARA FRANCIS
LARRY ATEN
BING STAFFORD
Special Guest Star
TOR JOHNSON
playing a double Role as the Beast
Featuring
TONY CARDOZA » ERIC TOMLIN » MARCIA KNIGHT
With JOHN MORRISON » JIM OLIPHANT » LINDA BEILEMA
GEORGE PRINCE » ALAN & RONALD FRANCIS
WRITTEN & DIRECTED BY
COLEMAN FRANCIS
PRODUCED BY
ANTHONY CARDOZA
A CINEMA ASSOCIATES RELEASE

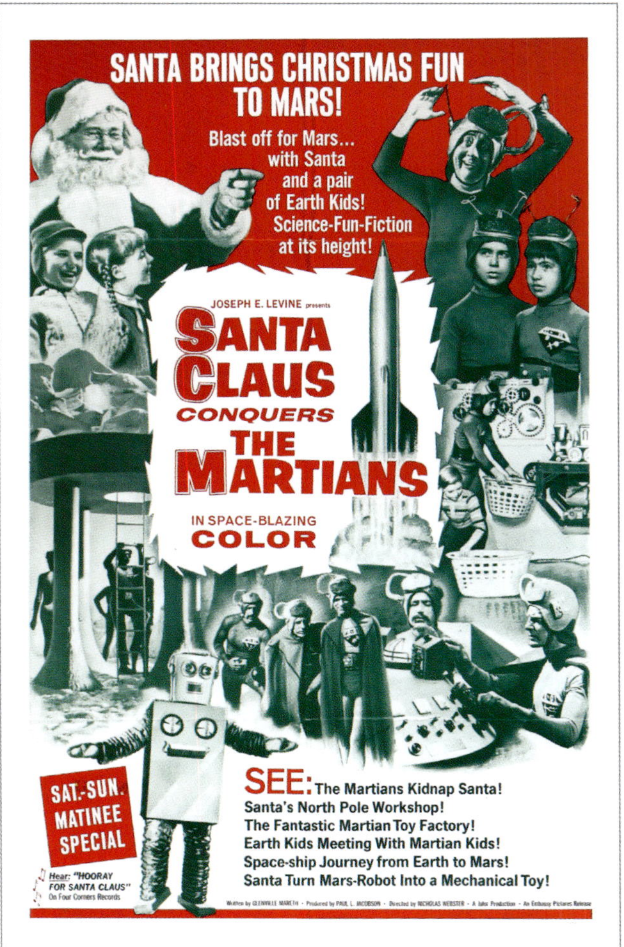

SANTA BRINGS CHRISTMAS FUN TO MARS!
Blast off for Mars... with Santa and a pair of Earth Kids! Science-Fun-Fiction at its height!
JOSEPH E. LEVINE presents
SANTA CLAUS CONQUERS THE MARTIANS
IN SPACE-BLAZING COLOR
SAT.-SUN. MATINEE SPECIAL
SEE: The Martians Kidnap Santa!
Santa's North Pole Workshop!
The Fantastic Martian Toy Factory!
Earth Kids Meeting With Martian Kids!
Space-ship Journey from Earth to Mars!
Santa Turn Mars-Robot Into a Mechanical Toy!
Hear: "HOORAY FOR SANTA CLAUS" On Four Corners Records

"THIS PICTURE COULD SET OUR SPACE PROGRAM BACK AT LEAST FIFTY YEARS!"
-N.A.S.A.
MONSTER A GO-GO!
(the picture that comes complete with a 10-foot-tall monster, to give you the wim-wams!)
starring
PHIL MORTON
JUNE TRAVIS
AN ASTRONAUT WENT UP—
A "GUESS-WHAT"
CAME DOWN!
RELEASED BY B I & L RELEASING CORP.

MEXICAN MADNESS

In addition to releasing Hollywood's output, Mexico has a fascinating history of homegrown SF movies, a small sampling of which appears on the following pages. *La Nave de los Monstruos* (The Ship of Monsters, 1960) is as good an example as any of the bizarre delights of the Mexican version of the genre: a baffling mix which includes swim-suited Venusians on the hunt for male aliens, a smart-aleck robot, a vampire, a Cyclops, and a singing cowboy. As online critic Dennis Schwartz warned, "The more you think you understand, the less you actually do." Though there are uniquely Mexican elements that make their way into the films—not least the masked wrestler *lucha libre* heroes Blue Demon and Santo, whose ongoing franchises often veered into SF territory—it's the local take on US genre tropes that often stand out. This might be a version of Batwoman unlikely to be approved of by DC Comics, in *The Batwoman* (*La mujer murcielago*, 1968), or poster designs which reference American originals—compare the *La Nave de los Monstruos* poster (left) with *Destination Moon* on p78, and *Santo vs la invasion de los marcianos* (Santo vs the Invasion of the Martians, 1967) on page 251 with *Robinson Crusoe on Mars* on page 218.

¡JUSTICIERA!
MAURA MONTI
ROBERTO CAÑEDO · HECTOR GODOY
DAVID SILVA · CROX ALVARADO
CINEMATOGRAFICA CALDERON, S. A. presenta
LA MUJER MURCIELAGO
(BAT-WOMAN)
A COLORES
¡INVENCIBLE!
¡PODEROSA!
¡AUDAZ!
¡VALIENTE!
¡SEDUCTORA!
¡TEMERARIA!
FOTOGRAFIA SUBMARINA de Genaro Hurtado
Director RENE CARDONA
PRINTED IN MEXICO - IMPRESO EN MEXICO
www.zomboscloset.com

CINEMATOGRAFICA RA, S. A. presenta a:
BLUE DEMON · REGINA TORNE
AGUSTIN MARTINEZ SOLARES
ENRIQUE AGUILAR en
BLUE DEMON Y LAS INVASORAS
con
OSCAR MORELI
GRISELDA MEJIA · SANDRA BOYD
actuación especial de GINA MORETT
A COLORES
Dirección de GILBERTO MARTINEZ SOLARES
ARS UNA

LA CONQUISTA DE LA LUNA
en esta sensacional película
A COLORES
DOS COLOSOS ENFRENTANDOSE EN LUCHA SUICIDA!
SANTO
EL ENMASCARADO DE PLATA
contra BLUE DEMON en la ATLANTIDA
con JORGE RADO · RAFAEL BANQUELLS · AGUSTIN MARTINEZ SOLARES
Cinedrama: G. TRAVESI · Una película de JESUS SOTOMAYOR
Dirección de JULIAN SOLER

CLAVILLAZO ★ ANA LUISA PELUFFO
en
CONQUISTADOR de la LUNA
DIRECTOR: ROGELIO A. GONZALEZ ★ ARGUMENTO: JOSE MARIA FERNANDEZ UNSAIN
PRESENTADA POR:
DIST. SOTOMAYOR, S. A. · Estudios Churubusco · México, D. F.

Guillermo Murray
Adriana Roel
Rogelio Guerra · Jose Chavez
'Ferrusquilla' · Evita Muñoz
Jaqueline Felay
GIGANTES PLANETARIOS
C1368

LORENA VELAZQUEZ
GUILLERMO MURRAY
EL PLANETA DE LAS MUJERES INVASORAS
Elizabeth Campbell Maura Monti Adriana Roel
"Ferrusquilla" Rogelio Guerra Raul Ramirez
C1380

ESTUDIOS AMERICA, S.A. y PRODUCCIONES CORSA, S.A. presentan:
WOLF RUVINSKIS
JULIO ALEMAN
ARMANDO SILVESTRE
CON
ROSITA ARENAS
"NEUTRON CONTRA EL DR. CARONTE"
"EL TESTAMENTO DEL DR. CARONTE" y "FRENTE A FRENTE"
DE LA SENSACIONAL SERIE Neutrón "EL ENMASCARADO NEGRO"
BETO EL BOTICARIO · RODOLFO LANDA · ARMANDO BIANCHI · GRECK MARTIN
DAVID LAMA · "LOS DIAMANTES" · "LOS ASES" · "LOS REBELDES DEL ROCK"
Fotg. FERNANDO COLIN · Arg. y Adapt. ALFREDO RUANOVA · Música ENRICO CABIATI · Direc. FEDERICO CURIEL

¡SOLO SU VALOR, SU AUDACIA Y SU HEROISMO PUEDEN SALVAR A LA HUMANIDAD DEL FIN MAS TERRIBLE Y ESPANTOSO!
BLUE DEMON
DESTRUCTOR DE ESPIAS
A COLORES
con BLUE DEMON · CARLOS EAST · MAURA MONTI · artista invitado ALMA DELIA FUENTES
HECTOR GOMEZ · GUILLERMO ZETINA · JORGE RADO y BRUNO REY
Cinedrama: Alfredo Ruanova y Emilio Gómez Muriel · Director: EMILIO GOMEZ MURIEL
www.zomboscloset.com

SANTO
EL ENMASCARADO DE PLATA
en
SANTO VS.
LA INVASION DE LOS MARCIANOS
con WOLF RUVINSKIS - EL NAZI - BENI GALAN - HAM LEE - EDUARDO BONADA
ANTONIO MONTORO
RAFAEL GARCIA TRAVESI
MAURA MONTI - EVA NORVIND BELINDA CORELL - GILDA MIROS
DIRECCION ALFREDO B. CREVENNA
PRINTED IN MEXICO - IMPRESO EN MEXICO

MARIO BAVA

Though Mario Bava (1914–80) was only credited as cinematographer, his first film as director was *The Day the Sky Exploded* (*La morte viene dallo spazio*, 1958), which was also Italy's first SF movie. By 1965, AIP, who had distributed Bava's gothic horrors *Black Sunday* (1960) and *Black Sabbath* (1963) in the US, partnered with the director up-front to co-produce *Planet of the Vampires*, an SF/horror hybrid that has had a huge legacy, even if it was made on the cheap. Bava recalled: "Do you know what that planet was made of? A couple of plastic rocks—yes, two: one and one!—left over from a mythological movie made at [Rome studio] Cinecittà. To assist the illusion, I filled the set with smoke." That foreboding atmosphere, and elements of the plot have influenced successive generations of filmmakers. *Alien* (1979) "stole the giant skeleton from the *Planet of the Vampires*," admitted co-writer Dan O'Bannon, while director James Wan enthused that *Aquaman and the Lost Kingdom* (2023) was "very heavily inspired" by the film.

DISTRIBUZIONE
SIDIS
TERRORE NELLO SPAZIO
CON BARRY SULLIVAN NORMA BENGELL ANGEL ARANDA EVI MARANDI
E CON STANLEY KENT FRANCO ANDREI FERNANDO VILLENA MARIO MORALES IVAN RASSIMOV MASSIMO RIGHI RICO BOIDO ALBERTO CEVENINI
REGIA DI MARIO BAVA
TECHNICOLOR WIDESCREEN
UNA PRODUZIONE ITALIAN INTERNATIONAL FILM - ROMA COOPERATIVA CASTILLA CINEMATOGRAFICA - MADRID
REALIZZATA DA FULVIO LUCISANO
TRATTO DAL RACCONTO "UNA NOTTE DI 21 ORE" DI RENATO PESTRINIERO PUBBLICATO SUL N. 3 DI "INTERPLANET" ANTOLOGIA DI FANTASCIENZA

GERRY ANDERSON

"Adults over the age of 16 should be accompanied by children" was the charming instruction on the UK quad by Bill Wiggins for *Thunderbirds Are Go!* (1966). Writer/producer Gerry Anderson's hugely successful puppet-based British TV series was filmed in color, but the theatrical spin-off was nevertheless billed as "in colour!" as TV broadcasting was monochrome-only in the UK until 1969. The Italian poster (opposite), based on the alternate UK quad, focused on the Zero-X ship rather than the International Rescue craft that were less familiar in that territory.

Anderson (1929–2012) used real actors in *Journey to the Far Side of the Sun* (1969, a.k.a. *Doppelgänger*), an intriguing "adult" tale about astronauts finding a mirror image Earth—an effect achieved by flopping the negative! The film also flopped at the box office, alas, despite some effective poster designs, including Jan Mlodozeniec's primary colors in Poland (below center).

1
THUNDERBIRDS
I CAVALIERI DELLO SPAZIO
PRODOTTO DA
REGIA DI
DI GERRY ANDERSON · SYLVIA ANDERSON · DAVID LANE
UNITED ARTISTS
Transamerica
DEAR FILM
SUPERMARIONATION : TECHNICOLOR ®
REALIZZATO PER LA UNITED ARTISTS
Prima Edizione Italiana Anno 1967

FANTASTIC VOYAGE

Announced by 20th Century Fox as "the most expensive science-fiction film ever made," *Fantastic Voyage* (1966) rejoices in one of those simple-but-brilliant SF high concepts—a miniaturized submarine is injected into a human body—which everyone knows, even if they've never seen the movie.

The eye-catching US one-sheet design (right) had a similarly effective simplicity, and became an element of many international campaigns, including a particularly psychedelic Spanish poster by "Mac" (opposite). An exception was the UK quad (below) by Tom Beauvais, who remembered, "That was done for John Fairbairn, the publicity man at Fox at the time. He wanted me to make sure I depicted the ship inside what was meant to be an artery, which is why you can see things that look like blood vessels around the edge. I was quite pleased with that one."

LEON FILMS
VIAJE ALUCINANTE
CON
STEPHEN BOYD · RAQUEL WELCH · EDMOND O'BRIEN · DONALD PLEASENCE
ARTHUR O'CONELL · WILLIAM REDFIELD · ARTHUR KENNEDY
Producida por SAUL DAVID · Dirigida por RICHARD FLEISCHER · Guión de HARRY KLEINER ·
Adaptación de DAVID DUNCAN · Basado en un relato de OTTO CLEMENT, JAY LEWIS BIXBY ·
Música de LEONARD ROSENMAN
COLOR POR DE LUXE

20th CENTURY-FOX
présente / stelt voor
DEREK FLINT CONTRE TEGEN GALAXY
(OUR MAN FLINT)
JAMES COBURN / LEE J. COBB / GILA GOLAN / EDWARD MULHARE
PROD. SAUL DAVID / REGIE DANIEL MANN / SCENARIO HAL FIMBERG & BEN STARR
CINEMASCOPE
COULEURS KLEUREN DE LUXE

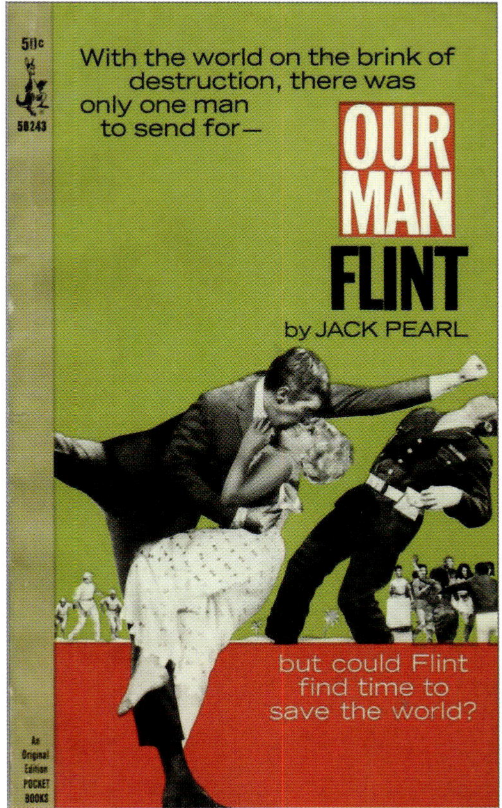

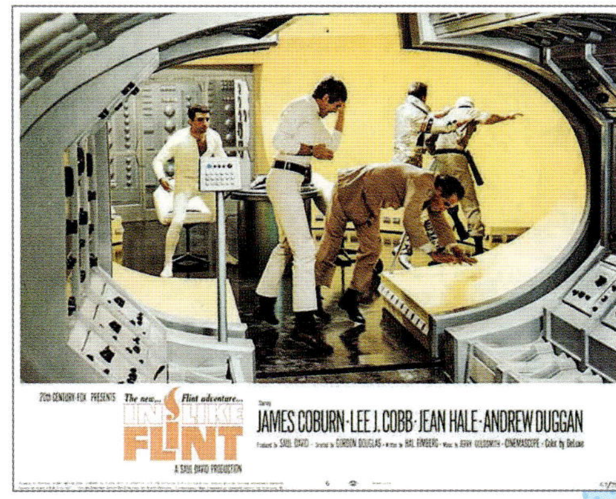

SPY-FI!

While the adventures of 007 himself tended to skirt the edges of SF, those of his '60s rivals were unafraid to fully embrace the genre. James Coburn's ultra-cool agent Derek Flint battled climate-disaster-inducing mad (but very polite) scientists in *Our Man Flint* (1966), and actually went into space in the sequel *In Like Flint* (1967), over a decade before Roger Moore attempted re-entry in *Moonraker* (1979). Coburn returned in *The President's Analyst* (1967), which saw the titular shrink hunted for his secrets by various spy agencies, though the true evil force in this remarkably prescient film is "The Phone Company" that plans to implant everyone with a wireless communication device. As its star noted proudly, the counter-culture classic "was named one of the finest political films of the decade by *The Sunday Times* in London."

The Flint posters were painted by American illustrator Bob Peak (1927–92). While the Belgian poster opposite is local artist Raymond "Ray" Elseviers's reproduction of Peak's US one-sheet for the first film, the UK quad for the sequel (left) used Peak's eye-popping original art. "I use color for mood and expressiveness," Peak explained. "Some of the things I do are calm, but most are not, so I prefer strong colors. Grays don't work too well for me."

Bond author Ian Fleming helped create *The Man from U.N.C.L.E.* (1964–68); episodes of the TV series were edited into feature films for international release (see overleaf), including *The Karate Killers* (1967), with Napoleon Solo and Illya Kuryakin on the trail of an alchemist's formula, and *How to Steal the World* (1968), in which they must foil a plot to release mind-control gas around the globe. European spy-fi filmmakers made do with bargain basement knock-offs like 077 in *Ypotron* (1966) and, unbelievably, Sean Connery's actual younger sibling Neil in *Operation Kid Brother* (1967, a.k.a. *O.K. Connery*), which imported supporting actors familiar from the "official" Bond films, and boasted a US one-sheet (see page 261) with art by Ron Lesser, doing his best to emulate Robert McGinnis's posters for *Thunderball* (1965) and *You Only Live Twice* (1967).

L'AGENTE DELL'U.N.C.L.E.
METRO-GOLDWYN-MAYER presenta una ARENA PRODUCTION
ROBERT VAUGHN - DAVID McCALLUM
CURT JURGENS - HERBERT LOM
TELLY SAVALAS
TERRY-THOMAS
JOAN CRAWFORD
GLI ASSASSINI DEL KARATE'
(THE KARATE KILLERS)
NORMAN HUDIS · BORIS INGSTER · NORMAN FELTON · BARRY SHEAR · METROCOLOR

MGM
Presents AN ARENA PRODUCTION in METROCOLOR
ROBERT VAUGHN
DAVID McCALLUM
Napoleon and Illya defy the most powerful menace of all!
HOW TO STEAL THE WORLD
BARRY SULLIVAN
ELEANOR PARKER
LESLIE NIELSEN
DANIEL O'HERLIHY
LEO G. CARROLL · TONY BILL
Screenplay by NORMAN HUDIS
Directed by SUTTON ROLEY
Produced by ANTHONY SPINNER
Executive Producer NORMAN FELTON

ERICH J. A. PIETREK zeigt
Gefährlichster Sonderauftrag für Agent 077 - schonungslose Härte im Kampf mit geheimnisvollen Gegnern
MIKE MURPHY
077 gegen YPOTRON
LUIS DAVILA
GAIA GERMANI
ALAN COLLINS · ALFRED MAYO · JESUS PUENTE
JANINE RENAUD · ALBERT DALBES · Regie: GEORGE FINLEY
Ein exzellenter erregender Shocker in TECHNICOLOR und TECHNISCOPE

UN FILM PRODUCIDO POR JOSE FRADE
JANO.
YPOTRON
LUIS DAVILA · GAIA GERMANY · JANINE REYNAUD
DIRECTOR GEORGE FINLEY
COLOR

Titanus
DARIO SABATELLO
NEIL CONNERY
DANIELA BIANCHI
ADOLFO CELI
O.K. CONNERY
AGATA FLORI · BERNARD LEE
ANTHONY DAWSON · LOIS MAXWELL
YACHUCO YAMA
ALBERTO DE MARTINO
TECHNICOLOR TECHNISCOPE
UNA PRODUZIONE D.S.

NEIL CONNERY
IS TOO MUCH
SUCH CLOSE FRIENDS...
SUCH BEAUTIFUL ENEMIES...
DANIELA BIANCHI
ADOLFO CELI
in "OPERATION KID BROTHER"
IS TOO MUCH FOR ONE MOTHER!
with
AGATA FLORI · BERNARD LEE · ANTHONY DAWSON · LOIS MAXWELL
YACHUCO YAMA · Screenplay by PAUL LEVI and FRANK WALKER · Produced by DARIO SABATELLO
Directed by ALBERTO DEMARTINO
TECHNICOLOR® TECHNISCOPE®
RELEASED THRU UNITED ARTISTS
A Transamerica COMPANY
Copyright © 1967 United Artists Corporation Printed in U.S.A.

PLANET OF THE APES

20th Century Fox was keen to stress the heavyweight pedigree of its "unusual and important motion picture" adapted from Pierre Boulle's 1963 novel. No disposable escapism here: *Planet of the Apes* (1968) was serious, grown-up SF, as the very wordy posters made clear. Just a few key character images made their way from the first US one-sheets (above) into many of the international campaigns, though some artists, especially from central Europe, didn't get the memo: both Czechoslovakia's Vratislav Hlavaty (see page 265) and an unknown Romanian artist (see page 264, bottom right) went completely off-piste. The Polish poster (opposite), while certainly not spoiler-free, was a typically impactful work by the distinguished artist and caricaturist Eryk Lipiński (1908–91), who was imprisoned in Auschwitz for faking documents as part of the Polish resistance effort in World War II.

ERYK LIPINSKI 69
CHARLTON HESTON
w amerykańskim
filmie przygodowym
Reżyseria:
Franklin J. Schaffner
w pozostałych rolach:
Roddy Mc Dovall
Kim Hunter
Maurice Evans
PLANETA MAŁP

猿人間が制する恐怖の惑星の秘密は!? 230光年のかなたの大宇宙スペクタクル!
チャールトン・ヘストン
PLANET OF THE APES
日本S.F作家クラブ特選
猿の惑星

PLANET DER AFFEN
Wird der Mensch einmal andere Wesen um sein Leben bitten müssen?
Twentieth Century-Fox zeigt
eine ARTHUR P. JACOBS Produktion
mit CHARLTON HESTON
RODDY McDOWALL
Regie: FRANKLIN J. SCHAFFNER
Ein Farbfilm
TWENTIETH CENTURY-FOX

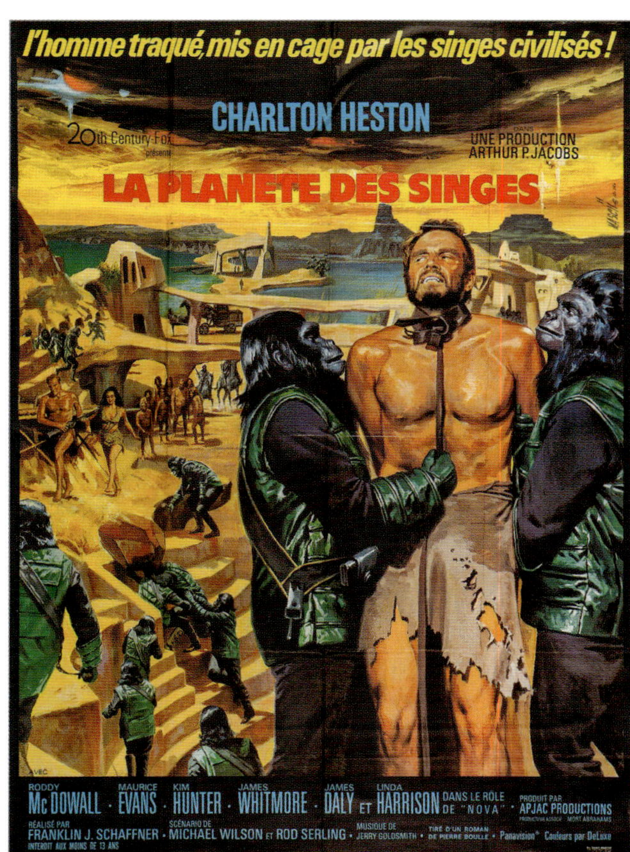
l'homme traqué, mis en cage par les singes civilisés!
CHARLTON HESTON
20th Century-Fox présente
UNE PRODUCTION ARTHUR P. JACOBS
LA PLANETE DES SINGES
AVEC
RODDY McDOWALL · MAURICE EVANS · KIM HUNTER · JAMES WHITMORE · JAMES DALY ET LINDA HARRISON DANS LE RÔLE DE "NOVA" · PRODUIT PAR APJAC PRODUCTIONS
PRODUCTEUR ASSOCIÉ MORT ABRAHAMS
RÉALISÉ PAR FRANKLIN J. SCHAFFNER · SCÉNARIO DE MICHAEL WILSON ET ROD SERLING · MUSIQUE DE JERRY GOLDSMITH · TIRÉ D'UN ROMAN DE PIERRE BOULLE · Panavision® Couleurs par DeLuxe
INTERDIT AUX MOINS DE 13 ANS

PLANETA MAIMUTELOR
O PRODUCTIE
A STUDIOURILOR
20 TH. CENTURY-FOX
REGIA:
FRANKLIN J. SCHAFFNER
Cu: Roddy McDowall
Kim Hunter, M. Evans
Linda Harrison
CHARLTON HESTON

PLANETA OPIC
! FILM USA !
REŽIE:
FRANKLIN J.
SCHAFFNER
UTOPICKÝ PŘÍBĚH
s CHARLTONEM
HESTONEM
V HLAVNÍ ROLI

BARBARELLA

"She is not a so-called 'sexually liberated woman,'" said Jane Fonda in 1967 of her upcoming role. "That would mean rebellion against something. She is different. She was born free." Though few would claim *Barbarella* (1968) as a feminist statement these days, it remains a colorful, campy time capsule from the '60s at their swingiest.

The US 24-sheet (above) is the best showcase for the key art by Robert McGinnis, perhaps better known for several James Bond campaigns, and his very first movie commission, one of the most reproduced film posters of all time: *Breakfast at Tiffany's* (1961). A veteran of over 1,400 book covers, McGinnis was still working into his '90s, admitting simply, "I don't know what I would do, if I ever stopped painting." European posters included the UK quad (left), created by Renato Fratini (see p98) at the peak of his £1,000-a-painting London career, and the Czech one-sheet (opposite bottom left) by local comics artist Kája Saudek.

未来40,000年の男は？ 女は？ そのセックスは？
鬼才バディムが、豊かな想像力と、鋭い表現力で
宇宙に描くS・F映画のエロティック・ファンタジー!!
テクニカラー〈パナビジョン〉
バーバレラ
BARBARELLA
ジェーン・フォンダ
ジョン・フィリップ・ロー
マルセル・マルソー
デビッド・ヘミングス

JANE FONDA
w komedii fantastycznej
BARBARELLA
reżyseria: ROGER VADIM
W POZOSTAŁYCH ROLACH:
JOHN PHILIP LAW,
DAVID HEMMINGS,
UGO TOGNAZZI
I INNI

JANE FONDOVÁ
Francouzský film
jako neohrožená COMICS vá hrdinka
režie: ROGER VADIM
"BARBARELLA"
HISSSS
Groan
Roar!
PURRR-MEOW!!

DINO DE LAURENTIIS PRESENTA
JANE FONDA in
BARBARELLA
UGO TOGNAZZI · ANITA PALLENBERG · MILO O'SHEA
MARCEL MARCEAU · CLAUDE DAUPHIN
DAVID HEMMINGS "DILDANO" JOHN PHILLIP LAW "PYGAR"
DIRETTO DA ROGER VADIM
PRODOTTO DA DINO DE LAURENTIIS
PANAVISION · TECHNICOLOR

OVERTAKEN BY EVENTS...

With the Apollo program in full swing, it's amazing that NASA had the time or inclination to co-operate, as they did, with two movies chronicling space missions gone wrong. *Countdown* (1967) starred James Caan as an ill-prepared astronaut on a rushed moon shot designed to beat the Soviets. Its director Robert Altman was fired for delivering footage with overlapping dialogue (which nonetheless went on to become his trademark). *Marooned* (1969) featured a command module crew low on fuel and running out of oxygen, and won an Oscar for its meticulously researched visual effects, but the film was soon forgotten when, not long after its release, the real-life Apollo 13 announced, "Houston, we've had a problem..."

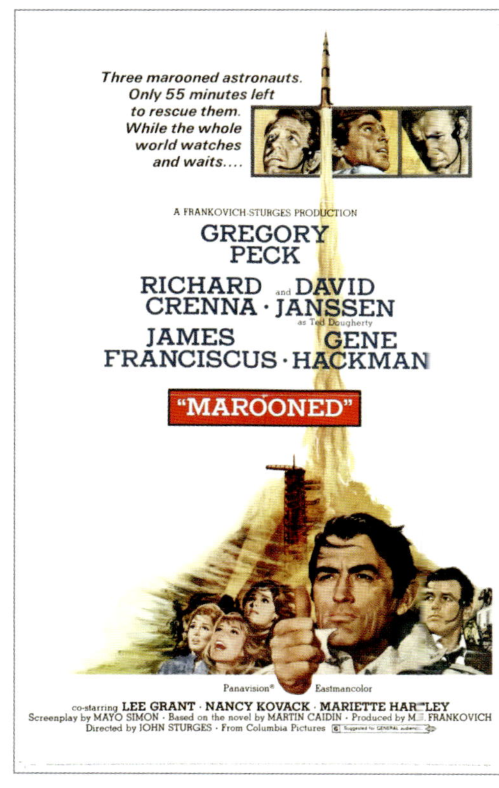

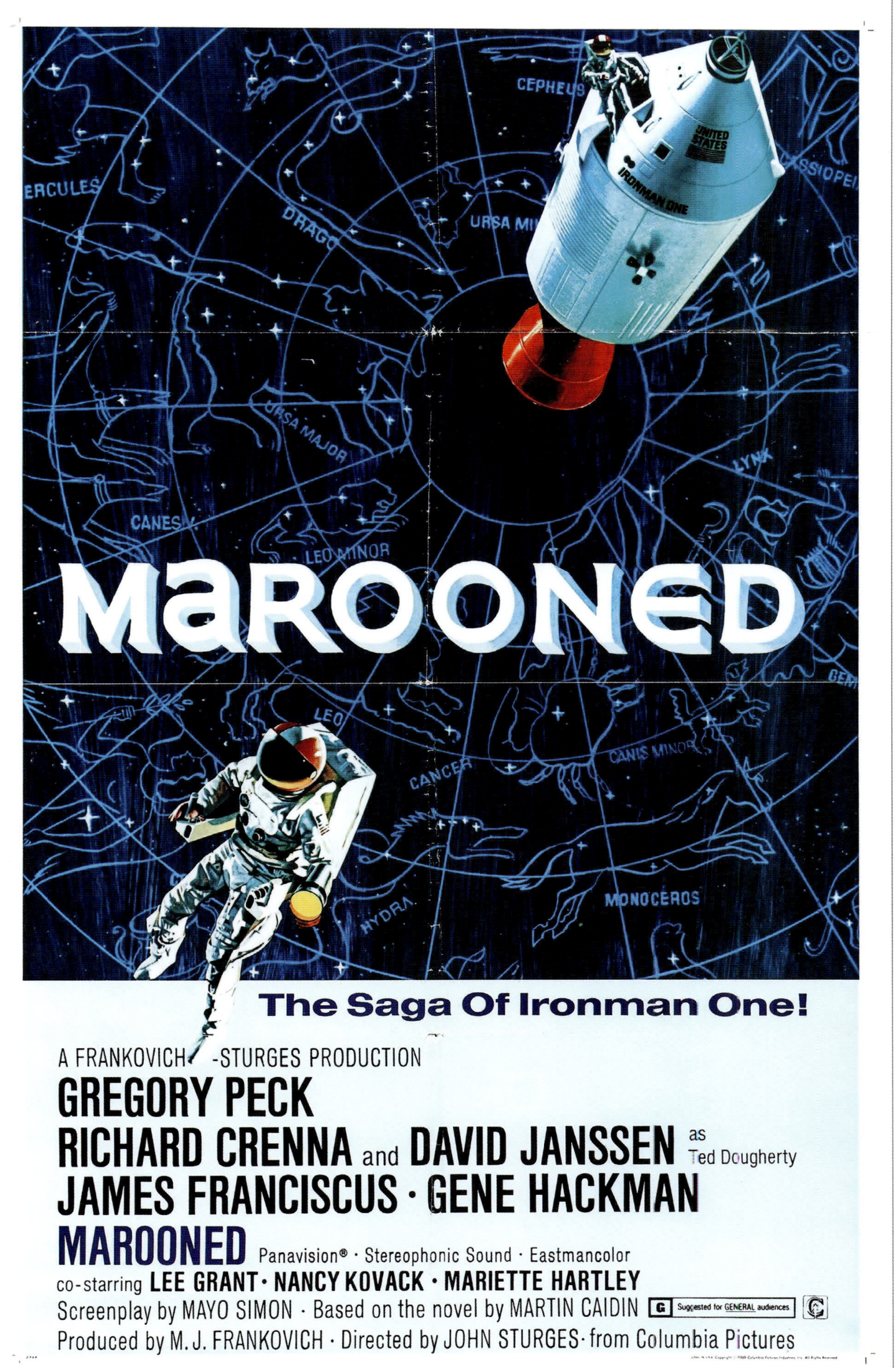
CEPHEUS
UNITED STATES
IRONMAN ONE
ERCULES
DRACO
URSA MI
SSIOPE
URSA MAJOR
LYNX
CANES
LEO MINOR
MAROONED
LEO
CANIS MINOR
CANCER
HYDRA
MONOCEROS
The Saga Of Ironman One!
A FRANKOVICH-STURGES PRODUCTION
GREGORY PECK
RICHARD CRENNA and DAVID JANSSEN as Ted Dougherty
JAMES FRANCISCUS · GENE HACKMAN
MAROONED
Panavision® · Stereophonic Sound · Eastmancolor
co-starring LEE GRANT · NANCY KOVACK · MARIETTE HARTLEY
Screenplay by MAYO SIMON · Based on the novel by MARTIN CAIDIN
G Suggested for GENERAL audiences
Produced by M. J. FRANKOVICH · Directed by JOHN STURGES · from Columbia Pictures

KUBRICK'S INFLUENCES

As he prepared to make *2001*, Stanley Kubrick famously watched practically every SF film made up until that point, so it's not surprising that the list of his alleged influences is lengthy. The orbiting wheel station in *Conquest of Space* (1955, see p82) was surely an inspiration, and after seeing the 1964 World's Fair Cinerama attraction *To the Moon and Beyond* he promptly hired its SFX crew. The Czech production *Ikarie XB-1* (1963, released in the US as *Voyage to the End of the Universe*) also made an impression, with Kubrick of the opinion that it was "a half step up from your average science fiction film in terms of its theme and presentation."

DRAMA KOSMICKÉ LODI
IKARIE XB-1
ČESKÝ FILM
námět a scénář:
P. JURÁČEK J. POLÁK
režie:
JINDŘICH POLÁK
kamera:
JAN KALIŠ
hudba:
ZDENĚK LIŠKA
HRAJÍ: nár. umělec Z. ŠTĚPÁNEK, nár. umělec F. SMOLÍK, D. MEDŘICKÁ, laureátka st. ceny KG, R. LUKAVSKÝ,
I. KAČÍRKOVÁ, O. LACKOVIČ a j.
ROTREKL 63 ©

the ultimate trip
2001: A SPACE ODYSSEY
MGM PRESENTS THE STANLEY KUBRICK PRODUCTION
MGM

2001: A SPACE ODYSSEY

The reaction to the first public screening of *2001* was so bad that a shell-shocked Stanley Kubrick retired to his bed for three days. "An epic drama of adventure and exploration" promised the initial 1968 release posters, with their photorealistic art by Robert McCall, but many critics disagreed: "A film that is so dull, it even dulls our interest in the technical ingenuity for the sake of which Kubrick has allowed it to become dull," sniffed *The New Republic*.

Some were entranced though: MGM ad man Michael Kaplan realized the young counter-culture crowd was showing up repeatedly, as they found the climactic, kaleidoscopic Star Gate sequence an excellent accompaniment to the taking of rare herbs and proscribed chemicals. As John Lennon cheerily admitted, "*2001?* I see it every week." A new marketing approach presented itself. Kubrick associate Jay Cocks recalled, "The cosmological conundrums of *2001*, which bid for a time to be its undoing, became instead a selling point and a rallying point. In Mike Kaplan's magical advertising phrase, *2001* became 'the ultimate trip,' and if you weren't hip enough to take it, you weren't worth taking seriously." Suitably trippy posters with the new tagline appeared for the 1970 re-release of the film. Printed to be "wilded" in urban areas, pasted up on empty walls and hoardings, few copies have survived.

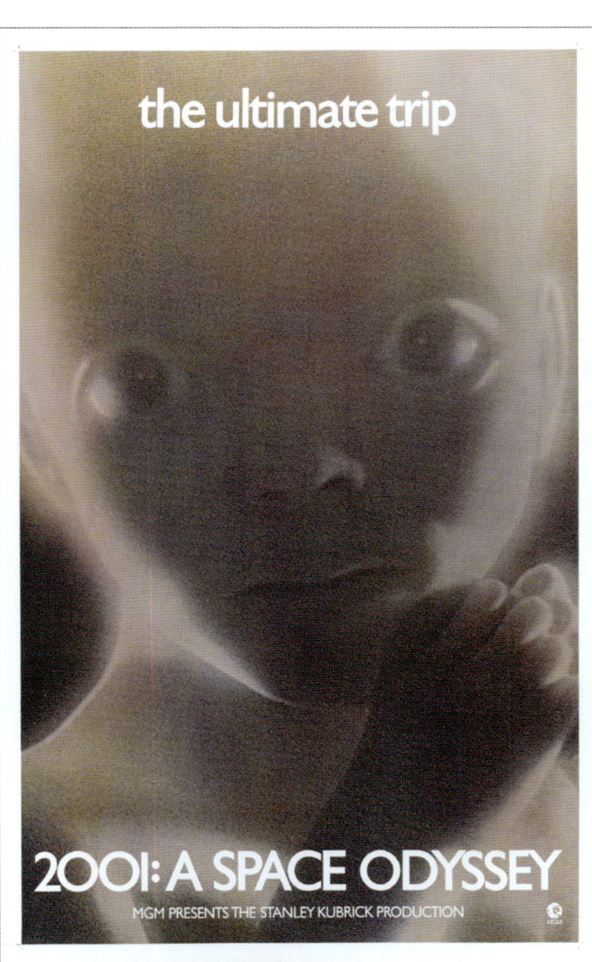

THE
1970s

Mark Salisbury on *Dark Star* and *Logan's Run*

While the early 1970s was a boom time for American studio and independent cinema, the sci-fi genre was, initially at least, still caught in the collective shadow of two behemoths released at the tail end of the previous decade: Stanley Kubrick's *2001: A Space Odyssey* (1968) and Franklin J. Schaffner's *Planet of the Apes* (1968). As the '70s wore on, and the summer of *Jaws* (1975) begat the era of the blockbuster, two new films were released that would rewrite the SF genre financially, aesthetically, and creatively.

PREVIOUS SPREAD: Detail from an Italian poster for *Solaris* (1972), art by Renato Casaro, dubbed "the Michelangelo of the movie poster."

BELOW: The US one-sheet for *Dark Star* (1974) riffed on *2001: A Space Odyssey* (1968).

In 1977, writer-director George Lucas's *Star Wars* blitzed the global box office on its way to becoming a cultural phenomenon, selling toys and lunchboxes aplenty, introducing a universe and characters that continue to this day. While Lucas preferred the term "space opera" or "space fantasy" for his galactic adventure, Ridley Scott's *Alien* (1979) fused together horror and sci-fi to create what its director called "*The Texas Chain Saw Massacre* of science fiction," although writers Dan O'Bannon and Ronald Shusett's inspirations were more Edward L. Cahn's *It! The Terror From Beyond Space* (1958) and Mario Bava's *Planet of the Vampires* (1965).

Alien hit box office gold, and together with *Star Wars* gave rise to realistic, lived-in spaceships that were in stark comparison to Kubrick's pristine, all-white affairs. Though Scott, his production designer Michael Seymour, and art directors Roger Christian and Les Dilley all deserve credit for the look of the *Nostromo*, *Alien*'s spaceship, praise must also go to co-writer O'Bannon, who pioneered the lived-in, worn out aesthetic and "truckers in space" crew vibe several years earlier with John Carpenter's debut feature, *Dark Star* (1974).

Starting out as a $6,000, 45-minute, 16mm student project at the University of Southern California film school in 1971, *Dark Star* was ultimately expanded to feature length and released theatrically in 1975, with a final budget of just $50,000. As well as being the film's co-writer, production designer, and special effects supervisor, O'Bannon played Pinback, one of four bombed out, bearded, hippie astronauts aboard the *Dark Star*, on an interstellar mission to

ANNOUNCING
THE BREAKTHROUGH PRESENTATION OF STANLEY KUBRICK'S CLOCKWORK ORANGE FOR THE MILLIONS WHO WERE NOT ALLOWED TO SEE IT UNTIL NOW!
STANLEY KUBRICK'S
CLOCKWORK ORANGE
A Stanley Kubrick Production "A CLOCKWORK ORANGE" Starring Malcolm McDowell • Patrick Magee • Adrienne Corri and Miriam Karlin • Screenplay by Stanley Kubrick
Based on the novel by Anthony Burgess • Produced and • Directed by Stanley Kubrick • Executive Producers Max L. Raab and Si Litvinoff • Original soundtrack available on Warner Bros. Records
From Warner Bros A Warner Communications Company
R

FINAL SAN SIMIAN SENTINEL

Vol. 1, No. 1 "THE TRUTH SHALL MAKE YOU FREE!" JANUARY 1 Weather: Snow Flurries

BATTLE FOR THE PLANET OF THE APES ACTION HOT IN LATEST OUTBREAK!

SETTINGS: PASTORAL AND PERILOUS.

CAMERA CATCHES NEW CONFLICT.

FIRST FAMILY OF APE CITY!

HE IS WHERE THE ACTION IS.

LAPSUS LINGUA

LIKE TOPSY SERIES "JUST GREW"

J. LEE THOMPSON

ARTHUR P. JACOBS

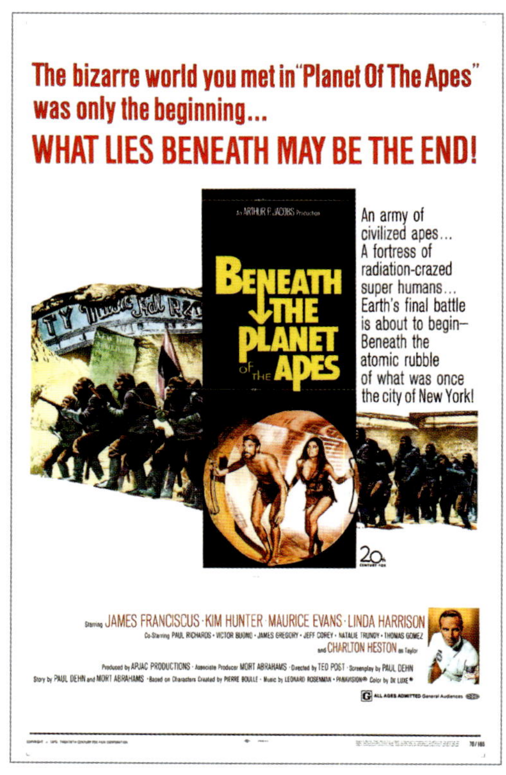

GOING APE

Even before a long time ago in a galaxy far, far away, there was a worldwide SF movie franchise phenomenon that ran to multiple sequels, spin-offs, lunchboxes, and a bestselling toy line. While Charlton Heston returned for a brief appearance in *Beneath the Planet of the Apes* (1970), the star of *Escape from...* (1971), *Conquest of...* (1972), and *Battle for the Planet of the Apes* (1973) was Roddy McDowall as the chimpanzee Cornelius, and then his revolution-leading son Caesar (the character later reimagined by Andy Serkis).

In 1975, all five films returned to the big screen in a huge "Go Ape!" event, as promoted by action figure company Mego (opposite), to tie in with the debut of an Apes TV series, again starring McDowall. He remained enthusiastic about his simian adventures: "The parts are good, and there's the challenge of communicating through the [ape makeup] appliances... Masks are in the oldest tradition of the theater and there is something exciting about reviving an ancient art."

MEGO®
WANTS YOU TO...
GO APE!
PLANET OF THE APES
BENEATH THE PLANET OF THE APES
ESCAPE FROM THE PLANET OF THE APES
CONQUEST OF THE PLANET OF THE APES
BATTLE FOR THE PLANET OF THE APES
MEGO® WILL GIVE AWAY FREE "APE" MOVIE TICKETS.
See your daily newspaper for details and theatre starting times.
PG
20th CENTURY FOX
PRINTED IN USA

残酷と恐怖のSF宇宙大アクション
地球は生きていた!?
猿と地下人間に支配されて
西暦3955年 我等人類文明の末路
すさまじい戦慄をみなぎらせて 再び 永遠に 地球が死んで行く
BENEATH THE PLANET OF THE APES
パナビジョン
デラックスカラー
続 猿の惑星
チャールトン・ヘストン■ジェームス・フランシスカス■リンダ・ハリソン■キム・ハンター
モーリス・エバンス■ポール・リチャーズ■ビクター・ブオノ■ジェームス・グレゴリー■デビッド・ワトソン
製作アーサー・P・ジェイコブス■監督テッド・ポスト■脚色ポール・デーン■撮影ミルトン・クラスナー■音楽レナード・ローゼンマン

大宇宙を、目もくらむ
白色の閃光が走った
真赤な炎となって溶け去った地球
その時、このドラマが始まった!
2300光年の時を逆流する意外な事実が……
衝撃のSFアクション〈猿〉シリーズ第3弾!
ESCAPE FROM THE PLANET OF THE APES
新 猿の惑星
ロディ・マクドウォール■キム・ハンター
ブラッドフォード・ディルマン■ナタリー・トランディ
エリック・ブレーデン■ウィリアム・ウィンダム
サル・ミネオ■リカルド・モンタルバン
監督ドン・テイラー■製作アーサー・P・ジェイコブス
脚色ポール・デーン■原作ピエール・ブールの小説による
音楽ジェリー・ゴールドスミス(フォックスレコード)
パナビジョン■デラックスカラー

★S・F史上空前の恐怖スペクタクル!
今!あばかれる恐怖の謎!
我が地球はかくして『猿の惑星』と化した!
CONQUEST OF THE PLANET OF THE APES
最新作〈猿シリーズ〉衝撃の第4弾!
猿の惑星 征服
新方式TODD-AO-35
デラックスカラー
ロディ・マクドウォール
ドン・マレー
リカルド・モンタルバン

■第1作より実に6ヶ年!
地球の未来を予言した驚異のエンドレス・ドラマ
いまその全貌を明かす完結篇の登場!
最後の猿の惑星
BATTLE FOR THE PLANET OF THE APES

ANNO 2670
ULTIMO ATTO
20th CENTURY - FOX presenta UNA PRODUZIONE ARTHUR P. JACOBS ANNO 2670 ULTIMO ATTO
con RODDY McDOWALL · CLAUDE AKINS · NATALIE TRUNDY · SEVERN DARDEN · LEW AYRES · PAUL WILLIAMS
e JOHN HUSTON nella parte del Legislatore Diretto da J. LEE THOMPSON Prodotto da ARTHUR P. JACOBS
Produttore associato FRANK CAPRA JR. Sceneggiatura di JOHN WILLIAM CORRINGTON e JOYCE HOOPER CORRINGTON
Racconto di PAUL DEHN Basato su personaggi creati da PIERRE BOULLE Musica di LEONARD ROSENMAN Panavision® Colore De Luxe®

CHUCK HESTON, SF STAR

Charlton Heston followed up *Planet of the Apes* with a brace of major studio SF movies in the early 1970s, both based on novels. *The Omega Man* (1971) was the second version of Richard Matheson's *I Am Legend*, though the author lamented, "I don't know why Hollywood is fascinated by my book when they never care to film it as I wrote it." (The 2007 Will Smith version was similarly unfaithful.) Harry Harrison's *Make Room! Make Room!* also got a tie-in edition when the overpopulation thriller *Soylent Green* was released in 1973, featuring John Solie's US one-sheet art on the cover (also used internationally, as on the French poster opposite). Though Harrison found Heston to be "very professional and a nice guy," he had to admit that "they gutted my book like a dead fish."

LA WARNER BROS. PRESENTA

CHARLTON HESTON

1975: OCCHI BIANCHI SUL PIANETA TERRA

(THE OMEGA MAN)

UNA PRODUZIONE WALTER SELTZER

E CON ANTHONY ZERBE - ROSALIND CASH

TECHNICOLOR® PANAVISION®

SCENEGGIATURA DI JOHN WILLIAM E JOYCE H. CORRINGTON

PRODOTTO DA WALTER SELTZER DIRETTO DA BORIS SAGAL

DEAR INTERNATIONAL DISTRIBUZIONE

A KINNEY LEISURE SERVICE

AVVERTENZA

GRAND PRIX DU FESTIVAL
DU FILM FANTASTIQUE
D'AVORIAZ 1974
RIOT CONTROL
RIOT CONTROL
RIOT CONTROL
INTERDIT AUX MOINS DE 13 ANS

SOLEIL VERT
METRO·GOLDWYN·MAYER présente
CHARLTON HESTON · LEIGH TAYLOR-YOUNG dans
"SOLEIL VERT" (SOYLENT GREEN) avec CHUCK CONNORS · JOSEPH COTTEN
BROCK PETERS · PAULA KELLY et EDWARD G.ROBINSON
Scénario de STANLEY R.GREENBERG d'après un roman de HARRY HARRISON · Musique originale FRED MYROW
Produit par WALTER SELTZER et RUSSELL THACHER · Réalisé par RICHARD FLEISCHER
METROCOLOR·PANAVISION · DISTRIBUE PAR CINEMA INTERNATIONAL CORPORATION
Visa Ministériel n°5728

The year is 2024...
a future you'll probably live to see.
2024AD
2024AD
2024AD
NO ONE ADMITTED AFTER PERFORMANCE STARTS...
IT HAS TO BE SEEN FROM THE BEGINNING!
a boy and his dog
an R rated, rather kinky tale of survival
LQ/Jaf presents 'A BOY AND HIS DOG' starring DON JOHNSON · SUSANNE BENTON and ALVY MOORE
with a special appearance by JASON ROBARDS co-starring HELENE WINSTON and CHARLES McGRAW
Produced by ALVY MOORE · Written for the screen and Directed by LQ JONES · Based on the award winning novella by HARLAN ELLISON
Music by TIM McINTIRE and JAIME MENDOZA-NAVA · Technicolor®
R RESTRICTED
Under 17 requires accompanying Parent or Adult Guardian

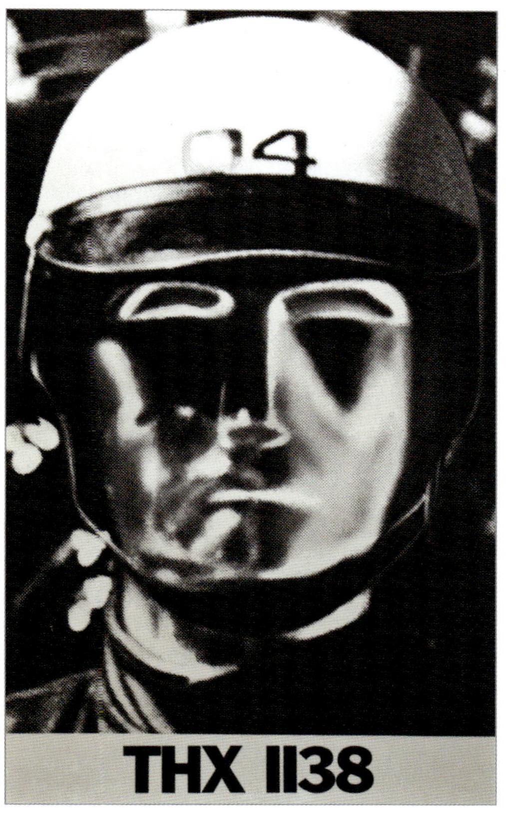

FUTURE SHOCKS

Cinematic visions of a post-apocalyptic future as the 1970s began included the alarming sight of Sean Connery in thigh boots and a red posing pouch in John Boorman's bonkers fable *Zardoz* (1974), and the relentless android policemen of *THX 1138* (1971); George Lucas's debut feature didn't cause much of a stir at the box office, but his time would come.

Actor L.Q. Jones, better known as one of Sam Peckinpah's regulars, turned writer/director for *A Boy and His Dog* (1975), adapted from Harlan Ellison's darkly comic novella. Robert Tanenbaum's one-sheet features a nice rendition of a pre-*Miami Vice* Don Johnson as Vic, alongside his telepathic mutt, Blood. (The artist's best known one-sheet is another spot-on likeness, of Paul Newman in 1986's *The Color of Money*.) The influence of *A Boy and His Dog* has had a long tail: according to video game developer Jesse Heinig, it inspired the *Fallout* series (1997–) "on many levels, from underground communities of survivors to glowing mutants."

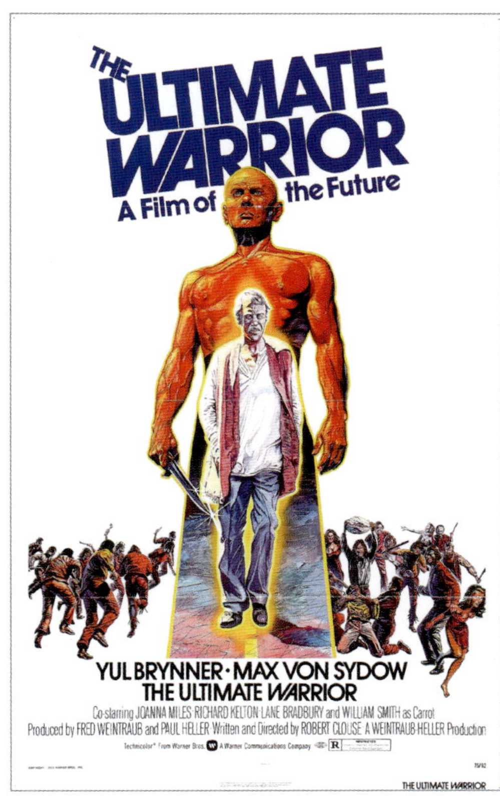

SOLARIS

Soviet filmmaker Andrei Tarkovsky described Kubrick's *2001*, with its focus on technology, as cold and impersonal: "Phony… a lifeless schema with only pretensions to truth." In adapting Stanislaw Lem's 1961 novel of space travelers communing with a sentient planet, he hoped to bring real emotional depth to an SF film, and the languid, lyrical *Solaris* (1972) certainly succeeds.

The bold Russian one-sheet opposite was unknown in the West until a copy surfaced in 2013. It's been attributed to Mikhail Romadin, also the film's production designer, who once commented, "A good painting is done from corner to corner, with equal tension in every square centimeter." The Italian posters (right and far right) were by Renato Casaro, who remembered, "My process has never changed much. I speak to the producer or director and give them several sketches and they choose one or two. *Solaris* was an easy one to do. Unfortunately, I never met Tarkovsky himself."

НА XXV КАННСКОМ МЕЖДУНАРОДНОМ КИНОФЕСТИВАЛЕ ФИЛЬМУ ПРИСУЖДЕН
БОЛЬШОЙ СПЕЦИАЛЬНЫЙ ПРИЗ
ХУДОЖЕСТВЕННЫЙ ФИЛЬМ В ДВУХ СЕРИЯХ
СОЛЯРИС
ПО ОДНОИМЕННОМУ РОМАНУ СТАНИСЛАВА ЛЕМА. СЦЕНАРИЙ Ф. ГОРЕНШТЕЙНА И А. ТАРКОВСКОГО
ПОСТАНОВКА АНДРЕЯ ТАРКОВСКОГО
ГЛАВНЫЙ ОПЕРАТОР ВАДИМ ЮСОВ, ГЛАВНЫЙ ХУДОЖНИК М. РОМАДИН, КОМПОЗИТОР Э. АРТЕМЬЕВ
В РОЛЯХ: ДОНАТАС БАНИОНИС, НАТАЛЬЯ БОНДАРЧУК, ЮРИ ЯРВЕТ
АНАТОЛИЙ СОЛОНИЦЫН, НИКОЛАЙ ГРИНЬКО
ПРОИЗВОДСТВО КИНОСТУДИИ «МОСФИЛЬМ»
Художник М. Ромадин Редактор Н. Новосельцева «Рекламфильм». Москва, Сущевская, 29 Подп. в печ. 29.XII.72 г. Цена 10 шт. — 57 коп. Заказ 1369 Тираж 102000

IN VERSIONE
STEREOFONICA
CON GLI INCREDIBILI EFFETTI DEL
FUTURSOUND
CANZONI ORIGINALI CANTATE DA
JOAN BAEZ
2002:
la seconda odissea
CON BRUCE DERN · CLIFF POTTS · RON RIFKIN · JESSE VINT
JOAN BAEZ
PETER SCHICKELE
SCRITTO DA DERIC WASHBURN & MIKE CIMINO E STEVE BOCHCO
REGIA DI DOUGLAS TRUMBULL
MICHAEL GRUSKOFF
UNA PRODUZIONE MICHAEL GRUSKOFF/DOUGLAS TRUMBULL
UNA ESCLUSIVITA HERITAGE ITALIANA
TECHNICOLOR
PREMIO OSCAR PER GLI EFFETTI SPECIALI DI 2001: ODISSEA NELLO SPAZIO

SILENT RUNNING

"*Silent Running* will become the object of cult worship by the young romantics of the Tolkien–Vonnegut generation," *Newsweek* correctly predicted in 1972, a quote Universal used in their newspaper ads for the initial release of this heartfelt, eco-themed film, ahead of its time then and an increasingly relevant classic over half a century later.

Japanese–American artist George Akimoto's US one-sheet art, based on an original sketch by Joseph Smith, was also used on the soundtrack album cover. It manages to make the act of planting a tree look dramatic and exciting—though to be fair, it's an excellent evocation of the story of Freeman Lowell (Bruce Dern) and his feisty robot drone helpers (an acknowledged inspiration for R2-D2) protecting the last of a cemented-over future Earth's greenery in deep-space biodomes. It's certainly more accurate than the actionably mendacious Italian marketing campaign, which took the fact that director Douglas Trumbull won an Oscar for *2001: A Space Odyssey*'s special effects and ran with it, re-titling *Silent Running* as a full-blown sequel to Kubrick's film!

THE ART OF MAC

"I worked with gouache and not oil because it dried in ten minutes and that allowed me to deliver on time, since the orders used to always be from one day to the next," Spanish artist Macario Gómez Quibus (1926–2018) once remembered, and no wonder: in a career spanning decades, "Mac" created around 4,000 film posters. Inspired as a young man by the work of nineteenth-century painter (and fellow Catalan) Mariano Fortuny, Mac's instantly recognizable style combined bold brushstrokes, a colorful palette, and often striking use of light and shade.

"I had to see the films to do it well," he recalled. Major studio pictures would be screened for him to select shots for reference: "I would watch it sitting in a chair with a button that I pressed when I saw a frame that interested me." Often, he would have to rely on just a synopsis and some black and white photos "and I would do the composition and color it." That might explain why on his poster for *Silent Running* (1972), Bruce Dern's flightsuit is not blue, as it is on screen.

"I never thought about money, that's why they exploited me so much," he admitted of his work-for-hire existence. "I delivered the posters, but none of them were ever returned to me; I didn't charge royalties either: they paid me once and that's it." At least he had his fans: Mac's portrait of Charlton Heston as Moses hung in the actor's office, and in 1977 George Lucas personally requested art for a *Star Wars* poster. Alas, it arrived too late, and remains unseen in the Lucasfilm archives, probably in a crate next to the Ark of the Covenant.

PARAMOUNT FILMS PRESENTA
naves misteriosas
(SILENT RUNNING)
Bruce Dern
Cliff Potts · Ron Rifkin · Jesse Vint
DIRIGIDA POR DOUGLAS TRUMBULL
GUION DE DERIC WASHBURN Y
MIKE CIMINO Y STEVE BOCHCO
PRODUCCION: MICHAEL GRUSKOFF
DOUGLAS TRUMBULL
TECHNICOLOR®
UNA PELICULA UNIVERSAL
70 m/m
UNIVERSAL PICTURES
DISTRIBUCION PARAMOUNT

LOST WORLDS OF THE '70S

The Valley of the Gwangi, released toward the end of 1969, was still in theaters worldwide as a new decade of lost world epics began. Ray Harryhausen created the special effects, finally bringing to the screen the cowboys and dinosaurs story originally conceived in the 1940s by his mentor Willis O'Brien. The French poster (opposite, bottom center) used Frank McCarthy's art from the US one-sheet.

You may remember actor Doug McClure from his top-billed roles in the stirring adventures *The Land That Time Forgot* (1974) and *At the Earth's Core* (1976)—and yes, he was the inspiration for the "You may remember me from such movies as *Stop the Planet of the Apes, I Want to Get Off!*" star Troy McClure in *The Simpsons* (Doug was reportedly a big fan). Tom Chantrell provided the action-packed UK posters for both of these Edgar Rice Burroughs adaptations from Britain's Amicus Productions.

Across the pond, Paramount and producer Dino De Laurentiis gambled a huge $25 million budget on *King Kong* (1976), a remake with then-cutting-edge ape effects from Rick Baker and Carlo Rambaldi, and a sly script from Lorenzo Semple, Jr., best known for the campy *Batman* TV series. This version removed the dinosaurs from Skull Island (the budget was already high enough!) and replaced the Empire State Building with the recently opened dual-tower World Trade Center, which duly featured on the posters. American artist John Berkey painted various key scenes, used internationally (top right), on the US one-sheet (center right), and on a text-free door panel poster (far right). Berkey, who had turned down an offer from Stanley Kubrick to work on *2001*, would go on to accept a request from George Lucas: to paint some of the earliest promotional images for a project called *The Star Wars*.

"Ten Tons of Animal Fury Leaps from the Screen" promised the one-sheet for the quickie 1976 cash-in production *A*P*E* (total budget: $23,000), along with the legally required disclaimer "Not to be confused with *King Kong*." The actual remake's tagline really swung for the fences, even by Hollywood standards, hailing it as nothing less than "The most exciting original motion picture event of all time." It wasn't, of course, but at least it made money: De Laurentiis banked a record $19.5 million for US TV rights alone.

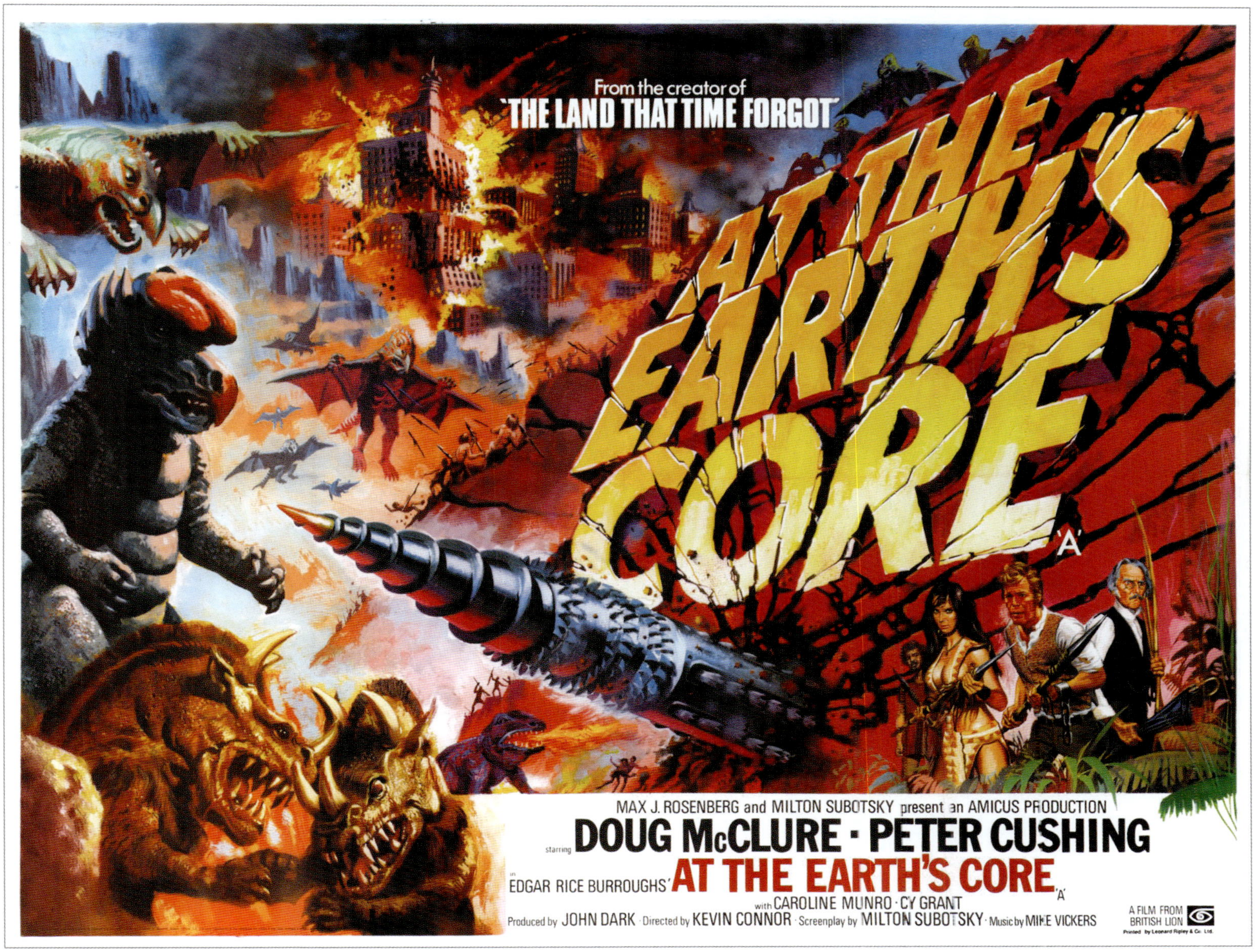
From the creator of
'THE LAND THAT TIME FORGOT'
AT THE EARTH'S CORE
'A'
MAX J. ROSENBERG and MILTON SUBOTSKY present an AMICUS PRODUCTION
starring DOUG McCLURE · PETER CUSHING
in EDGAR RICE BURROUGHS' AT THE EARTH'S CORE 'A'
with CAROLINE MUNRO · CY GRANT
Produced by JOHN DARK · Directed by KEVIN CONNOR · Screenplay by MILTON SUBOTSKY · Music by MIKE VICKERS
A FILM FROM BRITISH LION
Printed by Leonard Ripley & Co. Ltd.

AT THE EARTH'S CORE
地底王国

LA VALLÉE DE GWANGI
TECHNICOLOR
DYNAMATION
JAMES FRANCISCUS · GILA GOLAN · RICHARD CARLSON
RAY HARRYHAUSEN
JEROME MOROSS
WILLIAM E. BAST
CHARLES H. SCHNEER
JAMES O'CONNOLLY

FROM THE AUTHOR OF TARZAN
THE LAND THAT TIME FORGOT
THE LAND THAT TIME FORGOT Starring DOUG McCLURE
And JOHN McENERY · SUSAN PENHALIGON
Screenplay by JAMES CAWTHORN and MICHAEL MOORCOCK

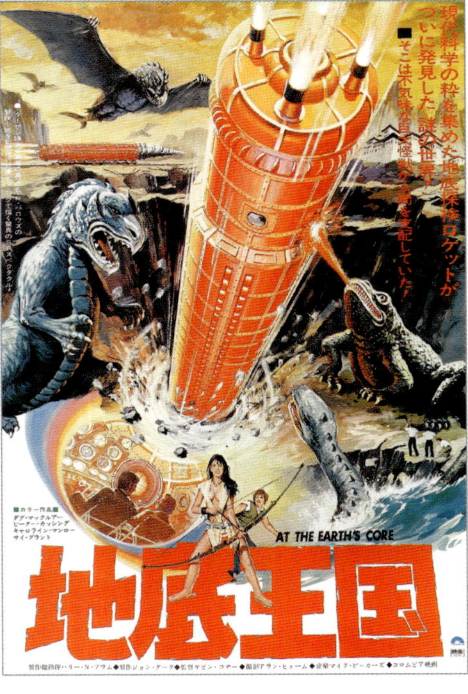

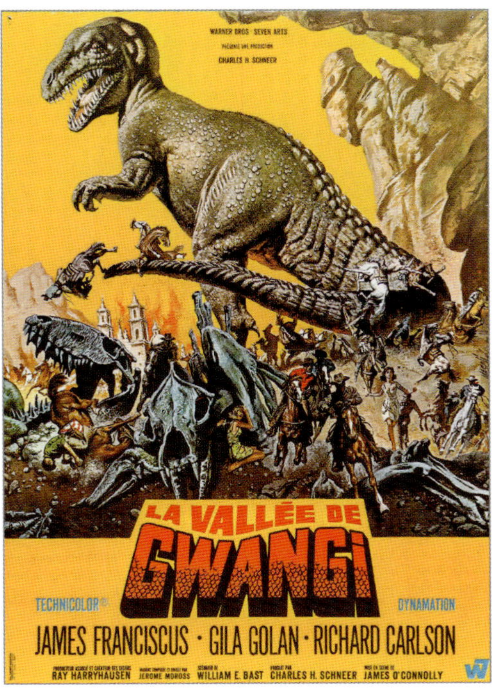

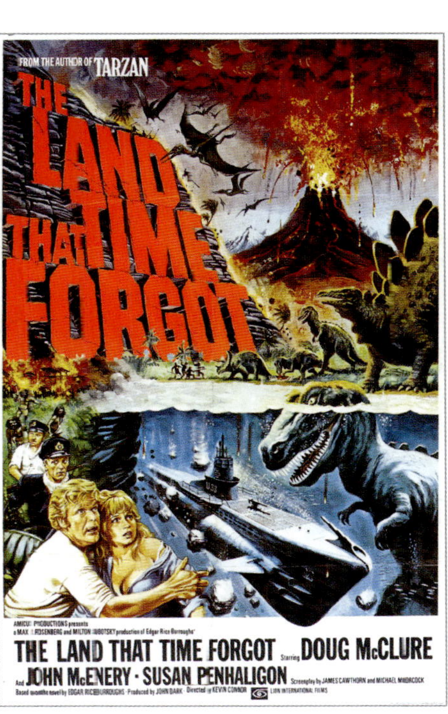

WICKED GAMES

Rollerball and *Death Race 2000*, both released in 1975, share the same premise: a famous player of an ultra-violent sport in a dystopian future rails against their fate and subverts the system. Bob Peak's airbrushed portrait of James Caan's Jonathan E. on the US one-sheet (bottom left) was unsurprisingly reused by the Japanese distributor, which also rather pointlessly tried to recreate it in photomontage. The French went their own way, though the art by Jouineau Bourduge still emphasized brute force (opposite). An advance teaser poster, printed on silver Mylar, featured a sketch made by Peak during filming on set (far left), and the artist also created "in universe" match posters (left) as a promo giveaway.

Producer Roger Corman's pedestrians-mean-points *Death Race 2000* starred David Carradine as Frankenstein, front and center on one of Tom Chantrell's finest UK quads (see page 300, top), though the Japanese posters preferred to focus on vehicular destruction and co-star Sylvester Stallone.

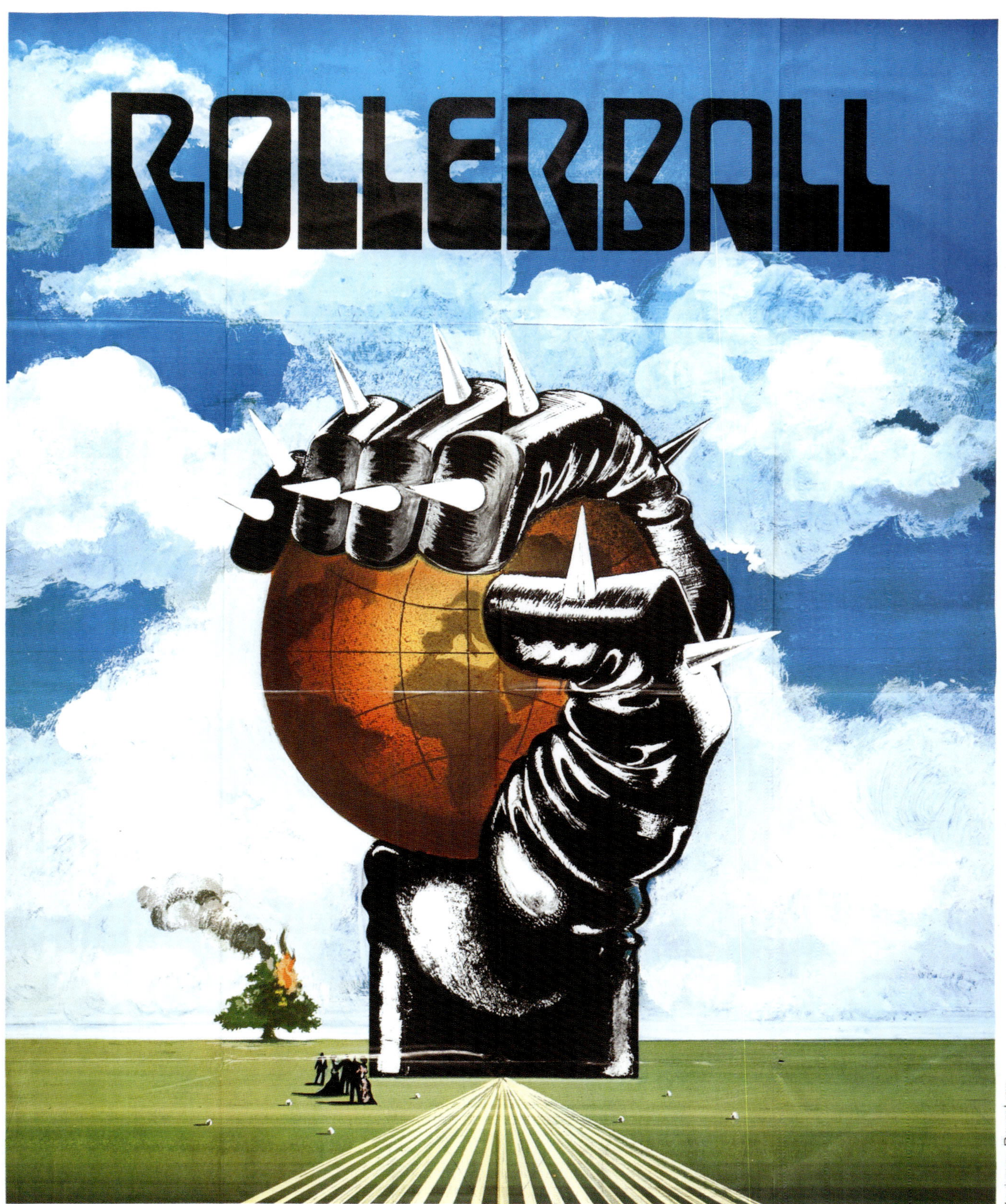

JAMES CAAN
dans
un film de NORMAN JEWISON "ROLLERBALL" avec JOHN HOUSEMAN
MAUD ADAMS - JOHN BECK - MOSES GUNN - PAMELA HENSLEY - BARBARA TRENTHAM
et RALPH RICHARDSON scénario de WILLIAM HARRISON musique dirigée par ANDRE PREVIN
producteur associé PATRICK PALMER produit et réalisé par NORMAN JEWISON
TECHNICOLOR distribué par LES ARTISTES ASSOCIES United Artists

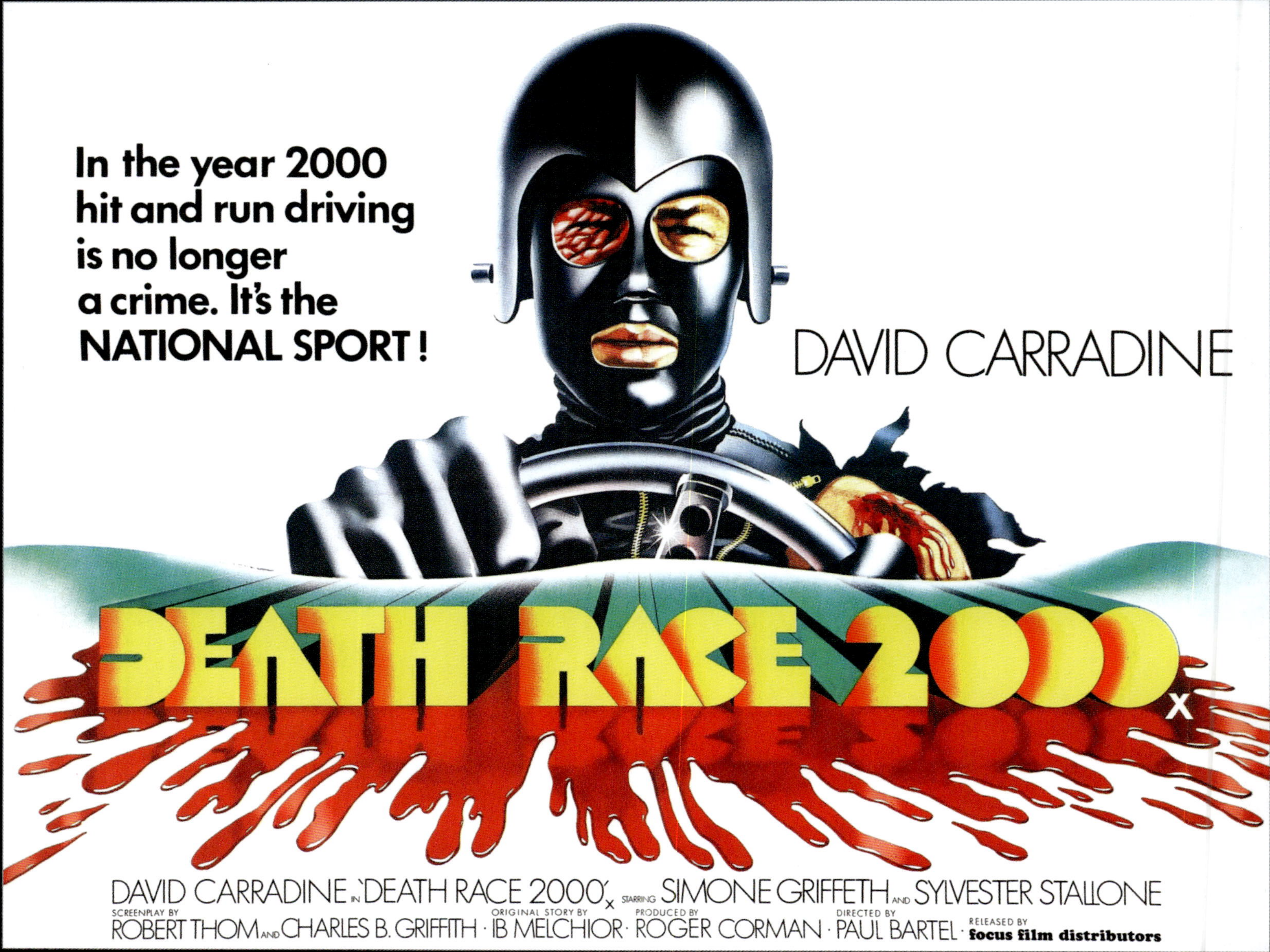
In the year 2000
hit and run driving
is no longer
a crime. It's the
NATIONAL SPORT !
DAVID CARRADINE
DEATH RACE 2000
X
DAVID CARRADINE IN 'DEATH RACE 2000' X STARRING SIMONE GRIFFETH AND SYLVESTER STALLONE
SCREENPLAY BY ROBERT THOM AND CHARLES B. GRIFFITH · ORIGINAL STORY BY IB MELCHIOR · PRODUCED BY ROGER CORMAN · DIRECTED BY PAUL BARTEL · RELEASED BY focus film distributors

YILMAZ FİLM
altan yılmaz sunar
david carradine
simone griffeth
sylvester stallone
TV.DEKİ "KUNG FU" DİZİSİNİN DEV AKTÖRÜ
"ROCKY" FİLMİNİN UNUTULMAZ OYUNCUSU
YÖNETMEN:
PAUL BARTEL
DEATH RACE 2000
FRANKESTAYN
RENKLİ TÜRKÇE

David Carradine
FRANKENSTEINS
Todes-Rennen
(DEATH RACE 2000)
Im Jahr 2000 ist mörderisches Autofahren kein Verbrechen mehr, sondern ein Nationalsport!
mit Simone Griffeth · Sylvester Stallone · Louisa Moritz · Don Steele · Regie: Paul Bartel
Eine Produktion der New World Pictures, New York · Constantin-Film

アメリカ大陸を引き裂いて
恐怖のスーパーカーが突っ走る！
シルベスター・スタローン
デス・レース2000年
DEATH RACE 2000

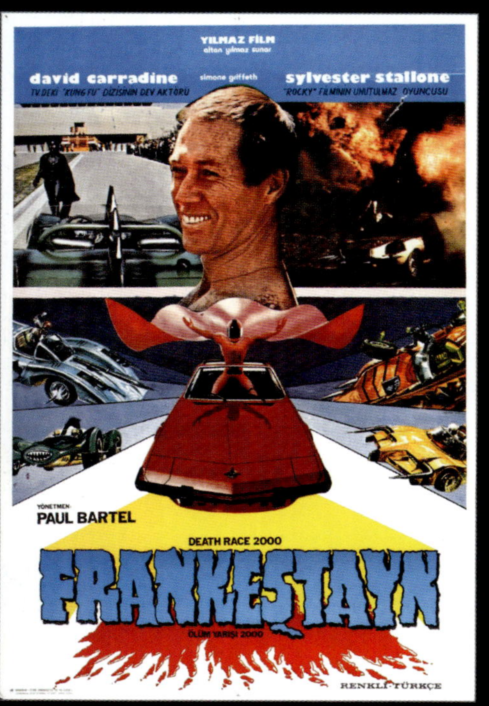

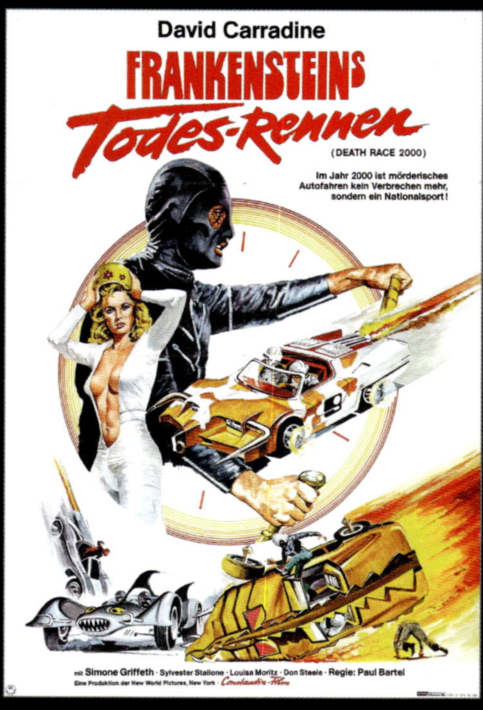

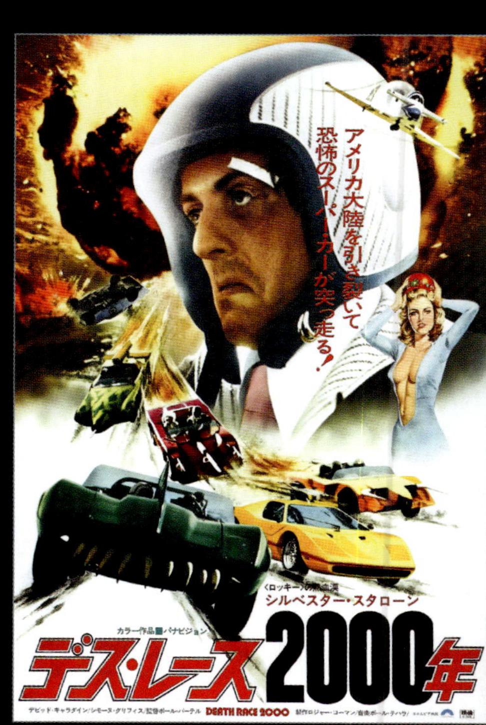

21世紀の恐怖が爆走する!!

驚異の超近代マシンが
激突する死の大レース!

デビッド・キャラダイン
シモーヌ・グリフィス
シルベスター・スタローン
マリー・ウォロノフ
監督 ポール・バーテル
製作 ロジャー・コーマン
音楽 ポール・チハラ

コロムビア映画
Columbia Pictures

DEATH RACE 2000

カラー作品／パナビジョン

デス・レース2000年

[映倫]

It's not nice to fool with Mother Nature...... it can be HORRIFYING!
EVEN TO THEM!
COLUMBIA PICTURES Presents
A ROBERT D. WEINBACH Production
THE MUTATIONS
DONALD PLEASENCE · TOM BAKER · BRAD HARRIS · JULIE EGE · MICHAEL DUNN
SCOTT ANTONY · JILL HAWORTH
Screenplay by ROBERT D. WEINBACH and EDWARD MANN · Executive Producer J. RONALD GETTY
Produced by ROBERT D. WEINBACH · Directed by JACK CARDIFF · COLOR
"THE MUTATIONS"

This film is filled with...
SHOCK
...VICTIM AFTER VICTIM DIES HORRIBLY IN THROAT-CUTTING ORGY!
AFTER SHOCK
...UNNATURAL LABORATORY EXPERIMENTS PERFORMED BEHIND BARRED DOORS!
AFTER SHOCK
...ONCE AGAIN HE WILL CHANGE SEXES AND KILL, KILL, KILL!
WARNING!
THE SEXUAL TRANSFORMATION OF A MAN INTO A WOMAN WILL ACTUALLY TAKE PLACE BEFORE YOUR VERY EYES!
PARENTS: Be sure your children are sufficiently mature to witness the intimate details of this frank and revealing film.
DR JEKYLL AND SISTER HYDE
An American International Release
STARRING RALPH BATES · Co-Starring MARTINE BESWICK · Also Starring GERALD SIM · LEWIS FIANDER
PG · in COLOR
Screenplay by BRIAN CLEMENS · Produced by ALBERT FENNELL & BRIAN CLEMENS · Directed by ROY WARD BAKER · EMI Film Productions Limited presents A Hammer Production

IZARO FILMS
EL HORROR DE FRANKENSTEIN
RALPH BATES · KATE O'MARA · DENNIS PRICE · VERONICA CARLSON
DIRECTOR: JIMMY SANGSTER
TECHNICOLOR

embryo
エンブリヨ
わたしは人間じゃないの?!
わずか4½週間で胎児から大人に……
しかし、愛を知ったその日から
ビクトリアの体に異常が!!
製作アーノルド・H・オーゴリーニ/アニタ・ドーハン
監督ラルフ・ネルソン
脚本アニタ・ドーハン〔番町書房刊〕
撮影フレッド・コーエンカンプ
衣裳モス・マブリー
音楽ジル・メレ
ロック・ハドソン/バーバラ・カレラ/ダイアン・ラッド/ロディ・マクドウォル
ジョイパックフィルム

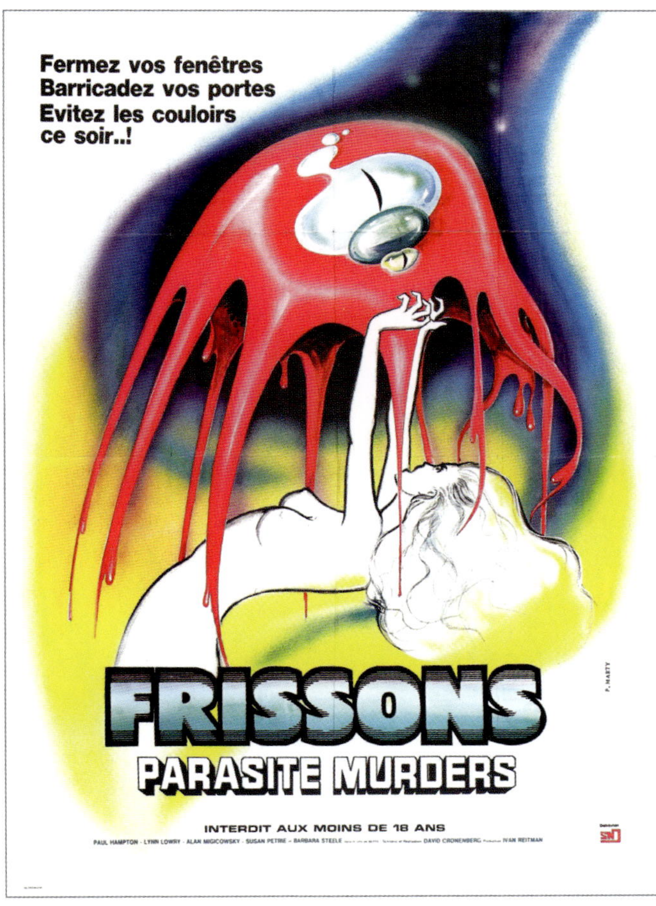

MAD SCIENTISTS REBORN

Increasingly explicit sex and gore accompanied the experimentations of a new generation of mad scientists in the '70s. "I'll create a race of plants that can walk, and men that can take root," declared Donald Pleasence in *The Mutations* (1974) as he crossed an abducted buxom coed with a Venus flytrap. *The Horror of Frankenstein* (1970) was a reboot of Hammer Films' series with younger star Ralph Bates as Baron Victor and future Darth Vader Dave Prowse as his Monster, who featured on the Spanish poster (opposite, bottom left) by "Jano" (Francisco Fernández-Zarza Pérez, 1922–92), a titan of Spain's poster artists, whose career began in the 1940s. Bates also starred for Hammer in *Dr. Jekyll and Sister Hyde* (1971), which adds gender transformation to the classic tale. The US one-sheet is festooned with warnings that hark back to the promoter Kroger Babb's "sex-education" exploitation films of the '50s, though strangely does not actually show Bates and his co-star Martine Beswick, who as *Variety* noted, "bear a strange resemblance to each other making the transitions entirely believable." *Embryo* (1976) starred Barbara Carrera as the lab-grown result of geneticist Rock Hudson's research, in a story with more than a hint of *Alraune*.

Filmed under the unimprovable title *Orgy of the Blood Parasites*, but actually released as *They Came from Within* and *The Parasite Murders*, the film now best known as *Shivers* (1975) featured a mad doctor who has created a parasite as "a combination of aphrodisiac and venereal disease that will, hopefully, turn the world into one beautiful mindless orgy." A gift to poster artists (as this page shows), it was an early example of David Cronenberg's particular brand of body horror, still unsettling audiences decades later in *Crimes of the Future* (2022).

MICHAEL CRICHTON

Under the pseudonym John Lange, Michael Crichton (1942–2008) had started writing pulpy novels while he was still a medical student, but it was the first two books under his own name that launched him as the bestselling king of techno-thrillers. Movie adaptations soon followed. Robert Wise directed the killer-microbes-from-space drama *The Andromeda Strain* (1971). "When Bob Wise set out to make the movie, his researchers assumed that everything was true," Crichton remembered, "so they went out and found all the things the book talked about—the underground laboratory, the computer programs, the biometrics security. After a while I stopped telling people that I had made it all up, because it turned out that it was based on true things. But I didn't know that when I was writing the book."

Director Mike Hodges said the look of *The Terminal Man* (1974) was inspired by the American realist painter of *Nighthawks*, Edward Hopper; Warner Bros. marketing, however, required a more dynamic style for the one-sheet (opposite), provided by Scottish-born artist Ken Barr, known for his DC and Marvel comics work and fantasy book covers.

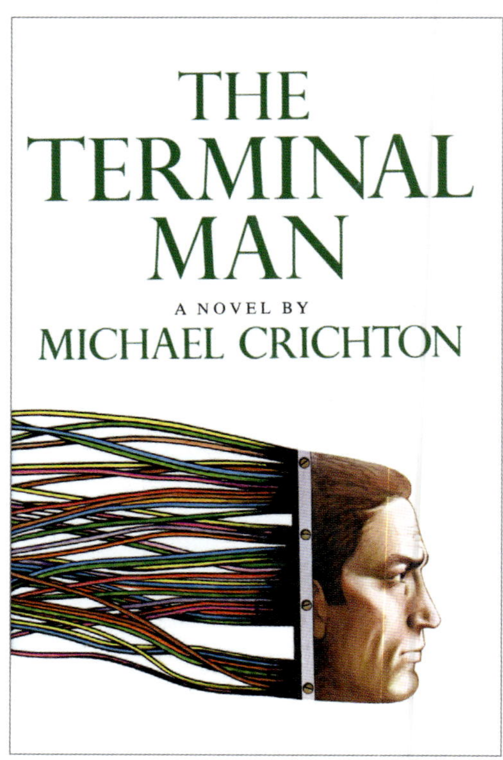

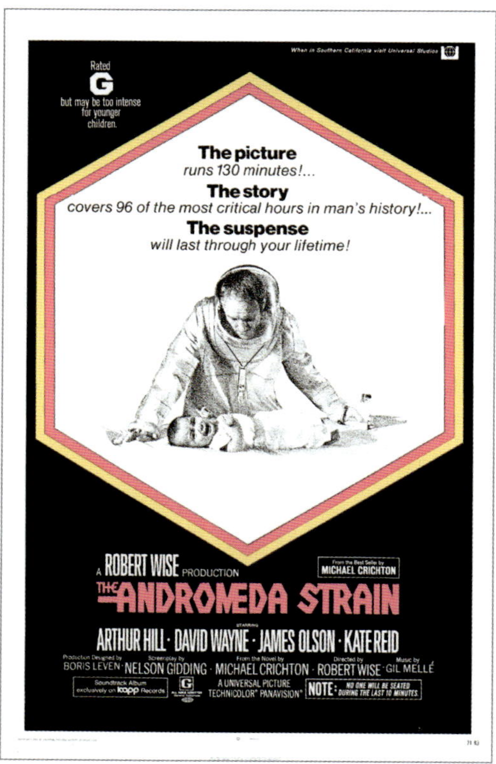

Harry Benson is a brilliant computer scientist.
For three minutes a day, he is violently homicidal.

GEORGE SEGAL: THE TERMINAL MAN

JOAN HACKETT Co-Starring RICHARD A. DYSART · NORMANN BURTON · JILL CLAYBURGH

Screenplay by MIKE HODGES · Based upon a novel by MICHAEL CRICHTON · Produced and Directed by MIKE HODGES

Technicolor® · From Warner Bros. A Warner Communications Company

PG Parental Guidance MAY NOT BE SUITABLE FOR PRE-TEENAGERS

74/2

THE TERMINAL MAN

BAD ROBOTS

"Boy have we got a vacation for you: Westworld, where nothing can possibly go worng!" ran a tagline for novelist Michael Crichton's cinematic debut as director. Working from his own original screenplay ("It didn't work as a novel… it's a movie about people acting out movie fantasies"), with a tight $1.3 million budget and 30-day schedule, Crichton ended up with MGM's biggest hit of 1973.

The US one-sheet (opposite) was one of a handful of movie posters by comic book superstar Neal Adams (*the* Batman artist of the '70s). The grid effect on the title logo hinted at a memorable "first" in the film: it cost $20,000, took four months, and resulted in scant seconds of robot POV footage, but as Crichton proudly recalled, "*Westworld* was the first feature film to process imagery by computer. We obtained a sort of blocky, animated effect that was remarkable in 1973." CGI was born. Crichton was not involved in the disappointing sequel *Futureworld* (1976), but returned to the themepark-gone-worng theme in his franchise-spawning 1990 novel *Jurassic Park*.

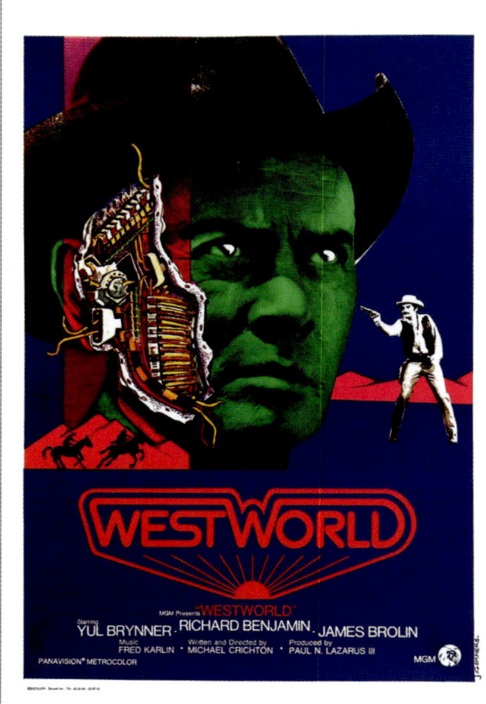

WESTWORLD
...where robot men and women are programmed to serve you for
...ROMANCE
...VIOLENCE
...ANYTHING
MGM Presents "WESTWORLD" Starring YUL BRYNNER RICHARD BENJAMIN
JAMES BROLIN · Music FRED KARLIN · Written and Directed by MICHAEL CRICHTON · Produced by PAUL N. LAZARUS III
PG PARENTAL GUIDANCE SUGGESTED
PANAVISION® METROCOLOR

THE MAN WHO FELL TO EARTH

David Bowie was perfectly cast as a visiting alien in *The Man Who Fell to Earth* (1976). "My one snapshot memory of that film is not having to act," he recalled. "Just being me was perfectly adequate for the role. I wasn't of this earth at that particular time."

British artist Vic Fair of the Downton ad agency created the UK quad (right) under pressure, knowing that rival companies were also after the job: "So that made me double my efforts and I actually completed the design in one night! The composition of the shapes was important to me. The only thing I don't really like about it is the figure that's dropping down at the bottom and I should have improved on that, really. I am fond of it and like its simplicity. I do see other minor things I should have fixed but that's always the way with jobs done like that—it's impossible to be fully satisfied."

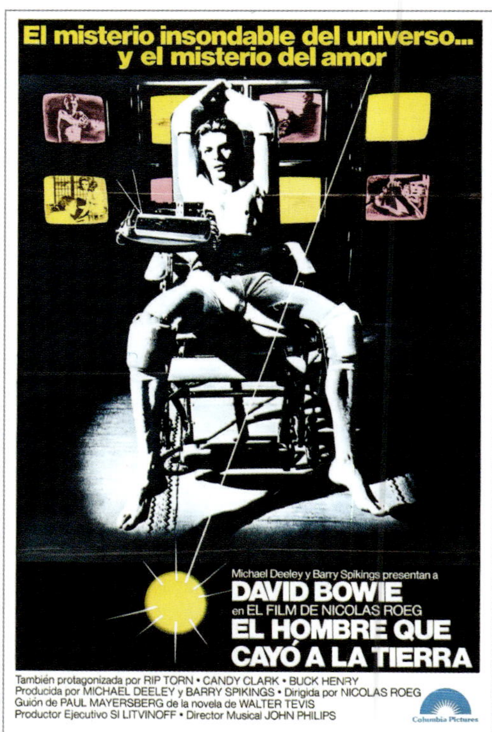

You have to believe it to see it
David Bowie in
The man who fell to Earth
Cinema I & Cinema II

A MAN HAS CREATED A MACHINE.
NOW THE MACHINE WANTS TO CREATE
A MAN . . .
Demon
Seed
MGM presents a HERB JAFFE PRODUCTION
JULIE CHRISTIE in "DEMON SEED" co-starring FRITZ WEAVER
Produced by HERB JAFFE
Directed by DONALD CAMMELL Screenplay by ROBERT JAFFE, ROGER O. HIRSON
Musical Score Composed and Conducted by JERRY FIELDING
Filmed in PANAVISION® and METROCOLOR®
MGM Distributed by CINEMA INTERNATIONAL CORPORATION

THE END OF AN ERA

SF cinema was ticking along, if not in particularly rude health, in 1976 and early 1977. There were still B-movies, including a run of natural-world-gone-mad tales, such as Bert I. Gordon's loose adaptation of H.G. Wells's *The Food of the Gods* (1976), with its rather graphic one-sheet by then up-and-coming artist Drew Struzan. April '77 saw the release of MGM's techno–horror *Demon Seed*, the last major studio SF production before the genre changed forever—in fact filmgoers leaving the theater may well have been given an advance promotional handbill (bottom right) for the movie, released the following month, which was responsible for that change...

Even though *Star Wars* (1977) ushered in a new "modern" era of SF films and filmmaking techniques, it was rooted in what had gone before, whether it be the Flash Gordon serial-style storytelling, or indeed an approach to marketing which embraced, even as the franchise continued into the twenty-first century, fully painted posters (many by Struzan) rather than bland Photoshop collages.

Coming full circle, it's fitting that George Lucas himself was happy to acknowledge the enduring influence of the film that began it all, *A Trip to the Moon*: "Méliès's grand adventure gave us all the opportunity to dream. The art of film has come a long way since that time, but the spirit never changes. We will forever use the medium as a means of exploring the unknown and the impossible—following in the tradition that was set more than a century ago."

Key to Non-US Posters/Lobby Cards

The images in this book are not all individually captioned, as most are self-evidently US film posters and lobby cards. What follows is a key to the images that do not fall under that category. For each page number, the relevant images are listed left to right, starting at the top. Artists (A:) are given where known. Re-release posters are marked "rr."

26: c1900. Paris Exposition Universelle Poster inspired by *The Astronomer's Dream* (*La Lune à un mètre*, 1898). A: Louis Abel Truchet; 1892 poster for a production of Jacques Offenbach's opera *Le Voyage dans la Lune*; Illustrations for the novel *Around the Moon* by Jules Verne (1870). A: Émile-Antoine Bayard.

27: *A Trip to the Moon* (*Le Voyage dans la Lune*, 1902). Production sketch. A: George Méliès; Original preparatory sketch for a poster. A: George Méliès; Hand-colored film frame.

28: Illustration for the novel *Voyages très extraordinaires de Saturnin Farandoul* (1879). A: Albert Robida; *The Extraordinary Adventures of Saturnino Farandola* (*Le avventure straordinarissime di Saturnino Farandola*, 1913). Tinted film frames; *20,000 Leagues Under the Sea* (1916). US newspaper ad; *Conquest of the Pole* (*À la conquête du pole*, 1912). French poster; *The Edison Kinetogram*. 1910. Trade magazine cover featuring *Frankenstein* (1910); *Algol* (1920). German poster.

29: *Himmelskibet* (1918). Swedish poster; 1920 trade ad for US release of *Himmelskibet* (aka *A Trip to Mars*); *Aelita* (1924). Russian poster.

30: *The Master Mystery* (1918). US Trade ad; US Trade ad; French poster. A: Francisco Tamagno; French poster.

32: *Metropolis* (1927). US trade ad. A: 'Cabliky'; US trade ad; German trade ad from UFA exhibitor's book. A: Otto Hunte; 1929 Japanese program. A: Sewge.

33: German 3 sheet. A: Heinz Schulz-Neudamm; Australian daybill. A: Bernie Bragg.

34: French poster. A: Boris Bilinsky; Swedish one-sheet. A: John Mauritz 'Moje' Åslund; US three-sheet. A: Glenn Cravath (attrib).

35: US window card, detail. A: Glenn Cravath (attrib); Swedish magazine cover; 1926 German first edition novel, pub August Scherl. A: Walter Reimann; 1927 British novel, pub Readers Library. A: Aubrey Hammond; German program magazine. A: Werner Graul.

36: *Woman in the Moon* (*Frau im Mond*, 1929). Swedish one-sheet. A: 'Est'.

37: German program magazine; Dutch novel, pub Nederlandse uitgevers-maatschap.

38: *L'Atlandide* (1932). French poster; Swedish one-sheet. A: Eric Rohman; *Alraune* (1930). German poster; *Gold* (1934). German poster; Japanese poster.

39: *Alraune* (1928, aka *Vampyren*) Swedish one-sheet. A: Eric Rohman.

40: *High Treason* (1929). US herald interior; Japanese program.

41: US herald cover.

42: *Just Imagine* (1930). US herald; US sheet music.

44: *Frankenstein* (1931). 1932 Spanish poster.

46: *Bride of Frankenstein* (1935). US pressbook back cover.

47: *Doctor Jekyll and Mr. Hyde* (1931), Swedish one-sheet. A: Gösta Åberg.

48: *The Lost World* (1925). US newspaper ad.

50: *The Mysterious Island* (1929). French *grande*. A: George Mercier; Swedish one-sheet.

51: *King Kong* (1933). French four-panel. A: C. Finel; *Son of Kong* (1933). US herald.

52: *F.P.1* (1932). Swedish trade ad; German textless export poster. A: W. Reil; *The Tunnel* (1935, aka *Transatlantic Tunnel*). Pressbook cover.

54: *Things to Come* (1936). UK trade ad; UK crown poster.

56: 1953 rr Italian two-*fogli*; 1953 rr Italian four-*fogli*; Spanish poster; c1950s Mexican lobby card.

57: Swedish one-sheet. A: John Mauritz 'Moje' Åslund.

58: *Flash Gordon* (1936). 1951 rr Swedish one-sheet.

60: *Flash Gordon's Trip to Mars* (1938). Circa unknown Mexican lobby cards x2.

62: *Buck Rogers* (1939). US pressbook cover and interior page.

63: Pressbook interior pages; *The Amazing Adventures of Buster Crabbe* No. 2, Feb 1954, pub Lev Gleason. A: Alex Toth; *Buster Crabbe* No. 5, July 1952, pub Famous Funnies Publications. A: Frank Frazetta.

65: *The Phantom Empire* (1935). Circa unknown Mexican lobby card.

66: *The Undersea Kingdom* (1936). Turkish poster; *The Lost City* (1935). Mexican lobby card.

68: *The Man Who Lived Again* (1936). US pressbook cover.

70: *The Ape Man* (1943). US herald.

71: *Bowery at Midnight* (1942). c1950s UK rr poster.

73: *Fiddlers Three* (1944). UK door panel (detail); *Szíriusz* (1942). Hungarian poster; b&w film still; *Time Flies* (1944, aka *El tiempo vuela*). Argentinean promo image.

75: *Dr. Cyclops* (1940). c1950s Italian rr two-*fogli*. A: Carlantonio Longi.

82: *Strange Adventures* #1, Aug-Sept 1950, pub DC Comics. A: Howard Sherman.

83: *Rocketship X-M* (1950). Italian four-*fogli*. A: Angelo Cesselon.

84: *X-15* (1961). French poster. A: Roger Soubie.

85: c1950s Mexican lobby cards for *Conquest of Space* (1955), *Destination Moon* (1950), *First Man Into Space* (1959), *Project Moonbase* (1953), *Rocketship X-M* (1950), *X-15* (1961).

86: *The Day the Earth Stood Still* (1951). Promotional Gort mask; Pressbook front and back cover.

88: Belgian poster; French poster; c1960s French rr poster; Italian four-*fogli*. A: Giamarra.

89: Danish one-sheet.

90: *When Worlds Collide* (1951). US novel, c1952 edition, pub Dell. A: Robert Stanley; US trade ad; Spanish poster.

91: French *grande*. A: Roger Soubie.

92: *Captain Video* (1951). US pressbook cover.

93: c1950s Mexican lobby cards for *Radar Men from the Moon* (1952), *Commando Cody* (1953), *Flying Disc Man from Mars* (1950), *Zombies of the Stratosphere* (1952), *Satan's Satellites* (1958), *Captain Video* (1951).

94: *The Thing from Another World* (1951). Italian *photobusta* x2; Japanese poster. A: Miya; UK pressbook cover and interior.

95: 1961 Italian rr two-*fogli*. A: Sandro Simeoni.

98: *Invaders from Mars* (1953). Mexican lobby card; Belgian poster; Italian four-*fogli*. A: Renato Fratini.

99: Italian two-*fogli*. A: Renato Fratini.

103: *The Crawling Eye* (1958). Italian four-*fogli*. A: Basilio Morin.

104: *The War of the Worlds* (1953). Mexican lobby card; US novel, pub Pocket Books; Italian *photobusta*.

106: Belgian poster; Danish one-sheet. A: Kurt Wenzel; Japanese poster; c1956 Italian four-*fogli*. A: Franco Fiorenzi.

107: French *moyenne*. A: Claude Venin.

108: *The Flying Saucer* (1950). Mexican lobby card.

110: *Godzilla* (1954, aka *Gojira*). Japanese posters x2; Spanish poster. A: Macario 'Mac' Gómez Quibus; German poster; Italian poster.

111: UK quad; French poster. A: A. Poucel; Bulgarian poster; Czech poster; Polish poster. A: Alicja Waszewska-Lauman.

112: *The Giant Claw* (1957). Italian two-*fogli*; *Rodan* (1957). Italian two-*fogli*; *The Monster that Challenged the World* (1957). Italian two-*fogli*. A: Giuliano Vittorio; Italian four-*fogli*. A: Giuliano Vittorio.

113: *Godzilla Raids Again* (1955). Italian two-*fogli*. A: Angelo Cesselon.

114: *Them!* (1954). Italian four-*fogli*. A: Luigi Martinati; Japanese handbill.

117: *Beast of Hollow Mountain* (1956). Belgian poster; *Untamed Women* (1952). Mexican lobby card; *Two Lost Worlds* (1951). Belgian poster. A: Wik; *The Monster of Piedras Blancas* (1959). Mexican lobby card.

119: *It Came From Beneath the Sea* (1955). Italian two-*fogli*. A: Alfredo Capitani; Australian daybill.

120: *Earth vs. the Flying Saucers* (1956). Italian four-*fogli*. A: Anselmo Ballester; Italian two-*fogli*. A: Anselmo Ballester.

121: *20 Million Miles to Earth* (1957). *Amazing Stories*, pub Ziff Davis; Italian two-*fogli*. A: Anselmo Ballester.

122: *It Came From Outer Space* (1953). UK quad; French poster. A: Xarrié.

124: *The Quatermass Xperiment* (1955, aka *The Creeping Unknown*). Polish poster. A: Marian Stachurski; Belgian poster; Italian four-*fogli*. A: Carlantonio Longi.

125: *Quatermass 2* (1957, aka *Enemy From Space*). UK quad; Italian two-*fogli*. A: Giuliano Nistri; Mexican lobby card; French *grande*. A: Clement Hurel.

126: *Flight to Mars* (1951). Italian *locandina*; *The Angry Red Planet* (1959). Italian four-*fogli*. A: Sandro Simeoni.

127: *Red Planet Mars* (1952). Mexican lobby card.

130: *This Island Earth* (1955). US novel, 1955 edition, pub Shasta; Italian *locandina*; Italian four-*fogli*. A: Arnaldo De Amicis.

131: Italian two-*fogli*. A: Arnaldo De Amicis.

133: *Day the World Ended* (1955). Italian four-*fogli*.

138: *Earth vs the Spider* (aka *The Spider*, 1958). Mexican lobby card.

140: *Invasion of the Body Snatchers* (1956). US Newspaper ad; pressbook page; US newspaper ad; Italian *locandina*. A: Alessandro Biffignandi.

141: Italian two-*fogli*. A: Alessandro Biffignandi.

142: *Forbidden Planet* (1956). US novel, pub Bantam.

144: Mexican lobby card; Italian two-*fogli*. A: Averardo Ciriello; Japanese press sheet; Italian *locandina*.

145: Italian four-*fogli*. A: Averardo Ciriello.

150: *1984* (1956). US novel, c1956 edition, pub Signet; UK pressbook.

151: *The Gamma People* (1956). Belgian poster.

153: *Beast From Haunted Cave* (1959)/*The Wasp Woman* (1959). 1960 UK quad; *The Fly* (1958)/ *Return of the Fly* (1959). c1960s UK quad. A: Jock Hinchcliffe.

155: *Boom in the Moon* (1946). c1950s Italian four-*fogli*. A: Carlantonio Longi.

158: *The Incredible Shrinking Man* (1957). US pressbook pages.

160: *Beginning of the End* (1957). US pressbook; *4D Man* (1959). US pressbook; *The Fly* (1958). US pressbook; *Curse of Frankenstein* (1957) US pressbook (detail).

161: US Newspaper-style heralds for *The Day the Earth Stood Still* (1951); *The Man From Planet X* (1951); *Attack of the Crab Monsters* (1957); *Beginning of the End* (1957).

165: *The Brain* (1962). Spanish poster.

166: Japanese posters for *Super Giant* (1957); *Super Giant Continues* (1958); *Super Giant: The Space Mutant Appears* (1958); *Super Giant: The Spaceship and the Clash of the Artificial Satellite* (1958). French *grande*.

167: *Super Giant* (1957). 1961 Italian two-*fogli*. A: Arnaldo De Amicis.

172: *I Married a Monster From Outer Space* (1958). Italian four-*fogli*. A: M. Cupizzi.

173: *The Blob* (1958). Italian four-*fogli*. A: Sandro Simeoni.

174: *The Killer Shrews* (1959). Mexican lobby card.

175: *Robot Monster* (1953). Mexican lobby card.

176: *The Space Children* (1958). Belgian poster.

179: *Devil Girl from Mars* (1954). Mexican lobby card. A: Rodolfo Aguirre Tinoco; *Queen of Outer Space* (1958). German poster. A: Ernst Litter; *World Without End* (1956). Pressbook page.

180: Belgian posters for: *The Land Unknown* (1957); *The Black Scorpion* (1957); *Kronos* (1957).

181: *The Monolith Monsters* (1957).

182: *The Deadly Mantis* (1957); *The Monster That Challenged the World* (1957); *The Incredible Shrinking Man* (1957).

183: *4D Man* (1959).

184–7: UK quads for named films, NB *Invasion of the Hell Creatures* is UK aka for *Invasion of the Saucer Men* (1957). Artists uncredited except *The Fly* (1958) and *Return of the Fly* (1959). A: Jock Hinchcliffe.

188: B&W 10x8 publicity stills from: *The Deadly Mantis* (1957); *The Fly* (1958); *The Monster That Challenged the World* (1957); *Voodoo Woman* (1957); *The Mole People* (1956); *I Married a Monster From Outer Space* (1958); *The Colossus of New York* (1958).

189: *It! The Terror From Beyond Space* (1958).

190: *The Invisible Boy* (1957). Italian four-*fogli*. A: Silvano 'Nano' Campeggi; *Tobor the Great* (1954). Belgian poster.

191: *Tobor the Great* (1954). Italian two-*fogli*. A: Carlantonio Longi; Mexican lobby card; *The Colossus of New York* (1958). Italian four-*fogli*. A: Mauro Colizzi; Mexican lobby card.

192: Japanese posters for *Half Human* (1955); *Rodan* (1956).

193: *The H-Man* (1958); *The Mysterians* (1957); *Varan the Unbelievable* (1958); *Battle in Outer Space* (1959).

194: *The Mysterians* (1957). UK lobby card. A: Robert Rigg; French *grande*.

195: *Battle in Outer Space* (1959). Belgian poster.

196: *On the Beach* (1959). US novel cover, c1959 edition, pub Signet; Polish poster. A: Andrzej Krajewski; US pressbook pages.

197: *The World, the Flesh and the Devil* (1959). US herald; Belgian poster.

204: *The Time Machine* (1960). US newspaper ad; French *grande*. A: Roger Soubie; Finnish poster.

205: Italian two-*fogli*. A: Silvano 'Nano' Campeggi.

206: *Latitude Zero* (1969). Polish poster. A: Andrzej Bertrandt & Marian Stachurski.

207: *The Lost World* (1960). Belgian poster; *Journey to the Center of the Earth* (1959). c1960 French *grande*. A: Boris Grinsson; *The Lost Continent* (1968). French *petite*.

208: *Konga* #4, Dec 1961, pub Charlton. A: Steve Ditko; *Reptilicus* #2, Oct 1961, pub Charlton. A: Dick Giordano.

209: *Reptilicus* (1961). c1963 Italian two-*fogli*.

210: *The Giant Behemoth* (1959). c1960 Italian two-*fogli*. A: Sandro Simeoni; *Gorgo* (1961). c1970s Spanish rr poster. A: Francisco Fernández-Zarza Pérez, aka Jano.

211: *The X from Outer Space* (1967). Japanese poster; *The War of the Gargantuas* (1966). French *grande*; Mexican lobby cards for *King Kong Escapes* (1967); *Ebirah, Horror of the Deep* (1966); *Son of Godzilla* (1966).

212: *Village of the Damned* (1960). Mexican lobby card; Belgian poster.

213: Italian two-*fogli*. A: Silvano 'Nano' Campeggi; French *grande*. A: Roger Soubie; *Children of the Damned* (1964). UK quad; Italian *locandina*.

214: *The Day of the Triffids* (1962). UK quad. A: Bill Wiggins; US pressbook.

215: Italian four-*fogli*. A: Sandro Simeoni.

216: *Matango* (1963). Japanese poster.

218: *Robinson Crusoe on Mars* (1964). Mexican lobby card.

220: *The Last War* (1961). Japanese poster.

222: *First Men in the Moon* (1964). US herald.

223: *Quatermass and the Pit* (1967, aka *Five Million Years to Earth*). UK quad. A: Tom Chantrell; French *grande*. A: Boris Grinsson; French *petite*. A: Boris Grinsson.

224: *The Mind Benders* (1963). Italian *locandina*; *Invasion* (1965). UK quad.

225: *Unearthly Stranger* (1963). UK pressbook cover and pages.

226: *Dr. Who and the Daleks* (1965). UK quad. A: Bill Wiggins; US comic, pub Dell.

227: *Daleks' Invasion Earth 2150 A.D.* (1966). UK quad. A: Bill Wiggins; French *grande*. A: Michel Landi; Australian daybill; Italian *photobusta*.

228: *Alphaville* (1965). French poster; Japanese poster. A: Kiroku Higaki; Polish poster. A: Andrzej Krajewski; Danish poster.

229: French *grande*. A: Jean Mascii.

230: *The Manchurian Candidate* (1962). Japanese poster.

231: *Seconds* (1966). UK quad; French *grande*. A: Arsen Roje; *The Face of Another* (1966). Japanese poster.

232: *Fahrenheit 451* (1966). Finnish poster; Hungarian poster. A: Gyorgy Kemeny; US novel, c1966 edition, pub Ballantine; German poster.

233: Japanese poster. A: Kiroku Higaki.

234: *Nebo Zovyot* (1959). Russian poster.

236: French *grandes*. A: Constantin Belinsky, for: *Danger! Death Ray* (1967); *Dinosaurus* (1960); *The Creature From the Black Lagoon* (1954); *Latitude Zero* (1969); *Mister X* (1967).

237: *Destroy All Monsters* (1968).

238: Italian posters for: *Lost Continent* (1951). c1962 rr two-*fogli*; *This Island Earth* (1955). c1964 rr four-*fogli*. A: Arnaldo De Amicis; *Reptilicus* (1961). Four-*fogli*.

239: *4D Man* (1959). Four-*fogli*. A: Sandro Simeoni.

240: *Rodan* (1957). c1968 rr two-*fogli*. A: Mario Piovano.

241: *Rodan* (1957). c1968 rr four-*fogli*. A: Mario Piovano; *Dr Cyclops* (1940). c1961 rr two-*fogli*; *The Projected Man* (1966). Four-*fogli*. A: Angelo Cesselon; *Women of the Prehistoric Planet* (1966). Two-*fogli*; *Earth vs the Spider* (1958). c1962 four-*fogli*.

243: *The Green Slime* (1968). Italian four-*fogli*. A: G.D. Stefano.

244: *The Human Duplicators* (1965). Mexican lobby card.

245: *Moon Zero Two* (1969). UK quad; Belgian poster.

248: US release titles (where available) given first. Mexican posters/lobby cards for *The Robot vs. the Aztec Mummy* (*La momia azteca contra el robot humano*, 1958); *La nave de los monstruos* (1960) x2.

249: *The Batwoman* (*La mujer murcielago*, 1968); *Blue Demon y las invasoras* (1969).

250: *Santo contra Blue Demon en la Atlántida* (1969); *Conquistador de la luna* (1960); *Gigantes planetarios* (1966); *El planeta de las mujeres invasoras* (1966); *Neutron contra el Dr. Caronte* (1963); *Blue Demon destructor de espias* (1968).

251: *Santo vs la invasion de los marcianos* (1967).

252: *Planet of the Vampires* (1965). Mexican lobby card; Spanish poster. A: Enrique Mataix.

253: Italian four-*fogli*. A: Averardo Ciriello.

254: *Thunderbirds Are Go* (1966). UK quad. A: Bill Wiggins; *Journey to the Far Side of the Sun* (1969). Polish poster. A: Jan Mlodozeniec; Danish Poster

255: *Thunderbirds Are Go* (1966). Italian two-*fogli*.

256: *Fantastic Voyage* (1966). Japanese poster; UK quad. A: Tom Beauvais.

257: Spanish poster. A: Macario 'Mac' Gómez Quibus.

258: *Our Man Flint* (1966). Belgian poster. A: Raymond 'Ray' Elseviers.

259: US novel, pub Pocket Books; *In Like Flint* (1967). UK quad. A: Bob Peak.

260: *The Karate Killers* (1967). Italian two-*fogli*. A: G.D. Stefano; *How to Steal the World* (1968). UK quad; *Ypotron* (1966). German poster; Spanish poster. A: Francisco Fernández-Zarza Pérez, aka Jano; *Operation Kid Brother* (1967, aka *O.K. Connery*). Italian *locandina*.

262: *Planet of the Apes* (1968). UK quad.

263: Polish poster. A: Eryk Lipinski.

264: Japanese poster; c1970s rr German poster; French *grande*. A: Jean Mascii; Romanian poster.

265: Czech poster. A: Vratislav Hlavaty.

266: *Barbarella* (1968). UK quad. A: Renato Fratini.

267: Japanese poster; Czech poster. A: Kája Saudek; Polish poster. A: Jan Mlodozeniec; Italian *photobusta*.

268: *Marooned* (1969). UK program; *Countdown* (1967). Belgian poster A: Raymond 'Ray' Elseviers.

271: *Voyage to the End of the Universe* (1963). Czech poster.

280: *Logan's Run* (1976). Japanese poster; *Slaughterhouse-Five* (1972). Japanese poster; *The Stepford Wives* (1975). Italian *locandina*.

282: *Battle For the Planet of the Apes* (1973). US newspaper-style herald; *Conquest of the Planet of the Apes* (1972). Italian two-*fogli*; *Battle For...* (1973). Dutch poster. A: Kurt Wenzel.

284: Japanese posters for *Beneath...* (1970); *Escape...* (1971); *Conquest of...* (1972); *Battle For the Planet of the Apes* (1973).

285: *Battle For...* (1973). Italian two-*fogli*. A: Alberto Spagnoli.

286: *The Omega Man* (1971): US novel, c1971 edition, pub Berkley; Japanese poster; Italian *locandina*. A: Averardo Ciriello; *Soylent Green* (1973). US novel, c1973 edition, pub Berkley.

287: French *grande*. A: John Solie.

289: *Zardoz* (1974). Japanese poster.

290: *Solaris* (1972). Italian four-*fogli*. A: Renato Casaro; Italian two-*fogli*. A: Renato Casaro; Russian export poster; Czech poster; Japanese poster.

291: Russian poster. A: Mikhail Romadin.

292: *Silent Running* (1972). Italian four-*fogli*.

293: US soundtrack album cover. A: George Akimoto; Italian photobusta; Japanese poster.

294: Spanish posters, A: Macario 'Mac' Gómez Quibus, for: *Godzilla* (1954); *Dr. Who and the Daleks* (1965); *Beneath the Planet of the Apes* (1970).

295: *Silent Running* (1972).

296: *King Kong* (1976). Japanese poster. A: John Berkey.

297: *At the Earth's Core* (1976). UK quad. A: Tom Chantrell; Japanese poster; *The Valley of the Gwangi* (1969). c1970 French moyenne. A: Frank McCarthy; *The Land That Time Forgot* (1974). UK one-sheet. A: Tom Chantrell.

298: *Rollerball* (1975). US promotional print. A: Bob Peak; Japanese posters x2.

299: French *grande*. A: Jouineau Bourduge.

300: *Death Race 2000* (1975). UK quad. A: Tom Chantrell; Turkish poster; German poster. A: Roger Boumendil; Japanese poster.

301: Japanese poster. A: Seito.

302: *The Horror of Frankenstein* (1970). Spanish poster. A: Francisco Fernández-Zarza Pérez, aka Jano; *Embryo* (1976). Japanese poster.

303: *Shivers* (1975, aka *The Parasite Murders*). French *grande*. A: P. Marty; Italian two-*fogli*.

304: *The Andromeda Strain* (1971). US novel, c1971 edition, pub Dell; Japanese poster; *The Terminal Man* (1974). US novel, 1972 first edition, pub Knopf. A: Paul Bacon; Japanese poster.

306: *Westworld* (1973). Belgian poster. A: J. Gommers, Polish poster. A: Jan Mlodozeniec; *Futureworld* (1976). UK quad.

308: *The Man Who Fell to Earth* (1976). UK quad. A: Vic Fair; Italian two-*fogli*; Turkish poster; Spanish poster.

310: *Demon Seed* (1977). UK one-sheet.

INDEX

CONTRIBUTORS

NICK JONES is a writer and editor based in Lewes, East Sussex. As author, his books include *Guardians of the Galaxy: The Ultimate Guide* and *DC Comics Cover Art*, and as co-author, *Marvel Universe: Map by Map*, *The DC Comics Encyclopedia*, and *The Mysterious World of Doctor Strange*. As editor, his credits include the illustrated biographies *The Art of Neil Gaiman*, *Alan Moore: Storyteller*, *Osamu Tezuka: God of Manga*, and *The Art of Movie Storyboards*; the graphic novel series *DC Heroes & Villains Collection*, *Dan Dare*, *James Bond*, and *Wallace & Gromit*; and the magazines *Star Trek Explorer* and *Mixmag Update*. A former dance music journalist, he has edited numerous music books, including *Listening to the Music the Machines Make*, *The Life and Times of Matt Johnson and The The*, *I Am Damo Suzuki*, and *Electri_City: The Dusseldorf School of Electronic Music*. He blogs at www.existentialennui.com.

STEPHEN JONES lives in London, England. A Hugo Award nominee, he is the winner of four World Fantasy Awards, three International Horror Guild Awards, five Bram Stoker Awards, 21 British Fantasy Awards and a Lifetime Achievement Award from the Horror Writers Association. He has written and edited more than 160 books, including the acclaimed illustrated histories *The Art of Horror*, *The Art of Horror Movies*, and *The Art of Pulp Horror*; the film books of Neil Gaiman's *Coraline* and *Stardust*, *The Illustrated Monster Movie Guide*, and *The Hellraiser Chronicles*; the non-fiction studies *Horror: 100 Best Books* and *Horror: Another 100 Best Books* (both with Kim Newman); and collections and anthologies including *Necronomicon* and *Eldritch Tales* by H.P. Lovecraft, *The Mammoth Book of Folk Horror*, *The Mammoth Book of Halloween Stories*, *The Lovecraft Squad* and *Zombie Apocalypse!* series, and 31 volumes of *Best New Horror*. You can visit his website at *www.stephenjoneseditor.com* or follow him on Facebook at "Stephen Jones-Editor."

KIM NEWMAN is a writer, critic, and broadcaster. His many books include the award-winning series of *Anno Dracula* vampire novels, the BFI Classic volumes on *Doctor Who*, *Cat People,* and *Quatermass and the Pit*, the *BFI Companion to Horror* (as editor), *Nightmare Movies: Horror On Screen Since the 1960s*, *Apocalypse Movies: End of the World Cinema*, and *Ghastly Beyond Belief* (written with Neil Gaiman). He is a regular contributor to *Sight & Sound*, and his column "Kim Newman's Video Dungeon" appears in *Empire* magazine. His website is at www.johnnyalucard.com.

ADAM NEWELL, who curated this book (and wrote the mini features scattered throughout its pages), is a longtime editor and project manager of movie and art-related books. Titles he's helped bring to print over the years include *The Art of the B-Movie Poster!*; making of tie-ins for *Star Trek*, *Alien*, and *Planet of the Apes* films; David Hughes's *The Greatest Sci-Fi Movies Never Made*; Stephen Jones's *The Art of Horror* series; Gallery 1998's *Crazy 4 Cult: Cult Movie Art*; Marcus Hearn's *The Art of Hammer*; and Pete Tombs's *Mondo Macabro: Weird & Wonderful Cinema Around the World*. Wearing his other hat, he runs a second hand bookshop in England's Lake District, called Withnail Books.

DR. MARGARET A. WEITEKAMP is chair of the Space History department at the Smithsonian's National Air and Space Museum in Washington, D.C., where she curates the Social and Cultural History of Spaceflight Collection encompassing some 5,000 pieces of space memorabilia and science fiction objects. She is the author of numerous scholarly articles as well as the books *Space Craze: America's Enduring Fascination with Real and Imagined Spaceflight* and *Right Stuff, Wrong Sex: America's First Women in Space Program* (which won the Eugene M. Emme Award for Astronautical Literature from the American Astronautical Society). In addition, she wrote an award-winning children's picture book *Pluto's Secret: An Icy World's Tale of Discovery*, in collaboration with David DeVorkin and illustrated by Diane Kidd.

MARK SALISBURY is a journalist, author, and screenwriter. A former editor of *Empire* magazine, he has written numerous film books, among them the acclaimed *Burton on Burton* and the *New York Times* bestselling *The Case of Beasts: Explore the Film Wizardry of Fantastic Beasts and Where to Find Them*. His other books include *Being Bond: A Daniel Craig Retrospective*, *Crimson Peak: The Art of Darkness*, *Alice in Wonderland: A Visual Companion*, and *Prometheus: The Art of the Film*. He also co-wrote the script for *Makers, Mysteries & Magic*, an audio book about the making of *Fantastic Beasts: The Crimes of Grindelwald*. A contributing editor of *Screen,* he also edits its biannual *World Of Locations* magazine and can be found on Twitter as @mark_salisbury.

ACKNOWLEDGMENTS

The Editor would like to thank all the contributors for their enthusiastic co-operation on this project. Thanks are also due to Paula Clarke Bain, Drs Jonathan and Emily Clements, Adam Ferguson, Sharon Gosling, Sam Jary, Paul Simpson, and Martin Stiff.

SOURCES

In addition to the various credited reviews and quotes from pressbooks, the following sources proved very useful in compiling this volume.

BOOKS

Branaghan, Sim. *British Film Posters: An Illustrated History*. British Film Institute, 2019

Duval, Gilles and Séverine Wemaere, ed. *A Trip to the Moon: Back in Color*. Technicolor/Groupama Gan, 2011

Frank, Alan. *Sci-Fi Now*. Octopus Books, 1978

Frayling, Christopher. *Things to Come (BFI Film Classics)*. British Film Institute, 1995

Gross, Edward and Mark A. Altman. *Captains' Logs: The Unauthorized Complete Trek Voyages*. Little Brown, 1995

Jones, Stephen. *The Art of Horror Movies (Expanded Edition)*. Applause, 2022

McGilligan, Pat. *Backstory 2: Interviews with Screenwriters of the 1940s and 1950s*. University of California Press, 1997

Peary, Danny. *Cult Midnight Movies: Discover the 37 Best Weird, Sleazy, Sexy, and Crazy Good Cinema Classics*. Workman Publishing Company, 2014

Ryfle, Steve et al. *Ishiro Honda: A Life in Film from Godzilla to Kurosawa*. Wesleyan University Press, 2017

Schwam, Stephanie, ed. *The Making of 2001: A Space Odyssey*. Random House, 2000

Turner, George E. and Michael H. Price. *Forgotten Horrors: Early Talkie Chillers from Poverty Row*. Barnes, 1979

Warren, Bill and Bill Thomas. *Keep Watching the Skies! American Science Fiction Movies of the Fifties*. McFarland, 2016

MAGAZINES

American Artist (Bob Peak interview in September 1962 issue)

Cinefantastique (Article by Stephen Rebello in March 1988 issue)

Popular Mechanics (March 1930 issue)

Psychotronic Video (James Coburn interview in issue 9, 1991)

Sight and Sound (1967 interview with Fritz Lang)

Starlog (Nigel Kneale interview in issue 139, 1989)

FILM

The Man Who Drew Bug Eyed Monsters (Reynold Brown documentary, 1994)

WEBSITES

acidemic.blogspot.com
archiviosandrosimeoni.com
artofthemovies.co.uk
b-westerns.com
beladraculalugosi.wordpress.com
bfi.org.uk
blackmaskmagazine.com
britposters.com
budapestposter.com
centuryfilmproject.org
cometosweden.se
criterion.com
cstonline.net
dennisschwartzreviews.com
denofgeek.com
designcurial.com
digital.lib.ku.edu
downthetubes.net
dvdtalk.com
elpais.com
filmonpaper.com
filmsite.org
forcesofgeek.com
framescinemajournal.com
guidafumettoitaliano.com
ha.com (Heritage Auctions)
hammerhorrorposters.weebly.com
iamlegendarchive.blogspot.com
indianriverposterco.com
johnberkey.com
lambiek.net
latimes.com
learnaboutmovieposters.com
mauvais-genres.com
michaelcrichton.com
michaelowencarroll.com
mjsimpson-films.blogspot.com
monsterbrains.blogspot.com
newyorker.com
nickcooper.org.uk
notesoncinematograph.blogspot.com
penguin.co.uk
pixels.com
planetoftheapes.fandom.com
postersmo.blogspot.com
publicdomainreview.org
pulpinternational.com
scifist.net
screeningthepast.com
sensesofcinema.com
sf-encyclopedia.com
slate.com
startrekfactcheck.blogspot.com
stvmcqueen.tripod.com
tanenbaumart.com
tapatalk.com
terrordaves.com
terrortrap.com
theguardian.com
thehollywoodinterview.blogspot.com
thesaucersthattimeforgot.blogspot.com
trailersfromhell.com
vantagepointinterviews.com
wikipedia.com
wrongsideoftheart.com
youtube.com
zipcon.net
zomboscloset.com